NEWS IS MY JOB

A Correspondent in War-Torn China

Edna Lee Booker

With a new introduction by Patricia Luce Chapman,
Edna Lee Booker's daughter

News Is My Job
By Edna Lee Booker

ISBN-13: 978-988-8422-24-1

HISTORY / ASIA / CHINA

First printing January 2017

EB082

This book was originally published by The Macmillan Company in New York in 1940, with the copyright attributed to Edna Lee Potter.

This edition with a new foreword is published by Earnshaw Books in Hong Kong and the copyright is held by Edna Lee Potter's daughter, Patricia Luce Chapman.

Published by Earnshaw Books Ltd. (Hong Kong)

A VISIT WITH
ACE WAR CORRESPONDENT
EDNA LEE BOOKER,
MY MOTHER

MY MOTHER WAS BORN with all the characteristics necessary to become a great war correspondent. I'm sure she began running before she could crawl.

On the surface there was the charm of a pretty girl with blonde curls, a dimpled smile, a soft Southern manner, and a sense of fun that teased from blue eyes. The charm masked a diamond-hard drive when she was after the story.

She was optimistic, she was fearless. A seasoned correspondent by age twenty-two, nothing stopped her. She didn't speak Chinese, she knew nothing of the country, she was alone when she ventured to China, decades before Women's Lib. It was often dangerous but in 1922 she secured a dream story: a personal interview with a fierce War Lord. Actually, two of them. J. B. Powell, editor of the *China Weekly Review*, wrote that "Edna Lee Booker was the first woman foreign correspondent to be granted a personal interview with both Marshalls Wu Pei-Fu and Chang Tso-Lin."

She used any mode of transportation necessary to reach her objective. She travelled on mule, on trains carrying troops, on one train carrying corpses, on river boats, wheelbarrows and rickshaws; she was strafed in a Chinese rice paddy and shaken in Japan when she scooped the world on the massive 1923 Kanto earthquake. In a sedan chair, she visited the Hakka people in a remote and mountainous part of China for a story. Of this visit she once told me: "It was hilarious. I had two sets of carriers. We swayed up and down mountains, plunged across torrential rivers. Once I was nearly dropped into a ravine—the carriers stabilized the *chaise* at the last *minute*. I was terrified but laughing at the ridiculousness if I had perished there in that way. Of course the carriers laughed too in the Chinese reaction to danger."

An early experience had fired her passion for journalism. While her parents Jessie May Livingston and John Calhoun Booker had moved from Kansas City, MO, to California around 1910, they sent their daughter back to Kansas City for a college education. She attended an unlikely college: Scarritt Bible and Training School for Women (now the Scarritt Bennett Graduate Center in Nashville, Tennessee). Here, young women were trained to be Methodist social workers and teachers. In the big city, she would be sheltered by her Moore grandparents.

Grandmother Moore's father Rufus Moore's twin brothers or cousins, I don't know which, worked at a Kansas City newspaper. One was nicknamed Squib, she told me; the other, Squibdoodle. I can't find their real names or the name of the newspaper.

"It was very exciting for me," she told me, "to visit them in their office. Sparks of hot lead shavings littered the floor around their working stations."

I don't know if she worked there as a writer or just swept up the shavings; but I do know that printer's ink ran in her blood from then on.

Her first recorded work experience on a newspaper came, apparently, on a summer vacation from college in about 1920.

Author Adela Rogers St. John mentions her in her book *The Honeycomb*, published by Signet Books in 1969. The scene: the offices of the *Los Angeles Evening Herald*.

FOREWORD

In the old kitchen chair in front of my old recurring typewriter I tried to think. Out of the corner of my eye I saw our club editor, Edna Lee Booker, sliding off into peripheral dimness and I said, 'You come back here. I may need you'. As a favor to Bookie, I had gone the day before to Pasadena or Poker Flats to speak to some Godforsaken women's luncheon club. They had asked Bookie to get a speaker. What with those old biddies on the *Times* or the *Examiner*, Bookie had said to me, I have trouble getting any club news first, or exclusive. I'd like to do them this favor. Bookie was then about twenty years old. So I said yes.

Mother also worked at the *San Francisco Call-Bulletin* and wrote the Class Play before graduating in 1922 from Scarritt. Her school assignment then was teaching the Bible and Christianity at the McTyeire School for Girls, in Shanghai, China. What a opportunity—to get a trip to China! But to be trapped teaching school with no freedom to work as a journalist!

She set about preparing to finesse the teaching role into a route into journalism, and secured a position as foreign correspondent with the International News Service.

With that posting in hand, she set sail for Shanghai in 1922, a 22-year-old who spoke no Chinese, had few contacts there, and was alone. Soon after settling in, she was signed on as, in her words, a "girl reporter" for the *China Press*, then the leading American daily in China.

China was at that time a choice assignment, viewed as a highly-prized foreign posting. The nation, struggling to recover from the Opium Wars, the 1900 Boxer Rebellion and the collapse of the Manchu empire, provided exciting material. Magazines

vii

and journals were churning out stories that attempted to interpret events in China. The international world craved information about China, and so the world's great newspapers started sending and hiring full-time correspondents backed up by an army of stringers. In addition to the *China Press* there were long-running publications such as J. B. Powell's *China Weekly Review* and Edgar Snow's short-lived *Democracy*. Carl Crow was the founding editor of the *Shanghai Evening Post and Mercury*.

Into this mix bounced my mother, an imaginative, fearless, and unstoppable force. The *New York Times*, in its review of her first book, *News is my Job*, February 25, 1940, wrote of her:

> "In the next two decades, during which she traveled
> some 50,000 miles to cover civil wars and to talk
> to those who made them, ...Throughout these two
> decades the "girl reporter" was on the spot, plunging
> into the chaos with a portable typewriter and with a
> nose for news, and often returning to her quarters in
> Shanghai with a triumphant smile and a scoop."

Marriage and children slowed her down. Her businessman husband and my father, John Stauffer Potter, had come to Shanghai in 1917 after a decade in Philippines as a Thomasite teacher sent by President Taft to establish an American school system in the new U.S. territory. Her first child, a son, John Stauffer Potter Jr., was born in 1924; her second, a daughter, me, Patricia Lee Potter, in 1926. But despite learning how to be a mother and an elegant hostess, helped by a houseful of servants and eventually a governess for me, she was never out of touch with her press contacts.

She bundled us all off in 1939 to the northern coastal town of Shanhaiguan, not then known as a vacation resort, when she wanted to see and write about what was happening with the Japanese in the area where the Great Wall touches the sea. On the way north we stopped in Beijing for several days. She found a college girl to take care of us while she conducted a series of interviews with the U.S. Ambassador and other American and Chinese officials. In Shanhaiguan I once watched her, after we had trudged up a mountain ostensibly to see a famous pagoda, interviewing several monks in their saffron Buddhist robes, with the help of a young interpreter who had come along with us on this jaunt. The next summer she took us all up to the British-run seaside town of Wei Hai Wei on Japanese-occupied Shandong Province, enabling her to cable stories to New York and to gather authentic material on Japanese techniques used to suppress the Chinese people. Because of the Japanese military presence she had to be very cautious in her research. She hired an elderly Chinese teacher to come to our bungalow by the back door, supposedly to teach us Mandarin. But she learned from him what was happening in the homes, the private lives, of the villagers. No other writer could match her subsequent cables. She began her second book, *Flight From China*, with what she had learned.

Another time, a notable scoop was an impromptu interview with Haile Selassie, the Emperor of Ethiopia, the Lion of Judah, the legendary 225th successor to his legendary ancestors King Solomon and the Queen of Sheba, when we stopped at Djibouti on the Red Sea on a trip to America in 1935. We had passed an Italian troop ship, which fired up Mother's nose for news. She just couldn't resist it and so obtained a ticket to the inland capital, Addis Ababa, secured approval for an interview – all this from a freighter with twelve passengers. She then headed off immediately for the overnight trip. Left uncared-for were Johnny age ten, and myself, aged eight. I believe there is a special press room in Heaven for reporters whose drive for the story overcomes their obligations as parents. But we children had fun watching the activity at the port and enjoying our independence. Mother returned the next day just before we set sail again, and cabled home a brilliant scoop about the Ethiopian preparations for resisting the coming Italian invasion of their country.

News Is My Job was written on and off over those years. Published by Macmillan in 1940, it was an Alternate Book of the Month Club selection. The book hit the market just as interest in China was peaking. It garnered rave reviews.

Mother especially prized this comment from the great Lin Yu-tang: "A swell job. A cavalcade of modern Chinese history."

And this from Kirkus:

The International News Service sent her to China in 1922 and – with intervals she has been there ever since, so this record covers seventeen years, for she was homeward bound when war was declared in September. From Shanghai she went into the interior, she interviewed the war lords, she was in on a notorious bandit kidnapping case, she was there for the Japanese earthquake, she was there at the psychological place at the psychological moment, whether that seemed to be a place for a woman or not. There is good descriptive material, and she has a facile pen. She knew Snow and the other top-notchers and they respected her ability and gave her equal breaks. The book is good reading and she's done a first-rate job, without quite the decisive note that some of the men's journalistic records have, but with a quality all her own.

During World War II, my mother and us two children were in New York, while my father was trapped in Shanghai and eventually imprisoned in a Japanese internment camp. She turned her energy and skill to finding ways to support the three of us. Most of our funds had been frozen by the Japanese, the stocks and bonds they had invested in the New York market had to be sold sparingly, saved for emergencies or for my father's possible escape or release from China. Mother gave lectures about China all over America; her best-selling book brought in royalties. Brother John worked in a Massachusetts cranberry bog one summer while I put my training from our Shanghai tailor into altering wedding dresses at Bergdorf Goodman. Mother found an Italian seamstress who made many of our dresses and somehow she managed to present me to the public at the leading debutante ball; Johnny was frequently my escort. I knew few of the other children.

At that time, she also began to write her second book, *Flight From China*, the second half of which was completed by my father about his experiences in Shanghai and in the Japanese prison camp at Pootung (Pudong) after we had left him there in November 1940. This book, too, was well received.

Following the Japanese defeat in 1945 and after my father recovered physically from the ordeal in the Japanese camp, he went to work as an executive with the Bank of China in New York. But soon after the war, he returned to Shanghai, followed by my mother and brother. I had married and stayed in the United States. As our home had been ravaged by the Japanese, they moved into the spacious, recently-vacated ground-floor apartment of the architect Laszlo Hudek in his Hubertus Court.

But after a few years of relative peace in Shanghai, it was clear to my mother that our China life, our home, had to come to an end. She returned to New York in 1949. My father was smuggled out in 1950. My brother moved to Hong Kong.

Now mother began another stage of her life. Worried about her husband, then still stuck in Communist Shanghai, she prepared for his eventual return to a relaxing life in the country. She found a beautiful home on a five-acre piece of land on Lake Agawam in Southampton, on Long Island in New York State. I had married well, and my father-in-law advanced the funds to purchase it. Pao Hai – "Potter's House on the Water " – became the family home for the next two decades.

In Southampton she got right into action. A few years after joining the Southampton Garden Club, a member of the Garden Club of America, she was awarded the "Horticultural Committee Award" for "horticultural achievement within the Club." She covered Garden Club events for the *Southampton Press* and lunched regularly at the Bathing Corporation of Southampton, watching her grandchildren compete in races.

She lost much of her drive after my father died in January, 1970, at age 87. Theirs had been a true love story. She could not live at Pao Hai without him, and so moved to Washington, D.C. to be near me and my children. Her son Johnny and the Potter grandchildren were then living in Singapore.

For many years she fought old age with angry determination but finally quit trying. I believe that she was bored beyond toleration with the inabilities that, in her nineties, her age had condemned her to. Perhaps even more, without her husband life had lost its value. But maybe the most painful part for her was missing the action that she saw daily on television in the invasion of Iraq in 1993, and was frustrated that her unwieldy fingers could no longer clack rapidly on the keys of her old Remington typewriter. She made up her mind that she would not eat. And she would not, no matter how we tried to coax food into her. She died in October 1994.

The sweetness between my parents continues. Mother selected for my father's gravestone the line: "*Good night sweet prince.*" After she died, we chose the balance of that sentence for hers, "*and flights of angels sing thee to thy rest.*" They now lie side by side again in Southampton.

Patricia Luce Chapman

Texas

2016

NEWS IS MY JOB

A Correspondent in War-Torn China

Edna Lee Booker

Generalissimo and Madame Chiang Kai-shek in their garden

Acknowledgment

Some of the material contained in this book has appeared in *Cosmopolitan Magazine* or in the *China Weekly Review* and has been used by a number of newspaper syndicates and radio programs. My thanks are due to their editors for permission to reproduce it here in different form.

I should also like to express my appreciation to Mr. H. S. Latham of the Macmillan Company, Mr. Don Moore of *Cosmopolitan Magazine*, and Mr. Barry Farris of the International News Service for their most valuable suggestions.

Also to Ruth Sterry and Lavinia Graham Timmons, the finest newspaper women I have ever known, for their friendship during "cub" days.

And I make grateful acknowledgment to foreign and Chinese friends in the Far East for material, photographs, letters placed at my disposal. The English-Chinese Colloquial Dictionary by Sir Walter Hillier is used as authority for the Romanization of Chinese words, except when a dialect other than Mandarin is indicated.

Edna Lee Booker
Shanghai, China

To

My Husband

John Stauffer Potter

CONTENTS

ILLUSTRATIONS

PROLOGUE
SHANGHAI GLAMOR

OUT OF THE MOONLIGHT which silvered the Whangpoo came junk after junk. The orange flickers of lanterns hanging at their masts touched the widespread sails with magic, and lighted great red eyes carved high on their bows.

My friends on the tender from the Pacific liner, anchored at the mouth of the river, were laughing in a gay little group. But I was scarcely aware of those others, so keenly conscious was I of the action that surged about us. They had lived long in the East, were returning from home leave, but to me it was all new.

Out there the river teemed with life: strange, mysterious, oriental.

A long boat train towing cargo barges chugged past—low-lying like a string of children's blocks. Gayly lighted river steamers churned up saffron spray with their side paddles: steamers which had once plied the Mississippi. Freighters such as Joseph Conrad wrote of, a "P. and O." from London, a liner flying the Tricolor of France lay, steam up, at their berths. Tiny mat-hooded sampans bobbed alongside battleships anchored amidstream. And just around the bend in the river, which was tortuous as a dragon, rode a great fleet of Chinese fishing boats. Their masts rose stark and black like the lines of a Rockwell Kent etching.

Harsh whistles announced our arrival at Shanghai.

I forgot the picturesque Whangpoo in the lights of the city.

Along the river, the Bund stretched like a well laid out park and, beyond the grassplots, the flowers and the trees, rose in silhouette the city's massive buildings. On the Customs Jetty, firecrackers, like dancing fire devils, created a sharp din, and in the waiting crowd I glimpsed Chinese children juggling two-edged knives, turning acrobatic handsprings.

At last I had arrived in China, my Flowery Kingdom!

I had come as a foreign correspondent for the International News Service of New York and as a "girl reporter" for the *China Press*, leading American daily in China. California friends, with whom I had crossed from San Francisco and was to live while in Shanghai, hurried me ashore, into a motor car. I had wanted to ride in one of the wild rickshaws, but as we left the Bund and turned onto Nanking Road my disappointment was forgotten in the picturesqueness of that famous street.

It was a shifting wheel of bright lights, gorgeous red and gold banners, gilded signs, and throngs of carefree Chinese. A joy in Shanghai swept over me as we rode out Nanking Road, Bubbling Well Road, and on out into the country. We stopped before an impressive residence, where a beaming watchman opened high gates.

Well back from the street, in tree-shaded grounds, rose a three-story residence of German architecture. The prominent German who had owned it had been evacuated from the city with his compatriots during the World War. My friends were enthusiastic about their Shanghai home; but I had hoped to live in a Chinese temple or a Chinese house, rather than in a handsomely appointed Herrenhaus. But it is only in Peking that foreigners live in the unutterably lovely old Chinese homes with their courtyards, ghosts and moongates.

My rooms—a study, bedroom, and bath—were on the third floor.

A few weeks later Nora Waln, author of *The House of Exile* and more recently of *Reaching for the Stars*, occupied an adjoining wing. We became good friends during those months and dreamed of a caravan trip into the far reaches of Mongolia. She too was romantic about China. Nora was gentle in manner, and her fair hair was always smooth. She sat at her typewriter for hours on end, writing and rewriting material based on experiences during a North China visit which she hoped would interest the editors of the *Atlantic Monthly*.

That first night in Shanghai, I was falling asleep under a great canopy of mosquito netting when the haunting song of a Chinese flute, a song poignant with the romance of old Cathay, plaintive with the mysteries of life-floated through my open window.

I had found China in the strange beauty of an ancient melody. And under its spell I drifted into dreams that were a prelude to the waking glamour of Shanghai.

- 2 -

A gentle-voiced Chinese woman awoke me.

"Time get up, Missie—bath leddy," she said softly as she threw back the mosquito-net canopy of my bed. "My belong Amah. Suppose Missie wantchee, my all time stop this side, my take care Missie."

A tall Chinese "boy," smiling, immaculate in a long white coat, appeared bearing a most attractive breakfast tray. "How you, Missie? Sleep happy?" he asked. "You likee Chinaside? My belong number two boy."

Like China? I, who since childhood had been romantic almost to extravagance in my feeling for China, replied enthusiastically, "I love China."

Amah was a strong, determined person with wise eyes set in a pleasant oval face. Her black lacquered hair was neatly coiled at her neck, and a sweet-smelling flower, a *Da Da Huo*, was caught just at the top of the chignon. She wore a short tight-fitting white grass linen jacket and straight shining black trousers. I liked her at once; and also at once I came to lean on her advice. I could not know then, of course, how definite a part of my life Amah was to become.

The patois which she and the other servants spoke was at first confusing. It was pidgin English. (The word "pidgin" means business, and pidgin English is a mixture of the English, Portuguese, Malay, and Hindi of the old clipper days.)

My luggage arrived. Amah, Snow Pine (the number two), and I unpacked. A coolie was called to hang my photographs. I wondered why Snow Pine did not get the tacks and hammer.

"This no belong my pidgin," he explained a bit reprovingly.

"Oh!"

No wonder the Robinsons required such a large staff of servants, if each one had his own pet pidgin. There was the number one boy, the number two, cook, small cook, Amah, coolie, number one garden man, small garden helper, chauffeur, wash coolie, house tailor.

I thought of Old Billy Yi, our Chinese Jack-of-all-work back on the California ranch in Cherry Valley, and hoped that he would never develop a pidgin complex. Snow Pine reminded me of a motion picture actor whom I had once interviewed. He couldn't do this and couldn't do that, because of "my public."

But I gave only casual thought to houseboys and coolies. I was eager to be off for the *China Press* office.

The siren of the taxi in which I rode into the city blasted a way through the amazing traffic of Nanking Road. By the glare of the hot sun the street was vivid, exotic in its splashes of red, gold, green; was Van Gogh in its coloring.

Crowds of Chinese strolled leisurely along sidewalk and street, alike indifferent to taxi horns and the jarring clang of bobbing trolleys. Rickshaw coolies, countrymen with baskets of ducks and cabbages which swung from bamboo carrying poles, pushers of handcarts piled high with rice straw, wheelbarrow men moved along. "He-ho-o — he-ho-o" was their rhythmic call. We stopped with a jerk as a troop of statuesque Indian Sikh police, with bright-colored turbans bound round their handsome heads, rode majestically past with banners flying; waited a bit longer, as three water buffalo filed by. Almost at once we became entangled in a wedding procession. The bridal palanquin, heavy with symbolic gilt carvings, rocked like a swing from the carrying poles. I wondered about the Chinese bride within. She was secluded like a princess in an old-time fairy tale.

"Today good joss day. Have got plenty wedding," volunteered the chauffeur. *Crash! Bang!* went the cymbals. The eerie notes of the pipes sounded shrill and high: Chinese wedding notes which came to be as familiar as the strains of the "Lohengrin" March. Strangely enough, it was also a good joss day for funerals.

Abruptly we stopped at a weather-beaten building in the downtown district, at the corner of Canton and Kiangse roads.

"This belong *China Pless*, Missie," the driver announced as he opened the car door. "Missie wantchee sign chit?"

"Sign chit?" I echoed, as he handed me a card and a pencil.

"Can do. Missie lite he name, by an' by shroff come catchee money. Any man Shanghai-side sign chit. Suppose Missie wantchee buy fur coat, nice piecee jade, cup tea — no got money. Maskee — can sign chit." (bill)

Under the spell of that friendly soft-voiced driver, I signed the chit (and thereby adopted that insidious custom of the Far East, the chit system), then entered the down-at-the-heel *China Press* building; found my way to the editorial department.

"Come in, Miss Booker," called a redheaded Irishman, J. Edward Doyle, city editor, years later to be known to America's radio world through his "Dialing with Doyle" in the New York *Journal and American*. His wide grin was infectious, cheering.

"Meet the gang!" he continued.

It was a brilliant group with which I was to be associated. Many of the men had New York and London reputations as correspondents; and they put out the best American newspaper in the Far East. Such writers as Thomas F. Millard, Carl Crow, and Nat Peffer had been among its earlier editors. George Sokolsky was a contributor.

I was the only "girl reporter" on the staff.

That first afternoon we talked of our previous newspaper adventures. I was young, my experience was limited; but I gradually lost my nervousness as I remembered days on the *Los Angeles Herald* and later on the *San Francisco Call Bulletin*, days when I had learned to turn out copy under pressure in the crowded city room. My desk was net to Adela Rogers St. Johns. Adela — brilliant, temperamental — covered Hollywood. It was she who showed me, a sixteen-year-old cub, "the ropes." There had been a year on the *Herald*, several months on the *Call*, two years in the South at a denominational college for young women — then had come an offer of a newspaper job in China.

China!

I had rushed into the *Herald* office with the news. Jack Campbell, city editor, said casually: "Why not represent the International News Service in Shanghai? I'll wire Barry Faris, our foreign news editor in New York." The reply came. I was to become a Far Eastern correspondent for Internews. It was as simple as that! Even so, it was only after friends invited me to live with them during the year I expected to be in the Orient that my family agreed to let me go.

I laughed, somewhat embarrassed, as I finished my tale, there in the *China Press* office.

"And here I am in the land of the Flowery Kingdom," I added jubilantly.

"Flowery Kingdom! Hell's bells!" sniffed the "Old Timer" on the staff.

"Must have some office cards printed for you," Doyle announced." The Chinese lay great store on calling cards; the bigger the better."

He called in the official *China Press* Chinese letter writer, an elderly man of scholarly appearance, who listened attentively as I repeated my name, backwards —

Booker Edna Lee. From the sounds he worked out a Chinese equivalent — Bo Ai-Ii. In this Chinese form, my name meant Precious Love Lotus. I was enchanted.

"Not bad," laughed one of the men. "The Chinese know me as Bundle of Virtue. What a moniker to hang on a newspaperman!"

I was assigned to a desk near a window — apparently the most desirable spot in the hot, shabby city room — and settled down to look over the files of the Shanghai newspapers. A Chinese office boy placed a glass of steaming tea and a dish of water melon seeds on my desk.

And so began my newspaper experience in China. The only order I received regarding my copy was that American prestige must be upheld — regardless.

"Face!"

- 3 -

That night cymbals and drums vibrated through a driving typhoon rain. The clamor seemed to come from the Chinese village back of our house. The peculiar rhythms and the whine of the wind kept me tossing about, staring wide-eyed into the

7

darkness. I turned on the lights and rang for Amah.

"What means this *bang-bang*?" I asked.

"Belong *Kwei Chieh*, Missie. Plenty ghosts come play-play." Amah began a Chinese ghost story so grisly that I kept the lights on all night. I knew that, if I turned them off, a headless devil would rush into my room on a blast of wind, sit down at my desk, and with his brush and ink write the names of those in the house doomed to die — the ghost of one who had been beheaded unjustly, one who roamed the world bent on vengeance.

In the morning the sun was bright and reassuring, and Amah's story of hungry ghosts seemed fantastic; but as I rode down to the office I soon realized that, while the advent of the ghosts might seem whimsical to me, a foreigner, their coming was very real to the Chinese masses and was woven into the very fabric of their lives.

Gay-colored paper clothing, exact replicas of the garments worn by the living, even to the tiny buttons which caught the high collars of the coats, and to the embroidery banding on the trousers, hung from clotheslines along the streets. Coolies passed carrying replicas of full-sized rickshaws, sampans, and motor cars, all made of bright tissue and thin bamboo strips. Heaps of silver paper money smoldered on the walk before small shop doors, while on the ancestral altars I glimpsed dishes of feast food, arranged just so.

Shanghai Chinese, and Chinese everywhere through the country, were celebrating the Festival of the Hungry Ghosts. Mr. Li, a Chinese member of the staff and a University of Missouri graduate, explained to me that every year on the first day of the seventh moon the gates of purgatory were opened, and ghosts in great numbers rushed forth to enjoy a month of feasting and merry-making on earth.

Dinty Doyle came to my desk.

8

"Want you to go over to the native city and cover the parade the City God is putting on for the hungry ghosts," he announced.

I smiled at him, thinking that this, my first assignment, was a joke being played on the griffin (that is, newcomer in China). But my editor was serious; acted as if a ghost parade was an everyday assignment: Mr. Li accompanied me.

Just a step across a street, and I was in an ancient Oriental city, with all of the color of the Hans packed into its maze of age-old, narrow passageways. All about was neglected age. Overhead the eaves of the tiled roofs from opposite sides of the narrow ways almost met, darkening the street, shutting in the moist heat. As we made our way into the crowds which had no beginning, no ending, simply flowed on and on, old China closed in. For a moment I was frightened, overwhelmed, seeing no foreign face in that sea of Oriental faces; then I lost my panic in the color of the life about me.

I longed to look into the bazaars offering porcelains, ivories, jades; to watch the makers of idols paint the great towering figures; to linger while a fat-bellied Chinese, naked to the waist, fried lion's-head dumplings — *shih tzu t'ou* — in vats of deep peanut oil. But Mr. Li hurried me on. Politely insistent, he led me past the bird market, and the fair which was going on in the wide courtyard of the City Temple. Jugglers in embroidered yellow coats were spinning bowls on the ends of chopsticks. Most of all I wanted to visit the famous "Willow Pattern" teahouse, the *Woo Sing Ding*, literally the Teahouse in the Heart of a Still Pool. But no! I resolved that I would come back again and again to the old city.

We little knew that a day would come when the old city would stand silent, dead, empty of all Chinese life; when only the tramp of the Japanese sentries would be heard through its deserted streets.

We were only just in time. The clang of gongs and the din of firecrackers announced the coming of the City God.

"Every city in China has its city god to whom the masses turn for help in plague, civil war, famine, and flood," explained Mr. Li.

Down the narrow street came a procession which breathed a spirit of things utterly foreign to me; of traditions handed down out of a remote past.

The City God was gorgeous in his embroidered robes, elaborate headdress, and he carried a scepter of jade, a symbol of his official rank. He "counted the souls" of the dead as he rode along on his gold and red palanquin through the city; for mingling with the crowds of Chinese onlookers, were the invisible spirits of the dead. If neglected they would bring calamities upon the people during the coming year — plague, fire, the death of newborn sons.

Following the City God came an equally spectacular figure, Prince Chun Shun, or Wang Shih, founder of Shanghai. The coolies swayed under the weight of his ornate chair.

Prince Chun, according to Mr. Li, lived during the time of the Three Fighting Kingdoms, 300 B.C. He was made governor of Kiangsu Province for having rescued the son of the King of Ts'u following his capture in battle by the ruler of a rival kingdom. One day when the Governor was riding over his domain he chanced upon a little fishing hamlet. Because of its strategic location he prophesied that the village would in time become an important trading center: Shanghai — Village on the Upper Sea.

Little boys in embroidered coats dropped silver paper money in his wake: money for the dead. And there were coolies who carried tables laden with feast food; others bore ancestral tablets for those who had died without family.

As the pageant moved on Mr. Li suggested we rest a bit in a *Shu Ch'ang*, Hall of Story-Tellers.

At the tables about us Chinese men sat— relaxed, content in their leisure. For ten coppers a man could enter a *Shu Ch'ang* where, provided with a bowl of hot tea, a supply of sun flower seeds, and a long water pipe, he could listen through the hours to legends of the past as recounted by pallid-faced storytellers. He could also be informed on affairs of the day. The grapevine had its center in the *Shu Ch'ang*. Through the centuries, in spite of Imperial decrees, Chinese story-tellers have by clever adaptation of tales from the Classics, spread the news of current affairs. Today the story-tellers are serving China very much as did their ancestors in times of stress. In their tales from the Classics they sometimes give information to the guerrillas, to spies, to farmer-soldiers, and although the Japanese militarist may be there listening he cannot hear the subtly worded message.

The story of that early Shanghai fascinated me.

Mr. Li told me of the Buddhist monk who came from India in about A.D. 221 and built the original *Lung Hua T'a*, Dragon Flower Pagoda. According to the recordings he came bringing a sacred "rainbow-colored" pearl believed to have been formed from the body of a holy man. He had enshrined the pearl under the roof peak. Aged Chinese villagers, however, held that the pagoda marked the head of a gigantic dragon which guarded the Shanghai district. So large was the dragon that its body stretched more than eight miles across the country, and shrines marked its eyes. The reach of the dragon indicated the rapid growth of the fishing and trading center.

Kublai Khan, in the thirteenth century, pronounced Shanghai a *hsien*, or city. The wealth of the Yangtze valley began to pass through the port. Mr. Li's eyes flashed when he told me of the looting and burning of Shanghai early in the sixteenth century by Japanese pirates: "dwarfs from the outer sea," he called them. Because of the "sea robbers" a city wall was built. There was no money after the sacking of the city with which to pay workmen, and so the magistrate issued strips of cloth stamped with the official seal as currency. Inside the crenelated wall with its watchtowers and guardhouses, its surrounding moat, sixteenth century Shanghai prospered.

It was not until the nineteenth century, with the coming of the "white barbarians," that Shanghai began to command world attention.

- 4 -

A map of the city hung on the wall near my desk.

Shanghai was actually made up of three "cities": the International Settlement, the French Concession, and the native or old Chinese city. Surrounding this triborough city were flourishing Chinese towns, which have since been consolidated into Greater Shanghai. (It is this Chinese Shanghai which now is occupied by the Japanese.) It was complex, this modern Shanghai, with its French, its International, its Chinese sections. Three separate units, each with its own form of government, yet together they made up the metropolis.

It was necessary for me, a newspaper reporter, to understand something of the Shanghai which I was to "cover." Some knowledge of its history is particularly essential during the present critical period of Far Eastern affairs. For information I dug into old diaries, newspaper files, histories; read copies of treaties between the foreign Powers and China; talked with old China residents; and studied faded, spotted maps. I found the story of the Shanghai beginnings utterly engrossing.

A British trader and a missionary arrived hand in hand in a

sailing vessel to knock at the gates of Shanghai one day in 1832. But the haughty *Tao-t'ai*, magistrate, very fine in his official robes, very secluded behind the high walls of his yamen (residence or office of a public official), refused to have any dealings with the "white barbarians from the outer sea." Ten years later, however, a British fleet arrived, captured, and · for a short time held, the walled city. It was only then that the *Tao-t'ai* granted the British a square mile of tide-washed land, a mud flat on the Whangpoo, outside the city walls.

The treaty between China and Great Britain signed in 1843 "permitted commercial intercourse being carried out at the Five Ports of Kwangchow, Foochow, Heamun, Pingpo and Shanghae, allowing merchants and others of all nations to bring their families to reside there . . ." Foreigners might rent this land in perpetuity and carry on trade, yes; but the *Tao-t'ai* wanted none of them, even insisted that "at each of the five ports opened, one English cruiser be stationed to enforce good order among the crews of merchant shipping, and to support the necessary authority of the Consul over the British subjects."

Thus, the beginnings of extraterritoriality in China.

The trade benefits gained by England's war with China were shared by the United States and by France. The French Government secured a Concession. The Treaty of Wang-hsia between China and the United States, signed on July 3, 1844, provided "that American traders and their families might be allowed to reside in the Five Treaty Ports for the purpose of carrying on mercantile pursuits without molestation or restraint."

Those early years were momentous in the annals of American trade in the Far East, for they marked the firm establishment of the "Open Door" policy for all nationals in the China trade.

There was nothing of the pioneer town about Shanghai ever. From the first, Shanghai had tone. Undismayed by mosquito-infested swamps, a river front washed by tides, those first traders, missionaries, government officials, and adventurers set to work filling in the river frontage, draining the swamp lands, building their homes, offices, warehouses, establishing their Protestant and Catholic churches, laying out a racecourse and a bowling green.

Early in 1853, Bayard Taylor, American author and journalist, arrived in Shanghai. He was, so far as I can learn, the first American correspondent to reach the city, and he sent his copy to the *New York Tribune* by clipper ships. I delighted in his journal, *A Visit to India, China, and Japan in the Year 1853*, published in 1855 by G. P. Putnam.

"The foreign settlement... extends along the river for three-quarters of a mile," he wrote. "The houses are large and handsome, frequently good examples of the simpler forms of the Palladian style, and surrounded by gardens. Along the water is a broad quay, called the Bund, which is the evening resort of the residents, and the great center of business and gossip. The foreign community, exclusive of the missionaries, consists of about 170 persons, 14 of whom are ladies. It is, beyond dispute, the most cheerful, social and agreeable community in China."

Of Commodore Perry's visit on the steam frigate *Mississippi*, Taylor wrote: "His presence and that of the *Mississippi's* officers, gave a fresh impetus to the social activities of the foreign population. Thenceforth there were balls, dinners, and other entertainments, in great abundance."

Ten years earlier the Bund had been but a tide-washed towpath, uninhabited marsh land!

The advertisements in early copies of the *North-China Herald* fascinated me. The luxuries of Paris and London were set down on a mud flat.

Large type proclaimed the arrival of perfumery, smelling

salts, hair dye, and snuff; of gold- and silver-mounted riding crops, walking sticks, colored kid gloves, and high silk hats for gentlemen; of keyed accordions, concertinas, with the latest music for the polkas, quadrilles, waltzes; of marble mantelpieces, gold moldings, Brussels stair carpets; of jaconet muslins, beplumed bonnets, feather boas.

During those first years the population of the Settlement was restricted to foreigners; few Chinese lived within the boundaries. But in 1853 thousands of Chinese swept into the tiny Settlement. They were refugees fleeing from the rumored approach of the "Small Swords," a branch of the Triad Society.

The idea of an entirely separate foreign settlement, quite apart from the Chinese life about, as laid down by the *Tao-t'ai* in the old city, was as if it had never been: Shanghai became a *city of refuge — a haven* open alike to men of all nationalities. Its spectacular growth dated from that time.

The Taiping menace of 1860-62 and the story of General Frederick Townsend Ward (heroic Yankee in whose honor the Emperor of China ordered the erection of a memorial temple in Sungkiang, and before whose shrine the Chinese still burn candles and incense) interested me especially. In the Public Gardens off the Bund I visited a monument dedicated to Ward and the forty-seven men, mostly Americans, who died while fighting with the Chinese Imperial forces against the Taipings. Essex Institute in Salem, Massachusetts, holds memorials of Ward, and the American Legion post in Shanghai is named for him.

Inscriptions on the plaques beside his Chinese gold and black spirit tablet on his shrine read:

"From beyond the seas came this rare man; for ten thousand miles stretches the fame of his deeds. His gray-jade blood remains. In Clouds-Center, oh, happy land, for a thousand autumns his cinnabar-red heart is proclaimed."[1]

The expression "cinnabar-red heart" is used to describe a loyal hero, while "Clouds-Center" is the old classical name for Sungkiang. Between ourselves, the American Ward must have been a dashing adventurer. "Gray-jade" blood? Never.

With the opening of the Yangtze to foreign trade in 1861 came the demand for steam tonnage. Paddle-wheel vessels, such as plied the Mississippi— *huo lun ch'uan*, fire-wheel boats, the Chinese called them— began to find anchorage among the Chinese junks, opium clippers, and sailing vessels off Shanghai. The coming of steam created a boom.

This was the time when the foundations of world-famed trading firms were laid; when fortunes were made in opium; when roads were extended, and massive brick mansions, substantial and spreading, with cupolas, spires, deep-set arched galleries were built. In those pretentious homes the dowagers of an earlier, smaller Shanghai reigned; laid down social customs which are the mode in Shanghai even today.

The taipans, heads of the great firms, boasted their victorias (open touring car that has a folding top) and stables. Every afternoon after tea their wives drove out to the Bubbling Well Temple by the *Ching An Ss'u*, Road of Quiet Peace Leading to the Temple.

Despite their protests the "light ladies" of the city, bedecked in picture hats, feather boas, imported gowns and carrying ruffled parasols, also drove out at five. Each sat aloof in her carriage after the fashion of the women of the demimonde in Paris.

Along the bridle path the young blades of the town galloped by, their eyes ever out for the "ladies."

---

1   Translation by Mrs. Florence Ayscough.

Even the important Chinese mandarins in their embroidered silken robes rode in the colorful pageant.

Life was formal, lived on a grand scale, and was very full of pleasure, during those gay seventies and eighties. The Town Hall was a center for community meetings (Ratepayers' Meetings, we call them today), for the elaborate annual balls given by the various nationals.

During those first twenty-odd years, the establishment of an American Settlement on the same basis as that of the British Settlement or of the French Concession, was much under discussion. And on July 4, 1863, during a gala Fourth of July celebration, boundary stones for an American Settlement in Shanghai were laid. Mr. George F. Seward, first consul for the United States, notified Congress of his action. But America was torn by civil war. Mails were slow; and before any considerable correspondence could be exchanged the American and British settlements were amalgamated into the International Settlement. Congress, so far as I could learn, neither accepted nor rejected the land grant.

This so-called "American Settlement" is known today, in 1940, as Hongkew. It is the "Little Tokyo" of Shanghai, where some 30,000 Japanese live. Although the fiction continues to be stressed in certain quarters that the entire International Settlement is still under the administration of the Shanghai Municipal Council,[2] 4.25 square miles of the 8.3 square miles of the Settlement proper not only is predominantly occupied by the Japanese and their troops, but is largely under their control and military domination. In this district are located many important American-owned industrial plants. Key industries that go to make up the vital manufacturing and shipping interests of the

---

2   "The International Settlement," a publication prepared by the American Association of Shanghai, August 30, 1939.

great port are located in this section now held by the Japanese military. Repeated representations, including Secretary Hull's strong note of May 17, 1939, have requested the return of this area to the International authorities, but to no purpose.

The government of the International Settlement was defined in 1869 in certain Land Regulations. These were based on the old New England "town-hall" form of city government. The taxpayers were the voters, and they elected representatives to the Municipal Council. (The present Shanghai Council stands unique in the world. An American is its chairman, and its fourteen members include five Chinese, five British, two Americans, and two Japanese. The Japanese are demanding larger representation on the Council, and in consequence a tense situation has resulted.)

Because of those first treaty provisions nationals of some fourteen of the Powers represented in Shanghai remain subject to the laws of their own countries through the establishment of special courts and judges. In 1939 Judge Milton Helmick made a notable contribution to the United States Court for China in establishing the China Federal Rules of Civil Procedure. Previous to this, the forms under which the court functioned were archaic, based upon the procedure for the United States Consular Courts of 1864.

Such was in part the social and political background of Shanghai.

As I came to know something of its past, Shanghai as a city began to take on meaning; I found myself becoming a part of it all.

- 5 -

Charming women left cards upon Mrs. Robinson and me, for calling was an established custom that played an important part in the social world.

18

There were not enough hours in the day. A new girl in town, I discovered, was "news." It was exciting to find my engagement book filled for days ahead with invitations to dinners, cocktail parties, tea dances; to be booked well in advance for the Washington's Birthday Ball in February, the Bal du Quatorze Juillet on Bastille Day; to be escorted to the races, the paper hunts, the polo games by men of different nationalities – older men who did not treat one with the casualness of the Westerner. I began reviewing my French, thought of studying Italian.

There was one man, an American, whose smile from the first day of meeting lit candles in my heart. I was to see much of John during happy weeks to come, and in the gayety of Shanghai was to forget for a time that news was my job, that I had dreamed dreams of a flowery Cathay.

I liked the late dinner hour, half past eight, and the custom of always dressing for dinner. A Chinese tailor who advertised fur coats "made from your skin or mine," made me lovely evening gowns from luscious Chinese silks, without a pattern, from sketches in French fashion magazines. A shoemaker, after tracing the shape of my foot on paper, turned out by hand, pumps copied from late New York designs. I learned how to ride a Mongolian pony; to chat casually of Ming porcelains; to accept "lap dogs," "monkey" jackets, hand kissing; to play mah-jongg "Chinese-fashion," according to the rules worked out by J. Babcock and A. R. Hager, American businessmen.

My newspaper assignments were varied, given to extremes, in that colorful city of the East and West. The Old Timer gave me some advice.

"Remember that news is your job, sister," he said. "Let Shanghai become your news oyster. Make every new experience grist for your typewriter; and turn it into copy."

After that the French Club became more than just a fascinating casino, where I was becoming proficient in the tango. It was a colorful news source. The terrace, from five o'clock on, was a gay gathering place such as is found in the Bois de Boulogne. Music — dainty, airy, French — floated about like notes from a jeweled music box.

The types there fascinated me. An enormous man at the next table with a rubicund face and a series of red chins, which in themselves told a tale of many *rijstafels*, was a rich planter from Batavia. The tall Britisher with only one arm was an adviser to a Chinese war lord. The bronzed chap just next was an American from Manchuria who had married the most beautiful dance-hall girl in Harbin.

I first saw the Baroness, one of the most exotic and notorious adventuresses who have ever drifted into Shanghai, there. I sent along an interview with her to New York — all surface patter, the kind the Sunday supplements feature — about her specially built bed, made from ornately carved gold and red panels salvaged from old Chinese temples; her salon, papered with gold-paper tea-chest wrappings; her bar, inlaid with semi-precious stones; her boudoir costumes, the robes of a one-time Manchu princess. But I did not write the story of her affair with a prominent Shanghai man, nor its tragic ending.

It was at the French Club also that an interview was arranged with the Cossack general, Ataman Semenoff, famed for his part in the Siberian drama, for his power over lamas and Mongols, when he arrived in Shanghai incognito.

He told me of his private armored train which carried his cavalry officers and his fastest horses. The last coach was luxuriously furnished with deep-piled rugs, silken hangings, couches draped with rich embroideries. He was a powerful man, and as many tales of daring clung to him as to Villa of Mexican border fame. He paced about, his hand within his coat in the

Napoleonic manner, as he told me of the time he and a Cossack private captured a heavily fortified station. After a bit he forgot the private, and I gathered that he had accomplished the feat single-handed!

All the world passes through Shanghai, and my stories included profiles of such celebrities as Marconi, Pavlova, Rockefeller, Jr., "Doug" and Mary, Heifetz, Einstein.

November brought Race Week and red persimmons, hot chestnuts, the chrysanthemum moon, and crabs from the Taiku Lakes.

At the office Few Words was doing a thriving business, for the Chinese, down to the last coolie, were investing in Champion Race tickets. At the house the servants pooled their money and bought a "big chance." The Champions carried a first prize of some $250,000 (Chinese currency). A year or so previously the first prize had gone to ten Chinese, the servants of one of the members who had bought the ticket for them.

Since the late forties the races had played a colorful part in the life of the city. Back in 1852 a *Herald* writer referred to the ladies as "bright jewels"; and an outstanding gown was "corded half-way up the skirt and trimmed with white passementerie." And I heard of the "Duchess of Hongkew" – a social leader who had created a sensation at one race meet by appearing in a red velvet creation with bustle, small train, and beplumed bonnet. The ladies were presented with programs of satin on which the race features were printed in gold; or perhaps the program was written on a lovely silk fan.

The Race Club was gay with flags and bunting. The band played, and crowds of foreigners and Chinese followed the ponies. I was to write a piece on the costumes. Many of the women imported their gowns from Paris and appeared in a new outfit each day. It was such fun going into the boxes of various members, meeting your friends, hearing the gossip of the course, placing bets with the club boys, congratulating the race winners. It was a gentlemen's club, and the jockeys were members or the sons of the members, non-professionals. And the Race Week tiffins! I give the menu of a buffet served by Mrs. "Billy" Coutts Liddell and Mrs. Vera McBain, two of the best known English racing fans in the Far East, and joint owners of the "We Two" stable:

Hot beef tea, piquant with a dash of sherry;
Boned capon blanketed in mashed chestnuts;
Tomato spaghetti covered with kidney and chicken livers;
Baked potatoes stuffed with sausage and topped with poached eggs, covered with curry sauce;
Cold Mandarin fish with a dressing of wild brown rice seasoned with saffron and sage;
Breast of snipe with pâté de foie gras;
Roast pheasant sliced on croutons spread with a sauce of ground woodcock, bacon, anchovy and truffles;
Shrimp curry done in cream and white wine, served with shredded coconut, roasted peanuts, raisins, diced hard-boiled egg, chutney, bits of Bombay duck;
White asparagus tips and cold roast beef with horseradish and caper sauce;
Young chicken, spitchcocked;
Prune soufflé—fresh and tinned fruits;
Cheese and coffee.

- 6 -

Life crowded fast. The Shanghai calendar is very full.
Mr. Li would protest, "Hurried men do not find wisdom."

He would advise me to meditate. "Time given to meditation is more precious than rarest jade," he would say. It seemed strange to hear a newspaperman advising anyone to meditate. Then he would tell me of his favorite singing cricket, "Golden Bell," to whose song he would listen for hours on end. One day in his pleasant way Mr. Li suggested that I study Chinese.

Study Chinese?

Dinty Doyle announced that foreigners "came over queer" who attempted to master Chinese; also that the dialects were as the sands of the sea. Mr. Li, however, arranged for my lessons and, before I had decided whether or not I would attempt to learn even a bit of the language, I found myself with a teacher: a teacher who arrived every morning at eight. On rainy days, however, fastidious house plant that he was, he never appeared.

Teacher Wang was a tall, slim chap with an oval face utterly devoid of expression, and he swayed as he walked — swayed like a young tree in the breeze; and I secretly called him Mr. Willow Tree. His long silken gown was autumn green; his overgown of black cloth was lined with fur. His voice was muted, like a zephyr whispering through the leaves. His long tapering hands moved gracefully back and forth, and now and then assumed a pose not unlike that of the carved hands of an ivory figurine. Teacher Wang was the very essence of a Chinese scholar of the old school.

Where should I find his counterpart among the modern young scholars of today — scholars who are flying bombers, leading guerrilla bands, fighting by the side of "common" soldiers?

Morning after morning I would drone words, phrases, sentences up and down the scale after my teacher, would study aloud as did the children in the old Chinese schools. I began to acquire a small vocabulary, and strutted each new expression; but after calling the duck we were having for dinner a "tender shoe" I subsided. As the days went by I glimpsed the poetic beauty and rich imagery of the language; and found the study of Chinese engrossing.

Mr. Li sent me a Chinese daily paper. Each morning Teacher Wang would give me the gist of the news. The political dispatches from the interior interested me not at all; nor did movements of the various war lords. They did not interest my instructor. He lived on a plane quite above the military. It was accounts of strange and, to me, fantastic events which intrigued, which made colorful copy.

There was the story of a haunted house, the ancestral home of the house of Chen, which the police ordered demolished because of the mysterious deaths which occurred there. In one of the courtyards — "the courtyard of death," a copy reader in the New York Internews office called it, when editing my copy — five coffins were found buried just below the surface. The coffins were removed, placed in little grave houses under the willows in the garden. After a time the Taoist priests announced that the spirits of the dead were at peace and the owner could rebuild his house. The mysterious click of mahjongg tiles, the echo of strange voices, the sound of chopsticks in rice bowls were never again heard.

One news item took me to a famous garden in the native city. The Chinese daily announced in all seriousness that a malicious fox spirit which haunted the garden was setting fire to the rice shops of the neighborhood. Again, I went to a cottage of mourning where a farmer had died from shock when he had inadvertently killed the god of his silkworms; and another day, to the ancient temple of Ma Chu, goddess of the boat people, to witness the ceremony of launching a proud, seagoing junk.

These were the stories in which I found my "Flowery Kingdom."

It was during a dinner at a Chinese restaurant, the Apricot Blossom Chamber, on Foochow Road that I first came into contact with Chinese relaxed, at play. It was then that I began to appreciate the capacity of the Chinese for pleasure; came to know something of their wit and humor; their joviality and friendliness. They were so leisurely in their dining, had such frank enjoyment in the many, many dishes which the "running-about" boys served. The Chinese about the tables in the private rooms laughed unrestrainedly; called out the count of the wine gambling games; listened or not to the shrill notes of the exotic singsong girls who sat behind their chairs. They made a great fuss over their little sons, who ran freely in and out of the rooms. Yet I saw no Chinese wives there, no beautiful daughters. I wondered if I should ever meet any Chinese girls.

There were no long after-dinner speeches – to all appearances no formality. But a Chinese dinner is most conventional in that every detail has been set for hundreds of years. Even the drinking of hot wine goes back to the time of Emperor Yu, about 2000 B.C.; the rules governing manners at the table, to the Chinese classic, "Book of Etiquette," written about three thousand years ago. We were long at the table. There was no hurry – time even for me to experiment with chopsticks, to inquire into the mysteries of bird's-nest soup and shark fins. Each main dish was brought on by itself to be commented upon, appreciated, explained. The "Gold Coin" chicken came down from the time of the epicure, Lord Chi Ksuen Kung. I had never before tasted such sauces.

Fall deepened into winter. According to the Chinese calendar, the season of "big snow," of "seven coat" weather, had arrived.

"Suppose snow come more early Chinese New Year time, belong plenty good joss," explained Amah.

Snow before the spring planting augured a full harvest, was a "good omen." There are, however, comparatively few marriages during the season of the "big snow." It is considered unlucky for snow to fall on a wedding day: if the bridal chair is covered with glistening flakes, sorrow is in store for the bride. White is the color of mourning.

Christmas trees, holly wreaths, Chinese lilies, red-berried heavenly bamboo, and yellow-flowered *lieh-mei-hua* appeared as if by magic along Bubbling Well and Nanking roads. Smiling Chinese dealers in flowers stood by, ready to bargain. Snowflakes of "good omen" began falling, and at the house the gardeners were twining the banisters with ropes of pungent cedar, setting up a towering Christmas tree, hanging wreaths of holly. The holiday season set in, and I was caught up in a gay whirl of eggnog parties, fancy-dress balls, the Christmas hunt, New Year's Eve dinners which moved on from the country clubs to the hotels and night clubs and back again. Everyone was friendly, merry. There was no time for homesick memories. Perhaps this is one reason why internationals so far from home make much of the Yuletime.

Because of its international make-up, the festivities in Shanghai began December 6, when in the German homes and schools Sankt Nikolaus arrived with sweets for the good children and whips cut from tree branches for the naughty; and it carried on until January 13, when the White Russians held their traditional New Year's Eve charity ball. And then came Chinese New Year with firecrackers and gongs and the Chinese in new outfits extending their smiling greetings. It was such fun!

I was asked to cover the Christmas vesper service at the Cathedral, to write of the Christmas spirit.

In the gathering twilight, the beautiful old church, designed after the early thirteenth century Gothic by Sir Gilbert Scott, and built approximately a century ago in spacious grounds in downtown Shanghai, seemed to stand, a substantial monument, for all that is best in life. Its stained-glass windows glowed with warmth; the illuminated cross, rising high over all, radiated a message of love for all mankind; while the chimes, with sudden joyous pealing, sang of peace, good will among men. Within, deep, stirring tones of the organ carried on the music of the bells, and there was candlelight; the high, sweet notes of choir boys; and the lifted voices of men and women gathered from all over the world. I was glad that the "little town of Bethlehem" had no geographic boundaries. The World War to "save the world for Democracy" was over; life was serene, secure.

John and I dined with British friends that evening. We lingered long at the table, talked in a leisurely way, as do internationals who have not yet lost the art of conversation, and enjoyed the old English ceremony of the port. I thought of the Christmas party at Mr. Wardle's, and decided to read again Dickens' "Pickwick Papers" in the light of a broader understanding.

The charm of life in Shanghai crept over me; cast its spell.

- 7 -

Into this delightful Shanghai, the Shanghai of the underworld burst like a sordid dream.

I was plunged into a "Clean Up the Trenches" campaign.

Those early twenties marked the culmination of a reform era in Shanghai's history. They were fighting years — years when the progressive, "right-thinking" forces of the city, both foreign and Chinese, fought to shed certain evil incubuses of the past, even as Sindbad the Sailor strove to cast off from his shoulders the Old Man of the Sea. During those weeks I made a readjustment of my acceptance of Shanghai as being only a glamorous, pleasure-loving, money-making city, a man-of-theworld port city; came to appreciate the depths of its foundations, the strength of its public opinion. I had believed Shanghai too sophisticated to grow ardent over a cause, to espouse a flaming reform crusade. This acclaimed "Paris of the East," "City of Adventure," had a steady keel. Before that campaign was over I learned of the gambling palaces, the old Alhambra and the Wheel; of the famous Kiangse Road district with its lush "girls," of the ornate opium establishments of Foochow Road which, years earlier, public opinion had succeeded, against terrific odds, in closing.

Across the Garden Bridge, in a section of what had once been known. as the "American Settlement," lay the Trenches.

It had dug in there half a century earlier under the "protection of American indifference," when gamblers, riffraff, cheap prostitutes from the Seven Seas had brazenly claimed American citizenship, and there had been no United States Court for China, only consular officials. In 1906 President Theodore Roosevelt had applied the "big stick"; ordered that undesirable Americans in China be "cleaned out," and that American prestige be restored. A United States Court for China was established.

· But efforts to rid Shanghai of the Trenches had failed. It was all very difficult. The district had spread; lay for the most part in Chinese territory, over which the foreign authorities had no jurisdiction. The Chinese officials allegedly received a substantial "squeeze" from certain foreign as well as Chinese interests which were determined to keep the district open.

The killing of an American seaman, a Chinese singsong girl, and a pretty half-caste during a brawl had brought the notorious Trenches again into the public eye; had stirred the International Settlement to action.

I drove one night with the late Dr. Frank W. Rawlinson, then chairman of the Moral Welfare Society and a member of the Vice Commission of the Shanghai Municipal Council, and members of his "Clean Up the Trenches" committee, out North Szechuen

Road. This important artery to the northern district of the city was patrolled by Settlement police, while the district itself, with its maze of narrow cross streets, alley ways lined with brothels, opium dens, dives, dance halls, was under Chinese control.

Despite my knowledge that I was on a "story," a fantastic feeling that it was all unreal crept over me. Here was a setting for a sordid Oriental thriller, but it had no place in my picture of Cathay.

Narrow alleyways, dimly lighted by red lights hanging over the doorways of low tenement-like buildings, stretched into the darkness. It was lurid. Figures slunk along: Chinese girls with painted cheeks; Japanese women with calcimined faces of the Yoshiwara, Tokyo type; faded hags of almost any nationality. The worn-out "ladies" of the China Coast loitered in those alleyways; sailors swung along with exotic half-castes clinging to their arms.

Jazz notes from half a dozen brightly lit cabarets and bars along more pretentious streets broke through the night: the Boxers' Cafe Buffet, the Palais Crystal Garden, the Eldorado . . .

Russian girls from Harbin, who spoke little English, but whose stock phrase was, "My Prince, ples, you buy little Sonya small bottle vine," were there. American girls from the old Barbary Coast and women from the dives of Marseilles acted as hostesses. They sat around tables placed along one of the walls. We chose a place near the door. With the first loud note of the mechanical piano player the sailors, tourists, men at the bar, made a mad stampede toward "the girls." Even as we watched, a quarrel started between a French and an Italian sailor over a dark-eyed girl in a red dress. Other Italian sailors stopped dancing, thrust their chests into the argument. French sailors began throwing bottles. In a moment the "spigs" and the "frogs" were at it. We hurried out as a chair leg hurtled past.

It was in such a brawl that the American sailor had been

killed.

In the groggeries of Pacific Street in early San Francisco many a man had been drugged, blackjacked, and shipped as a seaman on a hazardous "Shanghai voyage." So common did the impressment of sailors become that the verb "to shanghai" came into use, and Congress in 1906 passed an Act to prohibit shanghaiing.

Shanghaied. The very word envisioned errant yesterdays. Although the tea clippers and four-masters had long ago disappeared from the Whangpoo the sailorman was still fleeced in the Trenches.

We watched a long string of rickshaws file past, each with its sailor, headed straight for some brothel. The girls were a seasoned lot. It was play for them to lure a seaman into a dive, ply him with liquor or dope, perhaps prepare him a pipe, and later rob him.

Throughout the trial of those connected with the American sailor's death, strong pressure was brought to bear upon General Ho Feng-ling, military governor of the Chinese municipality. American and British government officials, Municipal Council leaders, the Moral Welfare Society, backed by some seventeen local organizations, missionary groups, the press, joined in the campaign. In the end it was this concerted public opinion which won. The edict, as published by General Ho, read in part:

"In response to agitation on the part of the foreign community, the Chinese authorities have resolved that the Trenches be closed within a month."

Newspapermen have a saying that murder stories run in threes. The adage held good in Shanghai.

The murder of a San Francisco girl in one of the notorious "houses" in Kiangse Road opened up the history of this famous district to me.

I was shocked to learn that so late as 1906, prior to the establishment of the United States Court for China, the term "American girl," was synonymous with "woman of the underworld" in port cities of the Far East. Under orders from President Theodore Roosevelt, Lebbeus R. Wilfley, former Attorney General in the Philippines and the first Judge of the United States Court for China, and Major Arthur Bassett, District Attorney, attempted to prosecute the "American girls" of the de luxe Shanghai establishments; to deport them from the city.

Foreigners and Chinese had crowded the courtrooms and streets on that exciting day in 1906 to see the "American girls," many of them famed for their beauty, culture, and charm, drive up in their carriages in answer to their summons. There were comparatively few unmarried, eligible women in Shanghai at that time, and these "American girls" set the fashions, lived in luxury, played an important part in the affairs of the city.

Before the Honorable L. R. Wilfley, Judge
U.S. People v. Minnie Kingsley, No. 16 Soochow Road; Maxine Livingstone, No. 53 Kiangse Road; Alice Duncan No. 2 Thibet Road; Dorothy Grant and Zaza van Buren, No. 10 Hong kong Road; Emily Moore, No. 53 Kiangse Road; Mona Monteith, No. 54 Kiangse Road; Alice Sherwood, No. 14 Soochow Road; Margaret Kendall, No. 10 Hongkong Road; . . .

The attempt to deport them was blocked, however, by the hurried marriage of the majority of the "girls" with men of other nationalities—Cubans, South Americans, Portuguese, Mexicans, Spaniards—and the automatic forfeiture of their American citizenship. Many of the "girls" had remained; carried on through the years. Shanghai had outgrown its Kiangse Road by the early twenties. A number of the houses were being torn down, giving way to business. Some of those women had died, were buried in the Bubbling Well Cemetery; others had made happy marriages to men of wealth and position; more than once a woman was pointed out to me as having come from "down the line."

I filled a notebook with their stories which I heard on every hand: I wanted to write those tales of real life—but I could not. They were beyond me.

There was the girl who during a brawl caused by jealousy in an old gambling palace, the Alhambra (now the Del Monte Café), startled everyone by tearing off her clothes and parading down the stairs from the gambling rooms into the dance hall, a veritable "Nude Descending the Staircase," yet who cared for, and educated, all Chinese girl babies left at the gate of her "house."

One famous woman had fled heartbroken to Paris when she learned that her paramour of years had married her younger sister.

The drama of many of these stories was laid in what was perhaps the most luxurious place of its kind in the Far East, "Number 16."

I heard gossip of the ornate ballrooms with walls paneled in satin brocade, and with long mirrors; of its Chinese rugs, chandeliers, gilded furniture, of its green and gold grand piano; and of the richly furnished "boudoirs." There was dancing and music each evening; dinner and champagne. The chits were determined by the number of empty champagne bottles, as in France by the number of saucers. Only foreign "gentlemen" were admitted, and even they had to send in their cards and be approved before being received.

"Someday," I thought, "I'll find time to think it all out. I'd label my thoughts, as Thomas Carlyle suggests."

- 8 -

I had almost given up the hope of meeting any high-class Chinese women socially. Foreign and Chinese business men cemented friendships during the many courses of a Chinese feast, but rarely did a Chinese woman attend such a dinner. Foreigners and Chinese did not meet socially in Shanghai, I was told, although they did in the diplomatic circles in Peking. I never saw a Chinese at the night clubs or the tea dances at the Astor House.

And then at a dinner given by the Honorable Edwin S. Cunningham, American Consul General, and Mrs. Cunningham, I met Miss Mayling Soong, youngest daughter of the House of Soong.

She was friendly, lovely in her Chinese satin gown, and grew radiant when she spoke of China and of America. She was very American in her speech and manner, but she was intense in her patriotism, impatient in her desire to serve her country. As she spoke I caught something of her spirit, and for the first time came to see China not only as a land of romance, adventure, fantasy — a Flowery Kingdom — but as a vital country struggling toward Democracy, toward a new life: a country with eyes looking westward.

I listened as she told me of her dreams for China, and we talked long together as will two young women who have much in common. A friendship which has carried on through the years was born. She invited me for tea and tennis a few days later. I was glad that I was to see more of this girl, my first acquaintance among the upper-class Chinese women of the city.

The Soongs lived in a large foreign-style house in the French Concession — a pretentious place with formal gardens and tennis courts. As the houseboy showed me into the drawing room, I knew at once that here was a home of peace and beauty, a home which, while preserving the best of old China, opened its doors to the modern spirit of the West.

Mayling Soong greeted me warmly. I liked her very much. She was warm and approachable, and she spoke my language. She was attractive in her semiforeign tennis togs. Her black hair, which was cut in a bang over a high intelligent forehead and arranged in a neat roll at the back of her neck, shone like satin; her deep brown eyes glowed with warmth. As we talked, Madame Soong entered.

Little has been written about this mother of the Soongs, but to me she was one of the remarkable Chinese women of her day. My first impression was of a woman of force and poise. She was a study in black satin jacket and skirt, with sleek black hair dressed in a neat chignon and alert, magnetic eyes set in a lined but serene face. There was a strength about this woman, sitting so erect in a carved blackwood chair, which had its source in a deeply religious nature. Madame Soong was a devout Christian, and her home reflected her piety. On the piano, which she played, a hymnal stood open. Biblical paintings hung on the walls. Religious periodicals in English and Chinese and a large family Bible were on a side table. In an upper story of the house was a chamber known as "Soong Tai-tai's prayer room." To this quiet place she retired daily to pray and to read her Bible. If the problem with which she wrestled was particularly close to her heart, she might remain there seeking guidance throughout the day and even far into the night. She prayed for her children, and she prayed for China.

Madame Soong was not a "first generation Christian." She had grown up surrounded by Christian influences, as had her mother before her. She told me something of her ancestry and of the early influences upon her.

Her maternal grandmother was a member of the historic

house of Hsu (in the local dialect, *Zi*). The Zi family had been Christian for more than three hundred years; from it the Zi-Kai-Wei (Siccawei) district of Shanghai derives its name (literally, *Zi-Kai-Wei* is "Homestead or Boundary of the Zi family"). One of Madame Soong's forebears was the distinguished Sui Kwang-ki (or Zi Kwang-chi), who in the Ming dynasty was converted to Christianity by Mathew (Matteo) Ricci. He assisted Father Ricci in translating mathematics into Chinese; became an influential cabinet minister; was an important ally of the early Christians in China. He was the first important Chinese official to embrace Catholicism and is known today as the father of Catholicism in China. About three years ago an impressive ceremony was held around his tomb in *Zi-KaiWei*.

Madame Soong talked of her girlhood.

With the family tradition of religion and learning, and her quick and brilliant mentality and avid desire for learning, she was given an education unusual for Chinese young women of her time. She studied the Chinese classics; worked over the formation of the difficult Chinese characters with her writing brush; delighted in painting, music, and embroidery lessons. At a missionary school for girls she studied English, devoured the foreign classics, and made the Bible in English her own.

She was married to a returned student, Soong Chia-ju. Her marriage had been arranged, according to old Chinese custom.

Soong Chia-ju, father of the now famous "Soong dynasty" of China, is to me one of the most important Chinese of the past generation, one of the outstanding patriots. His dramatic life story has for years been a tradition at Duke University (formerly Trinity College), where young Soong was the first Chinese student to enroll, and where at a recent commencement exercise he was acclaimed from the rostrum as one of the most distinguished alumni of the university. In his honor a monument is to be erected on the Duke campus by members of his family and by interested American friends.

Yet strangely enough little has been written of Soong. Perhaps this is due to difficulties in securing first-hand material on his life (or even to careless reporting) for Soong's ancestral home was in a little-known village on a coastal island. But the Soong clan was large, of some importance, made up as it was of shrewd, substantial farmers as well as of sea-faring traders.

In writing of Soong I have drawn my material from original sources in China and in the United States. My Soong profile is based on impressions gained from talking with his wife, Madame Soong, years ago; from his daughter, Madame Chiang Kai-shek, in Hankow in 1938; from Mr. James A. Thomas, for thirty-five years a leading American business man in China and today, retired, a resident of White Plains, New York, and a trustee of Duke University; from foreign and Chinese business men and missionaries who knew Soong; from material supplied by Duke University and from articles published in the *News and Observer*, Raleigh, North Carolina.

Soong's story shows him to have been a man of personal charm and magnetism, of courage and determination, ambitious for his children—his daughters as well as his sons. He had a shrewd business sense, unfaltering religious convictions, and a love of country which inspired sacrifice, even to the risk of his life.

Soong Chia-ju came from the village of Kui-san in Hainan off the coast of south Kwangtung. He was the youngest of three brothers, and had been adopted by a childless relative (a common custom in China, where the clan life of a family is closely knit).

This prosperous uncle and foster father, who was one of the early Chinese tea and silk merchants in Boston, took young Soong to America with him, expecting to train him in his business. His shop was a center for the first group of Chinese students sent to America by the Chinese government, and young Soong came to know such men as Tong Shao-yi, C. S. New, and B. C. Wen. (Years later Dr. New and Dr. Wen became Soong's brothers-in-law.)

He aspired to college, but his uncle had little patience with this ambition; he was a shrewd merchant, and he wished his "son" to carry on his business. But Soong had no interest in the tea trade and dreamed night and day of securing an American education. One day in 1880, when wandering disconsolately about the Boston harbor, he slipped aboard the United States cutter *Schuyler Colfax*, under command of Captain Charles Jones. His amazing adventures began that day. The captain, noticing the bright-eyed Chinese boy, talked with him, became interested in his ambitions, and, when his cutter sailed for Wilmington, he carried young Soong with him.

Captain Jones took the Chinese boy, to whom he had become greatly attached, to the Reverend T. Page Ricaud, pastor of the Fifth Street Methodist Church. And "Uncle Ricaud," as young Soong soon called the elderly minister, welcomed him into his home, tutored him, and a few months later was instrumental in securing a scholarship for his brilliant pupil at Trinity College. General Julian S. Carr, wealthy philanthropist who had given scholarships for a number of American boys, gladly provided one for "Charlie" Soong, as his college friends called him.

At Trinity, which in 1880 boasted only two buildings, six professors, and two hundred students, Soong was popular with the students and the teachers. Mrs. Braxton Craven, wife of the president of the college, became his devoted friend, assisted him with his lessons, opened her home to him. Years later Soong's family life in China was to reflect the influence of this American home. During his first year at Trinity he was baptized in the college chapel, and his career took on direction. Soong determined to return to China a missionary to his own people.

Encouraged by General Carr, Soong went to Vanderbilt from 1882 until 1885, and it was there that he was ordained for the ministry. Eagerly he sailed for the Orient, anxious to take up his work and to once again see his family in southern China. He had been away from his home for more than five years, and he had understood that he would be permitted to make a brief trip to Kui-san before beginning his work. The missionary in charge at Shanghai, however, refused his request. The warm cordiality which the North Carolina friends had shown was missing. From the first there was conflict between the two men. The American was an old-school type of missionary, one of the men who allegedly believed in keeping all "native" ministers suppressed, under the authority of the foreign missionary. A letter from Soong to James Southgate, leading Durham business man, explains something of Soong's emotional conflict:

"No, I haven't been to see my parents as yet. Dr _____ said I may not go until the New Year. I must bear this patiently, silent as a mouse. But when the fullness of time has come, I will shake off his assumed authority. The great mogul wanted to dismiss all native ministers from preaching a year ago. He ignores my rights and the equality to which I am entitled. I hope for a transfer . . ."

About 1892, after carrying on his teaching and preaching for years under great strain, Soong resigned and threw himself into the secret revolutionary movement led by Dr. Sun Yat-sen. Backed by Chinese patriots, among them young men who had gathered in his uncle's teashop in Boston, Soong opened a publishing house, primarily to print Bibles in Chinese. He married, and children were born, children who were brought up along the strict lines of the Southern Methodists: no dancing, mah-jongg, cards, wine in his home. His publishing house began turning out secret revolutionary literature, his home became a meeting place of the revolutionists. As the right-hand man of Dr. Sun, Soong served as secretary and treasurer of the "Young Revolutionary Society." More than once he and his family had to flee for their lives to Japan. Following the overthrow of the Manchus in 1911 Soong began the building of his fortune, the education of his six children (three sons and three daughters) in America. He erected a mission church and school, built a spacious home, one of the finest in Shanghai. In 1914, when General Carr visited China, Soong and all of his friends gave him a royal welcome, opened their homes to him.

Soong died in 1919 — a great man, whose image is stamped in the lives of his famous children today.

As the houseboy served tea there in the Soong home that day in 1922, Madame Soong spoke of her dreams for her children. She and her husband had early determined to bring them up as Christians, with ideals of patriotic service ever before them, and to have her daughters as well as her sons educated in America in order that they might be better fitted to meet life in a changing China. She had qualities in common with the outstanding mothers of history — forceful mothers who sacrificed, prayed, lived for their children. The three pretty little girls in their rich Chinese costumes attended Miss Potwin's private school in Summit, New Jersey, and on Sundays they had created a diversion when they filed into a local Sunday school. Later the eldest daughter, intelligent, clever Soong Ai-ling (Accomplished Years), and the flowerlike second daughter, Soong Ching-ling (Righteous Years), attended Wesleyan College for Women at Macon, Georgia; the youngest daughter, Soong Mayling (Beauteous Years), Wellesley

College. The sons attended Vanderbilt, Harvard, and Columbia, and achieved positions of prominence in government and business upon their return to China.

This is the background of the Soongs. And it is not extraordinary that with such a heritage they should be the outstanding family of China, and the three Soong sisters (now Madame H. H. Kung, Madame Sun Yat-sen, and Madame Chiang Kai-shek) the most influential women in the Orient.

I wonder now whether that youngest daughter of the Soongs — beautiful, as her brothers called her — had a premonition of her future greatness,[3] of the responsibilities which life was to thrust upon her.

Madame Soong left us. Mayling Soong and I picked up our rackets and hurried out to join her brother "T. V." on the tennis court. He had challenged the two of us.

---

3 TIME, the magazine, departing from its custom of selecting an individual as the outstanding personality of the year, in the December 5 issue named Generalissimo and Madame Chiang Kai-shek (Soong Mayling) as its "Man and Wife" of 1937.

Dr. Henry Noble MacCracken, president of Vassar College, in 1938 named Madame Chiang Kai-shek as one of the five most intelligent women in the world.

The Gold Medal of Honor of New York City Federation of Women's Clubs was presented to Madame Chiang Kai-shek in Chungking, April 14, 1939, in recognition of "her indomitable courage and leadership in the crisis of her native land."

Top. The City Wall of Shanghai as it appeared when the port was opened to foreign trade, 1842-43-built in 1544 as a protection against Japanese invaders after the looting and burning of the open city in 1543. (Courtesy R.V. Dent.) Bottom Left. The figure of Prince Chun Shun, founder of Shanghai, seated in his temple. (Courtesy North China Daily News.) Bottom Right. "Willow Pattern" teahouse and zigzag bridge, silent, deserted since the Japanese conquest of Shanghai, 1937. (Courtesy Richard Hubert)

PART I
WAR LORDS CLASH
(1922-1923)

ABRUPTLY THE CHARACTER of my news dispatches to New York changed.

China's war lords were on the move; were making large-scale preparations for civil war. According to dispatches coming into the city room from upcountry, war would break over China by early summer.

War lords? Civil war?

I had sent no political news to America during the months and knew little about the vast hinterland of China to which Shanghai was but a gateway. My reach had stretched only to the country about the city. As the men on the staff, all "in the know," discussed the possible consequences of such a war, I became impatient of my ignorance. Under the surface events were shaping, events regarding which I had no background of understanding. I began studying the wires which came into the office from correspondents in Peking, Mukden, Hankow, and Canton. Despite Teacher Wang's protests, I made him cull the political news from the Chinese dailies and explain it to me. I literally crammed Chinese history, studied the map of China. Shanghai was but a dot upon its far-spreading surface, a doorknob. The Chow cities jumped at me in my sleep: Foo-chow, Hu-chow, Hai-chow, Hang-chow, Soo-chow, Sui chow, Kwei-chow, Kiung-chow, Kiao-chow, and — who knew? — perhaps a Chow-chow. Chow cities without end. I familiarized myself with the names of the great war lords — feudal barons — and located their domains. Mr. Li and the men in the office answered my occasional question.

It was Mayling Soong, however, who found time, considered it worthwhile, to explain the China political set-up to me.

Painstakingly she drew a picture of the Chinese revolutionary movement. I began to find out something of China's cumulative revolutionary effort, which, after long, desperate years of struggle, was to result in the Chiang Kai-shek government of today. I could see the past grow into the present through her clarifying narrative.

Here it is in brief.

Late in the nineteenth century modernism was born in medieval China. An awakening took place as inevitable as the stir of spring. This new life, coalesced from many small group movements, engendered a Young China Revolutionary Society under the leadership of the ardent patriot Dr. Sun Yat-sen. Persecution followed. Sun, with a number of his followers, fled from Canton to Japan, where they drafted a platform which stressed the overthrow of the decadent Manchu Dynasty and the establishment of a Chinese Republic. (It seems ironic that Japan should have given shelter to the leader whose portrait she now tears in fury from the walls of the colleges and public buildings in the territory she conquers; that the very party which she today denounces should have been organized under her protection in 1904.)

A spirit of rebellion ignited Chinese leaders. In 1911 and 1912 the revolution became a *fait accompli*. The Manchu Boy Emperor (now the puppet ruler of Manchukuo) abdicated, and with great ceremony Sun Yat-sen was elected President of the Republic of China by a parliamentary body in Nanking.

But Yuan Shih-kai, Peking official with money and armies, by a dramatic *coup d'état* made himself President of China; discarded all pretense of interest in a democratic form of government, and set himself up in Peking as an absolute dictator. He appointed eighteen military governors from as many provinces to carry out his orders. Sun and his followers fled. A second revolution was well on its way when Yuan died.

China was at the mercy of the eighteen military governors, each of whom had a large army at his command. Each had learned from Yuan the trick of levying heavy taxes, of exploiting the people. Each fancied himself a second Yuan Shih-kai. Each thought that China was his oyster. Hence the birth of China's *war lords.*

The war lords began a struggle among themselves. The resultant civil wars of 1917, 1918, 1919, and 1920 threw China into chaos.

The republican ideals of Sun Yat-sen were ridiculed. Sun and his revolutionists fled to Canton. There they set up the South China Republic with Sun as President.

Thus China in 1922 was a divided nation. His Excellency Hsu Shih-chang was President of the Peking government, and Dr. Sun Yat-sen officiated as the idealistic President of the South China Republic, at Canton.

War lords Tsao Kun and General Wu Pei-fu of the Chihli faction and Chang Tso-lin, the Mukden tiger, were preparing to battle for the control of Peking. Dr. Sun and his young subordinate, General Chiang Kai-shek, were trying desperately to whip an army into shape.

American newspapers began playing up China's political movements. Barry Faris cabled me for a statement from Dr. Sun Yat-sen, and I in turn wired Dr. Sun in Canton. His telegraphed reply read:

I HAVE LAID IT DOWN THAT WE OF THE SOUTH CHINA GOVERNMENT HAVE GONE TO CANTON IN THE INTEREST OF A UNIFIED CHINA. WE WHO FOUNDED THE CHINESE REPUBLIC HAVE NEVER HAD A CHANCE TO RULE CHINA AS A REPUBLICAN STATE AND TO SHOW WHAT THE PROGRESSIVE SECTION OF THE NATION COULD DO. UNLESS THIS FACT IS REALIZED AND DEEPLY BORNE IN MIND, YOU – THE FRIENDS OF CHINA IN AMERICA – WILL SEE NOTHING BUT DISORDER AND FUTILITY AND INCAPACITY IN A PHASE OF THE NATION' S LIFE, WHICH I ASSERT, EXCEEDS IN PROMISE AND POTENCY THE RICHEST AGE OF EUROPEAN HISTORY,

CHINA MUST BE UNITED AND MODERNIZED IF' SHE IS TO SURVIVE AS AN INDEPENDENT STATE. A DESPOT, A WAR LORD, IS NOT BIG ENOUGH TO BRING THIS ABOUT. IT IS THE WORK OF OUR PEOPLE AS A WHOLE THROUGH A PARLIAMENTARY FORM OF GOVERNMENT. THE ARMIES OF THE SOUTH CHINA REPUBLIC ARE ASSEMBLING IN ORDER TO ENFORCE THIS LESSON OF PROGRESS ON PEKING'S VANGUARD AT WUHAN BEFORE THE SPRINGTIME PASSES INTO THE SUMMER. CHINA MUST BE UNITED ALSO IN ORDER

TO OPPOSE JAPAN.

In view of the situation in China today, the prophetic words uttered in 1922 by Sun, which I give verbatim, take on an unusual significance:

> JAPAN'S REAL AIM IN CHINA IS MASKED IN THE CONTENTION THAT SHE SEEKS IN CHINA ONLY ROOM FOR HER SURPLUS POPULATION AND THE RAW MATERIALS WITHOUT WHICH HER INDUSTRIES WOULD PERISH. BUT INTRAMURAL CHINA IS OVERCROWDED, AND THE CONDITIONS IN EXTRAMURAL CHINA – MANCHURIA AND MONGOLIA – ARE NOT SUITABLE FOR GENUINE JAPANESE, AS DISTINGUISHED FROM PURELY POLITICAL, COLONIZATION IN THESE REGIONS, AND OUR RAW MATERIALS ARE AVAILABLE TO JAPAN THROUGH REGULAR TRADE CHANNELS. JAPAN'S POLICY IN CHINA AIMS AT THE DOMINATION OF CHINA WITH HER MAN POWER AND HER NATURAL RESOURCES IN ORDER TO ENABLE JAPAN TO FORCE OPEN THE GATES OF AUSTRALIA AND AMERICA TO JAPANESE IMMIGRATION. THE FUTURE OF CHINA IS A VITAL – NOT AN ALTRUISTIC – CONCERN TO AMERICA.

The China political picture had become engrossing. My interest in picturesque feature stories to be picked up in Shanghai was gone. I wanted to get out into the vast country beyond the port, into the hinterland. But most of all I wanted to interview

China's war lords and revolutionary leaders. For days I toyed with the idea of writing Barry Faris what was in my mind. Instead I cabled.

Like a piston a wire shot back from Internews.

Jubilantly I read the cabled assignment aloud to the men then in the city room:

BOOKER SHANGHAI:
PROCEED HEADQUARTERS WAR LORDS INTERVIEW CHANG TSO LIN, HSU SHIH-CHANG, WU PEI-FU, SUN YAT-SEN, WU TING-FANG, LUCK INTERNEWS

"A little gal like you can't take on such an assignment," announced the cynical Old Timer. "That is a man's job."

"Yeh, you can't go into the interior at a time like this," broke in Dinty Doyle. "War may break before you can get back."

My elation was not in the least disturbed by their reaction. I was already off on a magic carpet for Peking, the capital of China, where President Hsu Shih-chang held audience in his palatial yamen. Away to Mukden, in far north Manchuria, to seek an interview with the mighty Marshal Chang Tso-lin, dictator of northern China—then deep into the heart of old China to Loyang, ancient capital of Cathay, where General Wu Pei-fu was gathering his armies—on, hundreds of miles south, to Canton and Dr. Sun Yat-sen. How I had dreamed of Canton! But not as racked by war. My dreams were of a Canton of old blue plates, deeply fringed shawls embroidered in enormous red peonies, early sailing vessels gallantly rushing before the wind.

That night in the midst of packing—Amah and I packed everything from bath salts to high-heeled silver slippers—I reread the cablegram. I wasn't worrying over possible danger ahead: I had no conception of the hardships such a trip would mean. No, my only fear was that I might fall down on the assignment.

The day following, I was off for Peking on the first lap of a journey of many hundred miles.

Friends came to the station to say goodbye but, until the train pulled out, kept telling me that I was quite mad. There was one, the American whom I had liked so much when I met him shortly after I arrived, who seemed to understand. I had seen much of John during the months. Although he too advised against the trip, he assisted me in many ways. He dispatched wires and letters to friends in the north asking them to look out for me and at the last moment, among other things, gave me a tin of insect powder.

"Why insect powder?" I laughingly asked.

As I waved a last goodbye to him from the rear train platform, an ache crept into my heart which did not lessen as the days, weeks, and even months went by before my return to Shanghai.

- 2 -

The picture from the train window as we jerked and bumped along was one of exquisite peace and beauty. Civil war? Absurd.

Stretches of young rice peeping through water-covered paddy fields, yellow rape as golden as California sunshine, peach orchards lacy with delicate pink blossoms lay on either side of the railroad. Every now and then we caught glimpses of vermilion-walled temples with curving roofs; of pagodas with tinkling wind bells rising tall and slender against a cobalt sky; and in the distance patched sails of junks moving lazily along an unseen canal. Out in the fields men were plowing with crude wooden plows while women, following in their steps, were dropping grain. Occasionally we passed a Chinese lad stretched out dreamily, contemplatively, upon the broad back of a water buffalo that he guided round and round a primitive water wheel on the bank of a canal.

I had been led to expect teeming millions living in misery and squalor; but from the car windows I watched with surprise and pleasure the tranquility, peace, and beauty of the Chinese countryside. Each little scene, each flashing incident of this normal China helped to make up a charming picture.

As we traveled northward the day following, the scene from the train windows began to change. Spring was late in the Shantung province. The brightness and joy of the south were gone, for famine was abroad in the land.

Everything was yellow as we journeyed toward Tientsin. The wind whirled great clouds of yellow dust. Grave mounds, always evident in a Chinese landscape, stood out in countless numbers against the bleak, barren yellow earth. The spring grain was not yet above the ground. Maybe there would be no spring grain. Flocks of black crows, miserable heralds of trouble, circled above.

Our train paused at a small station crowded with famine refugees. Two years earlier this land had been devastated by flood — now, by drought.

Four little girls were sitting in the thick dust by a well. They were just sitting — inanimate, dying — with their tiny clawlike hands folded over their faded cotton trousers. Their hair, which was unkempt and streaked with dust, framed pinched, old faces.

A woman came to draw water from the well. It was such a well as that by which Abraham or Jacob might have tarried, or by which Rebecca might have knelt to fill her pitcher. In a hopeless, spiritless manner she lowered a five-gallon oil tin which had been converted into a water pail. She drew it up — empty.

A portly Chinese in a padded silk robe stood watching the little girls as he puffed on his long water pipe. After a bit he offered the mother a few pieces of paper money. She looked at it listlessly; he added two or three pieces of silver. His coolies came and lifted the lifeless girls into his waiting cart; then drove away.

The woman stared after the cart. Against her leaned a boy-child. His coat hung on his thin frame, and his stomach protruded round and hard. ("Famine bellies," such deformed stomachs are called, and they come from a diet of roots, bark, dirt.) The mother had bound feet. It must have been torture for her to trudge on those crippled stumps from some distant countryside in her effort to save her children.

Her story as told to me by the Chinese was the story of thousands.

With the first indication of drought she had burned incense before the god of rain in the village temple. She had lighted fires of chamomile and wormwood for many nights in the courtyard. Her farmer husband had fastened over their doorway strips of yellow paper on which were written formulas of invocation to the dragon of water. She had helped sew the bright silken coat for the great rain dragon which was made by the villagers and paraded in a festival in his honor. But in spite of their efforts and the prayers of their priests the god of rain had remained aloof. In desperation they had set off with their neighbors for a larger, more prosperous village. They had come, not as a great ravishing band, but as helpless ones making a last effort for life. The boy-child must be saved...

I have always felt that I should have done something about those little girls. But what? They haunted me.

It was night when our train reached Peking.

The Tartar Wall—gray, massive, grim—loomed high against a moonlit sky. Peking—my dream city—was safe inside, tucked up, asleep. The great wall was on guard.

An English-speaking Chinese letter writer arrived at the

hotel early the following morning, and we dispatched letters pertaining to my interviews. The first was sent by messenger to the master of ceremonies of the Peking government, asking for an audience with His Excellency President Hsu Shihchang.

Then I was off on a four-day picnic—a large house party given by W. H. Donald, an Australian newspaperman and an outstanding figure in Peking, in his "temple" in the Western Hills. Mr. Donald, who in recent years has been the unofficial adviser to Generalissimo and Madame Chiang Kai-shek, was famous as a host and organized his picnics in a grand way.

His "temple," in reality a one-time Imperial hunting lodge, was perched high in the mountains far away from all things foreign and modern—yet life moved on in a sophisticated way. We dined by candlelight, enjoyed beautifully served dishes with appropriate wines, and wore evening dress. During the day we rode on donkeys over hills which through the ages have given shelter to holy men seeking to solve the mystery of life. It was an unforgettable experience.

Back at the hotel I found a long envelope from the presidential mansion waiting me; also one from E. Carlton Baker, formerly with the American Consular Service and at that time American adviser to Marshal Chang Tso-lin of Mukden. The first letter read:

Dear Miss Booker,

In reply to your letter of yesterday's date, I am directed by His Excellency, the President, to inform you that he regrets that he is rather busy with political affairs recently and could not find any spare time to see you.

Hoping this will not disappoint you anyhow, I am,

Yours respectfully,

WONG KAI-WEN

Grand Master of Ceremonies

The second letter informed me that His Excellency Marshal Chang Tso-lin was preparing to launch a great campaign against General Wu Pei-fu and in consequence was refusing all interviews. (Mr. Baker had, however, arranged for me to interview Chang's son, the young General Chang Hsueh-liang.)

I sank down on the nearest chair, uttering the Chinese wail of despair, "Ai-yah, ai-yah."

That evening I was taken by Mrs. Sam Young, wife of the Chinese consul-general at New York, to the ancestral home of a wealthy, official Chinese family. It was a splendid fete, with more than a thousand guests invited, in honor of the birthday of the Lao Tai-tai, Elderly Lady, of the family. I was delighted. This was my first glimpse of life behind the walls of a high-class Chinese family.

Chinese boys, wearing red coats embroidered in twisting golden dragons, blew shrill flutes and clanged brass cymbals as we arrived. Guests were entering the great red-lacquer, gold-trimmed gate in the outer courtyard. I was entranced.

We were in another world. Civil war might be at the city gates, but the sons of this ancient family were honoring their mother. This, in China, is of first importance. Crowds of Chinese strolled through the courtyards and rooms—laughing, talking, richly costumed crowds—happy in their merriment. In the great hall we glimpsed men feasting, being entertained by singsong girls whose shrill voices rose above the din.

Mrs. Young explained that the singsong girls live together in houses where they are taught the art of pleasing. For a few dollars they will attend a function, sing two or three songs, and then, like gayly tinted butterflies, flit on to the next party for which they have been engaged. They are always accompanied by their musicians and elderly chaperons.

We went on to rooms where guests were dancing. The syncopated music of an American jazz band echoed strangely through the courtyards of that ancient Peking house.

Dainty Chinese girls—Peking's inner circle—looking like a bouquet of sweet peas in their pastel silk and satin costumes, were dancing in an improvised ballroom with slim chaps wearing correct European evening dress. Smartly gowned foreigners of all nationalities, many representing their legations, were also there. In diplomatic Peking Europeans and Chinese mixed socially, and I delighted in meeting those charming girls. In adjoining rooms elderly Chinese men in satin robes, smoking long water pipes, were watching the dancers; and in connecting salons elderly women chatted—they were probably saying, "What is this generation coming to?"

In another courtyard cymbals banged and clashed as dozens of tumblers, acrobats, jugglers appeared. Lung Tung, one of the cleverest magicians in China, began to chant a rhythmic song. *Clang*, went the cymbals, and Lung Tung turned a somersault, produced a great bowl of water in which goldfish splashed. *Clang! Bang!* Another flip in the air, and he brought forth a fragile porcelain lantern encompassing a lighted, burning candle. And beyond there were Chinese actors from a Peking theater.

Presently we were taken by our host to meet his mother. It seemed strange that the lady for whom the elaborate affair was given was not present. But she was very modest and sent word to her guests that she was not worthy of such attentions and begged them to excuse her.

At the end of the Passage-of-Many-Turnings we came to the quarters of the Elderly Lady. There was no sound of revelry; no echo of modern music; no clanging of Chinese cymbals; no meeting of the East and the West. I felt as though I had stepped into a storybook of old China as we entered her quiet, spacious chamber.

A slight woman with a high-bred face was kotowing before the tablets of her ancestors. Incense floated, pale and sweet, toward the beamed, flower-painted ceiling. Red altar candles burned low, for the day was almost done. This was the aged woman's birthday, and she was honoring her forefathers. She came forward to meet us, slim and straight in black satin, and bowed us to carved blackwood chairs, while two giggling maids placed cups of steaming tea, dishes of candies, nuts, and small cakes on the tables by our chairs.

We offered our birthday congratulations.

This frail-appearing woman was the mother of eight sons; she had many grandchildren as well as a considerable number of great-grandchildren. They all lived in various sections of the establishment which the Elderly Lady ruled with a firm hand. She had permitted her sons to be educated abroad. Two of them were Harvard men. But, in her wisdom, she had seen to it that they were also well versed in the Chinese classics. She was glad that her sons were leaders among the young moderns of Peking. She would go to join her ancestors, when the day came, with a heart peaceful in the belief that in taking over the new her children would not cast out the old.

"Why is the heart of the honorable guest ruffled?" she asked in her quiet voice.

Strange she should know I was worried. In the flickering light of the ancestral candles, I found myself telling the Elderly Lady of my difficulties, of my failure to secure an audience with His Excellency President Hsu, and all about the news service in America which I represented.

She was immensely intrigued, and she sent one of the serving maids to call her eldest son.

Immediately she girded on her armor. She had changed from a polite hostess into a woman of power and personality. I could visualize her as equal to any danger or difficulty which might arise, for she was accustomed to intrigue, to diplomacy, to bringing off difficult undertakings.

"Do not trouble your heart," said the Elderly Lady. "I know that my son will take care of this small thing for you."

He did. He informed me that Dr. John C. Ferguson, American adviser to President Hsu, had only that day returned to Peking from the Washington Conference, and suggested that I see him.

Early the next morning I dispatched a letter of introduction to Dr. Ferguson. If anyone could help me untangle this Peking political puzzle, I thought, it was he. A reply came granting me an interview. My rickshaw coolie was waiting, and I was soon winding my way through the narrow hutungs which led to the Ferguson establishment.

Since 1891 Dr. Ferguson had served successively in advisory capacity under the Emperor Kuang Hsu, the Empress Dowager, the Emperor Hsuan T'ung, and in turn all the Presidents of the Republic up to that date. Besides his official activities Dr. Ferguson had made outstanding contributions to China along educational, art, and journalistic lines.

One of the Chinese newspapers in Shanghai, which my Chinese teacher, Mr. Willow Tree, brought me each morning, was the *Sin Wan Pao (News Report)*. In 1900 Dr. Ferguson, assisted by Mr. Wang Han-chee, formerly of the staff of the Nanyang University, had launched this paper. It had been a success from its first issue, and under the directing genius of Dr. Ferguson, who for years read every character printed, had become one of the two most influential Chinese newspapers in China.

Dr. Ferguson, who was known to the Chinese of all classes in Peking as *Fu Kai-sen* ("Happy and Prosperous Man"), was waiting for me in his garden, which was sweet with the scent of crab-apple blossoms and spring lilies. He was a tall man of commanding appearance, cultured and with great charm of manner.

He came at once to the point regarding my audience with His Excellency President Hsu. He advised me to write a second letter to Wong Kai-wen, then go to Mukden and if possible see Marshal Chang Tso-lin. In the meantime he would see what he could do. He was so calm and matter-of-fact about it all that my worries floated away.

After a time Mrs. Ferguson joined us. There was something very fine about Mrs. Ferguson, whose gentle face was framed with soft waving hair. She had come to China in the *City of Peking*, one of the early steamships, as a young bride—a pretty bride with a laughing face, just a bit proud of her fluted bonnet, her tiny waist, and her rustling silk dresses. During her fifty-odd years of married life in China she had made a home, borne nine children, welcomed grandchildren, four great-grandchildren, and bravely faced each new crisis— plague, revolution, antiforeign demonstration, Japanese invasion. Her attitude was not that of an exile crying out against living in a strange land, but that of a friendly settler, hands outreached to the people in this adopted country of her husband.

Dr. Ferguson showed me a copy of the Nine Power Treaty which had been signed at the Washington Conference, February, 6, 1922. As he read it to me, there in the peace of his garden, it seemed such a fine safeguard for China during those formative years of the Republic:

The United States of America, Belgium, the British Empire,

China, France, Italy, Japan, the Netherlands and Portugal,

Desiring to adopt a policy designed to stabilize conditions in the Far East, to safeguard the rights and interests of China, and to promote intercourse between China and the other Powers upon the basis of equality of opportunity, have resolved to conclude a treaty for that purpose. . . . The Contracting Powers, other than China, agree:

(1) To respect the sovereignty, the independence, and the territorial and administrative integrity of China; ·

(2) To provide the fullest and most unembarrassed opportunity to China to develop and maintain for herself an effective and stable government . . .

I was rather naïve about treaties then. So were the people of China.

That night I left for Mukden, headquarters of the most powerful of all the war lords, Marshal Chang Tso-lin; left with the hope that chance, or fate, or "joss" (luck) would somehow open the guarded gates of his great palatial yamen for me.

- 3 -

A note from E. Carlton Baker, American adviser to Chang Tso-lin, waited me at the hotel in Mukden.

Mr. Baker was very sorry, but it would be impossible for me to interview the Mukden war lord! Many noted personages — Russian princes, famous writers, government envoys — were being refused audiences. Chang was deep in preparations for war. Notes from the American consul, from the Chinese minister of foreign affairs, from three prominent American business men, men of influence in Mukden, were all the same. No interview!

Without a properly arranged interview there would be no

Left. Marshal Chang Tso-Lin, famous "Mukden Tiger," wearing his pearl-studded cap. (Photograph by author.) Right. The "Young General," Chang Hsueh-liang, eldest son of the great war lord. He figured prominently in the Sian kidnaping of Generalissimo Chiang Kai-shek in 1936. (Photograph by author.)

opportunity of seeing this "most powerful man in China." Secure behind the massive walls of his heavily guarded palace, he was the most difficult man in China to meet. Many attempts had been made upon Chang's life; consequently he saw very few persons even in peaceful times, and when he rode through the city the streets were cleared fifteen minutes before his approach. Then he whizzed by at sixty miles an hour in an especially built bullet-proof, armored car on the sides of which machine guns were mounted while guards rode strapped to the running boards.

The American consul, Mr. Taylor, called for me about one o'clock, and we drove in his car to the Baker residence for tiffin, where I was to meet Chang's son, the young General Chang Hsueh-liang.

As we entered the wide hall the telephone rang. The message delivered to Mr. Baker by the houseboy was that the young general was so busy dispatching troops that he could not come to luncheon. No interview with Marshal Chang. And now, apparently, not even with his son. And so far, no audience with the president of China. I must see these men. But how?

We were finishing tiffin when a smiling, boyish-looking young man in uniform, Chang Hsueh-liang[4] and a keen-faced, older Chinese in a long brocaded satin coat entered the dining room.

It was the young general accompanied by H. V. Kao, head of the Bureau of Foreign Affairs!

Mrs. Baker was equal to the occasion. Additional plates were laid, and in a few minutes we were all laughing over the informal situation. The excited houseboy had misunderstood the message from the official yamen.

As I watched the young general who sat across the table from me I could understand why he was such a favorite with

---

4   Who in 1935 figured so prominently in the kidnaping of General Chiang Kai-shek at Sian.

the foreign community of Mukden. He was most likable with his hearty laugh and friendly manner; and for the first time since I had been in the city faint hope of an interview with Chang Tso-lin began to stir in my consciousness. Young Chang was most modern in his outlook, and he was ambitious for China. At the local Y.M.C.A. school and at the Mukden Club, where he was a popular bridge partner, he had made friends. It was while we were in the Bakers' rose garden taking photographs after luncheon that I said (fingers crossed) to young Chang, 'I'm sorry that I won't be able to meet your famous father."

"Oh, would you like to talk with Dad?" he asked with interest.

"Well, I have traveled several hundred miles to see him for an important American news agency," I explained, "and now your Mr. Kao tells me it is impossible."

"Kao is an old fossil," laughed Chang Hsueh-liang. We both laughed. "Wait a minute, and I'll telephone Dad and see what he says."

In a short time he was back, and I slowly expelled the breath that I had held pent up during his absence.

"I've fixed it up with Dad. He will see you tomorrow afternoon at two o'clock."

I couldn't believe it!

All the ramifications of statesmanship, futilely invoked, for gaining me an audience with the Mukden tuchun had been waved aside through a comradely gesture by this dashing son of the war lord.

Mr. Baker and Mr. Kao called for me about half past one the day following, and we drove to Chang Tso-lin's magnificent palace. Soldiers stood at attention beside the heavily lacquered gates as we passed from the Spirit Wall (which kept out evil spirits from the House of Chang) and into the first courtyard.

It was very spacious and sunny. Peach trees blossomed by

the quarters where the gatekeepers and their families lived. An old man, wrinkled and bent, sat in the sunshine on a carved stone seat and smoked his water pipe contentedly. From the second courtyard we could catch a glimpse of the roofs of the yamen proper—golden tiled roofs with curved, carved corners. We passed another guard of soldiers, then followed the bowing servant into a hall which led to a spacious reception room of breath-taking beauty.

Lovely *famille-rose* enamel bowls filled with Chinese lilies, priceless scrolls portraying Chinese landscapes, rare terra-cotta tomb figures, carved blackwood furniture, silken rugs made up a room rich with the treasures of old China. Here were Ch'ien Lung porcelains, carved jade vases of mutton white, huge lacquer panels and screens with semiprecious stone insets, old bronze—treasures such as are sought throughout the world by museums and collectors. Chang's collection of porcelains was world-famous.

It was an impressive room, and I knew that Chang Tso-lin was not receiving me in his official military yamen, but in his own home. I again silently blessed the young general.

Marshal Chang Tso-lin entered.

Was this slim little man, with shining brown eyes, a kindly smile and gentle manner, a war lord? The Mukden Tiger?

He was wearing a short, black, cut velvet jacket over a long satin robe, and on his head was a black satin hat that had become famous throughout the Seven Kingdoms because of an enormous pearl of wondrous luster that glowed from the front of it—one of the largest and most valuable pearls in the world. He appeared a polished scholar with one of the gentlest speaking voices I have ever heard—and an engaging diffidence when he reached out to shake my hand. He placed us around a richly carved mother-of-pearl-inlaid table. There, surrounded by the glory and culture of ancient Cathay, Chang spoke. Mr. Kao acted as interpreter.

"China is sick," said Chang, "and, like a sick man, may need an operation. The operation will be painful, but I hope it will be justified by results."

I could see that Chang fancied himself in the role of the surgeon. As he talked I watched him, noted his alert, piercing eyes, his refined face, drooping black mustache, slim, ever moving, tapering fingers, and wondered wherein lay his amazing power: force which Lord Northcliffe, another outstandingly strong man, had felt.

Meeting Chang Tso-lin casually, you would have taken him to be a man who had lived his life in a quiet study poring over the Analects of Confucius. Yet he was called by his enemies a bandit! This was in part because he and his family had been outlawed by the Manchus on account of political differences. Chang first appeared in the limelight when, as a mere boy, he became the notorious leader of a powerful band of young fighters. Later he and his men won fame in the Russo-Japanese War when they fought on the side of Japan. Following the war, Chang threw his hat into the Chinese political ring. And thus began his spectacular rise to fame. ·

During the interview Chang Tso-lin praised the patriotism of Dr. Sun Yat-sen. I was surprised to learn that there was an understanding between them — that together they would attempt to drive out "the obstacle [Wu Pei-fu] who was preventing the reunification, the reconstruction, and the peace of China."

"I have no presidential ambitions," declared Chang. "I am working only for the good of China."

(And I could hear the men on the *China Press* scoffing; wondering what Chang Tso-lin was going to try to put over on China now.)

One of Chang's wives appeared in the wide doorway. With her

was an amah carrying a baby boy. The child was picturesquely dressed in a tiny-flowered, red satin coat and trousers, and on his head he wore a gayly embroidered good-luck band with a little gold Buddha in the center of his forehead.

Chang Tso-lin paid no attention to the pretty girl mother, for in conservative old China a Chinese woman has no place at an official interview. She had been curious.

As in all great establishments, the wives of the war lord lived in various sections of the home. Chang had a number one, a number two, and a number five wife. Number three and number four were no longer living. These women, who were said to be among the most beautiful in Manchuria, lived in seclusion behind the high walls of the palace and were seldom seen by the foreign women of Mukden.

Presently, my host picked up the fragile bowl of tea from the table to indicate, according to Chinese etiquette, that the interview was closed.

There was much bowing. Then Chang escorted us to the courtyard, an unusual courtesy, and smilingly permitted me to take his photograph. I think that he was most amused, for his eyes were twinkling. Mr. Kao told me in a loud aside that this was the first time His Excellency had ever been interviewed by a foreign woman, not to mention having his photograph taken by her.

I worked over cable and mail dispatches for New York as soon as I returned to the hotel.

But still another charming experience awaited me in the Chang chapter. Just before I left the hotel to take the train back to Peking, Mrs. Baker called. She presented me with the loveliest white-fox fur that I had ever seen. It was a personal gift to me from "the most powerful man in China," His Excellency Chang Tso-lin.

- 4 -

I returned to Peking with the confidence gained through a difficult task accomplished. I at once turned my attention to His Excellency President Hsu Shih-chang although, after having achieved an interview with Marshal Chang Tso-lin, I was no longer so worried over seeing the president of a tottering government.

Awaiting me at the desk in the hotel was a letter from Grand Master of Ceremonies Wong. Even before I opened it, I felt certain of his message. It read:

PRESIDENTIAL MANSION
DEPARTMENT OF CEREMONIES
PEKING, April 18, 1922
MISS EDNA LEE BOOKER,
Representative, International News Service,
New York,
Present.

In reply to your letter of yesterday's date[5] I beg to inform you that I have again laid your application before His Excellency the President, and His Excellency has consented to give you an interview at 3:15 on the 21st (Friday) at the Sze Chao Tong. But as you know, His Excellency is very busy and cannot be engaged very long.

Please arrange to come in a little earlier by the Fu Yao Gate at the Fu Yao Chia.

I am,

Yours respectfully,
WONG KAI-WEN

---

5   With Wong it was always yesterday's date no matter how long ago you had written.

Only those versed in Chinese etiquette could gauge the change of attitude from indifference in the first letter to respectful courtesy in the second. Accounts of my audience with Chang Tso-lin were played up in all of the Peking papers. Even the magazines commented on it, and I still have a clipping from a magazine article by J. B. Powell, editor and publisher of the *China Weekly Review*, in which he wrote (some weeks later), "Miss Booker has the distinction of having gained the first interview ever granted to a foreign woman correspondent by either Chang Tso-lin, Mukden's war lord, or Wu Pei-fu, China's national hero."

The driveway and long winding hall of the old Imperial Palace were lined with Peking soldiers when I arrived at the Fu Yao Gate of the Forbidden City according to instructions, a few days later. Seven high officials of the Chinese government, all wearing the formal afternoon dress of the European capital, received me in an ornate room adjoining the audience chamber. They were impressive, ceremonious, most formal.

Almost at once Isaac Marcosson, representative of the *Saturday Evening Post*, entered. He had an appointment for an interview with His Excellency for three o'clock; mine was for three-fifteen. He was an old hand at interviewing presidents, kings, emperors, but this was my first president. All the fine shades of official etiquette rose before me, causing me to be come very nervous; but Marcosson, who was looking most distinguished in his formal dress, was wholly unconcerned.

It seemed but a moment until Mr. Marcosson's interview was over and I found myself being ushered into a lofty audience chamber which was rich in its furnishings of old Imperial China. The seven officials accompanied me, and one of them presented me to His Excellency. President Hsu was in resplendent attire, wearing a richly brocaded short jacket of black satin over a heavy satin robe of Peking blue. He was a striking man with thick silver hair, an unlined yet strong face, and wide-set eyes which had a smile in them. He was a statesman possessed of a fair knowledge of world affairs and he had the polished manner and dignity of the old Manchu court. An oriental suavity even under the shadow of possible imprisonment or death (due to the complexities of Chinese politics) was presented by Hsu.

He offered me a hesitant hand, then with a graceful gesture indicated that I was to be seated. Hsu sat on what appeared to be a wide gold lacquer throne chair whose flat cushions were covered with tribute brocade, the officials and I on carved, straight-backed chairs which were flanked by small tables and grouped in set order about the throne chair.

Stage-fright swept over me as I sat there in silent, solemn state along with the impassive officials. Disciplining my thoughts, I began asking questions of His Excellency through one of the men who was acting as official interpreter.

"I have done all that I could do to prevent civil war in China," President Hsu stated in a most conversational manner. "For a number of years the Republic of China has been divided into rival camps, and we stand before the world a nation torn by internal strife. National unity is the first goal. If, out of the threatening war, union is the result, the price paid will not be too great."

When we rose at the close of the audience the high officials and I formed a semicircle in front of His Excellency and bowed very low. As we backed down the long, spacious room, we bowed again, and then again. There was absolute silence in the room, and the bows, which were punctiliously returned by President Hsu, were serious, ceremonial.

My audience was over.

Marshal Chang Tso-lin and His Excellency the President could now be checked off my list. Next week, I thought, I'll push on to Loyang and General Wu Pei-fu.

- 5 -

Just as I was going in to dinner with some friends that evening Upton Close, a Peking newspaperman and correspondent for the *China Press*, came dashing into the hotel lobby in search of me.

"The last train for Loyang leaves at midnight tonight," he hurriedly announced. "General Wu is going to commandeer all trains, you will have to step on it!"

He looked a bit wild. A khaki suit had been thrown on his lean frame; his red hair was bristling straight up; the freckles covering his long face seemed to stand out in accentuation of his excitement.

"Hundreds of refugees are crowding into the train. Be there within an hour." Handing me a package, he said, with a somewhat embarrassed smile: "My wife says you must wear these. It will be a rough trip." Then he was off."

The package contained a pair of khaki riding breeches, an old tam-o'-shanter, and a pair of warm gloves. I looked at them in amazement. I had had tea with Upton Close and his wife that afternoon, and they had seemed quite concerned over my wardrobe. While it did nicely for social Peking they were quite definite in their suggestions as to what I must wear on the trip to Loyang. I did not then appreciate their concern, and it was with distaste that I pulled on the breeches. They were ludicrously large; but the hotel amah managed with her needle and safety pins to take them in at the waist and shorten them at the bottom. There was no time to worry over my appearance, but I was glad nevertheless that my blouse covered the safety pins. I changed from dancing pumps to walking shoes, drew on the tam and my camel's-hair coat, and was off. The room coolies followed with my bags, hatbox, portable typewriter, and camera.

My taxi reached the station just in time. I shall never forget the expression on the newspaperman's face when he saw my baggage. However, he hurried me, baggage and all, through the crowd and into the train, which groaned under the load it carried. It was just ten o'clock when we pulled out, two hours ahead of the scheduled time.

We were off for Loyang to interview General Wu Pei-fu!

I planned to return to Shanghai, following my interview with Wu, by way of Hankow. Between ourselves, I did not wish to become involved in a Chinese war. The tension in north China was suddenly tightening. The warnings of my Shanghai and Peking friends and the admonitions of John began to seem less fantastic.

Upton Close and I crowded into a compartment occupied by soldiers and refugee civilians. There was a constant bustle of excitement during the long hours of the night. The train jerked and stopped—jerked and stopped. At Liuli, a small station several miles south of Peking, a number of Tsao Kun's soldiers crowded noisily onto the train. (Marshal Tsao Kun was Wu Pei-fu's commander-in-chief.) Some of them pushed into our compartment and sat on the floor. They had been directing coolies in the business of digging trenches.

Tsao Kun's soldiers were disheveled, dirty. They seemed very careless of their guns, always handling them, always pointing them about. They made me nervous. Our compartment was crowded, the air close and foul. Every few minutes the doors would rattle open, and two or three more soldiers would poke their heads into our compartment. Then they would bang the doors shut. Boys selling hot tea, watermelon seeds, green slices of pickled eggs, and small cakes crowded in every half-hour or so. The soldiers ate noisily, drank their tea in loud gulps, then belched intermittently. They would clear their throats and spit with a loud scraping hawk. One thin-faced fellow took off his coat, picked "cooties" from the seams of his padded garment and popped them. Two or three of the others joined in the sickening sport. They played Chinese finger games and laughed raucously. They smoked vile-smelling cigarettes. They slept fitfully — with their mouths open. One big fellow sitting at my feet swayed over against me in his sleep. I gave him a push. He half awoke, smiled sleepily, then with the constant jerking of that slow-moving train again fell toward me, and finally settled comfortably down on my feet. I sat unrelaxed, upright, waiting for I knew not what during those relentless hours.

Dawn finally came, and we stopped for a time at Paotingfu, headquarters of the Chihli party, which was commanded by Tsao and Wu. Some of the soldiers piled off; others crowded on; more refugees with their bundles, teapots, garlic, squeezed in. Then we were off on the next grueling stretch. By the second night the Hôtel de Peking and even Shanghai began to seem but fading memories, for only the train was real.

I was covered with the grime of travel; smoke, cinders, yellow dust had filtered in through the warped wooden sidings of that primitive coach. The Chinese woman sitting next to me, however, remained tidy and well groomed. She was dignified, composed. The train trip was unpleasant, very, but necessary; there was nothing she could do about it. Therefore, with the philosophy of her race, she met all of the vicissitudes calmly — quite wisely practiced the doctrine of *takuan* (detachment) and drank her tea as placidly, as gracefully, as if she had been sitting in the Perfumed Inner Apartment of her own home. When I realized how this middle-aged, really delightful Chinese woman had risen above the hardships of the trip, I began to try to do likewise. But it was difficult to maintain a semblance of poise when my body ached; my eyes were red and smarting from train smoke, from need of sleep; my face and clothing were covered with layers of dust. I decided to rise above it all by giving myself a clean-up facial of sorts. I took out a cold-cream jar and, while the soldiers watched me with concentrated interest, tried to clean my face. The cream rubbed off a dirty yellowish brown. One bold fellow stuck his finger into the jar, then streaked his unshaven cheeks while the others guffawed.

There was only one "dressing room" on our coach. It was a vile-smelling, cramped place, used alike by soldiers, coolies, women, refugees. There was a large "W.C." on the door, as well as Chinese characters. To reach it meant stumbling over the bedding, soldiers' baggage, spittoons, bird cages, and the Chinese who sat crowded together in the aisle. It was no place for a beauty treatment.

So ended my efforts in *takuan*.

The hours dragged on and on and on.

Sometime during that last night on the train most of the Chinese in our compartment got off at a small station. The newspaperman had long since discovered a more comfortable spot up with the engineer. Then the sweet-faced Chinese woman took a carefully wrapped package from her baggage. It was a pink satin pillow embroidered in purple, red, and blue birds, and she gave it to me with the suggestion that I stretch out on the seat and try to sleep. I was so tired that I did not even feebly protest. We were nearing Loyang when I finally awoke. A Chinese newspaper had been fastened over a corner of the window in an effort to keep out the glaring sunlight. The train boy brought towels wrung out of hot, scented water and a pot of steaming, refreshing tea, and I got off that train rested, eager, impatient to proceed at once to the headquarters of General Wu Pei-fu, my next war lord.

The spring sun was brightening the drab, crumbling walls of Loyang, ancient capital of China in Honan Province, as we left the station. The newspaperman hailed a mule cart with a blue-cotton-covered top, and we climbed in with our bags and typewriters. There were no seats, and we had to sit cross-legged on the matting-covered floor.

Our vehicle appeared harmless enough as we started bumping along over the ambling, narrow, dirt street. All went well until we suddenly hit a hole in the deeply rutted road. My head struck the framework of the cart with a blow for which I was totally unprepared. There seemed to be no way of bracing myself, of finding my lost equilibrium, of regaining my dignity. That cart and its mule seemed to have a penchant for the deep crevices which had been cut by the traffic of years.

The crowds on the street laughed at the spectacle of foreigners bumping along in a cart. (Strangers from across the sea are a novelty, for Loyang is off the path of tourists.) Small boys in short blue cotton jackets and trousers followed us very much as youngsters in America would have trailed a circus wagon. An old letter writer sitting in the market place, the coolies drawing water from the ancient well, a wrinkled seller of small cakes calling his wares, fat garrulous mending women sewing in the courtyard of the city's temple, all stopped their work to watch the foreigners go by.

This quaint city of Loyang with its simple, friendly people and their homely tasks, although then a country village practically untouched by western enterprise, was once a glorious city. During the Han Dynasty, some four thousand years ago, and again in the Wei Dynasty, sixth century after Christ, Loyang was the capital of China. Great palaces dominated it, and the pomp

71

and pageantry of court life were paraded before the populace. Li Tai Po and Tu Fu, two of China's most famous poets, sang of these days, and Tu Fu wrote:

Centuries ago Lo Yang fell, fell under the waves of invasion:
Men of the Capital changed color from sorrow.

And although rulers have gone, palaces crumbled into ruins, dynasties ended, the simple country people whose ancestors played their part in the days of luxury and grandeur still carry on.

We passed through the city gates and onto a wide, well made military road over the rolling lowlands to Wu Pei-fu's barracks. Green fields of young grain stretched from the city walls as far as we could see across the open country. From a cluster of the thatch-roofed mud houses partially hidden by clumps of verdant bamboo trees came the song of a lute. I thought again of Li Tai Po and his madrigal,

From whose roof does the voice of the jade flute come flying?
The spring breeze scatters the song into the city of Lo Yang.

We bumped on and on....

"Well, here we are," announced Upton Close briskly.

I awoke to the fact that we were at last in the domain of the great Tuchun Wu.[6] Suddenly this war lord of whom I had heard so much became very real.

We stopped before a large barracks with a jerk which threw me against the side of the cart. It was a staggering thump. I

---

6   The same general Wu Pei-fu who died a hero in December, 1939, after having resisted
    for two years the pressure of Japanese militarists to become the puppet head of the
    government that Japan hopes to set up in Japanesecontrolled China

had hoped to dismount from that fiendish cart gracefully, with dignity. Instead, I was so dazed and shaken that I could hardly stand, and had to be helped out by a most polished Chinese officer who awaited us.

- 6 -

The living room of the establishment was unpretentious when compared with Marshal Chang's spacious reception salon or the magnificent assembly hall of the presidential yamen in Peking. But it expressed the personality of General Wu. Books in blackwood cabinets lined the walls. I was amazed to see an oil painting of George Washington hung in a strong light near a window. On a table was a large, ebony figure of Kwan Yi, the legendary War Lord of China. He was riding his famous charger Red Hair and waving aloft his historic Blue Dragon sword. The figure stood on a brick-red satin table cover, and incense in an old cloisonné burner smoldered before him.

General Wu was smiling as he came into the room — a warm cordial smile of welcome. His striking, amber eyes were alight with interest and not assiduously veiled as oriental eyes so often are. I could see at once why Wu was the national hero of China — why men felt that he lived up to his name Pei-fu, the English version of which is Trust and Confidence. He inspired these qualities.

"The Little General," Wu was affectionately called. He was a slender, virile man whose winning personality in no way took away from his real character as a war lord. Although the officers we had met upon our arrival had been in uniform, Wu was wearing a dark green satin robe, over which was a short, brocaded satin jacket. He greeted the newspaperman as an old friend, then turned and thanked "the American writing lady for honoring his humble dwelling." He stated that I was the first

73

woman journalist he had ever welcomed into his home.

General Wu plunged at once into the business in hand. There were no wasted gestures, no court ceremonies to this interview. He seated us around the table presided over by the war god Kwan Yi, and asked me what I wished to know.

I had come to learn of his military plans, but curiosity was aroused over the portrait of America's first president hanging in the study of a Chinese warrior deep in the heart of old China. I asked about the picture.

"I have an extravagant admiration for the American hero, George Washington," said General Wu, moving to stand before the painting. (It was a copy of the Athenaeum portrait of Washington by Gilbert Stuart.) "Washington was an upright, cultured gentleman, a statesman whose integrity could not be assailed, a valiant soldier who fought, not for personal gain, but for the good of the people of America."

Without waiting for any response to that, General Wu asked shyly if I enjoyed reading poetry. On being assured that I did, he produced some of his own poems—charmingly arranged in Chinese characters done with artistic brush strokes. The first one was entitled "George Washington," and while I then sensed its meaning it was not until I was back in Shanghai and worked out a translation with Teacher Willow Tree that I really appreciated its depth. It read:

When I think of heroes, my mind brings me to George Washington.

He knew the force of the will of the people, and with their aid made a nation prosperous and strong

He united thirteen states into one strong body.

He appealed to the French people for support, and they responded. He hoisted the Flag of Independence,

And rang the Bell of Liberty.
He led the great cause of America's emancipation,
And won staunch supporters to his aid.
Military music is a source of inspiration to the people,
And stirs soldiers to energetic endeavor.
A new world was born in the Western Hemisphere.
Could any other man have filled the place of Washington?

"My great ambition is to do in a small way for China what the great American did for his country," stated Wu simply and earnestly. "I would unite the provinces of China, as Washington did the states of America, and make our nation prosperous and strong."

Then his eyes flashed. The poet, the dreamer, was gone. The fierce soldier tuchun was speaking. (The newspaperman, who had been bored by the introduction of poetry into a war interview, sat up with interest.)

"But, to unite China, we must rid the land of a bandit whose robber heart has never been reformed."

I remembered how a number of days earlier Chang Tso-lin had denounced Wu Pei-fu as "an obstacle to the unification of China."

An officer entered, saluted, and stated that the document formally declaring war on Chang Tso-lin and the Mukden forces was ready.

We rode to the barracks a few blocks away—rode in a Ford which seemed luxury after the mule cart.

General Wu's private staff was assembled around a table in a long dining hall of his military headquarters. The officers arose and stood at attention until General Wu and the foreign journalists were seated.

A large map of northern China lay on the table. Red and

blue flags dotted its surface until it looked like a complicated golf course with many more than the usual eighteen holes. The flags represented the armies of Wu and Chang placed in strategic positions.

A number of declarations lay ready to be wired to interested parties. One was addressed to "The Legation of Each Nation in Peking and for the Consulates of Every Country in Shanghai and Hankow." Wu read it in a loud and forceful voice:

"The ex-bandit, Chang Tso-lin, comes down from Mukden to run the Republic of China, disrupt the country, and overturn the law. His robber's heart has never been reformed. For a year or so past Peking has been deprived of governmental powers. Civil strife has been without cessation. Chang Tso-lin's motive has been through these things to establish selfish factions, grasp unto himself the powers of government, cut away the treasury, and commit every sort of action which will come under these heads.

"The agitators of oppression, the criminals who desire to restore the monarchy, the traitors of their country — all these he has taken unto his heart. Although in military and civil power Chang Tso-lin does not lack, yet his spoliation of the nation, and the poisoning of the lives of his people would place China without a ray of hope.

"Chang Tso-lin has taken his bandit troops, disturbed the environment of the capital; furthermore, he has without reason sent soldiers into Tientsin and made a drive upon Paotingfu.

"His bandits are clearly responsible for the plundering of the coasts of Shantung and the greater disorder of that province. The principle of demobilization of excess troops which was emphasized at the Washington Conference had its head lopped off by this man.

"Wu Pei-fu and these with him, working for political

righteousness in China, are unable to do otherwise than to take active measures for protection of the nation, to revive peace in the regions of Peking and Tientsin, and to fight for the lives and property of foreigners. We take upon ourselves the responsibility of guardianship.

"The war, once declared, will be quickly culminated, restoration of communication made, and a happy period of reconstruction will follow, which we believe will reward the hopes of the friends of every nationality who desire to see China united and at peace.

"May we ask every foreign friend, during the time required to drive out the bandit brigands, to observe strictly treaties according to international law. Above all things, not to give aid or furnish military supplies to the bandit troops.

"We send this telegram with our deep respects and hope that it will receive your careful attention.

"(Signed) Wu PEI-FU

"(Also signed) Tuchuns of Kiangsu, Kiangsi, Hupeh, Shantung, Honan, Shensi, and Shansi Provinces."

Another declaration which was addressed to the people of China explained the cause of internal strife and promised that the war would be of short duration. A third telegram was addressed to Marshal Chang Tso-lin. It was most polite, but what insults lay behind its poetic phrases!

Suddenly, General Wu began to chant a fierce, wild, marching song. The chant was taken up by the men at the table, by the soldiers who had drifted into the room and even by the boys who were serving tea. The slow tempo grew faster and faster, louder and louder, until the hall rang with a great frenzied war cry.

"I am starting north at once," said Wu. "I wish to surprise our enemy."

I had a fleeting vision of the trains of soldiers I had seen leaving Mukden, of the food supplies and ammunition. I did not think that Chang would be "surprised," but I did not say so.

"Would you and the young lady journalist care to go with us?" he asked Mr. Close. "Madame Wu is accompanying me to Paotingfu, our military headquarters. It would give her great pleasure to have you" — he turned to me — "as guest in our home there."

I accepted gladly. According to Chinese conventional etiquette, I should have waited until the invitation had been extended three times. I should have hesitated as unworthy of entering his magnificent establishment. I should have allowed him to protest that his small cottage was so humble as to be unworthy of a guest. But I realized that General Wu was not speaking idle words at such a critical time, and I accepted his first invitation. What a privilege it would be to visit in the home of a Chinese war lord, to take part in the life in the women's quarter of an old-established Chinese family!

Madame Wu greeted us as we reached the house. She was a large forceful woman, as vivid as one of the peonies which were blossoming in the courtyards. She was of the imperious, dominating Manchu race; a woman about five feet three — which is tall in China — and she was heavy-set, impressive. Gleaming black hair, snapping eyes, a large, full-lipped mouth, and a determined chin, gave an immediate sense of force. But I was almost as quickly aware of her very feminine flair for adornment, her quick eye for clothes. Her first glance took in every detail of my attire — and she didn't like it. My old tam especially seemed to annoy her. She promptly took it off my head, and her two amahs who were there to serve tea began giggling at my light hair.

Madame Wu herself was a Chinese picture, a study in purple,

gold, and black. Her black satin short coat and her long satin skirt were embroidered in purple. She wore purple silk hose and lovely purple and gold embroidered slippers, while her jewels — amethyst and gold earrings — completed a most effective costume.

Madame Wu, who was one of the most dominating women I have ever met, at once began preparations for departure. The Chinese say that "the hen does not announce the morn," but in the Wu family, I could soon see, Madame Wu made (at least) her own decisions.

Hearing that the leading officials and wealthy men of Paotingfu were sending their families to Hankow, and that the country people were fleeing like frightened sheep because of the news that Chang had threatened to level the city walls, Madame Wu decided to go with General Wu and show the "cowards" that she was not afraid.

I asked General Wu if I might dispatch a cable. He arranged for this, and the news that China was at war broke in New York almost before it did in the foreign ports of China.

The whole town of Loyang was out to see General Wu and his soldiers off to the front. Also, they were out to see if the astonishing news that Madame Wu was going with her husband could be true. (The tottering blind man, who was led through the streets by his faithful grandson; the amahs who drew water from the Flowering Plum Well, and the bean-curd vender who journeyed from door to door, had been spreading such news for days. But then they were notorious gossips.)

The crowds gave way as General Wu and members of his staff boarded the long troop train with its many coaches filled with soldiers. Madame Wu and I followed. With a quiet dignity she stood on the train platform and bowed slightly to the throng. On board she quickly adjusted herself to the train and did not complain over inconveniences. Her amahs, however, fussed from the time we left Loyang until we arrived at Paotingfu.

As we neared Paotingfu I began to think seriously of my decision to accompany Madame Wu. Instead of traveling south to Hankow and then down to Shanghai and safety—I was on my way north to the heart of the war zone: riding on a troop train en route to the military headquarters of Tsao Kun and Wu Pei-fu. I was going to live in the great house of Wu, behind the Orchid Door, for days. I wondered what adventures lay ahead? When we reached the station at Paotingfu a cable was handed to me. Internews had received my wire from Loyang, and I was ordered to cover the Chang-Wu war.

Thus I became a war correspondent in China.

At Paotingfu, a delegation of officials and members of the gentry awaited General Wu. Crowds of refugees bound for Hankow packed the platform. How weary they looked! For many of them had been waiting all night in the hope of a train going south.

As General Wu left the train an amusing comic opera military band, impressive in purple uniforms, great golden epaulets and plumed hats, began to play "Dixie" —a bit off tune, but still "Dixie."

But even while the familiar lilt of the old southern song rang in my cars another sound broke over us, a sound of menace that came, without definite words, from the sea of Orientals about us.

A hired assassin whose bronze face was twisted in a set smile hurled himself toward General Wu. There was the flash of struggling men; a shot. The man fell at General Wu's feet — dead.

What was I about to face?

-7-

Madame Wu and I were hurried through the muttering crowd into a closed, heavily guarded carriage. The loud bell on the swaying vehicle clanged constantly as it rushed pell-mell through the streets. My thoughts were so full of the oppressive experience we had just had that I saw little of Paotingfu; scarcely realized it when we stopped.

Soldiers stood on guard at the entrance of Wu Pei-fu's Paotingfu establishment as we entered the Great Gate. Madame Wu led the way. She paid scant attention to the bowing gate-keepers, the menservants, or the additional soldiers standing at attention in the inner court.

In the second courtyard the men of the family were assembled, and we were received in a most dignified manner. There was a young cousin, slim and aristocratic, who wore a brown satin robe. I was not surprised, when introduced to a middle-aged man who resembled General Wu, to learn that he was a relative. But whereas Wu had a dominating personality, this man was a dreamer who shuddered at the thought of war and spent his days in his study or in a garden with his flowers and birds. There was also an old uncle about whom clung the faint peculiar scent of opium. His hands trembled constantly, and the pallid skin of his face was tightly drawn over high cheekbones.

Almost at once we went on down a long passageway with devious turnings until we came to a door in the wall—a door as round as a great full moon—called the Orchid Door. This led into the women's quarters of the great house of Wu.

I was breathless with anticipation, sensed that life behind the Orchid Door was to be a delightful experience—perhaps the most colorful of all that would be painted on my treasured Chinese scroll. I remembered my brief visit to the home of Marshal Chang Tso-lin. I had felt life palpitating behind the high walls of his palace. Now my desire to learn something of the life within the

Inner Chamber was to be realized.

Before I left the house of Madame Wu I was to appreciate with amazement the cleverness of the Chinese women in handling men, domestic situations.

We paused a moment at the entrance of the women's apartments.

The scene framed by the Orchid Door of the Flower Wall was like a painting done on silk. The courtyard garden was typical of those delicately etched on round Chinese fans. It was all there—the artificial hill topped by a teahouse with a curved roof, the formal lotus pool in which goldfish flashed in the sunlight, the fantastic rockery which featured tall, honeycombed rocks with quaint designs that had taken dripping water more than a hundred years to carve. There were stiff rows of peonies blossoming in flower pots and a carpet of small colored stones arranged in symmetrical symbolic patterns. The garden was charming.

Three little children were running up and down the curving path which led to the teahouse on the hill. I caught a glimpse of their chubby faces, of tiny pigtails standing straight up from their closely cropped heads, and of lavender and pink silk coats as they played among the dwarfed pines and the azaleas which covered the sides of the hill.

Two young Chinese women, one in apple-green and the other in daffodil-yellow silk, swayed gracefully on their golden lilies to meet us.

Icy Heart, the one in green, was the wife of the young cousin, and she spoke a bit of English. I was glad; for although I had been studying Chinese every day for several months with Teacher Willow Tree in Shanghai I had barely skimmed the surface of the language.

Floating Cloud, the other young woman, was the wife of the elderly relative of Wu's who had met us at the gate. She was so lovely as she greeted us that I felt she must satisfy her husband's fine sense of beauty and poetry.

We went at once to a suite of rooms adjoining Madame Wu's. Here I was to live for a number of intensely interesting days: days so full of strange adventure and incredible experiences that this interlude within the Orchid Door was to seem a period of many weeks.

Four amahs bowed many times and greeted me with friendly chatter. They were unpacking my suitcase and were greatly amused at the strange garments worn by the foreign woman. Madame Wu arranged for these four to look after me while I was her guest. One good amah was a joy. But four! I was simply overwhelmed; but in spite of my protests the four amahs remained.

The room itself was pleasing and gave an impression of shining cleanliness. Long doors, set with squares of glass on which flowers and birds were painted, opened into the quiet courtyard; the windows, which were of iridescent shell, were heavily barred. The massive beams of the ceiling, called by the Chinese "Heaven Flower Boards," were painted in conventional designs of undulating dragons lifting their heads from the waves of the sea. The red, gold, marine-blue effect was startling.

A small blackwood table with a straight-backed chair on either side was placed in exactly the correct position against one of the walls. The bed with its silken curtains and embroidered satin cover occupied the opposite wall. The dressing table – a highly polished, beautifully carved piece of blackwood – was the only other article of furniture.

My chambers and courtyard, I was to know and love; but I was never able to find my way about the great house of Wu. The maze of rooms, courtyards, ancient wells, winding corridors, unexpected doorways, gardens, sections given over to various members of the family, unexplored passageways left me confounded. The house extended from one block to the next; I never knew whether I was coming or going, yet the plan was perfect to one familiar with Chinese architecture.

I had not undressed for days, and when Number One amah led me into the primitive bath adjoining my bedroom I gave a thankful sigh. A high, round Soochow *kang* was filled with hot, perfumed water which the pockmarked amah was tempering with cold water. After I had enjoyed a long, luxurious tub, rub-rub amah entered. She gave me a heavenly massage with sweet-scented oil. No wonder Chinese women were lovely.

My middy blouse and jodhpurs had disappeared. How good it seemed to shake the dust of the troop train forever!

The Number One amah had taken my dresses to be pressed. But Icy Heart, to the great delight of all, presented me with a lovely delphinium-blue silk Chinese costume embroidered in flowers, the short coat of which was fastened with pink loops caught over tiny balls of rose crystal. Icy Heart and I were about the same height, so that the trousers were perfect. There was a skirt; but Icy Heart and Floating Cloud were not wearing theirs, and therefore I did not try it on: in the seclusion of the women's quarters the women were *en famille*.

I sat down at the dressing table, and at once Number One began brushing my hair with a finished touch. The dressing table was most intriguing, for on its shining surface were a round magpie mirror of bronze, a beauty cabinet of black lacquer inlaid with silver, a jadestone back scratcher with a long ivory handle, and powder boxes of gold filigree inset with semiprecious stones. As I looked into the mirror I wondered how many Chinese girls had gazed into its clear, polished face, for it was very old.

Icy Heart, Floating Cloud, and I chatted and laughed as we watched Number One amah.

"Hair like rice straw," said the pockmarked one in a grumbling aside. I was just one more bath to her.

"No, more like sewing silk," answered the Number One.

"Eyes like blue glass" — more criticism.

"Yes, but skin like the fat of mutton."

The Number One liked me. She was trying to find something about the foreign guest which measured up to the Chinese ideal of beauty. The expression "mutton fat" is applied to a certain type of creamy white jade. It is greatly prized; and a complexion which can be likened to white jade is one of the finest gifts the Eight Immortals can bestow upon the girl-child.

After coiling my hair at the back of my neck, Number One began working on my eyebrows. With deft strokes, she twisted a strand of strong silk thread, which hurt less than foreign tweezers — and when she had finished, my eyebrows were as delicately arched as Icy Heart's and resembled the "new moon" and "willow leaf" of which the Chinese poets sing. Bushy eyebrows, according to Chinese books on physiognomy, indicate fierceness of temper and are not fitting for ladies.

Number One was very high-handed. She went right ahead with her work. A faintly perfumed white liquid powder, liquid rouge, an eyebrow charcoal, then she stood off to study the result of her efforts as impersonally as an artist working on a canvas. Number One had quite an air. Finally she gave a quick nod of satisfaction.

Just then Madame Wu entered the room. Her dark eyes were blazing with excitement.

I was at once drawn back from the land of fancy, from playing at being a princess in Cathay, to the actuality of being an American war correspondent with a particularly difficult assignment — a

Chinese war—ahead of me.

"General Wu is leaving for the front tonight!" she announced dramatically. "He goes to Changhsintien. He will attack the Mukden Tiger at dawn!"

Her eyes grew larger, darker; her broad shoulders squared. Here was a woman of such force that she herself looked capable of leading the army against Chang Tso-lin. Madame Wu was a Manchu, of the same race as Tz'u Hsi, the former Empress of China, and that adamant will which had characterized Old Buddha shone forth in this wife of General Wu.

The atmosphere of tensity which she had brought into the room was suddenly dispelled by the high, shrill laughter of the amahs. They had found my French-heeled slippers of blue satin.

Floating Cloud carried one of the slippers to Madame Wu, hoping to distract her from thoughts of war. She succeeded. For Madame Wu, who had the unbound feet of the Manchu women, was soon experimenting with the foreign footwear. There was regret—yet pride—in the eyes of the two younger women as they glanced at their golden lilies. Then they hastened to the assistance of Madame Wu. She had discarded her own satin slippers and had stepped into mine.

Taking a Chinese relative by each hand, she walked slowly back and forth across the room. The room sang with laughter. And Madame Wu, who a few minutes before had been torn with worry, was the merriest of all. A pair of black satin pumps with rhinestone buckles caught her fancy, and she tried them on, doing another tottering walk in them. In the midst of our merrymaking, a servant woman hobbled into the room, and announced the evening rice.

Stepping carefully from my pumps, Madame Wu resumed her own fascinating embroidered slippers and led us to the women's dining room.

A great mirror framed in black and gold which stood at the far end of the spacious room reflected a most picturesque scene and caught bits of the landscaped courtyards into which the dining hall opened. Even the wonderful looking-glass into which Alice peered before setting out on her thrilling adventures could not have portrayed a more charming picture. This mirror had a real personality and, according to Number One, was called the Bright One. It had more serious duties than just reflecting the beautiful faces of the women and amusing the children as they played with the golden carved dragon on which it rested. For the Bright One must ward off all roving demons and bring good luck to the family. And some clever Chinese even claim that they can see below the shining surface and read the future.

A baby organ imported from America, the joy of Madame Wu's heart, stood near. In the center of the room was a carved blackwood table about which we gathered for the evening meal. We were seated on barrel-shaped stools with marble inlay seats. There was no table linen. Fragile bowls filled with rice, painted porcelain spoons, ivory chopsticks, and a bowl of tea tightly covered "to keep in the heat," marked each place.

Four plates of cold food—appetizers—were in the center of the table. With her chopsticks Madame Wu began helping me to small pieces of chicken, slices of pickled eggs, thin bits of smoked ham, and diced pork. The cold dishes were removed by the serving women, and eight hot bowls were brought on: scrambled eggs with mushrooms; roast duck so tender that it fell to pieces with a touch of the chopsticks; fried shrimp balls; chicken with bamboo shoots and chestnuts; pork and red cabbage; bean sprouts; breast of chicken with walnuts; baked fish with marvelous sauce. Everything was delicious, for the Chinese rival the French as masters of cuisine. I felt awkward with the chopsticks. Every now and then one of the amahs would push a morsel of food, which she had softened by chewing, into the mouth of one of the youngsters.

Following the hot courses came an Eight Precious Things pudding. It was a marvelous concoction of steamed rice, lotus seeds, preserved green plums, candied cherries, dates, nuts, figs, and citron; and was served with an almond milk sauce.

While we were having our meal in the women's quarters the men of the family were enjoying a similar repast in another section of the house.

We were long at the table, but at last we strolled into the garden and watched the stars appear one by one in the square of blue sky visible from the Heaven Well (courtyard). Icy Heart and Floating Cloud soon left us, but Madame Wu and I remained by the Glowing Jade Pool. How still it was! Within the walls of the women's quarters no sound of the tramping of soldiers' feet or rumble of the supply carts could be heard. We were in a little world of our own—secluded, shut off from the life without the walls.

It was growing late; Madame Wu presently accompanied me to my room.

Learn Pidgin entered, carrying a bamboo cot. I discovered that she was to sleep in my room. Almost at once she closed the windows. She believed that evil spirits of the night roamed through the darkness looking for an open window or door. In the midst of a discussion with Number One as to whether the top red satin comforter should be arranged like a sleeping bag, into which I would crawl according to the Chinese custom, or spread across the bed as I wished it, I heard the faint echo of a bugle call.

There were sounds of hurrying steps down the corridors, the swish of silk, and a faint whiff of perfume. My amahs ran from the room to ask the cause of the excitement which was disturbing the household. I hurried after them through a maze of rooms and passageways and finally arrived at the front section of the great house.

Madame Wu, a group of soldiers, and the men of the family were talking excitedly. Almost at once General Wu entered. He paused just long enough to bid farewell to his family and to his foreign guest, then hurried away into the night. Wu was on his way to war!

We walked to the Great Gate and watched a long file of soldiers as they marched goose-step fashion towards the station. How sharply they were silhouetted in the starlight! On and on they came. Some of them looked not more than thirteen or fourteen years of age. They wore gray uniforms with wide red sleeve bands, and carried knapsacks on their backs. Fastened to the knapsacks were small trench picks, shovels, lanterns, teapots, oiled-paper umbrellas, alarm clocks, and hot-water bottles. It seems amusing now to think of a soldier carrying a fan, an umbrella, and a porcelain teapot to war, but there was nothing humorous in the situation that night.

Following the soldiers came two-wheeled carts loaded with bedding and supplies. Little boys ran by the side of the carts and trilled shrilly to the stubborn mules.

Behind the carts, like a caravan of death, came heavy wooden coffins suspended on poles from the shoulders of the coolies. I gazed after them in amazement. Madame Wu explained. The long stream of coffins gave the soldiers a sense of security. If killed in battle their bodies would not be left on the plain; their spirits would not roam throughout eternity, restless, forever seeking a place in the abode of their ancestors.

Then General Wu, the soldiers, the coffin bearers, vanished into the night. Only the majestic wall was left. It was like the cutting of a film: I wondered if it could have been real, or if it were but a gripping scene from some dramatic oriental motion picture.

I went back to my chamber—serious and saddened—knowing that war was soon to break almost at our gates; realizing that in a short time I too must follow Wu to the front. But I resolutely shut the picture of those coffins from my thoughts, opened the windows, and slid into bed to sleep under the watchful eyes of the dragons of the Heaven Flower Boards.

- 8 -

"Most Gracious Missie," said the Number One amah, as she handed me a small covered bowl, "here is your morning tea."

I was sleepy and had to look twice at the trim Chinese woman before I remembered. I was in the house of Wu!

It had been a strange night. Sleeping on a *kang* had been a surprising experience, for the *kang* with its brick and mud foundation, is so constructed that a fire can be built under it and kept burning during the bitter winter night. The satin-covered comforts filled with raw silk had misled me. It had been almost as uncompromising as the bunk of a hair-shirted anchorite doing penance.

Then there had been my undeclared war with Learn Pidgin over the windows.

I had awakened some time during the night and found the air heavy, the windows shut, so I slipped up and quietly opened the window nearest me. Toward morning I again awoke to find every window closed. Learn Pidgin was apparently asleep, and so once again I arose. But even as I sipped the tea which Number One had brought me I noticed that the windows were fastened. Almost at once, however, Learn Pidgin, who had evidently arisen at dawn, came into the room and with the greatest deliberation threw wide the windows to the sunshine. The demons of the night had fled.

I was new in China then and had had comparatively few encounters with that infinite patience of the Chinese: patience which wears down resistance as does water which falls drop by drop upon a stone. Now I never argue when I find myself in a situation over which I do not have absolute control. I just give in as gracefully as possible, thereby saving myself loss of face as well as a tremendous strain upon my disposition. This may sound like weakness, but it isn't. It is wisdom gained through experience.

"Will the Honorable Guest-One arise and accompany Wu Tai-tai to the temple?" asked the friendly Number One amah.

I hastened to prepare for the trip, slightly surprised that Madame Wu was leaving the house at such an early hour.

Supposing that we should be departing at once, I hurried with my dressing. But it was some three hours later that we finally started. It was difficult for me, an occidental, to learn that you cannot hurry the East, and to realize that in China "a few minutes" may mean several hours, while "a little way" may be the equivalent of many miles over a torturous road.

In the courtyard the three children were having their lessons with a pompous tutor. It was such a heavenly morning that I did not wonder that Precious Lotus was finding it difficult to concentrate. The youngsters were bending over a long, narrow study table. They were striving to write the difficult strokes which go to make up the beautiful old Chinese ideographs.

Small Sister and Young Brother were doing very nicely apparently, but Precious Lotus was restless. Her tiny fingers were finding the management of the writing brush tiresome. Her mischievous dark eyes were wandering to the butterflies dancing on the flowers or to a fat lark trilling in the sunshine. The unsympathetic tutor scolded her sharply, saying, "Is it not pleasant to learn with a constant perseverance and application?"

The tiny girl of five flew into a rage. She threw down her paintbrush, and the ink from the slab splashed her dainty pink coat. At once her nurse, who was sitting in the background knitting, ran for Floating Cloud.

The mother's face was calm as she met the child. She did not scold her, nor did she excuse her. She quietly led the little girl to her own section of the house. There, on a small table in the corner of the room, was a tall, graceful figure of Kwan Yin, the Goddess of Mercy, the Kindly One, who, it is said, harkens to the prayers of women. The figure was an especially lovely porcelain of *blanc de Chine.*

"Reflect upon the calm beauty of the Kwan Yin, my hasty child," said Floating Cloud. And the wee girl stood and looked up at the compassionate face of the Goddess of Mercy. "No lines of anger mar her countenance," continued the mother. "If you would be beautiful so that your honorable husband will sing of your loveliness, strive always to be calm like Kwan Yin."

In a few minutes, the child turned and said shyly, "The Gracious Lady smiled at me."

The nurse took her back, quieted and willing, to her task.

"As children we must learn the lesson of self-control," said Floating Cloud to me.

Icy Heart had already carried the morning tea in to Madame Wu, for she and Floating Cloud accorded the older woman the same attention that young Chinese daughters-inlaw give their mothers-in-law.

An old amah was smoothing Madame Wu's hair as we entered her quarters, with a brush dipped in a Chinese bandoline which was composed of resinous shavings soaked in warm water. Madame Wu turned her head from side to side, critically studying the effect. Her pretty young relatives who were fluttering anxiously about, and the three or four amahs assisting the Old One, watched apprehensively. Finally Madame Wu smiled. A momentary tension was broken.

Costume after costume was brought by the amahs from carved, red lacquer chests and offered to their mistress. They were lovely. Some were embroidered, others were of heavy brocades, while many of the velvets were cut in graceful bamboo, plum-blossom, and peony designs. Out of the shimmering rainbow of colors Madame Wu finally chose a black satin outfit. Small jadestone buttons were used for fastenings. Dozens of pairs of embroidered slippers were offered until Madame Wu decided upon a pair of black satin ones heavily stitched in gold and green to match her costume.

Another amah hobbled in, carrying a large lacquer case. Open, Sesame! And like the genie in the story the amah unlocked the jewel casket and revealed gems of dazzling beauty. A pair of long, dangling jade and pearl earrings, several pairs of bracelets, two long gold enamel hair ornaments, and numerous heavy gold rings set with jade or pearls, were carefully chosen.

When I expressed admiration for her lovely costumes and her jewels, Madame Wu said, with a shrug of her shoulders, that they were "of no importance."

At the great gate a carriage awaited us, and Madame Wu, Icy Heart, Floating Cloud, and I entered it. We set off with quite a flourish. Four horsemen rode as an advance guard and cleared the streets. Soldiers stood on the running boards, while a number of mounted soldiers brought up the rear. The amahs, carrying incense sticks and strings of spirit money, followed in a second carriage.

The wail of eastern music could be heard as we neared the high walls of the temple grounds. The pulsate rhythm of the large, lacquered fish-head drums and the chant of priests mingled strangely with the shrill bugle calls which vibrated from the military camp near the temple.

The soldiers ruthlessly scattered the crowds of the country people gathered about the temple gates as we arrived. Poor old things — slightly bewildered, yet resigned to the inevitable! They had come from many li[7] about Paotingfu. Their young sons, as well as farm hands, had been pressed into service as soldiers, cart drivers, trench diggers, coolies, and hustled away to the war. These relatives, many of them aged women and tottering patriarchs, had come to the temple in order that they might bow in supplication before the war god. They were little concerned as to the victor of the fray; their concern was for their spring crops; their prayers were for a speedy end of the war and for the safe, swift return of the men who were so sorely needed for the cultivation of the land.

Madame Wu, however, had come to pray for the success of Wu. Even as we entered the temple gates messengers brought a dispatch from Wu at Changhsintien Ridge. It read:

I go forth to eliminate the betrayer of the Chinese people from under heaven.

A chill of excitement swept over me. A few miles away the hills were echoing with the *rat-a-tat-tat* of machine guns. The war between Chang and Wu had commenced! I was at Wu's headquarters, yes, but I must find a way to get to the front.

Madame Wu received the news calmly and with dignity. She made no comment but at once led the way down the avenue toward the buildings of the Wu Shen Miao, the temple to the all-powerful war god.

---

7   One li is two-fifths of a mile.

Our little procession created much excitement: Madame Wu, like a haughty dowager in black satin; Floating Cloud, arresting in a soft lavender outfit embroidered in palest blue; Icy Heart, a flower in delicate pink satin, and a strange foreign missie. The three vivid Chinese women were like threads of richest color woven in a bit of old embroidery — woven in an old embroidery whose background was the faded blue and gray of the dress of the countryfolk. The women of the house of Wu were rarely seen outside the Inner Chamber of their home, and the villagers were delighted over the unexpected.

As we walked slowly along, the halting pace being set by Floating Cloud and Icy Heart, whose golden lilies permitted only the shortest of steps, the beauty of the gardens, courtyards, and various temple buildings came into view.

In our approach to the largest of the temple buildings we paused a moment to listen to the song of a blind minstrel who chanted to a great circle of country people. In a high singsong he was narrating the story of Kuan Ti. Then the murmurings of the crowd about our arrival caused the storyteller to sing of Wu Pei-fu. Madame directed the nearest guard to reward this blind raconteur.

The dual nature of Kuan Ti, which was described by the minstrel, was depicted in the Wu Shen Miao. The impressive central temple, with its gray walls and colored-tile roofs, was dedicated to Kuan Ti the god of literature. A near-by temple, also a gem of architecture, was inscribed to Kuan Ti the god of war.

The amahs had already placed the prayer sticks and red candles in the holders before Kuan Ti, god of literature, as we entered the first temple. The colossal, red-faced figure seated on a throne chair under an immense red satin umbrella seemed to me to be quite aloof from the pilgrims kotowing at his feet. He seemed unmindful of their offerings. He was wearing a bizarre costume of gold and red, and was holding a book. He was so huge that the Chinese were dwarfed. He had been made in Tientsin at enormous expense only the year before by special order of Tsao Kun.

The country people made way for Madame Wu and her relatives. It seemed a bit indelicate to stand around and watch them in their homage although I had a feeling that it was all more or less a form of ceremony with Madame Wu. Nevertheless, I wandered off.

The temple of Kuan Ti the warrior was even more elaborate. The hero, who was wearing startling armor, was mounted on a savage charger and was brandishing his magic two-edged sword. His black eyes glared in a most belligerent manner, as in the semigloom the lights from the candles played over his enormous brilliant red face in a lurid way.

I was surprised to note that the walls of this temple were not lined with lesser Buddhas, as is customary in Chinese temples, but instead with implements of warfare. War chariots, spears, lances, shields, and battering rams of ancient days were arranged on one side of the vast room. On the other side more modern weapons — rifles, cannons, machine guns — were shown. Scenes of historic battles were painted on marble wall slabs. These were beautifully done, and they told the life story of the famous hero in fascinating pictorial continuity. I began with a painting at the entrance and wandered slowly from one to another. Ever beside me were Number One amah and two soldiers. They were guarding the Guest One.

After a time Madame Wu entered and lighted her candles before Kuan Ti, god of war. . .

She was unusually silent during the drive home. Her large, expressive eyes were brooding and melancholy; and she failed to respond to the chatter of Icy Heart and Floating Cloud, for her thoughts were on General Wu. Mine were engaged on a plan for getting to the battle area. Upton Close had accompanied General Wu that first day, and I was concerned as to my copy. I did not wish to be "scooped" on my first battle as a war correspondent. I hoped to follow the progress of the fighting for a time, somewhere near the front, then rush back to Paotingfu and file a "first-person, eyewitness" story. Translations of actual war dispatches from the front were sent to me every few hours from the military headquarters in the city under orders of General Wu.

The click of my typewriter echoed strangely in the Hall of the Ancestors where I wrote my copy, prepared my cables, with the whole family, also the amahs, looking on.

It was with greatest difficulty that I persuaded the high-ranking officer who provided me with my war dispatches to convince Madame Wu that I must go to the front. It was late in the afternoon when she finally consented.

Sometime after midnight two heavily armed soldiers and two frightened amahs from the house of Wu accompanied me to the station. The amahs and I were shown into a private compartment of the long troop train, the door of which was closed, locked; then the two soldiers settled down in the aisle before the door to guard the Guest One.

Madame Wu had insisted on the guard and the amahs! I was off to war chaperoned by amahs! What ignominy for one who was tingling with the excitement, the adventure of being a full-fledged war correspondent! Although this dominant woman was most advanced in her ideas concerning her sex, still, I was in her charge. She felt that a retinue gave me face as well as offered me a certain protection. I appreciated her consideration — but to be accompanied by two amahs on a war assignment was almost too much.

It was yet dark when our train slowed on a siding.

The walls of the silent village beyond the Liu Li (river) were mysterious shadows; the towering gatehouse was but a giant ghost. Then as I climbed from the train a great fiery ball of amber flamed in the sky—a red sky which was soon to be reflected in the bloodstained battlefields below.

With the coming of the sun the valley sprang into life.

There was no mystery now. In the glaring light the humble walls of the distant village were harsh and yellow. I left the amahs drinking tea in the comparative comfort of the train compartment; and when I glimpsed the guards buying fat meat dumplings from a tall northern man who carried on his back a compact kitchen (including a glowing charcoal stove, pots of steaming food, and serving bowls) I slipped away through the maze of soldiers. I wanted to reach the gatehouse of the village and ran for it: a skeleton village whose inhabitants had been evacuated upon orders of General Wu.

From the vantage of the gatehouse on the wall I watched the panorama unfold.

Before me were Wu Pei-fu's thousands. In the immediate foreground were the abandoned trenches of yesterday—abandoned in Wu's advance on the enemy. Farther ahead stretched today's trenches crowded with men. Farther on, amidst the scattered grave mounds, were empty outposts. The grave mounds were the sacred resting places of the village dead. To the north, but four or five miles beyond Wu's forces, rose the sharply outlined hills of Changhsintien. Here in grim lines, on every ridge, Chang Tso-lin's Mukden hordes were deeply entrenched. Their batteries, discernible through my field glasses, commanded the plain from the heights. Here, too, an ancient pagoda, rising tall against green hills, was converted into a strategic war base.

This famous landmark, temple of worship for streams of country pilgrims, was now a prize coveted by enemies. The lovely valley lying between the two war camps was verdant after the spring rains. But its life was to be destroyed by fighting men—men whose blood, in reparation, would stimulate the blooming of another spring.

This no man's land stretched some hundred and twenty miles to the sea. It reached from Changhsintien, ten miles south of Peking (an isolated Peking whose protecting gates were tightly closed), to the very borders of Tientsin (a frightened Tientsin, whose foreign concessions were barricaded with sandbags and barbed-wire entanglements and were guarded by British, United States, French, Italian, and Japanese troops).

Suddenly, through the deep silence which covered the land, came a wave of excitement. It was almost audible. There was a gripping tenseness. Yet the stillness was so terrifying that the tiny chirp of a yellow bird perched on the curved roof of the gatehouse startled me. I reached out a hand to hush it.

Abruptly, shrill bugle calls rent the air. The weird minor notes echoed back from the distant hills.

Wu Pei-fu's soldiers swarmed from the trenches, which ran like long snakes through the fields of young grain. They poured from the tents, hastily fastening their uniform coats. They sprang from the box and coal cars which stood in a labyrinth of confusion on the sidings.

They then were off in Wu's famous, undulating formation on a slow run through the fields of millet. Down a forty-mile front they ran toward the empty outposts.

Death began mowing them down. The valley vibrated with the roar of cannons from the hills. It was as if the dragon who sleeps in the mountain were belching forth fire in a terrific rage, all the while beating his tail in crazed fury and shaking the earth

99

with shock after shock.

Then came Wu's guns in heavy retaliation.

Again Wu's men moved toward the enemy outposts. Their onrush was slowed by a withering shrapnel. It was as if a mighty farmer with a scythe of death were harvesting a crop of men instead of grain.

The sun was mounting high in the sky. The battlefield grew dim in the smoke of yellow dust. Yet I could see that Wu's men were slowly gaining ground. They were grappling with the enemy at the outpost. They were down to primitive hand to hand fighting. I was held in a numbing spell. Morning was merging into noon, but I had no conception of time or place. Time had ceased to exist. I was oblivious of everything but that panorama of death before me.

And then I saw the vultures. Scavengers, black and fat, sat in a long row beyond me on the top of the village wall. They were filled with the flesh of men.

"Missie, Missie!"

I was so startled by the sound of a voice that I cried out. Then a small Chinese materialized before my startled eyes – in the midst of blood and carnage, a Chinese sweet-cake seller.

"You – you belong who man?" I managed to stammer.

"No fear, Missie," the boy reassured me. "I belong small tlain boy. Just now I catchee plenty money. Sell soldier men cigalette and little cakes."

There was a whistle overhead. Another – and another. A long-range gun – Chang's forces must be taking my gate tower for a field telephone or some other sort of enemy armament. With this realization, I let go of the wall and dropped.

"Lun, Missie, lun chop-chop," shouted the train boy. He dropped his basket of cakes and streaked out of the village gate toward the deserted trenches just beyond.

I gathered myself up from the ground, my gaze following the running Chinese boy. He stumbled — fell. One of the bullets had found its mark.

In the gatehouse I found an old heavily padded robe, with which I covered him; then weighted it down with rocks so that the vultures could not find him. It seemed cruel to leave him there alone. I could hear him saying, "Lun, Missie, lun chop-chop."

I began to run, heading as I thought for the station. I knew, without official bulletins, that Wu had won the first victory. I wanted to put my story on the wire. At last I found myself at the railway station.

Out of the maze of trains at the junction one was steaming up. It was to carry wounded soldiers back to the hospitals at Paotingfu. From all directions the injured were being brought. Many of the suffering were borne on the backs of their comrades. Some were being jolted precariously along on narrow boards. Others were riding on doors. Only a few were coming in on stretchers.

At an impoverished Red Cross tent a pitiful handful of Chinese doctors rendered first aid to as many of the war victims as possible, but most of the wounded were taken directly to the boxcars. These cars had only a light straw covering on the floor, and the men were laid on this straw in rows.

I stood staring at the train. Suddenly, I realized that it was about to pull out and flung myself into the last car. I remembered the amahs and my guards — wondered where they were as the train pulled out and I sank down on the floor of that last boxcar. Wounded soldiers were about me. Slowly the train jogged along.

There was a weak tugging at my foot. My exclamation of fright was changed into one of compassion as I looked into a drawn, twitching face. The wounded man tried to speak, but he

NEWS IS MY JOB

could not. He tried to turn his head. I understood that he wanted a drink, and poured tea from the spout of his teapot into his mouth.

At the far end of the car, the screams of a war-crazed man broke forth. His contorted face was horrible to see in the gathering dusk.

Before my eyes a young chap was dying and I could do nothing to help him. He was thrashing back and forth in agony, his hands tearing through the straw at the heartless steel floor of the car. I closed my eyes. When I could bear to look at him again his hands were still; his torture was over.

I thought of the tales I had heard of previous Chinese civil wars. In the "old days" the Chinese summer war was a vacation of sorts for the troops. If it rained the opposing generals ran up white flags and had a few rounds of mah-jongg together. Only a few shots were fired (firecrackers played their part) and casualties were practically nil. Then the parties, in a very civilized and friendly manner, got together and talked things over. Maybe one of the generals was poisoned at a big feast given in his honor. Maybe he was bought off. But, whatever the method used to end the war, the men suffered little. That battle between Wu and Chang had then seemed a terrible example of modern warfare. How little I knew!

The rhythm of the wheels and the moans of the wounded mingled in a deadly dirge:

A crazy man and a corpse.
A crazy man and a corpse.
A crazy man and a corpse.

Over and over the wheels of the train seemed to grind out this monotone.

Suddenly there was a hard jolt. We stopped with a bump that

threw the suffering men upon one another – and again started up the screams of the crazed man. From a siding half a dozen more boxcars joined our already long train. I climbed out, desperate. I knew that I could not ride in that ghastly car for the rest of the night.

Already the heavens were bright with stars. Through the soft darkness I ran along the bank, peering into the different cars. At last I discovered one that seemed to carry only supplies. At least there were no wounded men in it. With a great sigh of relief, I climbed in and sat on a long rough box.

The train crept on into the night, and I swayed sleepily with its motion. Then I was wide awake, filled with a new apprehension I could not name, which tapped at my consciousness. Then I knew. The thoughts I had been striving to escape, almost unconsciously, clicked. I saw Wu, his soldiers, his supply carts, and his coffin bearers vanishing into the deep mists beyond the city walls of Paotingfu.

I was sitting on a coffin – riding in a car loaded with coffins. They were filled with the bodies of the dead . . .

The train slid quietly into the Paotingfu station. Stretcher-bearers from the hospitals wearing Red Cross arm bands looked into the car for wounded men. On the platform stood the amahs and my soldier guard anxiously waiting for the Guest One.

Two or three days later an ominous silence began to creep over Paotingfu.

The sun, which had been almost brazen in its brightness during the past few days, was now bleak and cold. Although it was early afternoon the day was dark, and a chill, damp wind whipped up eddies of yellow dust in the singularly quiet streets. Even the whistling pigeons circling overhead seemed, against the lowering sky, birds of ill omen. The whistle from the tiny pipes concealed under their wings was shrill, cheerless. No voodoo drums beat a warning, yet a premonition of danger seemed to sweep the city and country round about.

By that mysterious grapevine which with lightning speed spreads news throughout the vast hinterland of China, reports that all was not well at the front began to shake the morale of Paotingfu.

Little cliques began to gather in the bazaars. Silk-robed gentlemen strolling along the river bank outside the wall, ostensibly to give their favorite songbirds an airing, were collecting by the bridge. One by one, the shops were being nailed up. Many of the larger shops had left only the width of one board by which customers might enter.

At the station, crowds of refugees were again preparing to start south. They were sitting on their bulging rolls of bedding — stolid, quiet, patiently waiting hour after hour at the dreary depot for a train to Hankow. There was no schedule. Trains from the battlefront were coming in, car after car crowded with the wounded and dying soldiers.

Long strings of Red Cross coolies were meeting the trains. They were carrying the suffering on bamboo stretchers to government and mission hospitals. Never in the history of the city had so many wounded been brought back from battle. Even the schools were being converted into hospitals.

I seemed to be at one with the sun — bleak, cold, and wan. The thrill had gone out of my assignment as the sunshine had gone from the day. The horror of that long experience at the front from before dawn until after the stars had replaced the sun; the sight, for the first time in my life, of mangled men strewn over a blood-soaked field; the anguish in the eyes of those wounded wrecks on the troop train — all these had hit me hard in reaction.

The reports from the front were monotonous in their

discouragement. Wu's initial victory, of which I had been an eyewitness, had not been followed by a second advance. The Mukden forces were pouring a heavy rain of shells over no man's land. Wu's army was unable to gain ground. The Little General had been compelled to change his tactics. He was now playing a defensive game. He was waiting for reenforcements. The Invincibles, picked, experienced fighters from the army of General Feng Yu-hsiang, famous Christian General, were en route with several thousand additional troops. These would be thrown against the Mukden hordes. These soldiers were coming by forced march through Shansi, then by train from Honan; but the delay was costing Wu dear in men and munitions.

This morning the report had come in that Wu's army had been pushed back. Would Wu be forced to make a grand retreat? Would Chang Tso-lin's soldiers sweep upon Paotingfu in an orgy of looting, burning, killing, before the reenforcements arrived? These were the fears that were wrecking the morale of Paotingfu.

An invitation to tea at one of the mission stations came as a godsend. Perhaps it was just the gloom of the day that made me so depressed. Perhaps it was the sudden closed-in sensation—a gasping for breath—caused by the high walls of the house of Wu. The courtyards which a day before had seemed to me the essence of romance now appeared artificial, cold, unreal.

With the coming of that invitation from the missionaries I knew what was the matter. I needed to talk with my own people. There was only a handful of Americans in the city, missionaries, of good courage, long experience, and common sense. They would be able to size up the situation better than I. Perhaps they would be laughing at the idea of real danger. Just thinking about them steadied me.

I was anxious to be off. We did not start for the tea, however, until long after the conventional tea hour.

Within the house of Wu there was no unusual strain. The merry laughter of Icy Heart and Floating Cloud echoed through the gardens as they played with their children. Mahjongg tiles clicked, as in other days, in the quarters of the men. Only in Madame Wu did I notice sudden, far-away, brooding looks; these seemed to be against her will.

She, too, welcomed the invitation to tea. The women's quarters were in a whirl of excitement over her dressing. Costume after costume was brought, then discarded. The amahs were running about like children, the sarcastic words of their mistress adding to their confusion. Finally the storm died down. Madame Wu chose a lovely plum-colored velvet cut in elaborate phoenix design. Her accessories this time were diamonds.

I was already dressed when Madame Wu entered my chamber. With some misgivings as to its suitability for a mission tea, I had put on a black velvet suit, but my appearance did not please Madame Wu. She looked over my limited wardrobe, then, with a pleased smile, selected a semi-evening dress of cornflower-blue chiffon. At her command the amah brought my blue satin slippers.

I started to protest. A pale blue chiffon dinner gown at a missionary tea during a war in the interior of China! Incidentally, the dress was the first Paris model I had ever owned. I had purchased it at sale price because it was a small size, in a French shop in Shanghai. It was fragile, and I did not wish to ruin it; I wondered why I had ever brought it. Then I realized that this tea was an occasion to Madame Wu. She had made much of her costume. So, rather than offend her, I changed into the semi-evening outfit, resolving, however, to explain to the missionary women at the first opportunity. Floating Cloud came in with an exquisite pale pink satin coat embroidered in pastel flowers. The effect was lovely — for a dinner party.

But really the dress didn't seem to matter so much. I had a quickening sense that I should be getting into my old jodhpurs, packing a suitcase, and getting ready for action. What kind, I did not know. Just action.

As I stepped into the carriage with Madame Wu a messenger from the telegraph office handed me a telegram. It was from John in Shanghai, an unofficial communication from Mr. Cunningham. As we rode along to the missionary compound I read it:

EDDIE C. SUGGESTS YOU LEAVE PAOTINGFU IMMEDIATELY AS REPORTS FROM AMERICAN AND BRITISH LEGATIONS PEKING INDICATE WU PEI FU DEBACLE. TRY COME SHANGHAI VIA HANKOW AT ONCE TAKING EVERY PRECAUTION.

Madame Wu seemed to read the message through my thoughts.

Above the blasts of the rising wind which jerked the body of our carriage back and forth between its high wheels, she said most earnestly:

"The Honorable Wu will not fail. The Mukden traitor is sending out empty rumors."

Yellow dust, stirred by the wind as well as by the stamping of the horses' hoofs, seeped into our glassed-in carriage and settled upon our costumes. I wondered idly if that heavy, yellow powder would ruin the blue chiffon.

"In the game of bluff," she continued, "the Honorable Wu is a master. He will hoodwink his bragging enemy and laugh at his confusion."

I wondered. Mr. Cunningham would not have sent me such an urgent warning without reason. I knew, also, that unless John had felt there was real danger he would not have interfered with my work. However, Madame Wu might be right. I decided to hold my courage tight in both hands and, for the moment, adopt a policy of watchful waiting. I hoped the situation, in my mind at least, would be cleared up after a visit with my fellow patriots.

Madame Wu staged a grand entrance at the mission compound. An opera singer could not have done better. We arrived an hour late, with a heavy cavalry guard and a number of twittering amahs. Madame Wu swept into the living room of the missionary home, an impressive figure. Her alert eyes made a quick survey of the dresses worn by the women in the room. This was followed by an obviously pleased glance at the costume of her foreign guest. Then, like a grand dowager, she settled down to sip her tea complacently.

We sat in a circle around the simply furnished room, the ten or twelve missionary women, Madame Wu, and I. Gloomy light from the gray world outside caught the only high spots, strongly colored biblical mottoes which hung here and there on the whitewashed walls.

The hum of voices, which had died down as we entered, started again as soon as the soft-footed houseboys began serving tea. Madame Wu was the cynosure of all eyes, and the women, who spoke Chinese fluently, began questioning her about the war.

Two or three of the older women were strangely alike; white-haired, with kind faces, the light of sacrifice in their pale eyes. I knew that they were ready to face any crisis for the cause in which they gloried. They had been long in the mission field, and, come what might, they would remain at their posts. Some of the younger women, however, seemed to be needing the comfort of Madame Wu's reassuring words. A few of the young matrons were deeply worried, for they had little children.

Madame Wu wished to visit the Taylor Memorial Hospital maintained by the mission, where wounded men were being cared for, and the older women soon led her away on a trip of inspection. I had seen enough wounded men, so I remained at the tea. Some way the conversation turned to the appalling experiences of some of their predecessors during the Boxer uprising. The shocking massacre of those earlier missionaries was recounted.

A doleful accompaniment to the tales of horror was "Nearer, my God, to Thee, nearer to Thee," as sung in Chinese, in a dragging singsong by the native Christians. They were holding a prayer meeting in the mission chapel. Their voices echoed through the room.

(Each day during the war prayer meetings were held under the leadership, for the most part, of the native workers. The men of the congregation, which was composed of Chinese teachers, doctors, students, soldiers, servants – Chinese from many walks of life – knelt on the hard wooden floor on one side of the church. The women knelt on the other side. One after another, the men would pray, and now and then we could hear a Chinese Bible woman lifting her voice in fervent supplication. What a contrast was this simple chapel to the great, ornate temple of Kwan Ti! Motivated by the same heavy burden – War – the Chinese were gathering in both chapel and temple to offer prayers for the cessation of hostilities.)

As we sat listening to the singing – which, frankly, put me into the doldrums – the film seemed to cut back to 1900.

I could hear the Chinese Christians singing and praying then as now. I could feel the surge of unrest that was abroad. There had been no rain for months. The ignorant were claiming that the foreign devils had bewitched their rain gods. The missionaries had begun to hear of the Boxers, called by some the Big Sword Society; by others the Society of the Harmonious Fists.

"Sha-a — sha-a! Kill — kill!" the crowds which were beginning to gather would cry as they moved outside the mission gates. Now and then a rough street song would float over the compound wall:

"Soon will our Boxers brave
Wipe out the foreign devils.
Then the heavens will drop the rain,
Our children will eat rice in plenty."

The Boxer menace, which at first had seemed but a cloud in the sky, had suddenly swept over north China in a mighty whirlwind and had carried death and destruction in its wake. At Paotingfu the Boxers had struck first. Peking and Tientsin were able to fight for their lives. But in Paotingfu — isolated, unprotected Paotingfu, with the rails to Peking destroyed — the foreign missionaries and the native Christians were at the mercy of the fanatical hordes. About a mile north of the walled city stood the Presbyterian mission. It was surrounded by open farming country. Through the fields, taking care not to be seen, a Chinese Christian had run that hot, oppressive Saturday afternoon on June 30, 1900. He was wounded and he fell as he reached the mission gates.

"The Boxers! The Boxers!" he gasped.

Even as he spoke, the din of Boxers coming across country could be heard.

Dr. John Yardley Taylor, Dr. and Mrs. Hodge, young missionaries, and a number of faithful Chinese gathered in the home of Mr. and Mrs. Simcox. From an upper window the little group watched the Boxers draw nearer and nearer. With blood-curdling incantations the mobs advanced. Their long red banners, streaming in the hot waves of the wind, carried the inscription "*Pao Ch'ing Mien Yand*—Death and destruction to all foreigners and their works." They were at the gates.

They were inside!

Dr. Taylor pleaded with them. Mrs. Simcox begged for the lives of her three children—two husky sons, Paul and Francis, and her lovely baby daughter just a year old. Their appeals were lost in furious jeers, in taunting laughter directed at them by the Boxers. With cries of "Kill! Kill!" the madmen swarmed over the compound and applied their torches to the homes, the chapel, the hospital, the schools. In a short time the splendid plant lay a mass of charred ruins. The missionaries as well as their children were burned to death.

The day following this attack, the Boxers wreaked their vengeance on the American Board Mission and the China Inland Mission.

I was told that some of those doomed missionaries were saved by Christian Chinese. Others, however, were paraded through the city swinging from poles suspended from the shoulders of coolies. Finally they were imprisoned in a temple and tortured. The long knives of the Boxers ultimately brought merciful release in death.

"And now what is going to happen?" someone half whispered.

As we sat there in the gathering gloom, one of the men of the American Board Mission hurried in with a wire in code.

It was an unconfirmed report that General Wu Pei-fu and members of his staff had been killed at the front!

I could hear General Wu again saying to me: "I am a fatalist. I will not be killed until a shell with my name on it finds me." I must get back to military headquarters, where I could check the report of Wu's death.

We sought Madame Wu in the hospital. She had not heard the rumor, and was like a child in her enthusiasm over the X-ray machine. She was watching a doctor locate a bullet in a soldier; and it was some time before I could get her away.

I wanted to get out of my absurd evening dress and into jodhpurs ready for any emergency. News would be breaking at any moment; it came sharply to me that it might not be news from some other point: if Wu were really killed the backwash of war would engulf Paotingfu.

From the tragedy of the past we drove straight into the terror of the present. Paotingfu was in upheaval. As we entered the city gates we were engulfed in a sea of excitement. The rumor that General Wu had been defeated was sweeping the city, and already people were fleeing.

"*Ai yah! Ai yah!*" gasped Madame Wu.

The *mah-foo* whipped up the horses and, with our carriage rocking like a ship at sea, the huge bell clanging, outriders clearing the streets, we rode toward the house of Wu.

A drizzling rain which had started up while we were driving back, now began to pound down in great sheets. Through the rain I glimpsed shops which had been open as usual earlier in the day, boarded and barred; saw cart after cart loaded with household possessions; wheelbarrows carrying the aged and children.

As we entered the great gate the wailing of the amahs could be heard. The news of Wu's death had traveled fast. The chill of the deepening dusk invaded the rooms. Rain blotted out the gardens. The romance of that Chinese home, for me, had fled. It was desolate—a house of sorrow, of death. The tottering old uncle met us and quietly, protectingly, led Madame Wu into the

Hall of the Ancestors.

A messenger from the telegraph office was waiting for me. He had evidently been there for some time. He handed me a wire, a message from the Old-Timer of the *China Press*:

A WAR CORRESPONDENT WITH A HEAD IS MORE USEFUL THAN ONE WITHOUT. URGE YOU LEAVE PAOTINGFU AT ONCE AND SAVE YOURS.

I plunged back into the rain. Again the carriage bell clanged, and as we hurried toward the telegraph office I worried about Upton Close; he also was reported killed.

Yellow mud splashed my blue satin slippers as I jumped from the carriage. The wind drove sheets of rain against me, and the blue chiffon clung clammily to my ankles.

The telegraph office was in a state of confusion, and at first I could not grasp the reason for such an extraordinary excitement. A thin-faced operator explained.

"Wires finished?" I echoed his words for a moment uncomprehendingly. The operators began to close the crude little office. Paotingfu was isolated — cut off.

I decided to leave at once — on the first train out — for I must get to a telegraph station. There was only one line running from Paotingfu, for the tracks north to Peking had been destroyed. There were rumors of trouble in the south, but I decided to chance it. Secretly I blessed those cut wires — they gave me my "out."

- 10 -

An hour later I was headed south. The gateman from the

house of Wu had arranged for the train to wait until the foreign missie could reach the station.

Madame Wu, valiant, stout-hearted, fit wife for a Chinese war lord, refused to believe in the news of General Wu's death. With a shrug of her wide shoulders she dismissed the report. With a contemptuous sneer she declared the story to be but base propaganda sent out by Chang Tso-lin. But she had agreed that I should be off.

I felt so terribly alone, the only foreigner on that long train with its several hundred Chinese passengers. But after a time a young girl sitting next to me smiled in the friendly manner of Chinese countryfolk and a chap in a dark silk robe by the window spoke to me in English. He proved to be a graduate of Leland Stanford University and was most eager to talk of "dear old Stanford."

After some three hours' traveling the train slowed down, puffed a few times, then stopped on a siding.

According to the Stanford chap—who did not believe the report of Wu's death—General Feng Yu-hsiang's Invincibles were being rushed through to Paotingfu and from there to the front to reinforce Wu's forces.

"Feng is the vital cog in the war," he exclaimed. "I am certain that Wu's victory or defeat will depend on him."

We stood out on the platform of our train and watched carload after carload of soldiers pass. They were silhouetted against the blackness by the faint light of their lanterns and the glow from charcoal stoves over which they boiled water for their tea. I heard the rousing strains of "Onward, Christian Soldiers" come floating through the darkness and the rain. The music was that of "Onward, Christian Soldiers," yes, but the words were fiercely vindictive. They charged the soldiers to shoot when they glimpsed the whites of their enemies' eyes; to shoot to kill . . . to kill . . .

Across the station yard a troop train stopped with grinding brakes. General Feng himself was on that train.

From nowhere the Stanford chap produced an enormous umbrella of oiled yellow cloth, and with the rain swirling about us we cut through the mud, over the tracks, to the coach from which the lusty music throbbed. My escort explained the purpose of our visit to Feng's aide, who appeared on the train platform in answer to his call. Whatever else Stanford may have taught him, it had not taught him brevity of speech, for while I stood there in a mud puddle, he related all of his own life's history and much of mine as well. (This was correct procedure according to old Chinese custom.)

Finally—without further introduction—we followed the officer into Feng's private car.

A man in uniform over six feet tall, of brawny, powerful build, with fierce eyes hidden under thick brows, heavy cheeks, welcomed me as pleasantly as if the materialization of a young newspaperwoman out of the night were an ordinary occurrence. A number of officers were with him. Fresh tea was brought, and as we sat on the heavy benches which crowded the barren compartment we talked of the war. Feng laughed at the rumor of Wu's death. Two or three of the officers spoke English, several French, and with the aid of the Stanford chap and my limited Chinese we managed. Storm lanterns hanging over the table at which General Feng sat lighted a war map dotted with small paper banners (similar to the one I had seen at Wu Pei-fu's headquarters), an open Chinese Bible, and a hymnal.

I was interested in the hymnal especially. There were no music scores in it; only the columns of somewhat large characters printed on double sheets of fine bamboo paper. I complimented the men on their singing, and they broke forth into "Jesus loves me—this I know, 'cause the Bible tells me so." The others joined in, and soon this melody which I had always associated with the high voices of little children at Sunday School rang out with the fierce vigor of a fighting song. The pounding of the rain on the roof sounded like an accompaniment of battle drums.

As they sang I studied the militant Feng—the man out of the red-loess country—upon whom General Wu was depending. He was so obviously the war-lord-soldier of my imagination— neither Wu nor Chang had been—and yet I wondered about him. Whose hand was he really playing—his own or Wu's—in the intricate Chinese political drama? We talked for a moment longer; then the Stanford chap and I made our way back to our train.

The *clack, clack, clack,* of the bamboo sticks of a seller of *mien* (noodles) was heard. A round-faced boy and his traveling kitchen appeared. The aroma of noodles cooking in a soup of diced pork was irresistible, and my Stanford friend bought two steaming bowls. Over our noodles he told me much of General Feng, who was one of the most colorful and publicized of China's war lords.

Feng, who was a young officer attending the Military Academy of Paotingfu during the Boxer outrages, was most deeply impressed by the courage with which the missionaries and the Chinese Christians faced their deaths. Years later Feng was to remember those stanch Chinese when he attended a revival meeting conducted in Peking by Dr. John R. Mott of New York. During the service Feng was converted, and at once was hailed by the missionary world as the Christian General. Even then Feng was dramatic. His God was the militant God of the Old Testament, and he led his well disciplined soldiers forth to war to the music of Christian marching hymns. The reading of Scripture, songs of praise, and earnest prayer opened the day for Feng's soldiers. They were not allowed to smoke, drink, or gamble, and no light women were permitted to live near the headquarters. The soldiers attended a trade school and, when not actually engaged in fighting, were put to work making the shoes, uniforms, and so on for the army.

We talked—the Stanford chap and I—while those about us slept. The hours of the night flew past; then a cheerless sunrise announced the dawn. With the first rose-colored glow on the breaking clouds our train again started south. All morning we jerked slowly along through stretching farm lands, but about noon we reached Chen Tai, an important railroad and coal town.

I hurried at once into the telegraph office, anxious to send the cable which I knew would make front-page headlines in American newspapers from coast to coast. I also wired the Old-Timer at the *China Press*—asking him to relay the war news as it came into the office of the International News Service—and John. I did not know how soon I should be again in direct touch with news or with telegraph facilities.

Our train seemed most reluctant to leave Chen Tai station. There was much excitement. Chinese railroad officials were running about. An unusually heavy guard of Chinese soldiers lined the tracks. To my amazement, I noticed that they were climbing aboard two special boxcars which had been added to our long train. What did that mean?

Honan troops, instigated by Chang Tso-lin and his ally, Sun Yat-sen, had risen suddenly against General Wu. They were striking at Wu's very heart. They were striving to capture Wu's more or less unprotected home base, Loyang. Hundreds of soldiers who should have been rushing to the aid of the Chihli forces at Changhsintien Ridge were forced to remain in Honan to quell this unexpected insurrection.

There was grave danger that our train would not be able to get through the war zone.

The Honan troops were not the well disciplined soldiers of General Wu, General Feng Yu-hsiang, or Marshal Chang Tso-lin. They were notorious outlaws. They traveled in great bandit hordes from five hundred to ten thousand strong; they swooped down on rich Chinese villages, kidnapped the wealthy gentry, ravaged the women behind the Orchid Doors of the great establishments, carried off the maidens of the village, looted, burned. These were the soldier-bandits who destroyed missions upcountry, who kidnapped the missionaries, who held representatives of great oil and tobacco companies (when captured on their lonely business trips into the interior) for ransom. Some of these foreign men and women had been ransomed and finally released after days of harrowing suspense. Many, however, had vanished into the mysterious silence of the hinterland, their fate never disclosed.

In a few hours we were in the very heart of the bandit country. Our train crept along through the fields of grain; crept stealthily as if trying not to attract any attention, as if feeling its way. We were moving so slowly that I felt an urge to get out and push; to admonish the Chinese engineer to hurry — hurry — hurry.

We jogged on and on into the afternoon. We might have been riding through the rolling prairies of Kansas, or through the placid Barbizon country of sunny France. I relaxed; indulged in little cat naps lulled by the motion of the train. As if in a dream I noticed a group of soldiers crowding near the tracks just ahead — unkempt fellows — in ill-fitting uniforms but bristling with guns.

One minute — a mild landscape as peaceful as a painting by Millet. The next — bandit-soldiers blotting out tranquility.

"*Ai yah! Ai yah!*" cried a fat old countrywoman sitting across from me. She grabbed at her husband's wide blue sleeve as she pointed with trembling hand at the men leering into the train windows.

"*Ai yah! Ai yah!*" Her frightened moan was taken up by the

other Chinese in our compartment.

With a horrible scream of brakes the train stopped. It rocked as if it would jump the tracks. There was a deafening explosion. Dirt and timbers flew into the air. Window glass shattered and crashed. We, the passengers, shot to the floor in a mad scramble of legs, arms, bundles, suitcases, baskets.

The tracks just ahead had been blown up. A few more convolutions of its wheels and our train would have been derailed — wrecked. (The slow progress that had so maddened me had saved our lives.) In a panic the Chinese passengers hurled themselves through the windows and doors.

The soldiers who had joined the train at Chen Tai to see us through the danger zone at once took charge of the situation. From the train window I could see them rounding up the men who had fired the explosives, and who were now trying to escape through the grain. That our train had stopped, that it had not been wrecked as a result of their work, was a wholly unexpected development. They were unprepared for our escort of troops, and they were making a desperate effort to get away.

They were captured, however, and brought back — seven Chinese in tattered uniforms, and flung at the feet of the officer in charge. Two of them began talking wildly, kotowing, beating their heads on the ground, begging for mercy. One of the chaps, a good-looking young boy, began to laugh hysterically. The others were defiant; they looked like hardened Public Enemies One, Two, Three, and Four.

Without ceremony, the slim, trim officer in charge ordered the seven soldiers to be beheaded. One by one the men were forced to kneel on the ground. Their hands were tied behind them.

There was a flash of steel in the sunshine. A Chinese head rolled like a ball to the ground. Then another — and another — and another.

Swelling jeers from the gloating crowd marked each victim. I thought of the French guillotine—of the French peasant mobs.

The heads were retrieved from the ground and hoisted aloft on spiked bamboo poles. For nights to come my sleep was haunted by those ghastly Chinese heads: heads which dripped blood—heads which grinned at me from the tops of seven tall poles—heads which, in the glaring sunlight, appeared to be gruesome Chinese theatrical masks, props in some fantastic Oriental dramaturgy.

Heads and hearts. . .

Even as I watched a soldier tore off the coat of one of the headless bodies, and with his sword cut out the heart. And then another, and another, until the hearts of all seven victims had been removed. The heart of a brave man, a tiger, or a lion gives double strength to the one who eats it. (Years later I heard one of the luncheon speakers at a meeting of the Women's National Press Club in Washington, D.C., an American priest, tell of seeing a Chinese officer cut out and eat the heart of a Chinese Communist who had been executed upon orders of the authorities in his far-interior district.)

In the distance were rolling hills. I fixed my eyes on them, at first staring as unseeingly as those decapitated heads, trying desperately to blot out the nightmare of the past few minutes, then—suddenly—with acute attention.

Bandits! Through the fields of grain spreading from the base of the mountains, running lightly, swiftly, came swarms of Honan outlaws. Bullets whistled through the train. Bullets cut right and left into the stunned crowd of passengers and soldiers. The bandits were firing as they came.

Our soldiers sprang into action. Passengers ran into the train or crawled over the tracks and dropped behind an embankment on the other side. A train boy entered the compartment and pulled down the cloth blind. At the time his action did not seem amusing.

"More better lie down floor side, Missie," he advised quite calmly. "Wu Pei-fu gateman talkee me, my must take number one good care foreign missie."

He tore open a roll of bedding belonging to the fat country-woman, pulled out a blanket and stretched it on the floor. I flattened out on it, next to a countrywoman, reeking with garlic; then he piled boxes, fat bundles, my suitcase in front of us like a barricade. Bullets sang through the fabric blind and sank into the framework. They might have been hailstones so far as he was concerned.

I covered my face in my arms as I crouched there on the floor—my chin completely out of control—for what seemed hours. Light began to fade in the compartment. What would the night bring forth? Dangers that can be seen, recognized, faced by daylight, are bad enough; but dangers that creep up out of black shadows are far more difficult.

"No fear, Missie, no fear," said the calm voice of the train boy, who seemed to sense my fresh anxiety. "Plitty soon, my think so, any man must finish fightee. Sun go way."

We began to move.

Our train, which had sat there throughout the fighting, began backing. Passengers who had been hiding behind the embankment made a mad scramble to get aboard. The soldiers packed up their machine guns and swung onto the boxcars. In the fields the bandits stood and watched us pull out. We gathered speed, backed down the track to a siding where the engine was switched; then we were chugging back toward Chen Tai.

"But how—why?" I asked. I had supposed that our engine had been wrecked by the explosion, that we could not move. (Why else should we remain?) Apparently not, however, for we were chugging along gayly.

"All finish," announced the train boy with a broad smile.

He raised the blinds which were riddled with holes.

(A few years later, when covering a battle on the outskirts of Shanghai with two other correspondents, I was to remember the train boy who pulled down the fabric blinds to keep out lead bullets. We were in an open car. Without warning, bullets began flying across the road in our direction. In a flash the Chinese chauffeur was out of the machine putting up the side curtains. In spite of our protests he carried on. We waited there under fire until those fabric curtains, our protection from bullets, were in place.)

Fate seemed determined to keep me in north China; once again my plans for reaching Shanghai, via Hankow, were blocked.

At Chen Tai our engine settled down like a tired old horse that had had more excitement than is good for her, and refused to go. I filed wires to Internews and to the *China Press*, telling of the bandit attack. No one knew when the train would proceed to Paotingfu — certainly not for three or four days — no one knew when the tracks would be repaired and a train would again attempt to reach Hankow. No one knew any Chang-Wu war news. I was stymied.

Chen Tai is an important junction where a Frenchoperated train from Shansi province connects with the PekingHankow line. I decided to go farther into the interior, to Taiyüanfu, capital of Shansi, the model province of China, on the morning train. The impasse at Chen Tai would give me an opportunity to interview the powerful Yen Shih-shan, "model governor" of the province.

Yen was the only man appointed governor of a province of China in 1911 (the establishment of the Republic) to still hold that office in 1922. Although Taiyüanfu was a long day's journey farther into the interior of China, it was one of the few spots in the nation where peace and order prevailed. War Lord Yen spent millions of dollars for the construction of roads; the establishment of schools; the development of industry; the fighting of opium. I was eager to meet this man who was clever and diplomatic enough to ride successfully, for so many years, the waves of China's cyclonic political storms.[8]

Up through the verdant tree-covered hills of Shansi province the Chen-Tai train wound its way toward Taiyüanfu. Even now I feel a deep affection for that little French train. It had such a smoothly running engine; such clean cozy compartments brightened by photographs of scenic France; and such comfortable upholstered seats with a real bounce in them. An inviting diner served marvelous French food. What a surprise!

But Shansi was a series of delightful surprises.

All day we clung to the friendly mountain side as we climbed higher and higher. I sank back in my luxury — a whole compartment to myself — and even relaxed after a time. How pleasant not to be riding on a Chinese refugee train, not to be sitting on the edge of a hard wooden seat, waiting — waiting . . .

We arrived at Taiyüanfu at dusk — a tranquil, romantic dusk. The evening star was peeping over the highest pine, while a soft breeze which was gently stirring began to waft away thoughts of war, carnage, death. I caught myself listening. There were no raucous bugle calls; no sound of tramping feet of soldiers; no rumble of heavy supply carts.

A slim Chinese gentleman in a Bond Street business suit greeted me on behalf of Governor Yen and at once led me to a

---

8   In December, 1937, after days of desperate fighting in which the Chinese peasants resorted to pitchforks as weapons to aid the soldiers, the Japanese captured and destroyed much of the city and forced the Governor and Madame Yen to flee as fugitives from the province. They are now active in the Chungking government.

deluxe motor car. I had wired to Governor Yen only that morning, asking for an audience; and I had not expected to be met.

"His Excellency will receive you tomorrow morning," Mr. Wang, the Governor's secretary, informed me. "My wife, who is an English girl, will motor you about the city during the afternoon. In the evening Mr. Yen is giving a dinner in your honor."

Dinner with Madame Yen—an evening within the Orchid Door of the palatial house of Yen! I was delighted.

Wang had been educated in England and spoke with an Oxford accent; but, as we drove through the wide, beautiful clean streets, he spoke so proudly of his home city and province that he reminded me strangely of the American Babbitt. As I bade Mr. Wang good night at the entrance of the quaint, semi-foreign inn where I was to stop, I expressed my appreciation of his kindness. My unplanned venture into Shansi was not only to prove valuable from a news standpoint but also to add a delightful bit to my Chinese scroll—a charming bit of old, contemplative China.

Hotel boys picked up my typewriter case and my bullet-ripped, now thoroughly shabby, bags and led me along cool corridors into a spacious suite which opened upon a small private courtyard. In such a courtyard could the Fragrant One, Hsiang Fei, concubine of the Emperor Ch'ien Lung, have dreamed of her lost Dzungaria—have dreamed by the marble pool where the Heavenly Bamboo swayed in the gentle breeze, and where yellow birds chirped sleepy good nights. I too might have dreamed there in the moonlight—but I had glimpsed a big, old-fashioned brass bed in the adjoining room!

About ten o'clock the next morning a motor car called for me, and I was driven at once to the yamen of Governor Yen. As we entered the great gate and drove into park-like grounds the roseate walls of Yen's palace rose through the trees like a mellowed embroidery on old green satin. I was ushered at once through a lofty guest hall and into an impressive reception room where Governor Yen and Secretary Wang were at work.

"His Excellency is a bit concerned as to the proper etiquette for receiving an American woman newspaper correspondent," laughed Wang. "You are the first woman he has entertained in that capacity."

Governor Yen proved to be a man slightly above average height; of stocky build, with a determined jaw and alert eyes set in a rugged, broad face, with an eager, enthusiastic manner which was somewhat surprising. He was impressive in a plum-colored cut velvet jacket, black satin robe and black velvet shoes, and most gracious in his manner. As he talked I forgot the magnificence of my surroundings and was soon seeing, with him, his visions of a united, peaceful, progressive China. "When I became governor of Shansi," said Yen, "I determined to develop my province instead of armies."

I listened with keen interest while the Shansi leader outlined his tremendous program of reconstruction: a program which ran into the millions.

He spoke of roads constructed; of bridges built; of mountains reforested; of day schools and orphanages opened; of trade schools which trained soldiers to be self-supporting; of colleges of law, engineering, agriculture, and commerce. "More than eighty per cent of the children in my province are in school," he said with pride. He described the prize stock which he had imported from America, stressing especially the Merino sheep; he spoke with enthusiasm of the arid parts of his province which had been reclaimed along the lines followed in Imperial Valley, California; he told me of his experimental farms where he tried out grains and grasses from various countries; and of the miles of irrigation ditches which had been built in order that water might be brought from the Yellow River for the small farmers.

"Gambling in all forms is prohibited — even the game of mah-jongg is forbidden," he explained. His chief campaign, however, was against opium smoking. Opium growing and the smuggling in of the golden pills (small pellets of morphine) were punishable by death. "Perhaps Shansi will act as the leaven." Then he added, "But China is a very large loaf."

Madame Yen welcomed her guests in a spacious reception room of the women's apartments of the palace. She was a gracious, old-fashioned Chinese lady, most dignified in a black satin costume. Jade pins caught her smoothly coiled hair.

In contrast to our hostess young Chinese women guests, wives of high officials, were richly costumed, were radiant in pastel silks and jewels. They fitted into the beautiful old Chinese setting with its soft green satin brocaded wall hangings, round windows with delicate tracery, etched-glass wind lanterns and blackwood pieces. Two French women were among the guests. Mrs. Wang interpreted for Madame Yen. The dining room, one of many, was dominated by a foreign-style round table. I thought the dinner would be strained; it proved, however, to be most amusing, for the conversation was in Chinese, French, and English. The table was covered with fine Irish damask, and the serviettes, which were folded into designs of roses, birds, pagodas, peeped from the tall garnet-colored wineglasses. The intricately folded napkins reminded me of an amusing incident at a bachelors' mess in Shanghai some weeks earlier: It was the first time I had seen serviettes thus arranged, and I was told that the Number One had spent hours over the task. Reaching for my serviette, I heard a *cheep, cheep,* and a canary flew from my hand. From all around the table came loud *cheep-cheeps* as twelve bewildered birds flew wildly about the beautifully arranged table, overturning candles, flowers, nut and bonbon dishes. We returned to the drawing room, laughing, while the birds were captured and the table rearranged. The host, a man of great poise who had lived long in the Orient, shrugged his shoulders nonchalantly and exclaimed, "It is China." The Number One Chinese boy had doubtless tried to do something very special for his master's birthday.

Madame Yen laughed at my story with keen enjoyment and assured me that there were no canaries in her napkins.

After dinner coolies, carrying enormous lanterns of painted silk gauze suspended from long poles, led us into the gardens, which stretched on and on.

A low-hanging, full moon, like a pendant of luminous white jade, shone through the trees and transported me into an enchanted land. I was following mystic lights – the lantern bearers were unreal, but shadows . . .

Silently we wound our way around low terraced hills over which gnarled old pines, like bent pilgrims traveling to a mountain temple, seemed to climb – past a shrine to the Spirit of the Garden – and on to a beautifully arched bridge. It spanned a dashing stream which found contentment in a jade pool banked with willows below. Just beyond was the Pavilion of Golden Peace. It was a picture in a frame of bamboo, pine, and flowering plum trees. We rested here a bit and listened to the eerie music of distant phoenix-flutes while boys served us bowls of fragrant tea. It was all so unutterably lovely that I longed to loiter there ten thousand years.

After a time we moved on through the winding paths.

"Our gardens have a deep philosophical significance," explained Madame Yen somewhat shyly as we passed a number of huge stone figures representing Chinese historical characters. They loomed strangely there in the moonlight as they stood in a row by a Dragon Wall. I listened with deepest interest as this cultured Chinese woman explained many of the traditions, much of the symbolism, that has gone into the creating of the lovely gardens of China through the ages.

It was with reluctance that I finally bade Madame Yen good night; that I said good-bye to the China of my dreams.

I was sorry to leave Taiyüanfu,_but Governor Yen had received word that a train would be moving northward toward Paotingfu the following night. The tide of battle had turned. Wu with Feng's reinforcements was driving back the armies of Chang Tso-lin. I must leave early in the morning in order to make connections. At the inn I wrote a cable story on Governor Yen and advised Internews of my plans. After all I did have a job!

But the magic of the Yen garden was still upon me, and I lingered in the courtyard off my bedroom. Madame Yen had said that it was the "Season of Excited Insects," and there had been carved spirit screens at the entrances of her gardens to keep out evil genii. How delightfully whimsical it all was!

What part had I in the chaos of the plains below? I had glimpsed, as had Li Tai Po one moonlight night in the green jade hills, "another sky, another earth."

- 11 -

Everything was quiet about the Paotingfu station.

There were no flags flying; no gayly costumed military bands leading parades of marching soldiers; no crowds of jubilant villagers throwing their hats into the air and singing victory songs. There was no demonstration of any kind over the smashing triumph of the Chihli party and the success of General Wu Pei-fu. I tried to understand. I knew that the Chinese hated war; that their philosophers had, for centuries, preached its futility; that to them war was an unpleasant business that interfered with the rhythmic, harmonious routine of daily life. The civil wars between war lords were not of their making. They had seen war lords come, boastfully "showing too much edge," and they had seen them go and others "enter the stage." Their business was cultivating the land of their ancestors. "Let the miserable 'pigs' who have no other means of livelihood fight the battles of another for pay," reasoned the masses. "Men of substance have no part in war. Is there not a saying, 'Good iron is not made into nails, good men do not become soldiers'?" As I thought of these things I heard someone calling,

"Gracious Guest One, Missie, Missie!" Could that be the Number One amah from the house of Wu?

On his own the train boy had sent word of my arrival. Hence the familiar hack, the servants, and — when I reached the carriage — Madame Wu, Icy Heart, and Floating Cloud. They were there to welcome me.

In another moment we were swinging happily along, bell clanging, through the streets to the house of Wu. I noticed that the town had settled back to pleasant normalcy. The wrinkled old shopkeepers were smoking their long water pipes contentedly as they sat out in front of their little shops, now open. Ragged urchins were playing about the bazaar in the hope of making off with a long stick of sugar cane, a chunk of pork, or perhaps a red cabbage. Silk-robed gentlemen were again strolling in the shade of the weeping willow trees along the river bank as they took their little grandsons for a walk or their favorite birds for an airing. Thus Paotingfu was celebrating Wu's victory. The terror and fear that had gripped the city a week before was gone. The air was clear and calm as it is after a storm.

Madame Wu's dark eyes were glowing. Her face was alight with triumph, elation, happiness, as she told me the story of Wu's victory.

A plot had been hatched in the camp of Chang Tso-lin, she explained. Wu and his staff were to be blown up in a farmhouse which was serving as field headquarters near Changhsintien. The place had been mined, and the farmhouse completely demolished. But—General Wu was not in it. His spies had warned him just in time to enable him and all his staff to escape. (Upton Close had also been unharmed.)

Madame Wu, who was an excellent story-teller, laughed with keen enjoyment; then continued her tale.

When General Feng Yu-hsiang's Invincibles arrived at Changhsintien Ridge the fireworks started. Chang's defense fell before the fierce flank attack of the Invincibles and the carefully planned, well executed assault of Wu's seasoned fighters. In their flight the enemy had left cannons, tents, ammunition, food, supplies, horses, wireless, camels—spoils of war for the Chihli forces.

The routed army retreated toward Tientsin, and a second battle was fought a few miles from the city. Chang's forces experienced a second defeat and retreated beyond the Great Wall; Wu did not follow. To have done so would have been vulgar pompousness. It was not considered hanyang (good etiquette) "to push another to the wall." Also Wu was wise enough to know his own limitations.

It was delightful to be again in the house of Wu. The day following my arrival, I set out for the yamen of Marshal Tsao Kun. General Wu Pei-fu was there in conference. Now, thanks to Wu's decisive victory, Tsao Kun, as head of the Chihli party, was extremely important in China's political world.

Tsao Kun's palace was a modem semiforeign affair.

The reception room of the yamen was crowded. It was a large room, its walls lined with chairs, small tables, tall porcelain spittoons around which dragons curled. It was full of important-looking Chinese who were drinking tea, smoking cigarettes, and chatting, oh, so amiably! These politicians, office seekers, Oriental chiselers, were arriving on every train from many sections of the country. Paotingfu had suddenly become the mecca of China. Peking, for the moment, was forgotten. The mountain had moved to Mahomet. The world was beating a path to Wu's door.

I was ushered almost at once into an inner room. General Wu entered. His lined, gaunt face plainly showed the heavy strain under which he had been laboring. He accepted my congratulations with modesty. But he seemed careworn, worried, as if already the responsibilities thrust upon him by victory were weighing heavily. We sat down on a stiff French sofa with spindly, gilded legs. The room was a mixture of foreign and Chinese furniture, and it boasted many clocks of various periods and styles.

"I am sorry that China had to be burdened with civil war," he said. "Now one of the obstacles in the way of unification of China has been removed. There remains yet another."

I knew that he referred to Chang Tso-lin and Dr. Sun Yatsen, although he did not mention them by name.

"Do you think, General Wu," I ventured, "that in a short time efforts will be made to eliminate this other 'obstacle'?"

Wu sat lost in thought. When he said very decisively, "Yes," I realized that I must be on my way to Canton.

"What about Peking?" I asked.

"I am not a diplomat," answered the Little General. "I am a soldier. I do not want to go to Peking. I am doing my part in the tremendous task of reuniting the nation, in my role as a soldier. There are many worthy, experienced men in China who will aid in the establishment of a strong central government."

(And Wu had just said he was no diplomat.)

He continued: "I am in favor of recalling the last functioning

Parliament—of reinstating Li Yuang-hung as president—of checking all Japanese influence in China—of disbanding troops and putting the soldiers to work at building roads and on flood prevention projects, of wiping out banditry—of setting China's house in order so that foreign nations doing business with us will have a stabilized country with which to deal."

A difficult program to carry out in that chaotic year of 1922.

Marshal Tsao Kun came into the room. He was alert, purring. Even his long satin gown and rich velvet jacket seemed to have a jaunty, festive air.

Somewhat to my surprise he also stated that the former Parliament must be invited to return to Peking, and the former president, Li Yuang-hung, reelected. As Tsao talked so suavely, so pleasantly, I wondered what his furtive, half-closed eyes were really seeing. In Peking I had heard rumors of Tsao's presidential ambitions. We talked for a few minutes, then Tsao led me into his lovely gardens. There, against a background of honeycombed rocks which stood tall, slim, twisted, like strange rock formations in the California deserts, he permitted me to photograph him.

As I rode back to the house of Wu I thought of Li Yuang-hung, who was to be used as a pawn by Tsao.

I met Li Yuang-hung a few days later in Tientsin. He lived in a magnificent foreign establishment in the British Concession. He entertained lavishly, staged private theatricals in his own theater, which seated some five hundred guests, and he was very popular with the foreigners. He had even taken up dancing and skating. But Li was not a politician, he was a charming gentleman. He had not been able to cope with the militarists during his first venture into politics, and I doubted if he would succeed if he made a second attempt. With the establishment of the Chinese Republic in 1912 Yuan Shih-kai had been elected President and Li Yuang-hung named Vice President. But Yuan Shih-kai was not one to share honors, so Li was kept practically a prisoner in the heart of Peking. When Yuan died China remembered that she had a Vice President, and Parliament elected Li President. Li, however, lacked the force to control the crop of war lords which sprang up in China after Yuan's death; and they forced him from office, electing His Excellency Hsu Shih-chang President in 1918. Now the same militarists were throwing out Hsu and reelecting Li. And back of the complicated political drama was Tsao Kun pulling the strings. How long would Li last?

On my return to the house of Wu a telegraph messenger met me with a cable from New York:

CONGRATULATIONS EXCELLENT WORK.
NORTH CHINA. INTERVIEWS WAR LORDS
MOST SATISFACTORY. WAR COVERAGE
OUTSTANDING. PROCEED AT ONCE
SUNYATSENWARD. CABLING FUNDS AND
BONUS TO SHANGHAI, LUCK.
INTERNEWS.

I wanted to frame that cable. To me it was worth all of the hectic experiences of the past weeks. This was the second congratulatory bonus I had received from Internews; the first was for an exclusive statement from Lord Northcliffe, given me during his visit to Shanghai some months earlier, denouncing the Anglo-Japanese pact.

I decided that I must be off for Shanghai and Canton in the morning.

The reception room of the women's apartments rang with laughter. Mah-jongg tiles clicked. Voices — excited, happy voices — echoed to my chamber. Madame Wu was entertaining guests. The four amahs hovered about as I hastily changed into the blue chiffon dress. (I had left it a mud-spattered wreck upon my departure from Paotingfu; but Number One had cleaned it carefully, and it was as lovely a frock as ever.) And I joined the women at once.

Madame Wu was very gay. She was stunning in a red satin costume and—to my amazement—red satin, French-heeled slippers embroidered in gold. The village cobbler had surpassed himself. The Chinese guests were most impressed—envious.

I sat down to play mah-jongg with Madame Wu and two of her guests. I knew that they played for high stakes—that I was completely outclassed so far as knowledge of the game was concerned—but I did not care. I was still on wings over my cable.

One of the players was a lively little old lady who chattered incessantly.

"I am trying to persuade the honorable Chao that he needs a beautiful young concubine—a number four wife," she casually announced as she punged a Red Dragon.

Could I have understood?

"We have three women in our household," Madame Chao continued by way of explanation to me. "We need another wife to make a fourth at mah-jongg. The Honorable Chao is very old-fashioned. We live in the country and seldom go beyond the walls of our house. The Honorable Chao dreams always of more and more sons.[9] So I am arranging a fourth wife for him. I will give her a pair of my heavily carved gold bracelets. She will play mah-jongg, and she will bring me my morning tea. She can thread my embroidery needles. I like a pretty face about." And the elderly little woman, who had ruled her household for some fifty years, laughed merrily.

---

9   I learned that Chao was seventy.

"A fourth at mah-jongg!" I too laughed with delight.

Madame Chao had all the aplomb that goes with the "flower candle" — or first wife — of a wealthy Chinese establishment. Also she had given Chao two sons and one daughter. So she was doubly secure in her position. One of the sons was studying in America, his family living there with him. The other was in Shanghai, where he represented his father in business.

The number two wife had been blessed only with daughters, all of whom were married. The number three wife was childless.

What was Madame Wu thinking about the conversation? I knew that she had been a number two wife. But she "punged" and "chaoed" her mah-jongg tiles with her usual poise.

In the previous year three wives had lived in the house of Wu. I often wondered which apartments they had occupied — something of romance always seems to cling to the rooms of an old, old house.

When a very young man, Wu had been betrothed by his parents to a woman several years his senior. Their marriage had not been blessed with children, and, like all Chinese, Wu longed for a son. One day when in Shantung province he had met the present Madame Wu. He had fallen in love with her, and she later came to his home as his second but very much honored wife. The first wife was jealous, ill, and when the second wife failed to present the house of Wu with a son, or any child, she maneuvered to bring into the establishment a robust country girl as a third wife. Number Three — Lovely Blossom — was supposed to win Wu away from her Shantung rival, Number Two.

But the second wife was not one to be lightly set aside. Of a determined nature, and truly in love with Wu, she held her own against the country girl. And in time the first wife began to tire of the struggle for Wu's affection. The drama began to pall. More and more this elderly, now sickly, woman sought solace in golden dreams of her couch. The dominating second wife gained more and more control in the household. She prompted Wu to adopt two orphan sons of a relative. She cared for these lads and gave them the status of Wu's sons.

Toward the end of the year the delicate first wife died. There had been an elaborate funeral. Almost at once the third wife was banished. Madame Wu reigned supreme. And if I know anything about women, she will continue to reign as the only wife in the house of Wu.

Gossip had it that Marshal Tsao Kun wished to present Wu with a famous actress as a concubine following his victory over Chang Tso-lin. Wu was reported to have refused the gift. Was it that he wished to keep peace behind the Orchid Door, or did he hesitate to take the exotic creature into his home for fear that she might in time prove to be a treacherous spy? Through the years more than one Chinese in high political circles had been dragged low through the betrayal of a favorite concubine or a bewitching singsong girl to whom he had confided his secrets.

We played mah-jongg for hours. The elderly one was tireless. Round after round. When we counted our scores, I found that I had won a small sum. How had Madame Wu arranged this?

My visit behind the Orchid Door was over.

It was with real regret that I again parted from my Chinese friends; yet I knew that I must move southward. Madame Wu was leaving for her country home in Loyang in a few days; and I wanted a few hours in Tientsin in which to interview Li Yuang-hung, potential President of China, before sailing for Shanghai.

Shanghai—and then Canton.

The voyage from Tientsin to Shanghai was quiet and peaceful. Moonlight flooded the night on the first evening out. It shimmered across the dark face of the waters; it sprayed the decks of our ship with silver; it enveloped the world in cool enchantment. I began to relax from the high tension to which I had been geared in the past few weeks. Chaos and the tragedy of war lay behind me.

Each day of the trip brought new tranquility; much of the time I slept; and yet in the midst of some happy memory there would come unbidden the memory of General Wu Peifu's words, "The second obstacle must be removed before the unification of China can be brought about." I had a premonition that my days in Canton would not be as peaceful as I had originally thought, and I knew that my stay in Shanghai would be but a brief interlude in the stirring events of war.

A morning tide carried us up the yellow Whangpoo to Shanghai. It was good to see John and a group of friends waiting on the Bund to welcome me. Even the Old-Timer forgot to be nonchalant or caustic in his interest in my adventures upcountry.

I had tiffin my first day back in Shanghai at the American Consulate. Rhoda Cunningham had invited me to one of her famous curry tiffins-chicken curry, a pomelo salad and, for dessert, an Indian *Gu-la-ma-la-ka* which was served with fresh coconut milk and a thin syrup.

Mayling Soong was among the guests; and as soon as possible after tiffin we stole away to one end of the long room to talk over the political situation in China.

Miss Soong was searching in her questions as to my impression of the northern war lords; she was anxious that I be not unduly impressed by them; she was also most earnest in her explanations of the aims of the southern government. I am certain that it was Mayling Soong who laid the foundations for whatever understanding of present-day China I may have. She was so ardent, so intensely patriotic, so fine in her belief in China. Her enthusiasm struck a deep, responsive chord in me, and I began to glimpse an undercurrent of dynamic forces which were sending China forward; to realize that the apparent chaos in the land was the inevitable struggle which accompanied the transition period between the passing of an old regime and the birth of a new order.

When I told her of my plan to depart for Canton on the day following, she was glad. She, too, sensed a rising crisis in south China and she was eager for me to talk with Dr. Sun Yat-sen and her sister, Madame Sun, in order that I might present the cause of the Nationalists to America. She informed me that Eugene Chen was already in Canton, and that he would make all arrangements for me to meet Dr. Sun as well as Dr. Wu Ting-fang.

John saw me aboard the little coastal steamer *Soochow*, the day following.

I sailed with a light heart, thinking that my interviews with Dr. Sun and Dr. Wu were as good as accomplished and I should be back in Shanghai within three weeks. I could not then know that before I saw Shanghai again summer would turn toward autumn — Dr. Sun Yat-sen would become a fugitive on a gunboat — Dr. Wu Ting-fang would succumb from shock — and that I should have a most narrow escape from death.

The Old Timer advised the coastal steamer, saying that it spelled romance, for it stopped at such quaint, historic ports as Ningpo, Swatow, Amoy, Foochow. "With a spot of luck you may be caught in an early typhoon and shipwrecked on an island, or you may even be attacked by pirates from Bias Bay," he said. The transpacific liner was safe, luxurious; but it held slight hope of high adventure.

So when the little steamer, with its cargo of sheep, goats, and silver bullion, sailed from Shanghai at dawn two days later I was one of its eight first class passengers.

One glorious day after another drifted by: a cloudless blue sky; a magic ocean where flying fish cut through a shining mirror of deepest cerulean blue; enchanting islands where Lorelei might dwell. High-pooped cargo junks covered with gaudily painted dragons and phoenix glided by.

As we moved southward the indescribable charm of the voyage deepened. I thought of Conrad, of Maugham, of William McFee, of John Masefield. I dug their books out of my wicker book basket with its oil-paper lining, and now and then I dipped into a stirring tale. But for the most part I just sat in a long deck chair, my book half closed, and gloried in the beauty around me.

As we stopped at port after port, I caught flashes of a happy land whose seductive charm stood out in sharp contrast to the austere, harsh outlines of the north.

The fields of kaoliang and millet of north China gave place to flooded paddy fields where women cultivated young rice to terraced hills where the tea plant grows — to orange orchards whose perfumed blossoms mingled with the scent of jasmine and rose. Peking carts laboring over deeply rutted roads were seen no more. Instead, sedan chairs swung along on the shoulders of short, wiry, bronze-backed men.

The northerner is a rugged, broad-shouldered, rather simple-minded man accustomed to hard living, to soldiering, to combating floods and drought with their inevitable handmaiden, famine; the southerner is small, poetic, ultrasophisticated, a lover of the luxuries and refinements of life — yet, withal, of such a fiery temperament that Canton is sometimes called the hotbox of China.

And so the days drifted by...

At noon we would sit around the one big table in the

combination lounge, smoker, and dining room of the steamer and, over our coffee and cheese, listen to the captain spinning yams chosen at random from his many adventures during long years at sea. The conversation was never of the political problems which China was facing — never of solutions for those problems. Instead it was of pirates, smuggling, tiger hunting, typhoons, famous concubines, the Pirate Queen of Bias Bay, fan-tan.

They were enchanting: those stories told by the captain, by the tea taster from Foochow, by the charming Italian (who, I gathered, was going south to try to sell arms, munitions, and aeroplanes to the southern government), and by the English banker from Amoy. The Standard Oil chap of Canton, the mysterious Frenchman who carefully steered all conversation away from his purpose in life, past, present, or future, and the Bagdad merchant who dealt in everything from bean oil to lace and hair nets — these, too, spun tales of the China Sea. They made great feature copy!

"Have we any treasure on board?" I asked the captain one night as he finished an exciting account of a steamer which had been pirated some three months previously. The ruddy-faced Scotchman, who had sailed the China Sea for some thirty years, answered, "A wee bit."

The "wee bit" signified silver bullion worth some two million dollars. After I learned this, every Chinese fishing junk sighted off the port side spelled PIRATES in big letters, and I regarded with suspicion every disreputable-looking coolie glimpsed in the steerage. Incidentally the silver cargo explained the unusually heavy guard of Sikh police on board. Night and day, these towering Indians in brown police uniforms and bright red turbans paced the ship.

I was on the deck at dawn for our arrival at Canton. We had

come up the Pearl River from Hongkong by night, and I was out with the first light of morning to get a glimpse of this romantic old city.

As soon as our boat docked at Shameen Island, the foreign concession of Canton, I went to the Victoria Hotel, where I had made reservations.

- 13 -

The booming of cannons awakened me at dawn the next mooring.

Listening there in the old-fashioned English hotel on Shameen Island, I could hear not only the deep reverberations of cannons but a *rat-a-tat-tat* of machine guns. From a window I could see smoke and flames curling skyward in various sections of Canton. The sun was coming up in a red sky.

I had been in Canton only twenty-four hours. On the previous afternoon I had had an interview with Dr. Wu Ting-fang, prime minister of the south China government and twice Chinese ambassador at Washington, and with Mr. Eugene Chen, foreign secretary, in the yamen where Dr. Wu lived. As we sat sipping iced tea (a surprising drink to find in a Chinese home) in a spacious drawing room richly furnished in European style, nothing had been said of any immediate trouble; and I had been advised that an appointment had been arranged for me to interview Dr. Sun the day following (today). I hurried with my dressing then ran down to the lobby of the hotel. The manager, who was serving hot tea to other bewildered guests, explained.

During the early hours of the morning General Chen Chiung-ming, governor of Kwangtung Province and a once trusted supporter of Dr. Sun Yat-sen, had, by a daring coup, captured the forts of Canton. His armies had taken possession of the city.

Dr. Sun Yat-sen had been driven from the presidential

mansion and had barely escaped with his life. He was said to be hiding on one of his gunboats lying in the Pearl River!

Madame Sun Yat-sen was reported missing!

The presidential mansion was burning. The Treasury building had been looted. The governor's yamen, where I had had tea with Dr. Wu Ting-fang, was gutted with flames.

Some twenty-five thousand of Chen Chiung-ming's troops were in control of the city. Sun Yat-sen's army was *en route* northward on a punitive expedition which Sun had launched against the northern war lords; consequently Canton had been practically defenseless. Wily General Wu Pei-fu—I could see his hand in this overthrow of the Canton government. Again I could hear him saying, there in the military yamen at Paotingfu, "The second obstacle will have to be removed." This coup, by Sun's disloyal general, was the result.

"Now we are in for civil war," shouted a buyer of Canton shawls.

Hastily I drafted a long cable to the International News Service. The telegraph office was across the bridge from the British Concession of Shameen Island, in the heart of the old city of Canton. It was in the thick of the fighting. How could I hope to find my way there, file a cable? There was not a rickshaw to be had. The hotel porter refused to go with me, even for a substantial tip.

I was in despair. Here was a *scoop* handed to me on a silver platter, and I could not take advantage of the unique situation of being the only foreign correspondent in Canton that day.

Into the lobby came tall, broad-shouldered Paul M. Anderson— "Andy" Anderson, popular young Shanghai business man who was traveling in southern China for his company. Plunging into the heart of a Canton adventure appealed to him.

And so we set off. . .

Once across the bridge which leads from the lovely little island of Shameen, with its foreign consulate buildings and foreign homes, into Canton proper, I realized that we had set out on a hazardous undertaking.

Chinese soldiers, ragged, leering, squatty, guarded every main street corner. I had not been afraid of the northern soldiers; but these unkempt men, with their hard faces and careless manner of handling guns, frightened me. They were a rough lot — men who had been terrorizing the province of Kwangtung for months — "Andy" Anderson did not like them any better than I did. He hurriedly changed the route.

We left the broad, modernized main thoroughfare of Canton and dodged down narrow, sticky, hot back streets. Sometimes we would dart around a corner and wait until soldiers passed. All doors were barred and bolted. The streets were absolutely deserted save for occasional groups of men in ragged uniforms — and for the dead strewn here and there.

At last we reached the telegraph office.

Officers were on guard, but they let us in. The operators were surly, uncommunicative. They accepted my cable, however, and I was thrilled with the excitement of getting it off. Then the reality of civil war closed in. Mr. Anderson and I stood for a few moments in the doorway of the telegraph office, dreading to go out again into those streets. Even as we debated, there was a tremendous crash and everything rocked! Part of the telegraph station crumbled. Two shots were fired in the large main room.

"Run!" shouted Andy.

Like streaks we were off down the street — a street so narrow that the brightly painted signs of the shops almost met overhead. A hot mist rose from the large slabs underfoot, and drops of steam fell from the matting which roofed the street.

Suddenly at the end of the roadway, blocking the way, soldiers appeared. They began setting up machine guns. We turned to run in the opposite direction. Enemy soldiers blocked this exit. They, too, were setting up machine guns.

We whirled back, too late. Bullets from the machine guns began to pop, and we flattened ourselves against the door of a shop. After a bit there was a momentary lull in the firing. Was the skirmish ended? Then reinforcements arrived. Chen's soldiers started a charge down the street. They paid no attention to us. Their grim, set faces were intent on the men who were bearing down on them. Two of Sun's soldiers fell as they brushed by — one upon the other, in an inert heap.

My mind whirled. Yet I did not feel a part of that street fight, but rather a spectator of an exciting drama. I had no thoughts of death, of eternity — only stray little memories . . .

After a time — hours, it seemed — the firing in that immediate neighborhood ceased.

We started on. I dreaded those streets occupied by leering bandit soldiers — with guns cocked. We slipped around corners. Once I pressed into the narrow opening which sheltered a street shrine. Candles flickered before the garishly painted good-luck Buddha who, all unconcerned, sat there smiling a fat happy smile. When we did move it was always on the run. Bullets whistled by. But at last we reached the bridge leading to Shameen — and safety!

What about my cable?

A telegraph station was opened on Shameen Island during the morning. I had no way of knowing whether my wire had got off before the building had crashed; so I wrote a second account of the overthrow of Dr. Sun and filed it.

Two days later I received a stimulating reply cable from Internews. My first wire had got through. We had scooped the world by twenty-four hours on the story of the downfall of Sun Yat-sen and the South China Republic. I had been lucky.

The next few days brought Reuter men as well as European and American correspondents from all over the Far East. The tropic summer settled in, the civil war dragged on and on. . .

The foreigners living in Shameen at this time were worked up to a high degree of excitement. Many of the women and children left for Hongkong as soon as evidence of further fighting was seen. So grave was the situation that the Shameen Municipal Council issued a gun and fifty rounds of ammunition to every foreign man. Hundreds of thousands of dollars' worth of treasure was rushed from Canton proper by both Chinese and foreigners and stored on the island: a tempting bait to looting, lawless soldiers. Special plans were made to guard the settlement in case of a sudden rush attack. Church bells were to be rung and rockets fired.

Huge placard notices were posted conspicuously about the island:

EXPRESS
SHAMEEN MUNICIPAL COUNCIL
IN THE EVENT OF THE ALARM BEING SOUNDED
NONCOMBATANTS SHOULD AT ONCE PROCEED TO THE
BRITISH CONSULATE. WOMEN AND CHILDREN TO THE
NEW A. P. CO. BUILDING (LATE GERMAN CONSULATE).
SHAMEEN MUNICIPAL COUNCIL

My concern, however, was more over an interview with Dr. Sun Yat-sen than with these warnings. Sun was reported aboard one of his battleships at Whangpoa, some fifteen miles down the Pearl River from Canton. No small craft were allowed in the vicinity of the battleships. The American Consul was discouraging.

I must get an interview with Dr. Sun. But how?

A liberal cumshaw to my Chinese room boy brought the information that he had a cousin who had a cousin who was on Sun's ship, and would take me there.

It was an hour before daylight.

My room boy and I slipped quietly from the Victoria Hotel and down to the Shameen Bund. Dim lanterns were casting eerie lights on the dark waters of the Pearl River. A young Cantonese officer was waiting in a motor boat, and almost at once we were off on a run down the river to Whangpoa naval base, where the seven battleships of the South China Republic were at anchor.

We might be stopped, questioned, turned back, captured, fired upon . . . But we must take this chance. Dr. Sun Yatsen was reported to be on one of the ships. Should I be permitted to go aboard his ship and talk with him? I did not know.

As we crept cautiously along, occasional lights on the shore showed the splendid Bund with its modern buildings which stretched along the waterfront of Canton proper. (But behind the modern façade lived old Canton.) Only the dim outlines of the sampans, fishing boats, junks, houseboats, could be seen as we moved along. Yet I knew that for miles down the river and along the canals an immense boat city, sheltering some four hundred thousand Chinese, was asleep—but with one eye open.

Suddenly our boat swerved. We darted into a tiny opening between a Ningpo junk and a low barge which carried salt. The boatman shut off the motor. An enemy boat patrol was passing. After a time we were again on our way. Although the engine was heavily muffled its faint *put-put-put* seemed to echo through the still darkness. I thought that every soldier in Chen's army could hear it.

The faint light of early dawn began to disperse the darkness and to reveal open country, groups of picturesque farmhouses, tall banana trees, drooping willows . . . Rice fields stretched on and on until they reached the green hills and mountains surrounding the lovely valley through which the river flows. In the distance White Cloud Mountain emerged from delicately tinted mists to greet a glorious sunrise. The mountains, there in the golden morning light, looked peaceful and happy.

As we watched the sunrise, *the boom-boom-boom* of distant guns wrecked the beauty of the new day. It sounded like giants playing tenpins in the mountains. Our young official was aquiver with excitement. "Sun Yat-sen's men are attacking Chen's mountain outposts," he cried. We sped on.

Suddenly, without a moment's warning, bullets came sibilating about us. The guide and the Cantonese officer instinctively dropped to the bottom of the boat. They looked neither to the right nor to the left — just dropped. But like Lot's wife, I glanced behind us, even as I crouched low.

A junk carrying a load of soldiers was bearing down on us! The leader, a scarred-faced fellow with queue bound round his head, was gesticulating and shouting. Our boatman, with nonchalant unconcern, slowed the boat. He turned to the young officer, who had been recognized, for instructions. A nod from him, and the boatman opened the engine. We were off on a breath-taking race down the river.

Angry shouts came from the men on the junk. Simultaneously, a volley of shots. Bullets again whined past us. Then the boatman gasped, slumped forward; blood spurted down his bare arm.

It all happened so quickly that our boat careened wildly. A strong current caught us, headed us toward the treacherous sand bars near the shore. Acting wholly on instinct, I seized the steering wheel and with a turn which almost capsized us, headed the boat downstream. In another moment we should have been fast on a sand bar. The exposed hulk of a small British vessel which had cracked up on the shifting reefs was warning enough. Another shot or two, and the danger from the soldiers in the slow-moving junk was over! The currents bothered me, and I kept in the channel only by the feel and the color of the water.

The Cantonese officer and the guide were working over the wounded boatman. They had improvised a tourniquet with a handkerchief and a chopstick and had arrested the bleeding. They poured tea from a pot down his throat; slapped his face with a rough hand towel soaked with tea. In a short time, he regained consciousness; was again at the wheel. His steering showed long experience with the river. Sometimes we took a zigzag course, now close to the shore, now cutting a diagonal path toward the middle of the stream.

The Chinese were amazed that I could handle a motor boat, and were profuse with their compliments.

As we sped on, leaving a long wake behind, I thought of summer holidays in California. My brother-in-law had an obsession for motor-boat racing and lived at one time from one regatta to the next. His two youngsters cut their teeth on silver trophy cups. I had caught his enthusiasm. Flashes came to me of school vacations bright with days spent at Santa Barbara, Catalina, Ensenada. But I never had imagined that the day would come when the superficial knowledge I had of this sport would save me and others from possible death in far-away China.

Seven blue-gray cruisers — stripped, ready for action, smoke pouring from the funnels — loomed just ahead. The men fastened a large American flag to the bow of our little boat, and through a megaphone the Chinese official began calling. An officer of the *Po Pi Kui*, the boat upon which Dr. Sun was reported to be in hiding, answered. For at least half an hour the Chinese official in our boat and the officer above us on the battleship tossed questions and answers back and forth in the high Cantonese singsong. I was beside myself with impatience.

Finally, we learned that Dr. Sun was not on that particular ship.

We were allowed to proceed. Another battleship. Another long calling back and forth. Dr. Sun was aboard. The Cantonese official, taking my card and various credentials, climbed up on the ship. In a short time, he was back. Dr. Sun had given permission for me to go aboard.

My difficulties seemed over. But—there was no gangway. There was not even a swinging rope ladder such as I had seen pilots use. There were only iron rounds fastened to the side of the battleship. As I looked upward from the bobbing motorboat, the gray wall of the ship loomed high. Charlotte Greenwood would have loved it. She could have put on a regular "So Long, Letty" act as she nonchalantly stepped from one round to the next. But, not being built along Charlotte's lines, I was nervous, scared, as I reached for the first round and attempted to secure a footing. Then a welcoming voice called: "Why, how do you do, Miss Booker! Let me help you aboard."

It was Mr. Lil He had given up his job on the *China Press* to fight with Dr. Sun. I scarcely recognized the worn officer in tattered uniform as the well dressed young Chinese journalist who had always worn a flower in the buttonhole of his foreign business suit and was inclined toward canes. With his assistance I made the deck of the battleship and was shown at once into Dr. Sun's quarters. The square teak table at which Dr. Sun was working, and at which I was asked to be seated, was covered with writing materials. In the face of civil war, of the greatest personal danger, Sun was composed, was writing a message for the people of China. A few years later this message, amplified, gave the nation a new pulsating ideology. It grew into the now famous book, the *San Min Chu I*, which was based in part on Lincoln's "of the people, by the people, for the people."

The cabin was hot, cramped. A ship's boy stood behind my chair and fanned me with a large violet-colored feather fan. "Tell my friends in America," said Dr. Sun slowly, "that I am fighting for righteousness, humanity, democracy. I will die before I will give up the principle for which I have fought these many years."

Sun's eyes, which looked out from under heavy brows, glowed for a moment with an intense fervor, a fervor which quickly faded into sadness—always that patient sadness. There were sharp lines about his mouth, and his closely cropped hair and mustache were touched with gray. He was wearing a dark silk coat buttoned from the high collar straight down the middle, and baggy trousers.

Dr. Sun told me of his life, of the turbulent years of strife, exile, narrow escapes from death which he had experienced, and of his recent flight in the night from the presidential mansion. Dr. and Madame Sun had been awakened by the firing of guns at the very gates of their home. With only one bodyguard (the other guards were left to escort Madame Sun to safety) Sun had managed to evade his enemies, make his way to one of his gunboats in the river. The navy had remained loyal. Even as he fled, the presidential mansion burst into flames. (A number of Sun's guards were killed as they attempted to open a way of escape for Madame Sun, I later learned. It was only when she discarded her own costume and threw on the coarse dress of a countrywoman that she was able to escape.)

As Dr. Sun talked a young officer of medium height and slight build entered to receive certain instructions. He was somewhat handsome in a daring way with clear, dark skin, steady, quick-seeing eyes, trim mustache; yet there was nothing of the gallant, the ladies' man, in his manner. His was a rugged masculinity, an untamed force, and I sensed in him a man of quick decision, swift action, unwavering nerve. He bowed a bit awkwardly, saluted, then was off. He was Chiang Kai-shek, officer in the Nationalist Army and the devoted chela of Dr. Sun. The same Chiang who in a few swift-moving years was to become the great generalissimo of China.

During those long trying months Chiang learned from his leader much of patience under tribulation, of steadfastness to a cause despite ridicule, of courage which refused to admit defeat, of patriotism which put love of country before love of self; lessons which through the years have aided him in triumphing over situations which would have destroyed a weaker man.

Sun was never at any time daunted by the Canton debacle. But only a Sun Yat-sen could picture a united, modernized China in the face of the existing chaos; only a Sun Yat-sen could voice ambitions for a future China which were worthy of her past greatness.

A few days later I learned of the serious illness of Dr. Wu Ting-fang.

Dr. Wu, as premier of the South China Republic, was one of the most respected, truly patriotic men in China. Before the fall of the Manchus he had served the Court of Peking as Chinese Minister to the United States, was a close friend of President Theodore Roosevelt, and was famed in diplomatic society for his wit.

I talked with him for a few minutes in the home of a Chinese professor at the Canton Christian College. Wu was very ill. A Chinese symbolic character meaning Long Life was woven in conventional pattern in the silk of his jacket. Long Life—Wu's long life of eighty years was drawing to a close.

The fast-moving events of the past few days had been too much for the aged patriot. It had been a staggering blow to Wu to be awakened at dawn, that first day of the war, by rebellious soldiers filling his gardens and courtyards, to see smoke and flames engulfing his home. An attempt at flight was useless. When Dr. Wu had given up all hope, a motorcar floating white flags, with soldiers of the enemy victors standing as guards on the running boards, drove into the grounds. Wu was hurried to the car by this soldier guard and escorted through the city to safety under orders of General Chen Chiung-ming.

I asked Wu but one question: "What message shall I cable to your friends in America?"

"Tell my friends in America," answered Dr. Wu with a halting voice, "to take a long view of the Chinese Republic. A journey of five thousand li begins with a step. The road ahead may be 'weary to kill'; but Constitutionalism will triumph, and China will become a Republic in more than name. Maybe not today — but surely tomorrow."

He paused for a bit, then added:

"The general of an army may be defeated. But you can never defeat the progress of a right idea. The militarists will never succeed in wiping out the teachings of the father of the Chinese Republic, Dr. Sun. His doctrines will live."

As Dr. Wu was talking I thought of my cable:

PROCEED HEADQUARTERS WAR LORDS INTERVIEW CHANG TSO-LIN, HSU SHIH-CHANG, WU PEI-FU, SUN YAT SEN, WU TING-FANG.

This was my closing interview of the assignment, and a very sad one. It was, I believe, the last interview which the elderly statesman ever gave for publication.

Two days later Dr. Wu Ting-fang died.

After an impressive funeral service held in the Memorial Hall of the American Missionary Hospital at Canton, the flag-covered bier was carried in dignified silence to a barge draped with white symbols of mourning and banked with floral offerings. With solemn stateliness the barge, which was in reality a large Chinese houseboat, led a long procession of boats filled with relatives, officials, Chinese and foreign friends. Civil war was called off by both factions for that day. As the long procession moved down the river, foreign and Chinese battleships at anchor gave military salutes in his honor. A Chinese band played in one of the boats. The strains of Chopin's Funeral March echoed strangely there in the Pearl River.

The funeral barge of Wu Ting-fang moved slowly, majestically, down the stream with the ebbing tide.

The second period of the civil war began: a prolonged period which was characterized by strikes and their resultant disorders. The workers were in sympathy with Dr. Sun. One shop after another closed; guerrilla warfare made business impossible; disorders in the city increased.

The days dragged. Although political jockeying was going on underneath the surface, there was no news. The civil war might carry on for months, or it might end overnight. It was unpredictable. But, as one of the correspondents who had been rushed to Canton said, the story from a news viewpoint was "washed up."

Two days later, as I sailed from Canton for Hong Kong and Shanghai, I passed seven Chinese battleships anchored in the river. Dr. Sun was on one of them. Throughout that hot summer — day after day — he carried on.

As our steamer moved toward the open sea, I most respectfully saluted the refugee aboard his Chinese gunboat.

During the months I had been covering China's internecine wars, those long months spent far in the interior, China had been my world.

I thought of this world as the Pacific liner which I boarded at Hongkong cut swiftly through a rain-swept sea on my return voyage to Shanghai. China's seemingly boundless compass had awakened in me a tremendous respect; her strange, hypnotic charm had enveloped me; the kindness which had been shown to me by Chinese of all classes with whom I had come into contact had instilled in me a feeling of kinship. I liked the Chinese people. My months upcountry had given me an unshakable belief in those millions upon millions of intelligent, hard-working Chinese. I had the feeling that their roots were so deeply imbedded in the ages that despite the chaos which walked abroad over the land, surface chaos only, the Chinese masses would live—forever.

I was eager to return to Shanghai, now that my assignment was successfully completed.

John was there, and because of that, Shanghai had become home.

- 14 -

It was early fall when Dr. Sun Yat-sen quit the gunboat which had been his headquarters in south China for so many wearisome weeks and returned to the quiet of his unpretentious home in the French Settlement of Shanghai.

He was good enough to see me shortly after his arrival. As I entered the gateway I thought of the palatial establishments of the war lords which I had visited: there was nothing here of their magnificence. There was no guard. I was shown into a formal reception room which was furnished quite simply with Chinese furniture.

The months had borne fruit.

A new factor—Soviet Russia—had entered the picture, and I realized it almost as soon as Dr. Sun began to speak.

There was sorrow in his eyes as he told me of the refusal of Great Britain and of the United States to recognize the South China Republic or to aid the cause of the Nationalists. (To have done so would have involved many diplomatic niceties as America was still dealing with the farcical Peking government; also, by the terms of the Nine Power Treaty signed the year before, the United States of America, Belgium, the British Empire, France, Italy, the Netherlands, Portugal, and the then moderate government of Japan had agreed not to intervene in Chinese affairs; had agreed to let China work out her own salvation.) Dr. Sun told me of the recent visit of Adolph Joffe, one of the most successful of the Russian Soviet propagandists, and of the message of sympathy and good will which he had brought from Lenin—a message which was backed by a definite offer of aid to the Chinese revolutionists. The encouraging words from Russia were most gratifying to Sun after the rebuffs from America and Britain. I felt then (as I do now) that he had turned to Russia only as a last resort.

As we sat on the straight-backed Chinese chairs in his reception room, Dr. Sun talked of the years in which he had followed Russia's revolution. It was during his days of exile from China—days spent in London and in Paris—that he had first met Russian revolutionists, talked with them, read their literature. He spoke of the rise of the Russian peasants, of the workers, of Lenin.

After a time, Sun began to tell me of the masses of China. There was a hypnotic quality to his voice, a slow fire in his sad eyes, which wove a spell over me. Although I had talked with Sun a number of times, I felt then for the first time the strange power, the magnetic charm—a charm that could sway multitudes— which were his. He made me see China's throbbing hinterland with its millions of peasants who were being exploited by the "imperialistic" war lords: war lords who confiscated the crops to feed their armies, who drove the people to slow starvation by burdensome taxes, who pressed their sons into service as coolie-soldiers, who planted the opium poppy in the rich grain lands. He made me see lawless bands of bandit soldiers swarming at will over the country like ravaging locusts—burning villages, stealing women, garroting men. Famine was stalking abroad because corrupt officials put the funds for road building, dike repairs, reclamation of land into their own pockets; and such great industries as tea, silk, cotton, rice—in which China had at one time excelled—were slipping further and further down the economic scale because of these officials' greed. He made me see a peasantry sunk in illiteracy, struggling to wrest a livelihood from the land.

Dr. Sun gripped my sympathies as he said, slowly, tensely: "I will arouse the peasants, the workers. I will organize them. I will save them as Lenin has saved the masses of Russia."

Then he told me of the leaven of revolution that had been working for years in certain provinces of China. He pointed out that the terrible Boxer Rebellion and the overthrow of the Manchus were part of that awakening. In a voice vibrant with earnestness he declared that he was going to lead the Chinese masses in a revolution that would throw off the yoke of the war lords, of the "imperialistic" nations, and give China a government based on Democracy, Nationalism, and the Social Welfare of the people. He arose, a majestic figure, his eyes alight with an exalted purpose.

Madame Sun Yat-sen entered the room.

There was adoration in her glowing eyes; a shy gentleness, a reverence in her attitude when she spoke to him. I had been told that Madame Sun was lovely, but I had not realized how radiantly young, how exquisitely beautiful, how aflame with idealism she was. This flowerlike woman, in her delicate blue gown, so full of grace, charm, and dignity, was hard to imagine as a leader in a revolution. Yet she had dedicated her life to her husband, some thirty years her senior, and to the revolutionary cause for which he labored. She traveled with him, looked after his health, attended all party councils and mass meetings, edited his manuscripts, and criticized his speeches. Hers was a brilliant mind, and she fired the genius of her husband. But so soft of voice, shy of manner, retiring of spirit was she that few suspected the potentialities within the young wife.

It was then that Madame Sun told me of her escape from Canton several weeks earlier, describing the horrors of her flight through the bloody streets of the city, bullets flying about her, the dead and dying lying in her path. I could not know that this experience was but a prelude to a life fraught with drama.

I left the house uplifted, enthusiastic for the cause for which Dr. and Madame Sun stood. I wanted to go out and fight to right the wrongs of China's masses — to become a revolutionist (although with no more adequate conception of what was involved in that, in the Russian sense, than an average college sophomore had of what was involved in becoming a socialist).

I rushed into the office full of importance, hastened to my typewriter, and began a glowing cable. I forgot to count words, skeletonize copy, in my eagerness to write Sun's message.

The Old Timer came and looked over my shoulder. After a minute or so he commented:

"Great stuff you've got there, sister. Only trouble is, Sun's message of revolution has already been published many times over a period of years."

My fingers slipped from the keyboard.

"Thought you went to interview Sun as to whether he and his pals were going Red. Every reporter in town has been trying to see Sun and get a statement. You see him, and you come back and write a sob story about the Chinese masses."

I inserted a new cable blank into my machine and began to write:

SUNYATSEN BITTERLY DISAPPOINTED AMERICAS REFUSAL RECOGNIZE SOCHINA REPUBLIC OR GIVE FINANCIAL AID SAME LOOKS RUSSIAWARDS STOP ADOLPH JOFFE NOTED PROPAGANDIST ARRIVES SHANGHAI HOLDS MOMENTOUS MEETING WITH SUN STOP BRINGS PERSONAL GREETINGS EXLENIN ALSO GOODWILL MESSAGE EXRUSSIAN PEOPLE TO CHINESE MASSES ALSO PROMISES DEFINITE SUPPORT CAUSE STOP SUN RETURNS CANTON SHORTLY PLANS TRIUMPHANT ENTRY UNDER ESCORT GENERAL CHIANG KAISHEK STOP RUSSIAN ADVISERS LLASSIST[10] SUN REORGANIZE ARMY ALSO LAUNCH ORGANIZED PROPAGANDA CAMPAIGN TO AROUSE MASSES AGAINST MILITARISTS STOP LLFIGHT UNEQUAL TREATIES ALSO INFRINGEMENT CHINAS SOVEREIGN RIGHTS BY IMPERIALISTIC NATIONS STOP SUN

"Now quote Sun a bit, give them a little of your Chinese masses sob stuff, and you've got a story!" he advised. He puffed on his pipe as I wrote, then continued: "First thing a newspaper gal has to learn is to keep her mind, not her emotions, on the job.

---

10   Will assist.

As my friend Confucius once said, 'He who rules by his mind is like the North Star, steady in his seat.' "

- 15 -

In the spring I resigned from the *China Press* but kept my job with Internews. I was sorry to leave the *Press*, but John and I were to be married in March, and life was full. Elsie McCormick of San Francisco, and Irene (Corberley) Kuhn of New York and Paris had joined the staff of the paper and my resignation did not leave the Press without a "girl reporter."

It seemed a bit strange to be marrying there in Shanghai.

"Romantic!" my sister had written. But my parents had felt differently, and had cabled suggesting that I return to America and be married there when John could come over. But John's leave was not due for two years, and letters and cables finally resulted in messages of understanding.

John was a substantial, well liked American business man from Pennsylvania, active in the affairs of the American community. After college he had entered the United States government service and was appointed to the Philippines. Later he resigned and accepted a position in Shanghai.

His ancestors, like my own, had settled in the American colonies during pioneer days. His had chosen Pennsylvania, mine New York, Virginia, and Maryland. His father and grandfather before him had been churchmen. Other relatives had followed law and attained the bench. On his mother's side, for generations they had cultivated farm lands in Pennsylvania, had lived in the same roomy houses that their ancestors knew.

Ours was a conventionally beautiful church wedding with flower girls and bridesmaids. But even in my most romantic moments in America I had never dreamed of a honeymoon trip on a Chinese houseboat in far-away Hangchow.

To me there is no place so enchanting in the springtime. Perhaps it is because romance and happiness are forever associated with that city of "clear brightness," where the azaleas blossom in gayest profusion over the hills in the spring, and where pink-walled temples nestle in the forests of pale green bamboo on the "Peak That Flew Over" (from India).

We returned to Shanghai early in April.

Amah, full of dignity and pride, welcomed us at the comfortable house in the French Settlement where we were to live. And in a row behind her stood the other servants in clean white coats. Amah had engaged them. Her youngest brother, Ah Kun, a well built, pleasant-looking young man, bowed and said: "How you, Master? How you, Missie? My belong cook." To my surprise John spoke up, somewhat sternly:

"Any time, Ah Kun, you must say, 'How you, Missie? How you, Master?' Missie belong number one this side."

Another, Snow Pine, formerly with the Robinsons, bowed. "How you, Master? How you, Missie? My belong number one boy," he announced with pride, quite oblivious to orders.

Greatly to my amusement it was ever thus. To the Chinese the household revolves around the "Master." His wishes, his comforts, his likes, his needs are ever the first consideration in a family, but the custom had its compensations. John backed my every desire (a word from the "Master" settled any problem), and the house ran as smoothly as if we had been married for years.

The rooms downstairs were in order. Everything had just been stored in the house when we had left for Hangchow, and I had imagined that it would be necessary for me to direct the unpacking of furniture, of wedding presents, of dishes. But no — the boxes had all been cleared, cheerful fires were blazing, and the furniture was well arranged.

We had received such lovely gifts. Days before our wedding, presents had arrived from foreign and Chinese friends as well as from Chinese business acquaintances of my fiancé. I had noted each gift, and the list covered several pages. Gifts from Chinese of the old school came in pairs — two silver vases, two carved jadestone figures — as was the custom. A few of the extremely punctilious Chinese sent gifts in fours, such as scrolls depicting the four seasons; for according to old tradition the gods of marriage are four brothers, and all four must be honored. Someone sent us a pair of shining copper basins. The staff was shocked when I filled them with sand and used them for low flower bowls. They were, in reality, bath basins for the first-born.

We looked into the kitchen. Over in the corner a young boy, the "learn pidgin," was peeling potatoes. I came to know that this small person did all of the drudgery. Why should cook, an artist of the cuisine, be bothered with such things as shelling peas and peeling potatoes? Round of face, strong of build, immaculate in his starched white cap and apron, cook was a personage.

I watched, fascinated, as he frosted a cake for tea: a wonderful three-layer cake piled high with marshmallow icing.

With the flourish of an orchestra conductor wielding his baton, he smoothed the top of the cake with chopsticks. Chopsticks! Then "learn pidgin" handed him an old Chinese newspaper. Cook tore off a large corner and rolled it into a funnel. To my horror he turned a small bowl of pink whipped cream into the funnel and squeezed a long narrow ribbon from the opening onto the cake. I started to protest. Then I caught the intent expression on his face as he shaped the cream into roses with the aid of a turkey feather.

He was an artist before his canvas; and he turned out a cake worthy of a *pâtissier*.

The next day I bought cook an aluminum gadget for decorating cakes. We still have it, and it looks almost as new as on the day on which I bought it. In fact most of my foreign cooking devices, articles which in American magazines are guaranteed "to save the housewife time and labor," are arranged in neat rows on the shelves. Cook points to them with pride; but when he really gets down to work he uses chopsticks, stiff turkey feathers, and Chinese bowls of rough pottery.

But cook's artistic talent was sometimes most disconcerting — as on the day a very stiff bishop from New York came for tea and the boy brought in an elaborate cake on which cook had written, "Good luck, Jesus."

Cook did not seem to expect much of me.

Rather he treated me much as the experienced cook of a large Chinese family does the newly arrived bride of a son of the household. On the third day in the home, the young wife, according to old custom, puts on her flower-embroidered apron and goes into the kitchen to make a soup. She must be most careful that the bouquet please not only the taste of her husband but that of her mother-in-law as well. If she succeeds, she has made her gesture and won her laurels as a housewife.

Early in my married life, I too ventured into the kitchen. But when I discovered that Ah Kun fried chicken like a southern mammy, turned out Filets de Sole Meunière like a boulevard chef, a hot tamale pie like a fat señora, and a borsch like a Russian, I knew that we had a treasure, and decided to let well enough alone.

I learned something also of entertaining in Shanghai.

One Sunday afternoon at a Columbia Country Club tea dance John suggested casually that the whole party come to our home for dinner and bridge. Some ten persons accepted!

I smiled politely, but all the time I was trying to remember what was in the icebox. I had ordered only a light dinner. I knew that there were eggs on hand — no wonder cook bought eggs by the hundred! — and cold chicken. I heard John say casually to the boy serving our table, "Boy, telephone homeside, talkee cook ten piece man come dinner."

"Well," I thought, "this is on your head — you are the master!" True, but I was a bride — and nervous. When we entered our home I blessed the boy. Never by a flicker of an eyelash did he betray surprise or concern. "Can do, Missie," he confided in an aside to me.

The women fluttered gayly up to my room. When we came down to the drawing room, the men were laughing over their drinks. Snow Pine and the number two, both in long white coats and short henna-satin jackets, were serving tempting canapés. Everyone except the hostess was completely at ease as we entered the dining room.

The table was lovely. Candles gleamed over cut glass, silver, flowers. I tried not to stare at the flowers — I had never seen them before, nor the elaborate silver container which held them.

In a daze I watched the boys serve a delicious dinner: mushroom soup, Crab Louis, roast capon, rum ice.

I wanted to rush into the kitchen and embrace the cook. Everything was perfect. But all evening as we played bridge I kept wondering. How did he do it?

Ah Kun, upon being told by telephone of the impromptu dinner, had phoned the cooks of two or three of the guests and "borrowed" their dinners. From one home he had acquired the capon; from another the ice. Ah Kun would never let the "master" down, nor would he himself lose face.

When dining with friends the following Saturday night I was amazed to see the table set with my wedding silver. I saw the hostess give a slight start as she picked up her fork, and then carry on calmly. Her houseboy had decided that my new silver was "more nice" than "he missie's," and so he had borrowed mine.

Beyond the kitchen were the servants' quarters.

Their kitchen fascinated me.

Instead of a coal range such as we used, they had a three-hole stove made of brick and mud, freshly whitewashed and decorated with flower designs. In a niche above the stove was pasted a gaudy portrait of Tsao Wang (literally, the "Prince of the Oven," but universally known as the kitchen god). On his *tsao pan* (memory scroll) he wrote the good and bad deeds of the family during the year. He is perhaps the most universally respected god in China, and is known as the guardian of the hearth. On his birthday, the third of the eighth moon, the cooks' guilds in various cities burn incense at his shrines. And on the twenty-third of the twelfth moon all China sacrifices to him just before he sets off for heaven to make a report to the Jade Emperor as to the conduct of each family during the year past. From the time of Emperor Wu Ti in the second century B.C., he has played the role of censor of the household.

Months later, during the Chinese New Year season, I saw Ah Kun putting a bit of honey, a small ball of opium paste, and a drop of wine on the lips of Tsao Wang just before the ceremony known as the Burning of the Kitchen God, and wondered what cook had been up to! Usually honey alone is sufficient.

I did not worry over keeping house. I liked Ah Kun, and I had a feeling that he had "adopted" me.

John and I were enjoying a leisurely breakfast on the wide veranda which overlooked the garden one Sunday about a month after our return from Hangchow. It was spring; the moon was that of the Peony; and I was happy. The morning was as peaceful as a chapter out of David Grayson's "Adventures in Contentment." High hedges of viburnum, carefully boxed, shut in the garden from the outside world. The air was sweet with honeysuckle, syringa, and roses.

After a time Can Do Zung Kee, housebuilder and cabinet-maker, arrived. He was a gentle-faced, quiet-voiced man in a long gray silk coat, and he in no way disturbed the peace of the morning. He was making our furniture. We had supplemented our Chinese things temporarily with *lendee-lendee* pieces. Shanghai furniture houses did not carry large stocks from which selections could be made. Instead of going to the auctions (a recognized custom) or "taking over" the effects of someone going home, we preferred to have our furniture made, although this meant months of waiting.

Before our marriage, John and I dropped into Can Do Zung Kee's shop.

The fragrance of camphor wood, teak, and cedar filled the air. In a vacant lot, men stripped to the waist were taking turns drawing a saw some eight feet long through a great log of teak which was tilted over a sawhorse. Hour after hour they labored—such labor!—drawing the saw back and forth, back and forth through that hard, seasoned wood—a matter of days to saw off a single board. A large glue pot, smeary and dripping, gave odorous evidence of its presence over a small charcoal fire. At a bench a workman was busy with his homemade plane, drawing it towards him instead of pushing it from him. Another man was drilling holes with a tool which was whirled rapidly by means of a sort of bowstring. On a stool, a young woman sat nursing her baby.

Despite the primitiveness of it all, Zung Kee had smilingly, confidently, assured me, "Chippendale can do, Missie."

He had arrived at our house that May morning with a design for the dining-room chairs.

The telephone rang. Its jarring note broke the spell of the

springtime. Snow Pine brought me a message from my Internews assistant on the *China Press*.

What a story!

A band of some thousand bandits had derailed and wrecked the famous Blue Express train — the pride of China — at Lincheng, Shantung province.

Hundreds of passengers, including a number of wealthy and distinguished foreigners as well as Chinese, had been forced from their compartments at dead of night, in their sleeping garments, and driven at the point of bayonets and guns to the bandits' mountain stronghold; and among the missing was Miss Lucy Aldrich of the Rockefeller family.

Abruptly news became my job. A few hours later I was on the train headed north into the heart of the bandit country.

For the first time I began to wonder about a newspaper career and marriage. I might be away two weeks, or two months, and I had been married six weeks!

News was my job — but was it?

The kaoliang growing fresh and green on either side of the track as we entered southeastern Shantung was only about two feet high; by midsummer it would tower six to eight feet and provide ideal hiding places for the bandits. For many hundreds of years this mountainous district had been notorious. Its mountain strongholds had sheltered *hung-hu-tze* (redbeards) from Manchuria, *tufei* (brigands of local origin), and *chang doh* (strong thieves, robbers, who were part-time farmers, part-time bandits). The walled towns of southern Shan-tung were in constant terror of a visitation of the *tufei*. Sometimes a red warning sign was posted on the gate of a wealthy Chinese, an official, or even a mission compound demanding a large sum of money, particularly in the Tungchowfu, Lincheng-chow,

Tsaochowfu, and Yihsienfu districts. Again, the armed brigands swooped down on a sleeping village, kidnapped members of wealthy families, stole its young women, and looted the crops of millet, kaoliang, sweet potatoes, peanuts. It was a harsh, hard land. Winds, drought, flood, famine, banditry, civil war took their toll, and only the robust survived. Hence the sturdy, resolute Shantung farmer – the type of Wang Lung of "The Good Earth."

We crept slowly into Lincheng. Lying at the foot of the embankment, like a beetle on its back, was the Blue Express engine.

The intermediary between the bandit chieftain and the Chinese government was Roy Anderson of Peking, an influential American born in China. I learned he was at Tsaochung, a coal-mining town on a branch line running out from Lincheng, and hurried there.

A great wall thirty feet high, with towers at the corners and machine guns planted every few yards, surrounded the twenty-five-acre compound of Tsaochung. The top of the wall was patrolled by armed guards night and day, and powerful searchlights played over the surrounding district from the towers.

Mr. Anderson was astonished to see a woman there in the heart of the bandit country; but he invited me to tiffin in his private car, together with a group of officials of various nationalities. It was then that I was given the latest news.

The release of the prisoners, which during the first day had seemed imminent, had become problematical. The women had been released, but some twenty foreign men – eight Americans (among whom was J. B. Powell, editor of the Shanghai *China Weekly Review*), five Britishers, two Mexicans, one Italian, one Frenchman, and three of unknown nationality, as well as more than one hundred Chinese, had been taken deeper into the mountains; had been forced to climb up the precipitous heights of Pao Tze Kuo, to the Temple in the Clouds. (They remained there for some six weeks while the negotiations for their release dragged on.)

Miss Aldrich had been freed. I went on north by the first train and eventually caught up with her in Peking, where in the Rockefeller Hospital she was resting from her experiences. She was up and about her room, cheerful, amusing, apparently little the worse for her strange adventure. As she said, she had "marvelous stories for dinner parties for months ahead." Her story was fantastic. Fortunately the captors had no knowledge of her Rockefeller connection. They were demanding $2,000,000 ransom money from the Chinese government when they released her.

The *tufei* had struck at two-thirty in the morning, announcing themselves with breaking glass, blood-curdling yells, gunfire, crashing of compartment doors. Forced from the train in nightgown, kimono, and bedroom slippers, Miss Aldrich managed to hide two valuable rings, heirlooms, in the toe of a slipper. At the point of a gun she was prodded through the kaoliang along with a number of other partially dressed passengers, many of them barefooted. Through the darkness they trudged. By daylight the captives were in the foothills; although they were near exhaustion, the bandits' bayonets forced the party to greater speed. The rings cut into Miss Aldrich's foot, but she plodded on. Divided, and walking in file—a prisoner and a bandit, a prisoner and a bandit—they traveled on various trails to the Paotu Shan ("The Mountains Where the Tufei Live"). One Chinese, a frail elderly gentleman, who faltered was shot, and the spot later became known as the "mountain where the old one was shot in the neck."

The bandits halted to sort their loot and repack their

bundles. Ladies' evening gowns, hats with feathers and flowers, bedclothing, valuable rings, watches, door handles, wallets with money, papers from brief cases, toilet articles, portable typewriters, strings of bananas, tins of milk, were piled up in a great heap.

Miss Aldrich laughed at their antics. She laughed when one young bully waved a gun in her face, when another ate toothpaste which bubbled in his mouth, and still another danced around with a picture hat on the back of his round head, a pink satin corset about his slim hips. In the confusion Miss Aldrich took the rings from her slipper and hid them under a large rock, which she attempted to mark.

The bandits worked with speed; the sun was rising, and they must get on into the mountains. Government troops would be on their trail. The pull was grueling, for the trail was rough and steep.

Miss Aldrich slowed down the party. Rice cakes and hot tea did not stimulate her. They provided her with a donkey, but she slid from his back. Her release was unspectacular – the bandits, guarding their other prisoners, simply walked on up the trail and left her!

Miss Aldrich wandered alone about the mountains, seeking help. She met no one. It began to drizzle, and shortly after dusk she came upon an isolated walled village clinging to a hillside. Staggering along at the base of the wall, hugging it for protection from the rain, she came to the gates. They were shut, barricaded for the night, and no amount of pounding and calling could force the gateman, safe within the gatehouse, to open them.

After a time she stumbled upon a hut and crawled inside. When she awoke in the morning, hungry and suffering from exposure, villagers on their way to the fields ran in error. They thought she was a spirit. It was only when she began to make gestures indicating that she was hungry that a young Chinese, later held to be a bandit, ventured near. He led her into a mud-walled, thatch-roofed cottage. And while she rested, ate the hot noodle soup, meat dumplings, and tea which they brought her. A woman bathed her cut, swollen feet. Contact was made with the authorities and with the foreigners who were searching for her.

Miss Aldrich was concerned over her rings. One was a large diamond solitaire, the other a valuable emerald.

In the Peking hospital Miss Aldrich drew a map of the bandit trail, marking as best she could the spot where she had hidden them, and it was sent to the Standard Oil office in Tsinan, a short distance from Lincheng. Although the mountains were honeycombed with trails, covered with boulders and rocks, searchers were sent out on what came to be known as the jewel hunt.

As the train from Peking pulled into the station at Tsinan, a hilarious crowd met me.

"The Babcocks' houseboy found the crown jewels," someone shouted and I was carried off by Shanghai friends to the Tsinan Country Club (where the little international community gathered) to hear the story.

Feeling that his master, who was the number one of the Standard Oil office at Tsinan, would lose much face if the rings were not recovered, the houseboy set out to find them. The one clue he possessed was that the rings were hidden on the "mountain where the old one was shot in the neck." He could make few inquiries, however, for the country people, many of whom were bandits or related to bandits, were as suspicious as Kentucky mountaineers. A question or two, and he would be marked as a detective from the provincial government. The boy planned carefully. After hiring a bandit cousin as a guide and changing into a faded cotton coat such as a poor farmer might wear, he set off. For several days he combed the trail slowly and carefully. He forgot his dignity and lifted rocks, grubbed in the earth. After a week of hunting he sank down on the trail exhausted and discouraged: he must return to his master's house, a failure. As he sat bowed in misery, his hand touched a hard, round object, and then another. The bandit cousin was far ahead, no one else was on the trail. Even as he opened his hand he caught the fire of the jewels. Carefully hiding the rings in an inner belt, he made his way slowly, "sadly" down the trail. He did not betray his success to the bandit cousin by so much as a lift of an eyebrow.

I did not stay long in Lincheng. The story as I saw it read like a long exciting serial.

Weeks later, the final parleys with the bandit chiefs took place in the opium chamber of the bandit chiefs' headquarters, the air of which was thick enough with opium smoke to choke an ordinary diplomat—yet Anderson took it all in his stride. As a leading daily stated, "Roy Anderson emerged as the outstanding figure of the bandit situation and doubtless the lives of the foreign and Chinese captives were saved by his successful strategy."

Recently the original documents connected with the bandit negotiations were shown to me. Amazing documents: from the President of China, a bandit chieftain, and an American middleman. Most remarkable to me was that a foreigner had to sign a document guaranteeing the good faith of the Peking government. The bandits did not trust the promises of the government, promises, which even so were later betrayed.

The telegram from His Excellency President Tsao Kun read:

MR. ANDERSON:
You have acted as a negotiator in the Lincheng bandit case and, in spite of the hot weather and the hardships, have exerted

your full energy as a mediator. I greatly appreciate this. As the case has now been discussed and a solution has been found, please do not hesitate to give the several guarantees demanded by the bandits, in order that both Chinese and foreign captives may be relieved from danger at an early date. I greatly hope that the case will now be settled in this manner. I therefore send you this telegram, trusting that you will note the same.

TSAO KUN (Seal)

June 8, 1923

The document which the bandit chieftain signed with a great flourish in the opium hut read:

To MR. ANDERSON.

I, Sung Kwei-chi, representing all brethren here, beg to say that we are willing to be "called and pacified" and organized into a national army. From this time on, we will be permanently loyal to the country and commit nothing that will disturb the order of the army or hurt the reputation of soldiers. On behalf of all brethren,

I beg to make this important declaration that we have full confidence in Mr. Anderson, and to the person of Mr. Anderson we pledge that we will permanently observe the above things.

SUNG KWEI-CHI, Hsin * (Chop)

Witness:

KIANG CHIN-YUAN

SUNG FU-CHI

CHOU SIH-SUNG, ETC.

The letter which Mr. Anderson sent follows:

June, 1923.

TO THE MOST HONOURABLE CHIEF SUNG
AND ALL OTHER CHIEFS.

I, Roy S. Anderson, am an American citizen and a friend of China in life and death. As the brethren in the mountains are having hard times, as all Tan Chai have shown genuine sincerity in their actions and words in all the conferences, and as they are willing to submit, I am willing to guarantee that my brethren will be organized into an army and made officers and privates. There shall be no more than three thousand people and the number of unarmed men shall not exceed five hundred. The Government will undertake to support two thousand and seven hundred people while all Tan Chai shall make arrangements to pay the three hundred men, themselves. I am also willing to guarantee that after the brethren are "called and pacified," all their former crimes will be pardoned by the Government. After they are organized, their pay as agreed upon will be given to them according to their ranks, every month, by the Government. This guarantee shall be effective three years from the day of signing.

After you, my brethren, have submitted, you shall, for the sake of your country and fellow citizens, be loyal to your country and keep the order of the army, so that the whole nation, seeing that you are · serving the country, will praise your spirit of sacrifice.

ROY S. ANDERSON (Chop)

Witness:
KIANG CHIN-YUAN, SUNG FU-CHI, ETC.

- 16 -

Spring flitted by, then overnight came summer—a hot, sticky summer, whose days and nights were relieved only by occasional typhoon winds and rains. About the end of August the Chippendale chairs were ready, and Can Do Zung Kee's men delivered our new furniture. Amah called in a house tailor and we began a session of curtain making, using some of the rolls of sunshine gauze and heavy brocaded satin which we had received as wedding presents. We were measuring drapes for the dining room when I was called to the telephone.

Japan had been racked by a terrible earthquake!

A few hours later an urgent cable arrived from New York. Duke Parry, the International News Service correspondent in Tokyo, had not been heard from—he was probably either seriously injured or killed—I was to take an airplane at once for Japan and cover the earthquake disaster!

An airplane? Clippers were not zooming over the Orient in 1923.

An official relief ship carrying food supplies, medicines, clothing, was leaving for Japan at dawn, and Mr. Cunningham and John got me onto that ship, although they were frankly concerned about my going. As the ship pulled anchor and started on her way to Kobe, sadness at leaving home was mingled with the excitement of the biggest and most difficult assignment I had ever had—an assignment any newspaperman would have welcomed. I was the only woman correspondent given that job so far as I know.

Under a threatening sky, with murky clouds hanging low over the green mountains which backed the city, we docked at Kobe.

Kobe now occupied a position similar to that of a city behind the lines in time of war. Lorries flying Red Cross flags were at the wharves to rush off the urgently needed food, clothing, and medical supplies. I hurried to the Oriental Hotel.

The lobby and corridors were crowded with the first several hundred American, British, and European refugees who had been rescued from the devastated centers of Japan and brought to Kobe on the steamship *Prospect*.

Long lines of anxious men and women stood before information desks. At the American center a frantic husband was seeking word of his wife. An elderly man, whose veined hand shook so that he could scarcely fill out the request card, begged for news of his grandchildren. A young girl whose eyes had lost forever the smile of childhood was crying for her mother. The walls were covered with tragic little signs:

Will anyone with information regarding Mrs. — — — and child registered at the Grand Hotel Yokohama please report at once to — — —

Will anyone who knows the whereabouts of Mrs. — — — and children believed to be at Kamakura please call — — —

Sign after sign.

I asked at once for news of Duke Parry, the International News man in Tokyo. There was no information. I too filled out a card of inquiry.

The reception rooms of the hotel had been turned into outfitting stations. A man I had known in Shanghai spoke to me.

"I was lucky," he said grimly. "I was having a drink with some friends in the lobby of the Grand Hotel and stepped out on the street for a moment to give my chauffeur a message. As I turned to go back, the earthquake struck. I was thrown to the ground — stunned. The hotel crumpled in a great cloud of plaster dust. My friends were buried."

The ballroom, which had been converted into an emergency

hospital, was filled with rows of cots. I heard someone call my name. A woman with whom I had played bridge was lying there. I scarcely recognized the smart, poised person I had known in Shanghai in the shattered wreck tossing on the bed. Her hair had been clipped close to her head, her eyebrows and eyelashes were gone. Her poor face was blotched with scarlet scars.

"I had a ghastly time," she said in a husky voice. "I was down seeing friends off on the *Australia*. Suddenly there was a rumbling sound which seemed to come from deep in the earth – then all was confusion. My husband screamed, 'Earthquake.' The next I knew I was sitting in the water at the Bund. I looked toward the shore and thought that I must have gone crazy. Yokohama was gone!"

She paused, but after a bit continued:

"Sparks and burning particles began flying everywhere. Almost at once a great wall of flames rushed on the city. The heat was so intense that it blistered my face and I had to duck under the water every few minutes. I saw people running for the Bund, but many of them dropped before they got there. They were literally roasted alive. Then floating oil in the bay caught fire. We had to swim about to keep out of the way of that deadly flame and of the heavy debris. We were finally picked up by a lifeboat from one of the liners."

While many of the refugees gathered in groups excitedly recounting their experiences, their miraculous escapes, others sat alone. They were silent, unheedful of the milling throng. They stared into space. They were living over again the horrors of it all.

There was a feeling of mass calamity, mass tragedy, everywhere. A depressing heaviness in the air added to the general unrest. I felt myself falling under the mesmeric spell of that tense atmosphere. I had been in Kobe only a few hours, but it seemed like days.

When I finally slept that night I was in the throes of a nightmare. Someone had told me that shrill, warning cries of the pheasant hens in the zoos had been heard on the morning of the disaster, peculiar cries which the Japanese have long believed herald the coming of trouble, of earth tremors.

All night those warning cries rag through my dreams. What a night! I remember fighting sharks in the sea, trying to run through streets that jerked like bucking broncos, struggling to get out of a tunnel whose passage was blocked with dead bodies—echoes of tales I had been told.

I awoke in an absolute panic. It was unreasonable, I knew, yet I could not stay in that barren room with its white, cracked walls and listen to the rain pounding on the windows. So I dressed, ran down the dark hallway, and into the lobby below. It was three o'clock in the morning, but I was wide awake. With a relieved sigh I joined three or four other restless souls.

The sense of impending trouble stayed with me. Perhaps it was that sixth sense which is credited to newspaper folk. It was as if someone had been trying desperately to give me a message.

About five in the morning the lobby sprang into life. A refugee ship was expected. Ambulances, groups of nurses, doctors, and Boy Scouts soon assembled, and I went to the wharf with them.

A pitiful procession came down the ship's gangplank about an hour later. Only a few of the refugees were able to limp off without assistance. Some, whose heads were so bandaged that they could not see, were aided by the Boy Scouts. Then two or three hundred sick and injured refugees were carried off the boat on stretchers by American seamen. They were placed in ambulances and rushed to the hospitals.

One poor woman was there whose husband and children had been killed in Yokohama. The shock had crazed her, and she went about smiling insanely, saying that her husband was on one rescue ship, her children safe on another. She met every boat until she was mercifully sent back to America.

Hurrying back to the hotel, I dashed up to my room to write the first of the many cables I was to file on that eventful day. Wishing to refer to messages sent the previous day, I searched among my papers for the carbons; I could not find them. I looked everywhere — they were not in the room. I rang for the boy.

He bowed very low, sucked through his teeth, and politely said, "So very sorry."

During breakfast in the dining room, I almost forgot the incident in the excitement of seeing Captain Ariel Varges, ace cameraman of International Newsreel, who joined me for coffee. He was in a hurry to be off, however, to get back into the devastated areas for more pictures. He dumped six large tins of film on the table and asked me to take care of them. "Look after them," he said, "until I get back," and was gone.

I felt as if I had been asked to guard a sacred white elephant! They were heavy, unwieldy tins, twelve inches or so in diameter and about two inches thick. Two young Navy acquaintances who came into the dining room carried the films up to my room for me. Also they informed me that Japanese officialdom, according to the latest rumor, was threatening to confiscate all photographs and films of the disaster.

Almost at once a number of cables from New York were brought to me by an obsequious room boy.

"Ah-h-h!" he said smilingly with a great intake of breath as he noted the tins on the table. "Madame had earthquake picture fil-lums? No? Ah-h-h-h! So sorry, so glad." He bowed and closed the door.

One cable was for Captain Varges — a query from E. B. Hatrick, general manager of the International Newsreel Corporation regarding the earthquake pictures. There was also a wire from Barry Faris informing me that there was still no word from Duke Parry, and that I was to keep on shooting copy.

When I sat down to answer Mr. Hatrick's cable, there, by the typewriter, were the missing cable carbons! They had not been there when I had left the room.

At once that presentiment of trouble which I had felt so strongly the night before closed down upon me. Something was wrong. The cries of the pheasant hens of my dreams rang through my ears. Without losing a second I grabbed a suitcase, placed the films in it, and shot out of the room. The hall was empty, and I slipped down to the lobby without mishap.

In the crowd of refugees I located my Navy friends. One of the officers was from Virginia; the other, from North Carolina. I knew that I could depend upon them, and at once explained the situation. They advised me to get the films out of Japan. We called a taxi and dashed down to the docks. One of the officers took the suitcase, climbed into a gig, and headed for his ship in the harbor. He made the suitcase safe in his locker.

Within an hour we were back in the hotel. A great load had been lifted from my shoulders. Opening the door to my room, I came to an abrupt and startled stop.

Before my eyes was a scene of confusion. My papers were strewn over the floor. Had it been the wind? Then I noticed an open handbag which I remembered closing. Someone had been in my room! The films, however, were safe!

I wired New York at once, giving complete details. In a short time cables for Varges and for me began to arrive every half-hour or so. I was ordered to get on the first boat sailing from Japan for America and personally to bring the films to New York.

It looked as if the *Empress of Australia*, then anchored at Yokohama, would sail shortly with a shipload of refugees. So, after cleaning up all the cable news available, I boarded a relief ship going to Yokohama. The officers of the *Empress of Australia* were most kind. They took charge of the films and locked them in a deposit vault of the ship. Also one officer volunteered to take them to Vancouver. I did not wish to go to America unless it were absolutely necessary. So after more cabling to New York it was arranged that the officer should bring them. When the liner finally neared Vancouver some two weeks later an airplane picked up the suitcase.

That is the story back of the International newsreels of the Japanese earthquake. And often as I sit in comfort in a motion picture theater and shudder over the disasters depicted in newsreels taken in various parts of the world, I wonder what adventures have gone into the making of those pictures which run so smoothly before me.

It was about the 5th of September that I landed at Yokohama. All about was desolation. Sullen gray clouds seemed to fade into the blackened, prostrate land.

Although a ship's officer was with me, I was very nervous. There was something sinister hanging over that eastern coast of Japan, something menacing, as if Nature planned yet another visitation of her wrath. Walking was difficult. The streets and sidewalks were gone. Great piles of debris blocked our way. I simply could not believe that this barren waste which stretched on and on with only a handful of skeleton walls rising through the gloom was the teeming, bustling port city with half a million population which I had touched *en route* to China.

Japanese who had found safety in the environs of the city were stolidly plodding their way back through the ruins. Like the peasants of France, who during the World War returned to their beloved though demolished villages even before the last invader had marched out, the Japanese sought their city before the smoking ground had cooled, before the earth tremors had ceased.

Some of them had bricked up crude shelters down near the Bund and had their little charcoal stoves going, their kettles of water boiling for tea.

"*Shi-ia-ta-ga-nai* — It cannot be helped," they said.

Farther inland, the stench was nauseating. Little, as yet, had been done toward cleaning up the city. Yokohama was one great charnel house.

My escort's words were drowned by demoniacal yells from a mob of Japanese and Koreans ahead. The Japanese were attacking the Koreans. It was like a fantastic Japanese print — little blackened men, whose faces were livid with hatred, tearing their enemies to pieces. For a moment they seemed almost like pawns against that background of overhanging sky, of desolate waste, of unburied dead.

Then the fists of the big officer beside me doubled up; he muttered horrible threats under his breath, seemed to be ready to plunge into the midst of that battle. I grew frightened and was on the point of protesting — for a mix-up with a fanatical Oriental mob is an experience definitely to be avoided — when there came a hissing, groaning from deep in the earth.

There were cries of "Jishin! Jishin!" The earth shook violently under my feet. I sat down on the shifting debris — hard.

In the confusion the Koreans fled. The Japanese were right after them.

The disaster which had rocked eastern Japan had not only cut deep crevices into the earth; it had uncovered smoldering emotional depths in the people. It had brought to the surface the unceasing bitterness which many of the Koreans feel toward their conquerors the Japanese. There were rumors of pillaging bands of Koreans joining with the Japanese Red elements in an effort to overthrow the government. There were reports that the Koreans were looting, poisoning wells, committing arson as well as rape.

I managed to get on to Tokyo by a relief ship.

After the complete demolition of Yokohama, I was surprised to find sections of Tokyo more or less intact; to see a few tramcars running, some stores doing business, relief work well in hand, and the Imperial Hotel undamaged.

Although scattered districts of the city had not been destroyed, the loss of life exceeded that of Yokohama.

In the poorer districts the horrors were indescribable.

Any number of Yoshiwara girls were literally boiled to death in the water of the pools of the district where they had fled when the flames advanced.

Everywhere fear-maddened mobs had swept into open places. They had been trapped in those false havens. Thirty-three thousand people had perished in one small park. I glimpsed great masses of the dead. In a few places the bodies were so wedged together that some of them half stood, supported by the dead about them. In another congested center I saw the dead in gruesome, amazing positions. They had become entangled with fallen live wires, and had been electrocuted in those copper spider webs.

The military, however, were trying desperately to rid the city of corpses.

Sometimes even now I see those funeral pyres — flaming funeral pyres piled high with dead bodies. I hear Buddhist and Shinto priests in colorful robes intoning prayers, chanting burial rites. I smell again that horrible, unforgettable stench of burning human flesh.

There was a tenseness about, which was quite apart from that caused by the sudden disaster. The military had clamped down on the city, and a purge of all liberal thinkers, critics of the government, malcontents, was under way.

I saw students, university professors, workers, and I saw also Koreans, savagely cuffed about, manhandled, led away, against a background of charred ruins, of utter desolation.

The earthquake gave the military its excuse, its long awaited opportunity, to clamp down upon the country the grip of steel — to launch a wide campaign of suppression—to suppress the liberal movement which was just beginning to take form in Tokyo.

There had been rice riots, factory strikes, attacks on militarism in certain newspapers by professors of the Tokyo Imperial University, agitation by the Japanese Federation of Labor for the withdrawal of the Japanese soldiers from Siberia, demands for books of liberal writers, alleged reports of an attempt to overthrow the government, a soldiers' mutiny and ugly scenes in an arsenal, *dangerous thoughts*. . .

The military pressed down hard; began the grinding process so like that used in the days of the Shoguns, to crush any disturbing democratic tendencies abroad in the land, to destroy free thinking, free acting, on the part of the people. In Yokohama I had seen group after group of Japanese sitting among the ruins, as inactive as priests at meditation. They were doing little enough about rescue and relief for the less fortunate—they were doing nothing, so far as I could learn, towards ridding the city of its thousands of rotting, reeking corpses.

They were waiting for orders from *the military*.

But if the earthquake disaster uncovered the hatred of the Koreans, of unsettled social depths in the country, it also gave Japan a wonderful demonstration of the heart of America toward suffering humanity.

Feeling against America, was running high in Japan prior to the disaster. The Japanese press had been full of the part America had played in thwarting Japan's moves of encroachment in Siberia and in Shantung, China.

Then, to the great surprise of the masses, America extended a helping hand in their time of greatest need. President Coolidge had at once sent a cable expressing the sympathy of the United States. The American Red Cross raised $5,000,000 for relief work. The United States battleships raced toward Japan—not as enemies but as emissaries of good will, bringing food and supplies.

Rear Admiral A. E. Anderson and his fleet did a marvelous piece of relief work during those Japanese earthquake days.

When word of the Japanese disaster reached Dairen, where some seven destroyers of the Thirty-eighth Division of the United States China Fleet were on cruise, a number of American naval officers were lunching at the Dairen Club with a party of Japanese officials. A constant stream of messages giving authentic details of the disaster was received by the Japanese. Commander William Glassford, young, enthusiastic officer with a distinguished World War record,[11] fired with the realization of the need of his American countrymen in stricken Japan, figuratively cried, "What are we waiting for?" And the tiffin party broke up.

By four o'clock that afternoon the United States destroyer *Stewart* under command of Captain Mecleary was on the way to Japan. By six o'clock the other destroyers were off. Captain Gatewood Lincoln was taken aboard his ship on a stretcher from

---

11 Today a Rear Admiral with the United States Asiatic fleet.

a sickbed. The United States destroyers achieved the distinction of being the first to arrive in Japan. One ship was placed at Nagasaki, one at Kobe, another at Yokohama, and so on, in order that a radio chain might be established and the handling of American and other refugees from isolated coastal resorts simplified. Some two thousand persons were rescued.

I returned to Kobe on a relief ship which carried nearly one thousand refugees.

Duke Parry was at the Oriental Hotel. He had had a narrow escape, having been pinned under the ruins of his hotel for many hours, but had finally reached Kobe by a back way. He took over. I wound up my cables to New York and sailed for China at once. I couldn't leave Japan too soon.

- 17 -

There were a number of Russian refugees on the boat. I had been concerned over the fate of the White Russians there in Japan. There had not been a day during my stay in Kobe that Russian girls brave in remnants of finery, white-faced men with dazed eyes, mothers with children at their skirts, had not asked me for money to buy steerage tickets to Shanghai.

There were already several thousand destitute White Russians in Shanghai. They had arrived en masse by ship from Vladivostok several months earlier, arrived asking permission to land, to make Shanghai their future home. But while Chinese and foreign officialdom had debated the problem, the majority of the Russians had slipped ashore.

Because of this tremendous influx of Russians the very face of Shanghai was changing.

The morning the White Russian ships had arrived off Woosung, I had boarded a launch and gone down the river to get material for a human interest story.

I had no idea then that the story was to develop through the weeks, months, and even years ahead, into the most touching human interest drama which I have ever known. A drama of life and death, of courage and of despair. A drama whose end is not yet . . .

It began snowing as we neared the anchorage, and the vessels loomed cold and forlorn against a sullen sky.

Although faded flags of the Double Eagle were flying (probably the only place in the world), this was not a great fleet arriving with a fanfare of splendor. It was but a group of twenty-six Russian vessels of the old regime, all under a thousand tons, which included seven gunboats, four dispatch boats and nine transports, all as battered in appearance as the tramp steamers which sometimes limp into Shanghai. A Russian officer assisted me up the gangway of the flagship and led me into the dining room of the vessel, where a morning church service was being held. Impressive music greeted me: music in minor tones, which seemed to be at one with the dirge of the sea. An aged priest moved about the improvised altar where candles burned, and now and then a bell chimed. He was as self-possessed as though he had been conducting a ritualistic service in some great-domed Byzantine cathedral in Moscow in the days before the Church had been condemned, instead of on a leaking ship whose bunkers were empty, whose larders were bare, and whose passengers were ragged, hungry, cold.

After a time the officer took me to see Admiral Stark, the commander of the fleet. In his tiny cabin, Admiral Stark told me of the hegira of the White Russians now in his charge. He described the collapse of the White Russians in Siberia with the killing of Admiral Kolchak in 1920 by the Reds — of the desperate trek of the Whites across the vast stretches of Siberia into

Manchuria — of their life in Vladivostok until this city was taken over by the Reds — of their forced embarkation at Vladivostok for "God knows where."

The fleet had made for Gensan, Korea; but Korea was already overflowing with stranded Russians, and the governor general had refused a landing permit. The Japanese authorities at their next port of call, while denying the Russians the right to disembark, had contributed fuel, food, and clothing. The fleet had again set sail across the storm-swept China Sea and had staggered into Shanghai utterly spent.

As I rose to leave the cabin an unformed thought flashed through my consciousness, then was gone. It was an impalpable thought which just eluded me.

I was beholding for the first time in my experience large numbers of men without a country. I was seeing men who were not just refugees but victims of an ism, an ideology: Communism! In recent years I have again written of men without a country — German Jews — distinguished physicians, scientists, scholars among them — who fled to Shanghai following Hitler's first purge of the Jews from Germany and Austria. Sir Victor Sassoon and Mr. M. Speelman, heads of the Jewish Relief Organization in Shanghai, recently told me that by the early part of 1940 there would be some 30,000 of these refugees in the International Settlement. Nazism! And today the foreign areas of the city are crowded also with hundreds of thousands of Chinese refugees. They fear death from the sky and refuse to return to the farms and villages of their ancestors. Nipponism!

Shanghai was plunged into Russian relief work. All else faded before this very real problem of providing food, shelter, clothing, employment for these thousands of refugees who did not speak English or Chinese (though in many cases French); who had

Top left. Madame Sun Yat-sen. (International News Photos.) Top Center. Dr. Sun Yat-sen, President of South China Republic, 1922. (Photograph by author.) Top Right. His Excellency Hsu Hsih-chang, President of China, 1922. Bottom. Dr. Wu Ting-fang (second from the right), a refugee with missionary friends at the Canton Christian College after the capture of Canton by General Chen in 1923.

neither friends nor money; who were untrained, unskilled; who had come to stay.

The city spent thousands on her relief program, and she did a magnificent piece of work. The Russians themselves deserved tremendous credit for the orderly manner in which they tried to establish themselves under odds that were to me quite appalling. Most remarkable was the fact that there was no appreciable increase in crime. But these Russians were for coachmen, yard workers. Some because chauffeurs, riding masters, superintendents on building jobs, guards to Chinese of wealth who feared kidnapers. Positions in the big foreign hongs, banking houses, importing and exporting concerns, law offices, oil and tobacco companies, were limited in number; also they were filled by highly trained, experienced men specially sent out from "home" (Europe or America).

Even the Chinese women who worked in the foreign households as "missie amahs," "wash amahs," "baby amahs," "sewsew amahs," resented the Russians. One day I saw a seemingly gentle amah spit after a Russian woman who had been employed as nurse for the children of a friend. She had broken the rice bowl of the amah's cousin.

Some of the Russian women found work as nurses, French teachers, modistes, music instructors, clerks behind the counters of the innumerable Russian food shops selling sour cream, vodka, pickled fish, black bread, which began to open along Avenue Joffre, a few were employed as governesses in foreign and wealthy Chinese families. But literally hundreds of young girls entered the night life of the city as entertainers – girls who very often became the support of their husbands, parents, grandparents, in-laws, aunts, younger brothers and sisters. I do not exaggerate. I knew one little dancer who kept eleven adults going for months.

My copy for days was of these girls.

Many of them were lush, snow-white creatures, with hair the color of pale honey and eyes like violets in spring; and they sent the temperature of Shanghai's night life soaring. They were intoxicating, those girls, possessing a certain *quelque chose*. The day of the once famous "American" courtesans was gone.

Overnight, Shanghai became a cabaret town. A city of expensive night clubs where the most beautiful of the émigrés appeared as entertainers, it became also a city of tawdry, sordid dance halls.

The old Carlton closed. It opened again at once as a dance hall with Russian hostesses, a risqué floor show, and became a cabaret of the sailors.

Many of these Russian-owned cabarets failed because of the chits. They refused to employ Chinese shroffs (bill collectors) and, being unfamiliar with the chit system; they were unable to cope with the "George Washingtons," "Abe Lincolns," "Rudolph Valentinos," signed by certain of the patrons. The wise old Chinese Shroff, by a system all his own, can run down any number of "George Washingtons" and seldom fails to collect his accounts.

I saw a Chinese war lord, elegant in a long brocaded satin coat, accompanied by a bevy of dainty Chinese concubines, at a cabaret one night. He was a Shantung man, big and opulent and round of face, and he beamed on the Russian girls in the floor show. One girl in particular won his fancy, and he began throwing silver dollars at her dancing feet as he called "*Hao, hao* — Good, good!" A week or so later, when we again dropped into that particular cabaret, the pretty dancer had gone to Shantung with the war lord. He was reputed to have some eight Russian girls in his harem — enough to put on a floor show in his own ancestral hall. After a year or so he fled to Japan for political reasons, and was accompanied by his Russian harem.

It was intensely interesting to be close to history in the making; to be an eyewitness to events that move nations; to be familiar enough with the Far Eastern picture to know that the stage was set for even more gripping, drama.

Then one day, as if the director of an exciting, dramatic film had cried, "Cut!" the Oriental scene became unreal. I seemed to be watching it all from a great distance; impersonally. In my small world, the Far Eastern drama must fade before a new experience, purely personal, real, all-absorbing — an experience common to the lives of women.

- 18 -

Amah went about grinning like a Chinese porcelain cat. The whole staff seemed unusually cheerful and willing. I learned the reason one morning.

"My think so by an' by Missie catchee one piecee baby," Amah announced with a broad smile.

The quick words of reproof which sprang to my lips remained unsaid when I looked at the reflection of Amah's face in the gilded mirror of the dressing table. Her eyes were alight with hope and joy. I realized that, to a Chinese of the old school, motherhood was the purpose of marriage, that a union unblessed by children was considered a sad failure, that a wife who was not fruitful was soon cast aside, displaced by a second wife or a young concubine.

As Amah talked, I learned that she had gone to the Bubbling Well temple, lit red candles and burned incense sticks before Kwan-yin who answers the prayers of women; that she had struck the great temple bell according to the custom of Chinese wives who are praying for sons. Its deep mellow tone had vibrated through the *miao*. She had talked the matter over with one of the priests and had shaken the divining sticks from the bamboo tube. All of this she had done for me, and the signs had been favorable.

The amazing part of it was—I *was* going to have a baby.

As yet only John knew. We were happy over the thought of a son—wanted a little secret time in which to think about our babe-to-be. However, any foreign wife who tries to be shy and sentimental about the coming of a baby in China is in a difficult position, for the news is literally broadcast. Amah found it very difficult even to understand our reticence. To the Chinese I had acquired "plenty face." I was providing a link in the long ancestral line of my husband.

But as the days grew into weeks the overpowering weight of the Orient began to crush my spirit. Peculiar Chinese smells began to sicken me—incense, boiling peanut oil, opium. Sights on the streets which I had trained myself never to see began to loom up out of all proportion. The loathsome beggar women who thrust little maimed babies into the motor-car windows when we parked at the Wing On department store began to haunt me at night.

I was not well, and it was fatiguing to be gay and chatty through long dinners when my thoughts were full of baby dresses which I had found at the convent that afternoon, to listen to Russian entertainers singing away in the night clubs or watch them whirl and leap about the dance floor in mad dances which made me dizzy. Entertaining, all the formality of Shanghai's social life, its pace, its gayety, suddenly lost their glamour. It all seemed so unimportant. For we were going to have a baby! I longed for a clear blue ocean and sandpipers playing on the beach—for snow gleaming white on mountaintops—for purple shadows on desert wild flowers.

My husband, ever considerate, arranged for me to go to California; one of the men on the *China Press* staff took over the Internews job.

That time on the ranch in California was an interlude of contentment and peace. I missed my husband terribly, but I had a piece of work to do—and I felt so safe in America after the undercurrent of unrest which I had sensed in Shanghai. And the summer days drifted by—strengthening, life-giving days.

John Junior—Young Master—was born September first. The nurses in the hospital could not understand my joy at the clear light in his deep blue eyes. I was too happy to explain my Shanghai nightmares.

When "Young Master" was almost two weeks old a Los Angeles newspaperman called. He wanted an interview on the China situation. China situation? The exciting events which had been taking place in the Orient during the past few days had been carefully kept from me. I did not even know there was a "situation."

With consternation I read in his newspaper screaming three-inch headlines: "FOREIGNERS IMPERILED IN CHINA," "U.S. BATTLESHIPS RUSHING TO SHANGHAI."

The war lords of China were again on the march!

John Junior and I sailed for the Orient the first week in November. He was only eight weeks old, and relatives and friends were shocked by my taking him back to a country which was seething with discord, which was likened by the press to a smoldering volcano, the top of which might blow off any day. But I was impatient to get back to my husband in China. As I had regained my strength in the California sunshine, I had lost the weight of the Oriental depression. Once again the charm, the glamour, the allure of Cathay were calling.

John, friends, and our Chinese staff were down at the Customs jetty to meet us. Johnny cuddled into Amah's comfortable, experienced arms as if he belonged, and there was born an understanding and love between them which has never changed.

I was happy to be home; yet, as we drove along, my heart sank. It was the first time I had seen John in uniform, or Shanghai transformed into an armed camp.

The International Settlement and French Concession were heavily barricaded behind gates from which stretched miles of barbed-wire entanglements. Sandbag fortifications rose at strategic street crossings. Machine guns were mounted on buildings. Soldiers and marines in the uniforms of many countries paraded the streets. Foreign battleships were on guard in the river off the Bund.

"Nice little civil war the Chinese militarists have been having around Shanghai this fall," explained John casually. "It's about finished now."

Suddenly I wondered if I should not have left Johnny safe in the care of his grandmother, in the peace and sunshine of the California ranch. Our baby in a fortified war zone! He was such a little fellow to be facing life in a strange Oriental land torn by disorder.

"No fear, Missie," comforted Amah, "my look-see Johnny." When we reached home and I saw the baby comfortably installed in his sunny room with its jonquil-yellow and applegreen furnishings, I lost my anxiety. Do Zung Kee had achieved a great success in the nursery. He had brought in a Chinese artist who had decorated the walls in an enchanting manner with swaying bamboo, bright-colored birds on wing, dozens of gayly decked Chinese children, some carrying fantastic lanterns, others flying dragon kites. There was one big water buffalo on which perched a smiling Chinese boy—a buffalo and a boy—who were to become Johnny's make-believe companions in many an exciting adventure. They were rivaled in his affections only by a friendly striped tiger which was to personify the talkative tiger in "Little Black Sambo" when Johnny grew older.

So I hid my fears and tried to adopt the smart nonchalant attitude taken by all foreigners in Shanghai when civil wars loom; tried to shrug the war and its dangers away with a "Just the usual summer skirmish."

I had been back in Shanghai only a few weeks, however, when I began to sense disturbances of far greater import than the current civil war.

Could it be possible that China, so long set in her ways, who through some five thousand years had quietly absorbed, converted to her own, every new force with which the outside world had threatened her, was now to be converted to a radically new, completely foreign, ideology — the red doctrine from Soviet Russia?

This startling possibility, which would have been waved aside three years previously, was stark before us, and advancing!

PART II
"DARE TO DIE"
(1924-1932)

IT WAS ON A TRIP to Foochow where my husband was called on business that I first faced revolution in China.

We had been in Foochow only a few days when I began to hear about a tribe high in the mountains of Fukien—aborigines who, like Kipling's cat, walked alone. The Hakkas spoke their own dialect, had their own legends and customs, disappeared into the mountains on the approach of strangers; and the head of the tribe was said to be an aged matriarch. They were known also as the Dog-Faced people. Carl Crow in his "Handbook for China" says: "Their race is unmixed with Chinese and they worship a dog as their great ancestor." The women wore a headdress shaped like a Chinese junk on special occasions, and for every day daggers of pounded silver which they crossed in their chignons—"For protection from invading men," someone explained.

Old China with her legends had always intrigued me, and I became keen to visit this ancient Hakka' tribe: it sounded like colorful copy. However, it was a three days' journey by sedan chair to the nearest village, and it would be necessary to sleep in primitive Chinese inns.

As soon as I mentioned the trip, I began to hear of rebellious Chinese soldiers who had joined the bandit Reds who were infesting the interior. They were looting, kidnapping, killing. Bolshevism in that land of ancient legend and Dog-Faced people? I discounted the story as a port-city tale. John, on the other hand, was not in the least interested in roughing it in Chinese mountains for a week, and he did not believe in courting danger—"creating incidents," as he expressed it. Also there was good bridge to be found at the Foochow Club, and a fair golf course. However, his business satisfactorily completed, he put aside his prejudices and, because I had my heart set on the trip, agreed to go.

The number one boy at the American Consulate made the arrangements. He was one of the few Chinese of the city who knew the Hakka dialect and was tolerated in the village. Every sixth moon he went into the mountains to bring back stunning lacquer humidors, for which the Hakkas were famous. These were made from "ironwood," carved in striking designs and then lacquered. It took six months to make one.

With a local missionary who had offered to accompany us, we started off in our sedan chairs in single file: the number one boy, then John, myself, and the missionary bringing up the rear. There were some thirty sedan-chair bearers as well as the coolies who packed our rolls of bedding and food on their backs—quite a cavalcade. We passed through the ancient city gates and were soon winding our way through the rice paddy fields, past little clusters of farmhouses built among the bamboo and mulberry trees and the tall banana plants.

Late in the afternoon we entered a village near the foot of the mountains. The sky, blue when we left Foochow, had grown abruptly darker. We stopped at a tea shop for an early supper. It was a primitive place with pounded mud floor, but it offered a shelter. Curious Chinese packed in to watch the foreigners eating.

When it began to rain, the chair coolies put on great shaggy capes made of palm leaves and enormous straw hats lined with oiled paper, whose brims extended over their shoulders and served as umbrellas, and produced lanterns. We climbed back into our canopied chairs, and the curtains were dropped.

Darkness closed in quickly as we moved along. The bearers rested a bit before starting up the many hundreds of stone slabs which formed a stairway up the steep side of the mountain to the inn where we expected to spend the night—ancient slabs worn deep by the tread of many generations of feet; for this was the main pass from the other side of the mountains to Foochow. Some of the coolies went ahead, swinging lanterns that shone eerily through the rain. Occasionally one of my bearers stumbled, and I had visions of plunging down a steep mountain side; but the chair shafts rested on the shoulders of eight men, so that there was little danger.

Up, up, up we climbed. The swinging of the chair and the soft patter of the rain lulled me until I lost all sense of time and felt as if I were drifting in a phantom world. A commotion ahead awakened me just before the bearers lowered our chairs. In the dim light of the lanterns we saw the blackened ruin of a building.

It was—or had been—the inn.

In the courtyard the innkeeper and his two sons lay on the ground—dead. They had been shot. Rain was pounding on their twisted, upturned faces, on their coats. There was no sign of their women. They were in all probability comely and had therefore been carried off.

"Ai yah, ai yah!"

The Number One boy informed us that the inn had been burned—only an hour or so earlier, for the fire in the stove was still smoldering—doubtless by the bandit soldiers. He was very much excited and explained that the bandits were somewhere in the mountains. It was impossible to start back toward Foochow, for the chair coolies were exhausted from the climb and the rain, which at first had been warm and gentle, was taking on the proportions of a tropical mountain storm. The boy finally decided to take us to a secluded temple, where he hoped we could find shelter for the night.

We pushed on as silently as possible. The coolies were frightened—not so much at the Reds they might meet as at the ghosts of the dead men, which they believed were hovering about the inn. On and on. We climbed a last steep ascent, then stopped before a Chinese temple which through the storm loomed quiet and peaceful, a place of refuge. The bearers banged at the gates, implored the monks to open the gates. An acolyte finally appeared, bade us enter.

Once we were inside, the gates were promptly bolted. The chair coolies, upon instructions from the priest, carried our chairs to the rear of the rambling building and hid them away. We were led to a small room off the main temple. There was to be no evidence of foreigners about for the Reds to find. We did not even unpack our sleeping bags but stretched out upon worn hard benches used by the priests in their daily services.

From a little cup of vegetable oil hanging on the wall a taper cast a weird light over the room. In mysterious recesses huge painted idols loomed, idols with hideous faces and great burning-red eyes which seemed to glare down upon us. Occasionally a gong, deep and mellow, vibrated through the temple; but its music was lost in the crashing thunder and the pounding rain, while the wind in the pines sounded like harsh minor notes struck on harp strings. Occasionally bats swooped down from the beamed ceiling into the thin circle of light.

On impulse I slipped up and lit a row of red candles which were placed before the Protection to Travelers idol—not that I expected any protection from the red-faced figure which towered above me with drawn sword. John was in favor of burning candles before all of the idols—anything to lighten the chilly gloom! But the missionary tweaked out my candles and began to repeat the Ninety-first Psalm:

"He that dwelleth in the secret place of the most High shall abide under the shadow of the Almighty. . . . Surely he shall deliver thee from the snare of the fowler . . . . Thou shalt not be afraid for the terror by night . . ."

Suddenly the spell of his voice was broken. There was a tremendous pounding on the temple gates. Loud, harsh demands for entrance were heard.

The "Reds" had arrived—the terror by night!

A dozen or so men, apparently soldiers, clattered into the dimly lit main room, shaking the rain from their uniforms. They were heavily armed, and with them were two women: the elder was crying and moaning, but the younger was frozen in her fear; they sank down on the floor, a picture of misery.

The biggest of the men—a burly fellow with a cruel mouth and deeply lined, rugged face—cleared a square table near the entrance with one sweep of his arm. A priest brought tea and rice.

"The Dark Seventh One," whispered the missionary.

Although I realized to the full the danger of our position, yet I was caught up in the exciting drama and watched, breathless, from the darkness of our archway.

The men settled down to the business of eating. Two or three took out long water pipes and began to smoke; they laughed and talked good-naturedly. I wondered if they were really "Reds" and understood something of Communism, or if they were bandits. (The term was used indiscriminately during these early years.)

The simple meal was soon finished; then the leader and three of the others scattered mah-jongg tiles over the table and began to play. Silver dollars clinked. The rest stretched out on the floor and were soon snoring loudly. Breathlessly I watched. Then a priest came and led us to the comparative safety of a distant chamber.

My newspaper sense was spurring me on. I wanted to interview the notorious Dark Seventh One, to take his photograph!

All night the mah-jongg tiles clicked, but at dawn the leader and his men were off, headed toward a besieged town in the valley. Even so tension hovered over us, and John's eyes were still concerned; but never once did he say, "I told you so," or hold the experience over my head!

As we drank our morning tea the missionary described conditions in the province of Fukien:

For months the people had lived in complete panic. They were oppressed by the corrupt military and the civil authorities, by the bandits. Opium cultivation was enforced. Resistance by the farmers brought armed soldiers. Shopkeepers, fearing looting by troops, hid their goods away, carried on business behind shuttered doors. The boat people lived in constant dread of having their junks and barges commandeered; farmer boys, of being seized for transport duty; men of wealth, of being kidnaped, held for ransom; women, of being ravished; the village elders, of having to pay indemnities to first one descending force and then another. The richest towns had become pawns, to be fought over by provincial troops, bandit band. the armies of the "Reds." Behind the walls and stockades, the people lived in constant fear. News of the approach of soldiers, bandits, or Reds caused vast numbers to flee.

Foreigners as well as Chinese were caught up in that wave of chaos. Business, educational, religious activities were at a standstill. The papers were full of reports of atrocities against missionaries, representatives of foreign hongs, captains and officers of river and coastal steamers, even newspaper correspondents. The list of foreigners kidnaped, murdered, was lengthening.

Even so, only the most alert read the writing on the wall; realized that a definite revolutionary movement inspired by Moscow was beginning to take form in China. That early spring, when we glimpsed the bandits or Reds — whichever they were — in the mountain temple, the Red Army was still in embryo. But the borders of western Fukien and eastern Kiangsi were destined to become a stronghold of the Red forces of south China. From this section in 1934 the Red Army (grown to impressive proportions) started its famous six-thousand-mile "Long March" into the far interior — a march which ended at Yenan, Shensi Province, where a capital was set up in 1937 under the leadership of two remarkable men, Chu Teh and Tao Tse-tung.

Several weeks after our return to Shanghai I again glimpsed smoldering fire breaking into flame. In the settlement, life moved so normally that I was unprepared for the uncovering of that fire in a neighboring city.

We set off gayly for Sungkiang, ancient walled city twenty-five miles southwest of Shanghai, on a week-end houseboat trip, to visit the shrine of General Frederick Townsend Ward. As the *laodah* (head boatman) pushed off from the anchorage near the Garden Bridge, to tie up with a long boat train pulled by a steam tug, Snow Pine announced that the dragon which had been sleeping in the ground all winter had now lifted his head.

"Suppose dragon put he head up, Missie, bright spring sure have got," he explained.

But Snow Pine was wrong — there was to be no "bright" spring in China for many moons.

We moved leisurely along winding waterways, under carved, beautifully arched bridges, past quaint villages where women squatted along the bank to wash their rice and bean sprouts, teeming cities, open country. We sat out on the deck lazily content, watching the Chinese junks sailing along in all their dignity, chickens and babies tied on the poops, speculating as to the life of the pretty girl we had seen peeping from the window of a Chinese house perched on a canal bank. Was she Golden Flower, a favorite concubine, or was she the fortunate mother of sons, or was she only the pretty "slave" of the old mother? After dinner we watched the fireflies and lanterns gleaming on the shore, and after a bit John began to strum his guitar, to which we sang haunting Spanish melodies which he had picked up in the Philippines.

It was all idyllic, and I loved it.

Sometimes we went hunting on the islands and lowlands of the Yangtze estuary, where the guns produced handsome bags of geese, teal, pheasants, bamboo partridges; and there had been one delightful trip to the Ningpo Lakes which had given me two unforgettable glimpses of primitive native life, had shown me the resourcefulness of the Chinese farmer.

We were duck-hunting when we noticed a Chinese "hunter" standing up to his neck in the reeds. He wore a hat which was covered with branches; and on the water before him, anchored to his body by a rope, was a wooden float on which grass grew. Decoy ducks sat there, and a tame duck, fastened by a string, floated about. He moved quietly as he pushed the float ahead of him, into a bevy of unsuspecting ducks. Skillfully, he pulled a duck under the water, cracked its neck, flung it into a basket on his back, then reached for the feet of another, and then another.

It was cold at dawn the following morning as we set out.

Somewhat casually we watched a Chinese fisherman sitting

in his sampan wrapped in a blanket, huddled over a charcoal stove. Abruptly he threw off the blanket and slipped quietly, stark naked, into neck-deep water. He stood there, motionless as an old tree trunk. As we watched, he threw a large fish into his boat, and then another. Shivering, he climbed back into his boat, drew the blanket about him and roasted himself red over his charcoal brazier in preparation for his next jump into the water.

The heat of his body drew the fish!

Sungkiang was a quaint old city, and I anticipated new adventures which would enrich my Chinese life scroll.

We tied up at a village a few miles from the city. The men pushed off for a bit of shooting. One of the girls and I had a leisurely breakfast, then went for a walk on shore. The countryside was fresh and green, and the earth vibrant with awakening life. We noticed Chinese gathered in an open square before a village temple and stopped a moment.

A student in a long dark robe was talking loudly, excitedly. His young face was afire with earnestness, and he was swaying the crowd as does an itinerant actor. When he paused, there were loud shouts of *"Hao, hao!"* such as are heard in the Chinese theater when a performer pleases.

"We had better get back to the boat," said my companion quietly. "He sounds to me like a Communist agitator."

Even as we turned the speaker saw us; stared in amazed anger. He had been denouncing all foreigners to the villagers, and suddenly two of the hated ones had appeared.

"Yang kwei tzu — Foreign devils!" he shouted. The crowd surged toward us.

We hurried on, not wishing to create an incident. There was an ugly murmur as from the swell of an angry sea, then rocks and sticks began to fall about us. Fortunately we were wearing jodhpurs; and, throwing off all dignity, we tore along the narrow

Top left. Mao Tse-tung, famous Chinese Communist general of the Eighth Route Army, addressing his soldiers. (Trans-Pancific News Service.) Top right. Chou En-lai, Communist leader. (Trans-Pancific News Service.) Bottom. Eighth Route Army giving Communist salute in response to address by Mao. (Trans-Pancific News Service.)

Top left. Mass marriage as inaugurated by New Life Movement. Top right. Chinese soldiers learning a trade. Bottom left. Chinese soldiers attending classes in international affairs. Bittom Right. Generalis-simo Chiang Kai-shek addressing the nation by radio. (Trans-Pacific Photos.)

path along the canal which led back to our boat. Dogs snapped at us – vicious, mangy dogs which have an active hatred for all foreigners. Even as I ran, I could not believe that this was real, that we were being stoned and jeered. Only a month before we had passed that way, and the villagers had been friendly, kindly. During my long months in the interior three years earlier, I had been in the midst of civil war, of danger, yes; but there was no hatred directed toward me – no malice shown me just because I was a foreigner. I had experienced only kindness at the hands of the Chinese, never this frenzied abuse. We were near the end of our endurance when our men, with Snow Pine and the *laodah*, came tearing down the path toward us. The crowd fell back; but the experience left me weak in the knees, shaken.

Banners which we noticed on gateways, walls, further alarmed us with their revolutionary slogans: "Kill the foreigners," "Cancel all unequal treaties," "Seize the foreign concessions," "Comrades, arise against the capitalistic classes," "Exploited workers, organize." It was the last houseboat trip we were to take for many moons.

Back in the city we were in another world: a modern, safe, familiar world. There was nothing in its smooth surface to show that an organized revolutionary movement was gaining momentum in the hinterland, in Shanghai itself.

After the houseboat trip I set about picking up the China political picture, working out a series of articles on Russia's campaign to Sovietize China.

In Peking on my war-lord assignment I had heard much of Moscow's overtures to Peking, and at a large tea a distinguished-looking Russian had addressed me as "Comrade." I had quickly exclaimed that I was no "comrade." He was a member of a diplomatic mission seeking recognition of the Soviet government by China, and explained that Moscow had issued a manifesto in which the Soviet promised to give up all extraterritorial rights and special privileges of Russians living in China, to return all territory previously acquired from China, to restore control of the Chinese Eastern Railway, and to renounce Russia's Boxer Indemnity—all this if China would recognize Moscow. But strong pressure had been brought to bear upon the weak Peking government by the diplomatic corps, and the Soviet manifesto received little consideration.

When Adolph Joffe arrived in Peking in 1922 to urge recognition of the Soviet, he was so coldly received that he left for Shanghai to confer with Dr. Sun Yat-sen of the South China Republic. The diplomatic Leo Karakhan followed Joffe, bearing gifts and promises. He succeeded in settling the Mongolian and Chinese Eastern Railway question for the time, in concluding a treaty with Marshal Chang Tsolin; and early in June, 1924, he was received in Peking as Soviet ambassador to China.

What a furore this news created in Peking's diplomatic circle!

Karakhan and his staff had made a spectacular official arrival. They moved through the streets in a grand motorcade, horns sounding, flags of the hammer and sickle flying, and swung through the gates of the historic Russian legation with bands playing the *Internationale* They took up their residence in the one-time home of the titled representatives of the Czars. Red bunting enveloped the pretentious columns, while immense flags of the Soviet hung from the windows, balconies, and flagpole.

In this great establishment—a fit setting for the sumptuous functions of the Czarists, but scarcely in keeping with the doctrines of the Soviet—Karakhan reigned. From here he sent out his flaming denunciations of imperialism; proclaimed to the Chinese that the Soviet Union, alone of the world powers represented in Peking, desired China to become an independent nation, with full sovereign rights. And it was from here that Karakhan conducted a definite campaign to Sovietize China, until he was exposed by Chang Tso-lin many months later.

Almost at once we began to hear of Communist activity in Canton. Dr. Sun Yat-sen and the Nationalists were again in control of the city, following its recapture by General Chiang Kai-shek.

I began to fear Canton just a bit. Dispatches from there told of the reorganization of the Kuomintang to admit the Chinese Communists to membership in spite of the opposition of the more conservative members of the party, of the rightists; of the arrival in Canton of Soviet Russian military and political advisers; of the departure of picked Chinese students for Moscow; and of large loans.

A previous cable which I had dispatched containing a statement from Dr. Sun had read in part, "Sun Yat-sen bitterly disappointed America's refusal recognize the South China Republic or give financial aid looks Russiawards."

And Russia was fulfilling the promises made by Joffe and Karakhan.

Chiang Kai-shek, chief of staff of the army of the Kuomintang (Dr. Sun was commander-in-chief), was dispatched to Russia with letters to Lenin, Trotsky, and Chicherin.

What would the Soviet politicians do to him?

I remembered so vividly the officer I had met that stifling day on Sun Yat-sen's gunboat in the Pearl River off Canton. He it was who put aside face and took his turn in mopping down the decks when short of crew; who at the risk of death stole ashore on moonless nights to secure food and medicines for his commander; who resisted all overtures of the enemy to desert Sun. His eyes had been steady, appraising, and he had impressed me as being shrewd, as having a will of his own—a strong man.

I had admired him.

I followed the news dispatches from Moscow closely. Moscow welcomed Chiang as an envoy from Canton. For several weeks the reports were most friendly. Then Chiang exploded a bombshell. In addressing a body of young Chinese students in Moscow — ardent young men and women who had embraced with enthusiasm the doctrines of the Soviet — Chiang had boldly warned them against "lauding overmuch the works of foreign revolutionary leaders." He was greatly criticized for this speech, and shortly returned to Canton.

There was little in common between Chiang and the Russians; and from the first there was a subtle enmity between Chiang and Michael Borodin.

For months to come, Borodin was the outstanding foreigner in China. He came to Sun with letters of warm recommendation from Leo Karakhan.

Borodin (alias Berg, alias Grusenberg) was backed by an impressive record as a world revolutionist. As a child he had emigrated with his parents, Mr. and Mrs. Grusenberg, from Russia to America. He was educated in the public schools of Chicago, and began his adult life under the name of Berg as head of a business college. For years a voracious reader of Communist literature, he shortly closed his school and began his life work as a revolutionary agitator. It was upon his assignment by the Third International (organized international Communist party with headquarters in Moscow), to launch revolutionary activities in Mexico that Berg took the name of Michael Borodin. His success resulted in a similar mission to Scotland. The Scots made short work of the agitator Borodin: he was arrested, deported. In Turkey, however, as adviser to Mustafa Kemal Pasha, leader of the Young Turks and founder of the nationalist movement, Borodin achieved conspicuous success. The triumph of the nationalists in setting up a new government at Angora[12] securing a favorable treaty for Turkey in 1923 (Lausanne), abolishing the office of sultan, and establishing a republican government in Turkey with Mustafa Kemal Pasha as the first president was due, in part, to Borodin. Believing that China was ripe for Sovietization, Borodin — now one of the most experienced, diplomatic, high-powered, of all Moscow's propagandists — was rushed to Canton. His job was to ally China with the Union of Socialist Soviet Republics.

Such was the background of Comrade Borodin.

Dr. Sun was delighted with the big Russian, who hung on his every word, praised his writings, expressed his belief in the Three People's Principles. He glorified Sun, as it were, held him up as a light before the masses, hailed him as the · savior of China; he presented Sun before great audiences of students, of workers, of soldiers, and the magnetic personality of the aging revolutionist won over increasing numbers to the cause. Borodin 's subtle flattery must have been as balm to the man who had so often been received by the world at large as a "visionary," a "dreamer."

Borodin was made chief adviser to the Kuomintang. Through him, during the first National Party Congress held in January, 1924, the Chinese Communists were formally admitted into the party, despite strong opposition from the more conservative Nationalists as well as the rightists. He became the constant companion of Dr. Sun.

The Whangpoa Military Academy was opened by Dr. Sun. Chiang was appointed president, and Marshal Vasilii Bluecher (General Galen — who until a recent purge by Stalin was playing an important role on the Russo-Japanese frontier) and a number of other Ruction of Borodin. Students, farmers, workers, villagers were organized. And the youth we had heard firing the peasants

---

12   She presumably means Ankara

at Sungkiang with antiforeignism was but one of the thousands of propagandists working in the interior indirectly under the direction of Moscow.

Almost at once rumors reached Shanghai of friction between Chiang and the Russians, for the curriculum of the Whangpoa Academy was patterned after that which Trotsky had laid down for the Red Army of Russia. Chiang gave his time to his cadets. When he formed the First Army Corps, which was under his personal command, he chose as officers men who had not come under the leftist influence of Bluecher and Borodin.

It is essential that this Soviet infiltration of the South China government be examined in the light of subsequent events, as a background for the understanding of the complicated political picture in the Far East today — a picture in which Stalin is playing an important part.

But the world at large knew little of what was taking place in the interior of China; gave only casual attention to the tremendous activities of the Russians in Canton.

A truce of sorts was made between the Chang Tso-lin faction in northern China and the South China government.

Toward the end of 1924, Dr. Sun — who years before had been driven from Peking with a price on his head — was invited to the northern 'capital to discuss peace terms with Marshal Chang Tso-lin and the unification of northern and southern China. Dr. Sun, although sick unto death, set off on this mission; but the gallant old patriot, even as Moses, was not to realize his promised land. The afternoon papers of March 12, 1925, carried this Reuter's Pacific Service dispatch: "Dr. Sun Yat-sen died peacefully at 9:30 this morning, conscious to the last."

That night I took the train for Peking.

- 2 -

The northern capital was on edge, nervous, charged. It was as if a dust storm, blowing off the Gobi for days, had goaded the city to the point of hysteria: under the cutting, penetrating red sand, driven in great blinding clouds, the tempers of men flare quickly. Massive walls, built to keep out the "wolf from the north" and the "cock from the south," have little effect on red sand—nor on red ideology.

It was all unexpected to me, this electric atmosphere of jealousy, distrust, intrigue, bickering, violent hate; its rumors of bombing; its street incidents. And yet I should have known, if I had given serious thought to the *situation politique*, that for Sun Yat-sen there was no peace even in death. I sensed this tension first at the station when I stepped from the train into a vast multitude of Chinese; in the crowds that poured from the train. Delegations of students, labor leaders, politicians, bearing banners and flags, were there. In the crush I had seen the five-striped flag of China, the flag of the Kuomintang Revolutionists—red with a white sun on a blue field—and the blood-red banner of the Soviets: flags of conflicting beliefs brought together to pay tribute to the great Sun Yat-sen.

As I made my way through that mob, I felt the fierceness in its very sorrow, and the jealousy. Each faction wished to claim Sun as its own.

A controversy raged as to the form Sun's funeral service should take.

The Chinese Christians, backed by foreign missionaries, urged a simple Christian service, claiming Sun as a Christian. They held that, despite his turning toward Soviet Russia for political help, he had never renounced his belief in God and in the resurrection.

The old conservative officials and politicians of Peking, who thought in terms of face, held that nothing less than a gorgeous panoplied funeral procession would be fitting.

The Chinese Communists, backed by the Soviet Legation, fought for a service like that held for Lenin in Moscow a year previously, and bitterly refuted the claim of the Christians, Chinese and foreign. They wired Moscow for a pretentious glass coffin, a replica of that in which the embalmed body of Lenin reposes in state in a magnificent mausoleum. The Russians wished to connect the names of Lenin and Sun in the minds of the Chinese masses; to take advantage of the hysteria caused by Sun's death to further the cause of Communism in China. The political pressure brought to bear upon Madame Sun, Sun Fo (son of Sun Yat-sen), and the Soongs[13] was great. Nevertheless the family arranged for a Christian service in the privacy of the Peking Union Medical College chapel. The Soviet Russians announced that they would have no part in it. They, it seemed, would enter the picture only when the mammoth public procession formed. It was all most confusing.

Eugene Chen, leftist and head of the political bureau of the Kuomintang, was indignant, sarcastic over the rumors that Sun Yat-sen had in death repudiated his Soviet Russian leanings and turned toward Christianity.

"It is not seemly," Chen told me, "that the yet unburied body of Dr. Sun Yat-sen should be the subject of a dispute concerned with an alien religious rite. But historical veracity, as well as mere loyalty to the memory of the great leader of a great cause, calls for instant protest against the creation of a legend that he died more as a meek and penitent Christian than as a formidable leader of a revolutionary movement destined to restore China's strength and independence."

---

13   *Sun Yat-sen was married to Soong Ching-ling, the eldest of the Soong sisters, from 1915 until 1925.*

The Soviet legation took unto itself great importance. A steady stream flowed in and out. Somehow the illusion had been created that Sun Yat-sen lay in state under the banner of the hammer and sickle.

On the day of Sun's funeral the tension in Peking was electric; the streets were thronged; extra guards and police were called out, and I heard for the first time large groups singing the *Internationale*.

The chapel was peaceful after the confusion of the streets. The hush which comes with prayer filled the room with its Chinese and foreign mourners. An imposing framed photograph of Dr. Sun was banked with white flowers on the altar. His patient eyes seemed to look down upon us. Many were weeping. The massive coffin of Chinese hardwood (the glass coffin had not yet arrived), draped with the flag of the Kuomintang, was just beneath.

Out of the stillness came a surpliced choir of students from Yenching University, carrying tall lighted candles and singing a favorite song of Dr. Sun: "Sweet peace, the gift of God's love." They formed about the bier, stood there as the service, beautiful, impressive in its simplicity, continued.

"I am the resurrection and the life . . ." read the Reverend Timothy Tingfang Lew.

Outside, the densely packed thousands waited, waited until the choir boys led the mourners from the chapel. Madame Sun, so frail and appealing in her widow's dress, her enveloping veil, leaned on the arm of her younger sister, Soong Mayling, and of her stepson, Sun Fo; and there were Dr. and Mrs. H. H. Kung and others closely connected . . . Then came the great coffin borne by twenty-four pallbearers . . . The Christian service for Dr. Sun was ended.

Overhead airplanes circled, and as the long procession to the

Central Park, where Sun's body was to lie in state for some two weeks, got under way guns fired salutes at fiveminute intervals.

Thousands of Chinese crowded the line of march and detachments of police cleared the way. Those in the know, behind the political scene as it were, had the opportunity of observing the gamut of human emotion, of indulging many reflections, philosophic and political, on its strange make-up, for in the long procession following the bier were representatives of all political factions, bitter enemies. The coffin was placed in the great pavilion of the Central Park, which was banked with flowers, hung with flags. A great wreath placed before Sun's bier was flaming red — the gift of Ambassador Karakhan. Before that great multitude the reading of Sun's will began: "For forty years I have served the cause of the people's revolution . . ."

As I listened I realized that through the ages Sun Yat-sen would be hailed as the symbol of democracy in China, as the father of the Chinese Republic.

That night I dined with friends in their enchanting Chinese place off a quiet *hutung*. The spell of old China was over all.

It was as if the great spirit screen which rose tall and impressive behind the lacquer gates had shut out the tension of the day, the hysterical excitement of the streets. The "Drowsy Moon," hanging like a horn lantern over the willows, silvered to unreality the courtyards with their secrets of other days, the secluded garden where the Spirit of Spring was awakening in its sheltered shrine, and the low-roofed house with its upturned, carved, and ornamented corner eaves, latticed windows, and moon door. Over the aged gateman's ear hung a spray of willow — symbol of vitality, fecundity; protection against wandering ghosts. Within the spacious drawing room, that same sense of harmony with the ages prevailed: lacquered pillars of mellow Chinese red; faded flower symbols on old beams; golden-yellow tribute satin from the palaces, cushioning, softening the stiffness of the blackwood; porcelains, bronzes, ivories collected through the years. Even the hostess . . . She was speaking of a bit of carved jade which her favorite curio man had brought her that afternoon. Servants moved quietly among the guests, serving the *apéritif* in translucent cups of palest green jadestone, "small chow" — caviar *croûtes*, anchovy squares, prunes stuffed with "Peking dust" (mashed chestnuts) and sweet ginger.

I had arrived somewhat tense from my experiences of the past days, terribly concerned over the encroachment of Soviet Russia into China. There were so many questions I wished to ask these distinguished old residents; but during dinner the man on my right was talking of the festivals of the dusters of temple images, the artificial flower makers, the craftsmen in oil lamps, which were to take place at the Tung Yo Miao shortly.

"Man alive!" I wanted to shout. "Is China going Bolshevik?"

And then someone else mentioned that, on the 15th, scholars would confess their sins and make their offerings to the god of writing. With their gifts of ink slabs, writing brushes, paper, they would bow before the god of writing, or perhaps before the group known as the gods of literature. They would confess their sins, the chief of which was the misuse of the Chinese character, recite their accomplishments with the brush during the year, and pray for greater skill.

And just as casually someone spoke of the death of Sun Yat-sen. "It will probably mean the end of the Canton government," the host commented.

No one seemed to be greatly excited about what was going on outside. To these old Peking residents, who were steeped in the lore of China, it was but another incident in her long history. China would carry on . . . and on . . . regardless.

"But what of the new students?" I ventured. I could see them marching, marching—embracing doctrines which struck right at the heart of old China; at her virtues, philosophies, culture, home life, her very threshing floor.

The hostess dismissed them as "undisciplined addlepates."

In Shanghai I had heard many foreigners denounce the students as rowdies, young hoodlums, firebrands, troublemakers. And at a Chinese feast one night a splendid old Chinese gentleman, with troubled eyes, had declared that the students no longer "walked slowly behind the elders." He had sighed even as he had belched over his bird's-nest soup and confided that it was getting very difficult these days for a parent to guarantee the virtues of his children. They no longer asked advice of the "three old ones," and in consequence acted without discretion. I had felt sorry for him, for his sons were not only one generation ahead of him in their thinking, but literally centuries. And now my hostess had called the young of China "undisciplined addlepates."

I wanted to contradict her, rudely, fiercely. What did she who lived like an orchid on the glories of old China know of the eager-eyed, ardent youths who were reaching out so earnestly for an understanding, a part, of life in the modern world? Several tens of thousands of students, some only girls and boys of ten and twelve, were organized into an All-China Students' Union, with headquarters in Peking. In a chaotic land, torn by rival factions, with no central government, the organization of the students of all sections into a strong national unit was to me most remarkable. Practically every middle school and college in China had its Students' Union. In the large educational centers, Shanghai, Peking, Hankow, Canton, the many branches were controlled by students' city councils. The councils took orders from the National Union at Peking. The local organizations were kept informed of all activities through "committees of correspondence and telegraph." Into China had come a new force — a force destined, I believed, to bring about a regeneration, a second flowering of an aged country.

That force was the Chinese Student.

- 3 -

To understand the Youth Movement of China it was necessary for me to inquire into its history. During my research I came to know something of the thousands of young Chinese students who through the years have journeyed, a bit fearfully although eagerly, into a western world and have returned after full years, with visions of a New China ever before them — returned students.

Ninety-two years ago (1847) Yung Wing, a nineteen-yearold Cantonese protégé of the Morrison School, first English school in China, sailed on the clipper *Huntress* for New York — the first Chinese boy to become a student in America. He attended first a preparatory academy, later Yale University.

In his book, *My Life in China and America*, Wing wrote:

All through my college course in America, especially in the closing year, the lamentable condition in China was before my mind, weighing heavily on my spirits. In despondent moods, I often wished that I had never been educated, as education had unmistakably enlarged my mental and moral horizon, and had revealed to me responsibilities which the sealed eye of ignorance can never see, and the sufferings and wrongs of humanity to which an uncultivated and callous nature is less sensitive. Before the close of my last year in college I had sketched out in my mind what I should do. Determined that the rising

generation of China should enjoy the same educational
advantages that I had enjoyed, and that China through
western education should be regenerated, and become
powerful and enlightened, to accomplish that *object*
became the guiding star of my ambition. Towards this goal
all my mental resources and energies were directed.

Yung Wing returned to China full of purpose. Years later
through his efforts one hundred and twenty students were
sent to America; and he accompanied them as educational
commissioner. Dr. Wu Ting-fang was one of those hundred and
twenty boys.

With a twinkle in his eyes, Dr. Wu told me of the obstacles
placed in the way of the students. America, at that time, was a
little known, barbarian country lying somewhere beyond the
Huang Hai (Yellow Sea). American natives would scalp them,
eat their brains and eyes to gain wisdom. They might graft the
skin of wild beasts upon them and exhibit them in cages over the
country! They might die abroad. Furthermore, it was not filial
for them to go.

Nevertheless, the students sailed. Before they could finish their
studies, however, the government ordered them home, fearing
that they might acquire foreign ways; and upon their return it
kept them prisoners for a time in the old Examination Hall in
Shanghai. Some thirteen of them were eventually beheaded.

Shortly before the Sino-Japanese War of 1894-95, the
government sent some fifty students from the Foochow Arsenal
to Europe to study — not western culture, but western navigation,
the building of warships, military tactics.

The students and others, roused by the defeat of China by
Japan, launched a China Reform Movement under the leadership
of Dr. K'ang Yu-wei (he had the chief part in persuading Kuang

Hsu to issue the Hundred Day Reforms of 1898). They urged the overthrow of the Manchu government, a New Learning, the abolition of foot-binding, and laws prohibiting the sale and importation of foreign narcotics. Officials broke up their meetings, and a number of leading students were beheaded. Dr. K'ang escaped. Dr. Yung Wing, another outstanding leader, fled from the country, a price on his head; he died in America, an exile — but he lived in China, a symbol to the rising generation.

Then came the Boxer Rebellion. Following this period of confusion, thousands of students flocked abroad to study. A new era was born.

C. T. Wang, one of the students who went abroad during the early nineteen hundreds, was later to become Ambassador to Washington. Dr. Wang told me of that chapter in his life.

"An unusual movement took place in this particular decade such as the world had never before witnessed," he said. "It was the great exodus of Chinese youths, the flower of the nation, to foreign countries, with the fixed determination to learn what the world had to teach. The great Renaissance movement in Europe, which caused the Dark Ages to pass into oblivion, cannot even be compared with this spectacular phenomenon. Is it possible to point to any decade in preceding centuries when students of one nation, numbering tens of thousands, migrated to every part of the world to search for more light?" he asked.

"In 1906, in the city of Tokyo, Japan, alone, there were upwards of fifteen thousand students. Even in America and Europe, where only the most favored could go because of the greater difficulty in the mastering of the language, the longer distance, and the heavier expenditure, the number of our students rose from a few handfuls before 1900 to nearly ten thousand at the close of the first decade."

The students went to America, Europe, England, Japan.

They studied medicine, law, engineering, military and political science, philosophy, railroading, finance. Upon their return they organized clubs; debated, discussed, criticized fearlessly; worked out programs for the reform of their country; contributed their impressions of western life to publications in China.

It was of a regenerated New China that they dreamed. "I, and hundreds of other students," continued Dr. Wang, "returned to China in the full vigor of life, fresh from our studies abroad, determined to do our share for our country. Youthful enthusiasm was set ablaze by lofty idealism."

But the "lofty idealism" of those early students met with stern opposition. The traditions of old China, the deeply implanted superstitions, the corruption of officials, the conservative attitude of the Chinese masses, rose to defeat the students. The *Feng Shui* (Wind and Water Influence) objected to the building of railroads and the construction of telegraph lines because the "harmonious influences" of the countryside would be disturbed. In the *North-China Daily News* of July 23, 1869, seventy years ago, I read:

We regret to hear that the *Tao Tai* refuses to entertain the proposition of the Commissioner of Customs, supported by the foreign Consuls, at the instance of the Chamber of Commerce, for the construction of a line of telegraph between Shanghai and the Beacon. He says that similar propositions have previously been declined by the Provincial authorities, as being fraught with danger to agricultural interests and displeasing to the *feng shui*. He requests the Consuls to inform the mercantile community that China can dispense with telegraph wires.

Dragons living peacefully in the mountains did not wish to be disturbed by diggers for ore, drillers for oil. The first railroad, built in 1905 by one of Dr. Wing's students, Dr. James Tien-yu, a returned American-educated engineer, was torn up by enraged peasants. They were terrified of the *huo ch'e* (fire cart) with its *lung t'ou* (dragon head).

The conflict between the students and the Manchu government grew, and the students took an active part in its overthrow. During those exciting days of revolution the students cut off their queues, pulled down the dragon flags, hoisted five-barred flags of the Republic — flags whose colors stood for benevolence, righteousness, harmony, wisdom, truth. And in their patriotism they wrote a National Anthem:

Our ancient land is born anew:
Beautiful our Republic is, bright as the dew,
The rainbow-hued banner on high we fly;
Our flag, so sweet, waves in the now quiet air.

But Yuan Shih-kai, President of the new Republic of China, clamped down hard on the students, as did subsequent presidents.

For a time the students withdrew from politics and began the herculean task of educating China along modern lines.

They took positions in the mission and government schools in the hope of implanting western culture in students who were clamoring for modern education. The National University of Peking became the cradle of the educational movement; Dr. Tsai Yuan-pei of Leipzig University, Germany, was made chancellor. On the faculty of the university were nine members who had studied in France, six in America, five in Germany, five in England, three in Japan, and five in Chinese colleges.

Magazine after magazine came into being. Some five hundred were published in the hope of bringing the "thought tide" of the world into China. Their titles portrayed a new student life which looked out upon a great modern world, rather than back into a conservative old past: *The Renaissance, New Youth, Young China, The New Women, The New Culture, The Athletic Review* . . . They interested me, with their fiery articles: "Why Should the Old Family Rule Me?" "Women's Right to Matrimonial Happiness," "Rid China of Superstition," "What Is Truth, What Is Thinking?" "The Problem of the Chinese Language," "Should Women Vote?"

But these publications were written in the classical language of the scholars, and certain youthful editors determined to publish in the "popular" or vernacular language in order that their magazines might be read by the greater numbers.

Thus was the Literary Revolution of China launched.

Dr. Hu Shih, now Chinese Ambassador to Washington, had lighted the flame when a student at Cornell University by sending back to China an article, "Suggestions for a Literary Reformation in China."

What Dr. Hu Shih demanded for China was a "living, human, democratic, and scientific medium of self-expression — not solely a literature of and for the intelligentsia" but one that smelled less of classicism, and met more adequately the needs of everyday life.

Dr. Hu Shih told me of his experiments in writing poetry in the vernacular. He was the object of the jeers of the literati. His reply was a poem — in the vernacular:

Why is there a doubt about this literary revolution?
Raise the warrior's flag and be a strong youth.
It is important to break the record of the long past,
And to open a new path to the everlasting future;
To get rid of all that is decayed,
And to rejuvenate our life!
To create a new literature for the Republic of China,

To whom can we give this responsibility?

For poetic materials, have we not at our command this modern world!

Then abruptly the students of China plunged back into the political arena. When Japan attempted to seize Shantung at the close of the World War the students became front-page news.

Carrying banners which denounced as "traitors" certain Peking officials, fifteen thousand students marched through the city in demonstration against the Versailles decision. Thirty-three of the leaders were arrested. Overnight, students' unions were organized in Shanghai, Hankow, Foochow, and Canton.

The work of Dr. Yung Wing was bearing fruit. The awakening of the students through the years to a new method of action, of thinking, had made such an organization possible. It was the expression of a new consciousness, the beginnings of a new China.

Under their leadership a nation-wide anti-Japanese boycott was launched, inflammatory handbills distributed, mass meetings held. The agitation grew. The students demanded the expulsion of the "national traitors," the release of the students, the return of Tsingtao. Workers, public bodies, merchants supported the students. The result was the release of the "hero" students, the dismissal of the three "traitors" from office, and the refusal of the Chinese delegates at Versailles to sign the Peace Treaty. And the matter of Shantung was left open—to be settled at the Washington Conference.

Dr. Sun Yat-sen, as President of the South China Republic, had been quick to recognize the importance of the students' organization, to assume leadership of the movement and had tied it up with the Kuomintang. Representatives of the Union of Socialist Soviet Republics had set about the appointment of agents to work among the students—agents who, as clever propagandists, played upon their idealism, their patriotism; but the western world overlooked the importance of the Student Movement.

Knowing as I did the history of this movement, was it any wonder that I wanted to shout a rude denial to my dinner hostess in Peking when she dismissed the students as "undisciplined addlepates"? I wanted also to contradict the assumption that Dr. Sun's death would mean the "end of the Nationalist movement, of the Kuomintang, or People's Party."

Only that day of Sun's funeral I had talked with two of those thousands of marching students. A girl glowing with fire had cried:

"What is one life? What are ten thousand lives? We will struggle—fight—for our national salvation. We are not afraid to die."

And the other had solemnly declared:

"I will be a free ghost rather than a shackled slave of the militarists."

No, the Chinese revolution would not die with the death of Sun, for Sun lived, a shining example.

A few months later the world awoke to the power of the Chinese student.

- 4 -

Tension was growing in Shanghai.

There had been strikes and labor and student demonstrations in the Chinese city during the entire month of May. A Chinese workman had been killed by a Japanese foreman during a riot at a Japanese cotton mill. The strikers and the students had worked themselves into a dangerous temper over his death.

There were rumors that the students were to attempt parades and demonstrations in the Settlement. But no one was unduly concerned.

It was past noon on Saturday May 30, 1925, when the caddie packed up my clubs after a golf lesson at the Race Course on Bubbling Well Road. As usual my putting had been "off." It was a Whitsun holiday. Many of the foreigners were up the river at Henley for the Spring Regatta; others were attending the Spring Race Meet down at Kiangwan. Numbers were gathering at the cricket grounds for the match to be held that afternoon. I stopped at the clubhouse for a lemon squash and a sandwich, telephoned for the chauffeur to pick me up, then walked out toward the street.

I was surprised to see students marching down Nanking Road: youths in straight robes of pongee or dark silk; schoolgirls in short light jackets and dark skirts or trousers; and following them a motley blue-coated crowd of Chinese men. The students were carrying banners: "Down with Foreign Imperialism," "Citizens, Awake," "'Withstand Japanese and British Oppression."

At the corner of Thibet Road they stopped. One of the older students climbed up on a box and began a noisy, ranting speech. There was an eager, exalted expression on his refined face as he shouted: "The great powers are destroying China. Death is preferable to tame submission. Rise and fight the Japanese oppressors!"

An enormous crowd had collected. I was caught up in a surging sea of Chinese and carried into the street. All traffic was blocked. Then through that mob, like a football squad, charged the police. A broad-shouldered British bobby, brandishing his long club like a red-faced drum major, led his tall, grim Sikhs into the fray. I glimpsed their bright turbans and curled black beards over the sea of heads. Their clubs cleared the way.

The boy on the box began shouting louder—gesticulating more wildly as the police fought their way toward him. A young Chinese boy crowded next to me was chewing his handkerchief in excitement. Two girls on the other side began to sing in high quavering voices—now and then I caught the words:

"Red as flowers is the blood of the Revolutionists—
"All for sacrifice—all for sacrifice—
"Students, onward—students, onward—
"Dare to die—dare to die."

The refrain "Dare to die" swelled in chorus as classmates joined in the singing.

The police dragged the speaker from his box. Instead of resisting, he smiled triumphantly and calmly took a bow. The police escorted him and two other leaders to the near-by Louza Police Station on Nanking Road.

"*Hao, hao, hao!*" shouted the girl next to me.

"What is it all about?" I asked.

"We are protesting against the murder of Koo Tseng-hung by the Japanese imperialists," she replied in excellent English. "We want publicity for our cause. We want the city to know the conditions in the Japanese mills. We knew that, if we staged parades and meetings in the French and International settlements, students would be arrested."

I was pushed along with the crowd. From every direction Chinese were headed toward the Louza Station. The cells on both sides of the building were crowded with student agitators who had been arrested in various parts of the city. The mob began surging toward the gates. A foreign policeman was knocked down and manhandled.

"Arrest us! Arrest us!" came a cry. "Our comrades are in jail.

Let us join them!"

The mob surged toward the gates of the station. There was only a handful of police on duty — two or three British inspectors, a few Sikhs, some six Chinese constables — but they met each onrush of the crowd with their batons. They were forced back to the gates of the station amid excited jeers and delirious yells. Twenty years before, a similar mob — fired with fanatical zeal and anti-foreign hatred — had seized and burned the Louza Station. Now there were many guns and rounds of ammunition stored there, which must be protected. In desperation the officer in charge ordered the police to line up in front of the gates with fixed bayonets. He called a warning — which was lost in the cries. The mob was completely out of hand.

I whirled about in sudden panic. The Chinese were so intent on the fighting at the gates that they paid scant attention to me or the other foreigners who had been caught in the fray. Little by little I worked my way toward the edge of the crowd.

Then I heard a cry of "Missie, Missie."

There was Ah Ching, the chauffeur, fighting his way toward me. In a loud voice he began explaining to the Chinese that he had come to get his foreign Missie. Ah Ching told them all about his very good master who helped him pay the bills for the funeral of his first wife, and said that I was his Missie — and although I was only a foolish female one, of no particular consequence, still he must take me home. The crowd about us agreed. Ah Ching is a big Chinese with a bit of swank in him; he shoved right and left.

I heard jeer after jeer rising in a roar from the rioters behind us. They were making a final charge on the gates. In desperation the officer in charge gave the order to fire. A volley of shots, and then another. Bullets whistled. There was sudden silence.

Nine students had fallen dead on Nanking Road! Many

others were seriously wounded.

"Lun, Missie, lun," cried Ah Ching.

I saw white-flanneled men from the cricket grounds hurrying toward the scene; foreign police officers began arriving as we reached our car.

It had all happened so suddenly. Yet in those few minutes a date—May 30, 1925—had been stamped irrevocably on the history of modern China.

We drove to the Shanghai Club to pick up John. There was an air of excitement about that usually staid entrance. Groups of members were talking seriously as they waited for their cars.

"We're in for it," said John gravely. "The Reds will now deal the hand in this oriental game, and the sky will be the limit."

The news of the shooting of the nine students had spread like wildfire through a city already set for the conflagration. Crowds of Chinese swarmed the streets and sidewalks. They were yelling and jeering as they stoned tramcars, busses, motorcars. A brick just missed our windshield.

I could not believe it. The Shanghai I knew and enjoyed— where I felt as safe, as much at home, as I should have felt in any city in America—had suddenly vanished. I was living in a strange, unfriendly oriental world thousands of miles from nowhere. . .

It was a relief to enter the house, located in the quiet of the suburbs, after the turmoil of the downtown streets. I rushed up to the nursery. Johnny, who was then nine months old, was playing happily in his bassinet. He banged a battered duck in welcome. I picked him up and held him close.

Amah, immaculate in fresh white linen jacket and black flower-brocaded trousers, was knitting a sweater for "young master." She greeted me with a quiet "How you, Missie?" then continued: "Boy talkee foreign policeman shootee Chinese schoolboy. What thing, Missie? This no b'long plopper."

"I'm very sorry about it, Amah," I replied, then told her of the mobbing of the station.

"My savvy number one big trouble come Shanghai. Russian man talkee plenty nonsense. My too muchee fear."

John, as a member of the French Volunteers, was called out on duty. My heart sank as he changed into uniform, buckled on his club and gun—then told us goodbye. The baby went to sleep. The house seemed strangely quiet.

Outside was turmoil—and John.

Inside was only waiting.

For the first time I began to realize the courage it takes to wait. Heretofore I had been in the heart of the action, whatever it was. Raising a family and dashing over the Far East on newspaper assignments had not worked out; I had not realized, when I gave up my work as a correspondent—temporarily, I hoped—all that it would mean. As a newspaperwoman I, like my husband, should have plunged into the thick of things. I longed to get down to a newspaper office and pound out cables. I had joined the ranks of the women who wait, and I felt that I must learn a new brand of courage—a courage unstimulated by excitement, or action, by a dead line.

I was roaming restlessly over the house when cook came in, bustling with importance. He asked me to come into the kitchen. Had I walked into a grocery and meat market? Hams were hanging from a shelf; chickens with their feet tied were squawking sleepily in bamboo baskets; bags of flour and of rice were stacked on the floor. There were baskets of oranges, apples, pomelo, and a whole stem of green bananas, while in the cupboard were rows of tinned goods.

"What thing, Ah Kun?"

"Must catchee, Missie. Suppose no catchee, byw an' by no

can chow," he answered. "Tomollow any shop shuttee. Maybe shuttee one day, maybe shuttee one month—no can savvy."

I groaned, wondering just how much of this supply would filter out the back door. But as the days went by and we began to realize the strength of an antiforeign strike, I appreciated Ah Kun's thoughtfulness.

Monday found Shanghai paralyzed.

A general strike had been called by Chinese labor organizations, and there was a tie-up in practically every industry in the Shanghai area. A boycott was declared on all British and Japanese goods. British and Japanese boats stood idle at the docks. Monster mass meetings of students and workers were held at the public Recreation Grounds just outside the Chinese city. Many of the students wore black arm bands in mourning for their dead comrades. Thousands of banners and flags flaunting antiforeign slogans were carried. Large posters in lurid colors portrayed the Nanking Road shooting. One picture showed the agonized face of a young boy. Blood flowed from his bared chest. "He Dared to Die" was the caption.

In the International and French settlements the streets were ominously quiet. Overnight the Concessions had become armed camps.

Wild rumors flew about.

The Shanghai Consular Body was forced to appeal for naval reinforcements, as there was danger that Shanghai might be taken over by the rioting elements. Several hundred sailors and marines were landed. Before that long, hot, tense summer was over, twenty-two battleships stood on guard. A cordon of armed men was thrown around the boundaries of the two settlements — men protected by barbed wire entanglements, sandbag barricades, and deeply dug trenches. In the downtown districts war tanks rolled through the streets. Machine guns mounted on armored cars guarded important sections. Companies marched to strains of martial music – to the stirring notes of the bagpipes of the "Scotties." The British Light Horse and the American Troop paraded Nanking Road. Guards were placed around the water and power plants, the telephone and telegraph offices. Foreign volunteers replaced the striking Chinese.

Martial law was declared, and curfew.

From ten P.M. until four A.M. the streets of Shanghai were deserted. Only the dull steady tread of the squads of men on patrol resounded through the night – English, Scotch, French, American, Japanese, Portuguese, Italian, Filipino, with groups of Scandinavians, Germans, and others. Shanghai was a brilliantly illuminated phantom city. But although the bright lights blazed throughout the long watches of the night, they did not signify the gayety of a Great White Way. They burned for protection.

Reports from the interior told of incident after incident; of thousands of students on parade; of bands of Reds destroying foreign property, manhandling and killing foreigners. Reports from Hankow, Shameen, Canton, Kiukiang, Chungking, Nanking, Hongkong, Tientsin, Peking, all told the same story. The great back country was awakening, was uniting in a revolutionary movement which was sweeping no one knew where.

As the weeks went by, it became evident to foreigners and conservative Chinese alike that the uprising had passed out of the hands of the students. Another force gave the momentum to discontent. For that accumulated discontent was being organized, directed. Great Britain was left to bear the expensive brunt of the strike, a strike which cost her millions of dollars, which laid prostrate her great port of Hongkong before differences were finally adjusted.

Cooling winds of autumn brought relief, and for a few months conditions in Shanghai were almost back to normal.

But in the great back country Soviet Russia, allegedly unofficially, pulled the strings of revolution and xenophobia.

- 5 -

Eugene Chen had once said to me, "What Canton thinks today, all China will think tomorrow."

And the Canton of the spring and early summer of 1926 was turbulent, seething, torn with convulsions; a city of violence, riots, strikes, of intrigues, plots, assassinations; a city whose thoughts were as the cross currents, rip tides, rapids of the upper Yangtze; a city where Chinese and Russian Reds, Left Wing and Right Wing members of the Kuomintang, including the old reactionaries, four groups, were striving to gain control of the party, to determine its policies.

Cynical Shanghai was inclined to believe that the Chinese Revolution was doomed to die on its own doorstep—Canton.

Then early in July came the news that Chiang Kai-shek had been appointed Commander-in-Chief of the People's Revolutionary Army; that the much heralded "Northern Punitive Expedition" of the Kuomintang against the "militarists" was at long last under way.

How had Chiang Kai-shek, a Rightist, a little known figure nationally, practically unheard of abroad, been able to rise through party intrigues to such a position of command? What was the story back of the newspaper dispatches?

Out of Canton, Chiang burst upon the world—China's new strong man—commander of her revolutionary armies.

Fantastic stories were printed about him—amazing fabrications, some of them. Was Chiang just another war lord? Was he a Red? Was he an uneducated peasant from the mountains of Chekiang? Was he a Cincinnatus? Just who was

234

Chiang? Question after question.

I appreciated the background which was his only after talking personally with him, Madame Chiang, and Dr. Hollington K. Tong, graduate of the University of Missouri School of Journalism, editor and authorized biographer of Chiang; translating, with my Chinese teacher, certain accounts from Chinese publications; and after visiting Ningpo and the Fenghua district which is now known as "Chiang Kai-shek's country," and talking with the villagers and members of the Chiang clan.

Some hundred fifty miles south of Shanghai in the province of Chekiang lies the historic old port of Ningpo. A city of great antiquity, it is mentioned in Chinese literature as having flourished as early as 2000 B.C.; and for hundreds of years it has been a leading Buddhist center of southern China. Its rich legendary and heroic lore was expressed in ancient monuments, temples, pagodas, and tombs. Magnificent arches erected in memory of famous men of Ningpo — philosophers, warriors, rulers. scholars, engineers — who have played a memorable part in history, span certain of its streets. Portuguese traders established a prosperous colony in Ningpo in 1522, but eventually were driven out. The East India Company in the seventeenth century suffered a similar fate. It was only when the city was opened as a treaty port in 1842 that the foreigners were accepted. News of world affairs, brought by traders, fishermen, merchants, sailors plying back and forth from Ningpo to Shanghai, filtered into the wildly beautiful mountainous back country with its lakes, torrents, cliffs, and valleys.

Nestling in the foothills, on an ancient road leading into Ningpo, was the farming village of Chikow. Cotton, wheat, and rice fields stretched across the verdant valley and dimbed in regular terraces up the mountainsides.

The Chiangs were farmers of importance in the village, in the country round about; had been for generations. Chiang, the venerable grandfather – the Wise-Old-One – was renowned for his learning, and in the tea shops men gathered to hear his opinions on affairs of the Empire. To Chiang Su-an, his son and the head of a family of his own, men brought their troubles; unofficially, he settled their disputes. Madame Chiang Su-an, his third wife, was a woman of education, good family, refinement and a devout Buddhist. A son was born to her on October 31, 1887. There was great rejoicing.

When young Chiang was seven, China was defeated in a war with Japan. The grandfather ate much bitterness. He talked to him of the decadent court of Peking; of the yoke of the Manchus. The grandfather died, and then the father.

Madame Chiang, slight and frail in appearance, was left a widow with her children. With that remarkable generalship which characterizes the Chinese women, Madame Chiang, as head of the family, set about the uphill task of carrying on the honorable house of Chiang. She became a Spartan mother, and Chiang was made to shoulder responsibility, to do his share of the laborious work of the household, and received a rigid training under a strict disciplinarian. There was little time for play. When lessons and the drudgery of the farm were accomplished, Madame Chiang would instruct her son in the teachings of Buddha, instill in him sayings of wisdom.

"Learn to control your senses," she would urge as she sat spinning. "He who lives for pleasure becomes idle, weak. The wind will blow him down the mountain."

Or again, as they stood by Chiang's favorite rushing waterfall she would counsel: "There is no torrent like greed, no waterfall like the flow of senseless words. Do not be 'old-invain' when age makes you an elder."

Teachings which, years later, he inculcated in his famous New Life Movement.

Chiang was sent on to the higher schools in the Fenghua district. Although his mother hoped her son might become a scholar or a "tranquil one" (Buddhist monk), she gave way to his desire to be a soldier, and helped him prepare for the competitive examinations for admission to the Paotingfu Military Academy. Before Chiang passed his sixteenth birthday, however, she arranged his marriage to a young woman years older who fitted admirably into the life of the Chiang household: a daughter-in-law who was a source of strength to Madame Chiang.

Chiang successfully passed the Paotingfu Academy examinations, and was later sent to Japan to study advanced military science. He graduated from Shinbo Gokyo in 1909 and prepared to become a cadet in the Japanese military college.

Tokyo at that time was the center of a young Chinese revolutionary group whose pivot was Dr. Sun Yat-sen. At one of their meetings Chiang Kai-shek heard Sun make a passionate, magnetic appeal for workers in the Chinese revolution. He met Sun, talked with him, and a life friendship was formed between them — leader and disciple. With an exaltation of spirit, Chiang knew that his life had taken on a definite pattern; purpose.

"This," thought Chiang, "is what my grandfather would have wished — Chiang Kai-shek, Revolutionist!"

Events moved swiftly. The Revolution which was to result in the overthrow of the Manchu Dynasty broke in October, 1911.

Chiang, along with a number of other young patriots attending military school in Japan, broke away from their quarters, and in disguise reached Shanghai. There he joined a dare-to-die corps in the Fenghua district near his home; led an attack on the Governor's yamen; burned it down; saw Ningpo go to the revolutionists. He rushed to Shanghai, joined a band of a hundred dare-to-dies. With the fall of Shanghai, Chiang was made regiment commander of the Shanghai army.

The coup of Yuan Shih-kai and the resignation of Dr. Sun came as a hard blow to the young patriot.

Chiang returned to his village, sought his mother's wise counsel. Was the Revolution to be for naught? Had the east wall been torn away only to strengthen the west wall? Again it was his mother who dispelled his bitterness. "Is ice three feet thick frozen in a day?" she asked. "The road one generation opens, another generation will travel; by the trees one generation plants, another generation will find rest in the shade of thick branches."

"She taught me how to make the principle of filial piety applicable to the whole nation," said Chiang. "'From the family is built a nation,' she quoted to me. And she impressed upon my mind that to be merely a dutiful son does not fulfill all of the exacting conditions of the principle of filial piety; the principle demands also an unflinching devotion to the cause of the nation. Whenever I reflected on the conditions in which we two—a widowed mother and a fatherless son—lived in the shadow of cold realities, I could not but pray for the day when I should be able to fulfill my mother's wishes in a worthy manner."

Chiang began preparations for completing his military training in Germany, but when the revolutionists revolted against Yuan Shih-kai he threw himself into the work of the "second revolution," in 1913, and a third, in 1915; both failed. Several attempts were made to assassinate him.

A legend that his mother's deep piety, her sacrifices and prayers, were as a protecting wall about him, sprang up. It has persisted through the years because of Chiang's many escapes from death.

A few years later (May 5, 1921) when Sun Yat-sen set up the South China Republic in Canton, Chiang joined him.

News of the serious illness of his mother caused him to rush from the political excitements of Canton to his ancestral home. Madame Chiang Su-an died a month later, and for many days Chiang remained in the mountains. In the presence of death "state affairs cease"; there was a long period of mourning. It was shortly after the death of his mother that Chiang and his wife, by mutual agreement, were divorced. Although they had long been estranged there had been no final separation out of respect for his mother's wishes. Then Chiang returned to his military duties in Canton.

One afternoon late in 1923, Chiang, Kai-shek called at the home of his commander, where Dr. Sun, Madame Sun, and a young woman were having tea. Chiang was presented to Miss Soong Mayling, who was down from Shanghai on a visit to her sister. Chiang, the fearless one, who had risked his life any number of times in the cause of Revolution, was confused: *shou mang chiao luan*, the Chinese call it—"without control of hands and feet." The beautiful Miss Soong, with her charm, her wit, her smart appearance, was as a vision to the man whose life for years had been spent in the trenches, the battlefields of civil war. When she plunged at once into a discussion of the Revolution, displayed an amazing knowledge of the political situation in China, he recognized a fiery, patriotic spirit which matched his own. Always given to sudden decisions, Chiang knew that above all else he wished to marry Mayling Soong.

He confided in Sun; told him of his love for his sister-in-law; pleaded with his leader to intercede for him. Dr. Sun advised his impetuous officer to have patience. But Chiang urged his cause. Dr. Sun sought the advice of Madame Sun, and she in turn approached her sister.

"Not interested," was Miss Soong's sharp answer. The abrupt young man must be put in his place.

He might as well have asked for the moon. The beautiful Mayling, youngest daughter of the house of Soong, could have married any man in China. In Shanghai gossip had it that the "knights came riding" from all corners of the land. There was the son of a powerful northern war lord, a brilliant writer of international note, a diplomat destined for the courts of Europe, a man with millions back of him—suitors of wealth, of fame, of foreign education and training.

Unspoiled by their attentions, Mayling Soong had carried on her purposeful life in Shanghai—I met her often when she was engaged in social service work and women's club activities—and had left the matter of her suitors in the hands of a most capable mother.

Again Dr. Sun advised Chiang Kai-shek, in whom he had greatest confidence, to exercise patience. It was a hard virtue for Chiang to cultivate.

Five years passed before Chiang again talked with Miss Soong. Five years—but the influence of Mayling Soong had spurred Chiang onward. She in turn followed with ever increasing interest, and with growing respect, Chiang's meteoric progress—unheralded, unacclaimed—across China's turbulent sky. Occasionally he wrote long letters to her which revealed the simplicity, forthrightness, depth of his nature; the poetry in the soldier; the strong influence of his mother in his life; his passionate nationalism.

Then Dr. Sun died; and Chiang threw himself into the fight for control of the Kuomintang, a fight between the Nationalists, and the Chinese leftists and Russian Communists.

Such was the background of Chiang Kai-shek, the man destined to become the greatest soldier-statesman of modern China, and one of the outstanding men of the world. China's new strong man! Commander-in-Chief of the People's Revolutionary

Army.

I called at the Students' Union headquarters in the French Concession upon reading the Canton dispatch. How had Chiang accomplished his appointment as Commander-in-Chief? The students' grapevine, I knew, was a very reliable source of information. Little happened in China that the students did not know. They had a way of cracking delicate nutshells and getting down to the kernel — regardless. They were apt to brush aside the polite *lao kuei-chü* (old custom), the diplomatic phraseology with its references to the Classics, to historical and poetical allegories, and call a spade a spade.

George Sokolsky first put me in touch with the student group in Shanghai, and I knew a number of the young revolutionists rather well.

Several of the girls came to our house: bright-eyed, neat, attractive girls, most capable, serious in purpose. At first they were shyly formal; but as I came to know them better they laughed easily, talked freely (and how Chinese women can talk!), and grew confidential. They were interested in everything; were eager, alert, like plants which had been thirsting for water for a long, long time. They were poised, strong despite their slimness, determined. We talked of many, many things. Books by socialist and radical writers, Russian, European, American, were sought by them. The writings of Charles Darwin, Voltaire, John Dewey, Tolstoy, William James, Bertrand Russell were read as soon as they were translated into the Chinese.

When Miss Jane Addams arrived in Shanghai, I had tiffin with her and a number of these student leaders at the Astor House. Dozens of Chinese journalists, amazingly familiar with Hull-House and her life work among the poor of Chicago, had interviewed the sweet-faced, gray-haired woman. She had received a surprising ovation from the Chinese. In Peking I had gone with two girls to hear Mrs. Margaret Sanger lecture on "What Is Birth Control?" before several hundred young men and women students. Later a Society for Birth Control had been organized among the young women in the National University. A Society for Birth Control! How shocked our western universities would be if the coeds formed such an organization!

Over our tea the Chinese girls would inquire about women and children workers in American factories, mills; about settlement houses; about Margaret Sanger's ideas on birth control. They wanted to know about free love and soul kisses (and what about kissing anyway?), about God, and silk-embroidered undies. And were men really descended from monkeys? Did I think it worse for a husband to have concubines than for him to keep mistresses like foreign men? And what about divorce, and trial marriage? And why did foreigners like great clumsy dogs as pets when there were singing birds, and little silken dogs? And would I tell them about Mrs. Carrie Chapman Catt and her fight for woman suffrage?

Strangely enough, it was Mrs. Catt who had first interested me in China and her women, when I was but a girl in school. Mrs. Catt, who is my mother's first cousin by marriage, returned from a trip to China filled with her remarkable experiences there. As president of the International Woman Suffrage Alliance, she had attended in 1912 an International Suffrage Congress at Budapest, then had sailed for the Orient. While in Europe she had read a newspaper dispatch stating that the women of China had been given the vote and seats in the national assembly. She was immediately interested.

Upon arrival in Hongkong Mrs. Catt went at once to the American consul seeking information. He knew nothing about the report, was frankly skeptical, as were the British and the

Italian consuls. At the British consulate, however, she was given a letter to an influential foreign-educated Chinese at Canton who was one of the leaders in the Chinese revolutionary movement. Only recently at a Thanksgiving dinner at her home in New Rochelle, Mrs. Catt, now over eighty, with as great a charm and sparkle as she had during the years when she led the great woman suffrage movement in America, told her adventures in China on her quest for the new woman of China back in 1912.

"We secured a guide at a hotel in Canton and set out in rickshaws with our letter. We rode through narrow, crowded, winding ways, but at last we reached the home of the Chinese revolutionist. He said yes, there were Chinese women on the Canton Assembly, and directed our guide to take us to a meeting then in session, also he invited us to dinner that night to meet some of the Chinese women leaders.

"We got into our rickshaws again and set off. At last we reached the government building and were given seats in a balcony. During that afternoon we heard Chinese women speak as well as men before this large gathering. We were greatly surprised, pleased."

Mrs. Catt and her companion sailed for Shanghai. Her visit there left an impression upon the Chinese women leaders of that city which today, some twenty-eight years later, has not been forgotten. News of Mrs. Catt's interest in the women of the Chinese revolution preceded her.

"One afternoon I heard a gentle knock at the door of my hotel room, the whisper of soft voices, and the rustle of silk. A group of charming young Chinese women had come to call," continued Mrs. Catt. "They came in somewhat shyly, and I ordered tea. After a time they lost their timidity and began to ask questions. They were eager to learn something of the international woman suffrage movement, to hear about the fight the women of America

243

were making for the vote. But they wanted to know more than this, they were anxious for suggestions as to how best to lift the position of women in China.

"I visited Nanking and also Peking. In both cities I met Chinese pioneers in the woman's movement in China."

Mrs. Catt was an inspiration to these women. She advised with them in their gigantic task of educating the masses, of bringing about changes in laws pertaining to women, of forming anti-foot-binding societies. It was not surprising that the eager young daughters of those pioneers whom I came to know should ask about Mrs. Catt. She had been held up to them as an example through the years.

One day three of those Shanghai girl students had asked if I would go with them to get their hair bobbed like mine. It had been an adventurous experience, and there was a glint of tears back of their laughter. The elderly French coiffeur, who had lived in China during the days of seclusion for Chinese women, had muttered away in unprintable French as he clipped the shining black braids. He was as shocked as their grandfathers at their plunge into modernism. Within two years the boyish bob of Colleen Moore had penetrated far into the heart of changing China. Civil authorities had legislated against students bobbing their hair. A year or so later the bobbed head marked a girl as a Red suspect, in some cases caused her imprisonment and even death.

So I sought out members of the Students' Union's "committee of correspondence and telegraph" to inform me on the political crisis in Canton.

At the headquarters I was told the story of Communist Borodin and Nationalist Chiang Kai-shek in the first round of their dramatic fight for the control of the Kuomintang, of China.

Chiang Kai-shek, being very astute, longheaded, experienced in political life, determined that the hope of the Nationalists lay in action. As head of the Whangpoa Military Academy, he set swiftly to work organizing a campaign against the northern militarists, which years earlier had been outlined by Sun Yat-sen.

He met immediate and determined opposition.

Borodin, Bluecher, and certain Chinese Communist leaders proved strong obstructionists. They were in favor of an expedition against the northern militarists at some distant date, yes; but they played for time: time in which to strengthen the Communists in the Kuomintang and to oust Chiang; to consolidate the Red campaign in South China; to work out their own plans for the northern operations. Chiang, with a campaign vision gauged to the smallest details as well as to the panoramic whole, pushed his plans. Leaning hard on Dr. Sun's Three People's Principles — Nationalism, Popular Sovereignty, People's Livelihood — he urged all factions in the party to fight under the banner of the Kuomintang.

Two attempts were made on his life. He organized a secret service, learned of a third plot. With the swiftness, secrecy, ruthlessness for which he was to become famous, Chiang struck.

Without warning he threw a cordon of his Whangpoa cadets about the headquarters of the Bolsheviks, unofficially placed Canton under martial law. Russian advisers, military instructors, sympathizers, were arrested. Chinese Communists occupying high positions in the party were removed from office, replaced by more conservative members. Wang Ching-wei, veteran party member, pronounced leader of the Left Wing, and chairman of the pivotal Central Executive Committee of the Canton Government, fell "ill" and sailed for Europe on "sick leave." L'iao Chung-kai, able and sincere Left Wing official, was assassinated. Chang Ching-kiang, early party member who had contributed his fortune to Dr. Sun for the cause of the First Revolution, was made chairman in Wang's place (the same Wang Ching-wei, who, during the present SinoJapanese war, abandoned the party council at Chungking, and in an ill timed message issued December 30, 1938, urged Generalissimo Chiang Kai-shek to accept Japan's stultifying peace proposal).

Pessimistic reactionaries, disgruntled politicians, student leaders, Canton strike "racketeers," lesser military officers of doubtful loyalty, mercenaries, were brought to heel by Chiang. The Russian Communists capitulated.

Borodin, who had gone north allegedly to gain support to bring about the downfall of Chiang Kai-shek, returned—his plans completed—to find Chiang's coup a *fait accompli*. Borodin had the choice of falling in with the northern expedition under the leadership of Chiang, or of returning to Russia. Surface differences were smoothed out; a reconciliation of sorts was effected between Chiang (who fully realized his need of Russian support) and Borodin. Chiang Kai-shek was appointed Commander-in-Chief of the People's Revolutionary Army, July 9, 1926. He presented to the Central Committee carefully worked out plans for the reorganization of the army, for party finance, for a campaign of propaganda along the line of march.

One month later the now historic Northern Punitive Expedition was launched under the united front of the KuomintangCommunist Party; under their two banners, under two commanders, as it were, Chiang and Borodin.

The Revolution was marching on. . .

A cable arrived from New York, "Who is this man Chiang?" I unpacked my typewriter, oiled and cleaned it, and (my resolutions to keep out of the newspaper game forgotten) settled down happily to work.

- 6 -

Every Chinese civil war opens with the circulation of official manifestoes to the people, the officials, the representatives of foreign powers.

I read with keen interest the manifesto issued by General Chiang on the eve of his punitive expedition against the northern war lords. His official manifesto read:

The People's Revolutionary Army is soon to fight the armies of Wu Pei-fu at Hankow. Ours is a war between the people and the militarists; the revolutionists and the imperialists. We fight for the Three People's Principles. Men of China, will you arise and fight?

I will tell you why we march against the militarists led by Wu Pei-f u. For more than eighty years, since her defeat in the Opium War, China has bowed to Imperialism. The Taiping Rebellion was crushed only when the Manchus used foreign troops; hired men like Gordon to command their forces. The Manchus cried, "We will open our kingdom to the friendly Powers rather than give it back to our Chinese slaves."

We, the Revolutionists, succeeded in overthrowing the Manchus in 1911 in the first Revolution, and in establishing China as a Republic. But Yuan Shih-kai stole the Presidency. He was a betrayer of the Republic, a running dog [tsou kou] of the imperialists. From Yuan Shih-kai down to Tuan Chi-jui and Wu Pei-fu, the militarists have sacrificed China to further their own interests.

Now the masses are rising to free themselves from foot shackles [liao-tzu]. Wu Pei-fu is unsympathetic with the people's cause. He ordered the massacre of railway strikers. He did not protest the May 30th outrage. The shooting down of our students is the blackest spot in the history of our Revolution. We must defeat Wu Pei-fu if we would check the atrocities of the imperialists.

Wu Pei-fu tells the world he is fighting to crush Communism. Any movement for nationalism, popular sovereignty, people's livelihood, to him is Communism; also any fight against militarism. As a revolutionist entrusted with the sacred charge of fighting for the people of China, I will do my best. Men of China, rise up to save your country! All militarists in North or South China will be treated as comrades if they will surrender, come under the banner of the Kuomintang, fight to reach the goal set by our Leader, Dr. Sun.

I will endeavor to make the time of fighting short, but the Revolution must be fully executed, every obstacle uprooted.

Out of Canton marched China's revolutionary armies: armies which were made up of trained soldiers and young recruits; of workers and peasants; of propagandists and agitators; of conservatives and radicals. One hundred thousand men, picked units, from the eight army corps under Chiang's command, marched northward on Hankow—marched as on a crusade, two factions, unified by a spirit of patriotism, yet at odds . . .

Hundreds of students and members of propagandist corps were sent forward as vanguards along the line of march under directions from Borodin. They talked with the farmers, the villagers, the men of the cities; they enlisted the students in the schools, the coolies in the streets, the farmers in the fields. In the teahouses, the temple courtyards, along the roadsides, they proclaimed the cause of the Revolution. They distributed pictures of Dr. Sun; startling posters made by the students; and slogans, "Rise Against Your Oppressors," "Down with Wu Pei-fu," "China for the Masses," "Down with Imperialism!"

And everywhere they organized.

The now famous Communist, Mao Tse-tung, of whom Edgar Snow writes in his *Red Star over China*, worked with Borodin in forming Peasants' and Workers' Armies; in organizing a large-scale labor movement throughout the back country.

I met Mao Tse-tung in Shanghai before he had become a power in China as chairman of the Chinese Soviet Government and had set up his Red bailiwick in isolated Shensi. I had talked with Mao minus the glamour of a dangerous trip hundreds of miles inland. Mao in 1921 and 1922 was a Chinese radical, in his late twenties, just turning Communist.

He was a most earnest young man, as I remember him, in appearance no older than the students who grouped around him, with a face not unlike that of an American Indian — an American Indian with hair cut like that of a Left Bank artist. He had a high forehead, strong cheekbones, and a freedom of movement which made me think of rugged, open places. Beside him the two or three students present seemed effeminate; their silk coats, slim hands and pale faces, purposeless. There was little of the refined or polished about Mao. I was surprised to learn that he was well educated.

He came from the picturesque mountainous province of Hunan, where his family — hard-working, respected, frugal, middle-class people — had managed to acquire a few *mou* of farm land. As a boy he had been sent to the village school; worked in the fields. He attended a higher school in the capital, Changsha (an educational center which boasted a university in continuous existence for some seven hundred years); and from there he went to the provincial normal school. It was during those years that he met students who were reaching out toward liberalism. A year or so later at the Peking National University his radical tendencies crystallized into Marxism.

There was as yet no Communist party in China.

An "organizer" from the Third International arrived in Shanghai in 1921, another in 1922.

In the *China Press* office we heard talk — mostly rumors — that a Chinese Communist party had been secretly formed; but George Sokolsky, whose ear was close to the ground, told me of the organization meeting. It was attended by twelve brilliant Chinese, of whom Mao Tse-tung was one of the most outstanding. A group of overseas students established a branch in Paris. Mao was sent by the central party committee back to his home province, Hunan, to organize peasants, workers, students. The others were given similar assignments to strategic centers.

During the years immediately following the arrival of the Russian Soviet advisers, the growth of the Communist party was phenomenal. Thousands of workers and students were enlisted as propagandists in a far-flung network.

I next heard of Mao in Canton, where, with the forming of a Kuomintang-Communist *entente* in 1924, he was made head of one of the Ministries — the Publicity Board. And again when in 1926, at the time of the showdown between Borodin and Chiang Kai-shek, Mao was let out of office, along with a number of other Communists holding important portfolios in Canton. He returned to Shanghai; was ordered back to Hunan by the central party committee; rushed into propaganda work among the masses. He had worked among, corresponded with, the students of China for years; and from the Shanghai group I heard much of Mao as the Kuomintang-Communist armies headed northward.

Mao, as advance propaganda agent for the Communist party, was one of those responsible for their "triumphal march." He had long worked in Hunan; had been sowing his seeds of Communism among the peasants, students, workers of that province for five years. He advocated seizure of land from rich, oppressive landlords and redistribution among the people, laws against wealthy merchants, shorter hours and higher wages; and he had stirred up the students against missionaries and their institutions, against Christianity. When the revolutionary armies moved through Kwangtung and into Hunan the masses hailed them, "Saviors of the People," spread a smooth carpet before them.

Without firing a shot Changsha, important walled city, was taken. Chiang moved on toward Hankow, the strategic industrial, commercial, and shipping city of the middle Yangtze, to fight the forces of General Wu Pei-fu.

As Chiang headed on northward, the Communists took over the city and set their machine to working. Daily the workmen paraded. Trade unions were organized; strike and picket bands. There were now farmers' associations; committees of miners, of boat and train crews. Workers, even down to the unionized singsong girls, presented demands. Merchants, wealthy landlords, high-class Chinese with their families fled. Conservative Chinese began to view the situation with alarm. Changsha came under labor control. Christian institutions long established in Hunan were forced to close; were looted, burned, taken over, used as stables for horses, headquarters for soldiers. With the growing influence of the Left Wing of the party, and of the Communists, the city turned antiforeign! From all over Hunan the foreigners, whether in business or in missionary activities, were forced to flee.

Over the vast back country, like a consuming fire, spread the antiforeign propaganda of the radicals. News reaching Shanghai from the hinterland was shocking!

Mobs stormed schools, painted churches red; looted and burned; drove the missionaries, teachers, doctors to the safety of their gunboats on the Yangtze. From beyond the Yangtze Gorges, from the outermost mission posts, from the tributaries and canals, they came. Under cover of darkness they traveled without their possessions, by foot, sometimes in disguise; by wheelbarrow, along with their Chinese Christian workers; by sampan, junk, and sedan chair. Fighting, praying their way to the Yangtze, they and their children were taken on board river steamers, foreign gunboats, to safety. Business houses in Shanghai advised their representatives in the river ports to rush their families to Shanghai. The various foreign consulates sent out warnings to their nationals upcountry. Chaos was breaking over the Yangtze.

"Drive the foreigner into the sea" was the cry of the Chinese and Russian Reds.

Disheveled, exhausted, women and children refugees began arriving in Shanghai. There was a look about them which brought quick tears — a look which had nothing to do with their wrinkled appearance, but which sprang from soul-searing experiences. We met one of the river steamers. Friends were among that sea of white-faced refugees who crowded the rails as the ship docked; who poured off the rescue ship where they had slept on the decks, on the floors of the dining saloons, cabins, any place — slept in their clothes for many nights, their children held close — if they slept at all.

I interviewed a number of those refugee Americans, sent their stories to New York: real life, human interest stories, packed with tragic drama. But through that saga of violence and unloosed fanaticism shone now and then, like threads of gold, stories of faithfulness and love: stories of servants, Chinese friends and business associates, Chinese Christians, who had risked their own lives — and those of their children as well — to hide foreigners until escape was possible; had disguised them as Chinese; had got them away to safety.

Mrs. Holwill, wife of Mr. Claud Newton Holwill of an old

Pittsfield, Massachusetts, family, and American Commissioner of Customs at Chinkiang during those difficult years, told me an amazing story.

A year or so earlier, during a time when civil war had broken about Chinkiang, and thousands of peasants had poured into the walled city, Mrs. Holwill had opened the gates of the Customs compound to the Chinese refugees and had ordered her servants to provide hot rice and tea for them daily. The customhouse was in the tiny foreign settlement and consequently offered a certain protection. When the fighting moved on, the Chinese returned to their farms, their small shops, and life carried on in the outport as usual — for a time.

Then Chinkiang was caught up in antiforeignism!

A mob stormed the foreign concession. There was no warning; the gates were open; no word had reached the gunboats upriver. Down the street came yelling, screaming rioters, bent on destruction. Into each foreign house they swarmed, throwing furniture, books, dishes, everything they could lay their hands on, out of windows, doors, into the street.

Mrs. Holwill was alone in the big customhouse asleep. Her terrified amah wakened her, helped her to dress. But even as she threw on her clothes, the mob poured into the compound. On they came — boys, coolies, students, loafers, workers on strike, Communist agitators. A brick shattered a drawingroom window.

Suddenly out of the mob, and onto the steps, sprang a rickshaw coolie.

"No, no," he cried, pushing back the oncoming rioters. "This house we shall not enter. A good man lives here; he sheltered my old father and mother last year during the fighting; he gave our people rice and tea. This house we do not enter."

And even as Mrs. Holwill watched, spellbound, she saw the crowd pause, sway uncertainly, then turn and rush out of her gates, pellmell, into the house just beyond.

"I will never forget that old man calling out, 'A *ting hao jen*[14] lives here,' " Mrs. Holwill said.

Like a typhoon, the red terror born in Hunan swept down the Yangtze. A miasma of fear, of foreboding settled over the river ports; over Shanghai.

Johnny, Amah, and I sailed for California.

"Little Missie" was born there. Amah was painfully polite about this girl-child. But in her heart she was disappointed. A second son would have given the family much face; the care of a *Di-Di* (as a younger brother is called in Shanghai dialect) would have brought her additional éclat. I was thrilled over a little daughter, while John's cable from Shanghai expressed his joy.

We named the baby Patricia after a great-great-aunt Patricia Leticia Moore, who lived in Maryland during stirring times. I had always adored, been proud of that beautiful Irish ancestress, and I hoped that our Patricia would inherit her laughter, courage, charm. She had been a belle in Baltimore but had pioneered with an elder brother and an uncle through wild Indian country, into the untamed lands of southern Missouri. She had brought her personal slave with her, a gift from her father, who was a Baltimore slaveowner; and she brought also a favorite yellow taffeta ball gown! Her brother had owned a slave also, a great strapping fellow; but even at that early date he had set him free. He was an ardent abolitionist; but not so Patricia Leticia. She had permitted her young wench to marry her brother's freed slave, and somehow he had become hers, he and his descendants. Seventy-year-old "Aunt" Mahaley and her aged mother, old "Aunt" Lot, who boasted a third set of teeth and second sight,

---

14   Good man.

family servants of the Moores when I was. a little girl, had come from those Baltimore slaves! The stories about Patricia Leticia had been many, all exciting — more fascinating to me, as a child, than any found in my storybooks.

So our baby became Patricia, and she was to possess that same gift of easy laughter.

The days moved so slowly, there in California.

I followed with avid interest the newspaper dispatches from China; waited, with growing anxiety, for the days when letters from John arrived; wrote articles for the International News Service in New York, and for the Los Angeles *Herald*, on the China situation; played with our two-year-old boy, and baby girl. I was restless, nervous; my heart was in China, and I could not interest myself in the quiet, pleasant life on the Cherry Valley ranch.

Letters from John told me of the Leftist turn affairs were taking. More and more the radical elements in the Kuomintang, together with the Communists, were gaining power. The Revolution was running away from the Rightists; from Chiang Kai-shek. Following the fall of the Wu-han cities, the seat of the Kuomintang Government was moved from Canton to Hankow and Wuchang. It was dominated by Eugene Chen and Borodin. There was a growing impatience among the Leftists with Chiang's leanings toward moderation. There was jealousy of China's new strong man. Plots were laid against him. A reign of terror was instigated in the Yangtze to discredit him.

In March, 1927, at a meeting of the Kuomintang, now under Leftist control, Chiang was relieved of all party committee positions and reduced to the rank of an army commander, under orders from the Military Commission. General Bluecher's position improved, his power was increased.

As I read the newspaper accounts, pored over John's letters, listened to the radio, I wondered. Was Chiang Kai-shek to be railroaded out of the party? Was the removal of his command only a question of time? Was Chiang's star to set as quickly as it had risen? Was Chiang, who since boyhood had worked for China's Revolution, who had led the People's Revolutionary Army northward, to be set aside by party intrigue?

Chinese history is full of instances of men rising to fame only to be speedily torn down from their high estate. Few are the men in China who have been permitted to reach pinnacles, rare those who could maintain such eminence.

Then came a report stating that Chiang, surrounded by his loyal Whampoa cadets, had dug in at Nanchang, Kiangsi Province, while he determined his next move. A gunboat was kept in readiness to rush him to Shanghai if attempts should be made on his life.

I could not believe that Chiang would easily accept defeat at the hands of the Leftists. He commanded the finest cadets in China. They were loyal. Also he had the support of the conservative members of the party as well as of a number of lesser war lords who actively opposed Communism.

Chiang, from Nanchang, issued an explanation of his position. In the light of Japan's assertion in 1937 that she was fighting to rid China of Chiang and Communism, the address delivered by the Generalissimo to all China in 1927 is of special interest.

Later, Hollington K. Tong gave me an official translation of Chiang's address. I quote in part:

"Certain people allege that I have no more confidence in the Communist Party, and that I have even prohibited the introduction of Communist elements into the Kuomintang. As a matter of fact, *I have never supported the Communist Party*. As I said last year in the Whampoa Academy, I was only inviting other minor revolutionary organizations to join hands with us in the revolutionary movement. At that time, I made it a condition of their admittance that we reserved the right to suppress the movement if they should go beyond the limits and act with a view to endangering the Nationalist cause. In the interests of and for the welfare of the Kuomintang, I must suppress the Communist movement. It has gone beyond the limits."

The Nanking outrages by the Hunanese troops were the defiant answer to Chiang! The Communists hotly resented his bald manifesto. The final split between Chiang and the moderate Nationalists, on one side, and Borodin and the Communist elements on the other had come. The civil war in China took on three dimensions. The northern militarists were battling the southern Nationalists, and the two factions in the party, the Left and Right wings, were fighting not only the militarists but each other.

First dispatches reaching America were shocking. I read with horror the headlines telling of looting, raping, murder in Nanking. As I listened to radio reports I was beside myself: name after name of friends and people I knew by reputation came over the wire. Foreign consulates, missions, hongs were wrecked by the uncontrolled Leftist troops! Foreign women were outraged! Foreign officials and missionaries were killed!

It was an orgy of horrors—the climax, the blowing off of the lid, the eruption of the volcano, as it were—of the anti-foreign, anti-Christian policy of the Chinese and Russian Reds!

News came of the siege of "Socony Hill." Friends, the Hobarts, lived there—Mrs. Alice Hobart, wife of the manager of the company and a writer, had beautified that great house on the hill, landscaped its gardens. She wrote of her experiences during those days in her *Within the Walls of Nanking*.

The reports of that nerve-racking time came over the wire, reports relayed from the United States battleships off Nanking. Later I talked with the officer in charge of the U.S.S. *Noa* (Destroyer Number 343), Lieutenant Commander Roy C. Smith, Jr., and only recently when writing of this attack on Nanking I received permission to quote from his story (published in *United States Naval Institute Proceedings*, January, 1928) from the Board of Control of the United States Naval Institute, Annapolis, Maryland. His diary opens with an account of the Cantonese army battling at the outskirts of Nanking in an effort to capture the city (there had been a previous disastrous battle for the northerners under General Galen):

"The nineteenth also saw a new attack launched to the south of Nanking along the Anhwei-Kiangsu border . . .

"Early in the morning of March 24 it became evident that the Southerners had entered the city and were rapidly occupying all of it. We were still without word of any alarming incidents, however. . .

"But shortly the picture changed! . . .

"(About eight o'clock] armed uniformed bands of Southern soldiers were led by' officers and by local Kuomintang communists to all foreign property, schools, hospitals and missions, and systematically looted them and maltreated the foreigners there found. In one case Dr. Williams, vice-president of Nanking University, was robbed and then deliberately shot and killed by a Cantonese soldier. That these outrages were perpetrated by Southern troops is not open to question. Missionaries and others perfectly acquainted with Chinese languages and dialects recognized the distinctive dialects of the Southern provinces, Hunan, Yunnan, and Kwangtung, whence most of the Southern armies are recruited. The efforts of Chinese and propagandists at home and elsewhere to show these outrages to have been perpetrated by Northerners are wholly useless in face of plain facts. Their statements are all false and in most cases knowingly so. It is, however, quite likely that this was a Communist plot, and that the Communist wing of the Kuomintang, and not the more moderate element led by Chiang Kai Shek, was responsible. . .

"The unfortunate missionaries fled and hid before the storm. The one bright spot was the behavior of many servants and Chinese friends of the foreigners, who secured clothes and, at great personal danger to themselves, hid their masters or friends, and so saved many lives. . ."

The story of the hectic time at the Consulate is given by Lieutenant Commander Smith in the words of Ensign Woodward Phelps, U.S.N., who had been sent there in command of a small guard:

"'At about 0915 we heard that the British Consul General had been wounded and the British Consulate looted. . . The Consul and I decided to evacuate to Mr. Hobart's house on Socony Hill. They were telephoned of our coming. . . In the meantime, five missionaries had come in . . . At 0930 we set out with Mrs. Davis, her two young children, and a coolie carrying her two suitcases. . . Since we had about a mile and a quarter of open and hilly country to traverse, I expected we would have to open fire before arriving at our destination. Our only hope was that no large body of soldiers would be met. We had walked in single file, hardly 200 yards, when an armed soldier was met. The Consul spoke with him explaining that he was the American Consul and we Americans. The soldier smiled and motioned for us to pass on. The last man in our column had not gotten fifty yards past him when this soldier deliberately took aim and fired at us. From that time on we were pursued and potted at by from one of three or four soldiers who kept in the rear of us. . . The going was hard, particularly on Mrs. Davis and the children, but they bore up well. . .

"'At 1030 (according to signals about 1015) we arrived at Mr. Hobart's house to find there about thirty men and Mrs. Hobart.
. .

"'At 1300 we heard what we feared was coming: that the other houses on the surrounding hill were being thoroughly looted. Soon soldiers in twos and threes were seen in the vicinity and those coming to the house were argued with by Mr. [E. T.] Hobart, Mr. [J, K.] Davis and Mr. [J. Hall] Paxton, whose lives were continually in jeopardy. The first looters were bribed to leave. . . It was hoped that we could get in touch with responsible Kuomintang officials who would afford an escort to take us to the bund unharmed. . . . More soldiers kept coming to the house, until we were surrounded by anywhere from thirty to fifty Chinese. All the men had been gathered together in one room on the second floor in order to deceive the Cantonese as to how many foreigners were in the house. The women and children were in another room. It was known by this time that the aim of these soldiers was to kill all foreigners. The Consul quoted one of these soldiers as saying, "We are Bolshevists, we are proud of being Bolshevists, and we are going to act like Bolshevists." The Consul then came upstairs and said, "It's no use, get your arms."
. . .'

"During all the morning and early afternoon on the Hill, Mr. Hobart and Consul Davis had been arguing with these looters, most of the time with rifles, bayonets or pistols leveled in their faces or breasts. They gave up all the money they had and practically all that everyone else had, hoping to hold the men off until people outside could get into touch with responsible

Cantonese officials to end the disorder. . .

"Finally it was obvious that nothing more could be done. . . the Southern troops were bent on loot and murder and had worked themselves into the necessary rage and frenzy . . . The time had come to fight, and, reluctantly, Mr. Davis gave the order.

"The signal electrified us in the ship: . . .

"'1534-Z-D43 and *Emerald* V Socony. Commence firing, fire over our heads' followed by 'SOS,' 'SOS.'

"We at once ran up the signal to commence firing . . . I gave the order to fire. *Noa* thus got off the first salvo, two guns, Nos. 1 and 2, using flat nosed projectile. It landed right where it did the most good, one slightly to the left of the house on top of the Hill, and the other just over the crest, going down into the valley behind, whence most of the Chinese fire on the house was coming. The people in the house greeted it with a mighty cheer! . . .

". . . I sent the following signal to Commander Yangtze Patrol:

"'*Noa to Comyangpat*. 104. The Standard Oil house refuge of foreigners is being attacked. It is necessary to open fire with main battery. 1538.'

". . . At 1545 we could see men coming out of the house and throwing things out of the window. A mattress with white cover fell flat on the hillside below the house and I took this as a signal to cease fire, which I did. We watched the people come out with long ropes made of bed sheets, linen, blankets, anything they could find to tear up into lengths to knot together to serve as ropes to lower themselves over the sixty-foot wall below the house. There had been a rope there, with a boatswain' s chair, left by U.S.S. *Penguin*, but the Cantonese had stolen that. . .

". . . a signal from the Hill:

"'1555-Z-D433 V Socony. We are now trying to go over the wall below us, please send help.'

"We had already done so, and answered:

"'Socony V D43—Come over wall and come straight down toward beach to meet landing party.'

"Back again now to the party in the house, continuing Ensign Phelps' account of the actual firing and their escape over the wall.

"'. . . The gunfire was most effective and undoubtedly saved all of our lives. Missionaries in the interior who were being looted stated that all looting ceased when the bombardment commenced. At Socony Hill, the soldiers ran like scared rabbits . . . When the soldiers left, we made three ropes out of sheets, in order to get over the city wall at the base of the hill. A landing party from the ships had been sent for to meet us at the bund. Taking all necessary precautions, we made our way to the foot of the hill, stationing patrols to cover our evacuation from above. Armed men were first lowered over the city wall (about sixty feet high) to prevent any soldiers from getting at us from the foot. Then came the women and children followed by some unarmed missionaries. The last to leave were the signalmen, who maintained communication with the ships until the last. We still had about a mile of open country and one canal to cross before reaching the shore. . . However, the shell fire had so completely frightened the Cantonese that not a single armed soldier was encountered. At the canal we commandeered three large sampans and were ferried across to the other side. About 100 yards from the shore we were met by British bluejackets, members of their landing party, and it was only a few minutes before boats came to take us off, a total of forty-eight men, two women, and two children. We all escaped uninjured except Mr. Hobart, who broke his ankle when the rope broke with him in his descent of the wall. Had it not been for the shell fire, we would undoubtedly have all been massacred, since our ammunition could not have lasted long and the number of Cantonese soldiers around the house was increasing every minute.' . . .

EDNA LEE BOOKER

"It is the consensus of opinion among all refugees that only the opportune opening of fire by the ships saved the lives of all foreigners in Nanking."

I was terribly worried. John was on duty as a volunteer in an embattled Shanghai. Would this Red movement break over the city even as it had broken over Nanking? He had packed our curios, silver, linens—just in case an order for evacuation came.

The Nanking outrages, however, proved a boomerang to the Chinese and Russian Reds. The carefully laid plots against Chiang Kai-shek dissolved into nothingness. Chinese, not only in China but throughout the world, voiced their condemnations. Substantial, conservative Chinese arose to demand the overthrow of the Communist elements in the Kuomintang; regional war lords affiliated themselves with Chiang; even the masses of industrious hard-working Chinese in the provinces of the lower Yangtze turned to him. They too feared the Red excesses. The Nanking outrages broke the mesmeric spell which the Reds had laid over the Yangtze.

Chiang took a determined stand against the extremists.

Leading his loyal cadets, he swept down upon Shanghai where, backed by Chinese of influence and wealth, he instigated a time of "White Terror." Ruthlessly he hunted down the Red elements, and for days the streets of the old city literally ran with the blood of beheaded victims. In the month of April, 1927, some five thousand workers were reported executed. And months later I learned of the killing of a young girl revolutionist whom I had known rather well. She was so full of idealism, I wonder if she had understood what it was all about. The workers in and about Shanghai went under cover. Their headquarters were closed.

Chiang purged the Kuomintang and set up a new Nationalist government in Nanking.

The Hankow government of the Leftists was doomed. A counter-revolution was launched by one of Hankow's own generals. Borodin, General Bluecher, Eugene Chen, were forced to flee China, and even that truly great patriot the fragile and gentle Madame Sun Yat-sen left for Russia.

In Hankow had centered the hope of the Communists of the world.

Nevertheless, it had been impossible for Communist leaders to bring about a real social revolution, in the Soviet Russian sense. Private Chinese capital, properties, business enterprises, age-old traditions, inherent beliefs, love of peace, vested foreign interests (missionary as well as business), had played their part in defeating Moscow's ambitions in China. Borodin was held responsible by the Third International for not proclaiming Hankow a "Communist state." Trotsky, or even Lenin himself, could not have accomplished this. China's millions, with their deeply ingrained distaste for change, could not take on such a radically new ideology overnight. Borodin was a realist. He had grown up in Chicago. His first few months in the interior of old China had convinced him that the doctrines of Moscow had only scratched the surface. The Chinese Revolution was nationalistic, not communistic, in its last analysis.

Generalissimo Chiang Kai-shek emerged the man of the hour in China.

The first stage of the Chinese Revolution had been accomplished. The Yangtze valley had been conquered, and General Wu Pei-fu defeated. But there remained the powerful Marshal Chang Tso-lin and Peking before the unification of China under the Nanking government could become a *fait accompli*.

Chiang was an astute politician as well as a military leader.

At the height of his triumph he announced his decision to retire from the post of commander-in-chief of the Nationalist armies.

There was so much friction in the Kuomintang between the various factions that Chiang declared: "If by my retirement the dissension will heal, I should like to make it clear that I could be at home as a recluse. I still stand on one point only: the suppression of the Communists must be effected, for they scheme to wreck the party."

Again Chiang, the clever strategist! Before his enemies could tear him down from the heights, he had voluntarily abdicated his position. His resignation made a powerful appeal to the Chinese.

As one Chinese friend later said to me, "General Chiang's retirement, in the hope of saving the party from further internal strife, establishes a new precedent in China. His is an act of heroism." To my great astonishment the Chinese burst into tears. "In Chiang rests the hope of China. Who will carry on the work of Revolution? He must not be allowed to retire."

Chiang, accompanied by a bodyguard of some two hundred cadets, arrived in Shanghai from Nanking, *en route* to his ancestral home. Mass meetings protested his resignation. The Chinese press urged that he return to Nanking. Telegrams, letters from hundreds of organizations poured in upon him. But Chiang sailed for Ningpo.

High in the mountains beyond his native village of Chikow, Chiang sought peace. An ancient Buddhist temple hidden away among the pines and bamboo, near the summit of one of the loftiest peaks, became his headquarters. In the tranquillity of this lovely old monastery, where for generations the Buddhist monks have lived in prayer and meditation, Chiang put aside his uniform and donned a straight dark robe as simple as that worn by the priests. For the first time in five years—five war-torn, hard-pressing years—Chiang sought seclusion. Even as the monks, he sought guidance through meditation; and, like them, he lived abstemiously: neither drank Chinese wine nor smoked tobacco, was sparing in his diet. He retired at midnight and was up at five.

All China, as it were, began making its way up the picturesque trails of the mountain to Hsueh Tou Temple.

A constant stream of visitors sought out Chiang. And there, high in the mountains, where the mellow beat of temple drums and the musical chant of the priests told of a world far removed from machine guns and cannon, Chiang held daily conferences with party leaders. He was bitter over the disastrous effect the Soviet doctrines had had upon China's Nationalist movement, upon the Kuomintang government. There was no compromise with the Leftists nor with the radicals in the party. His words were unpalatable to those seeking concessions. His answers were sharp, stinging, definite. He could not be shaken.

Late in September, Chiang came down from his mountain retreat and sailed almost at once for Japan.

Chiang was off to ask Madame Soong, who was in Kobe recovering from an illness, for the hand of her youngest daughter, Mayling.

We returned to Shanghai from America just in time for the wedding of General Chiang Kai-shek and Miss Mayling Soong in December.

Radiantly beautiful, the bride-to-be told me of Chiang Kai-shek, and she was as excited as an American girl would have been over her wedding plans. Hers was to be a modern-style wedding, with flower girls and bridesmaids, and she was to wear a veil and carry a shower of roses. She was to arrive at the Majestic Hotel in a motor car decked with streamers, and not in the red-embroidered wedding chair of the old-fashioned bride. It was all most exciting, and many of the prettiest girls in Shanghai rushed in and out of the Soong home assisting "May" in her preparations.

Although many wondered at her choice of husbands, the bride was happy, satisfied.

Chiang Kai-shek, as the outstanding man of China, the leader of the Chinese revolutionary movement, was a different person from the young officer who had sought her hand five years earlier. Then she had replied, "Not interested." During the years following, he had risen high above the ranks; had become the hope of a New China. It was more than this. Letters from Chiang—in which he never failed to express his admiration for her—had convinced her of the sincerity of his purpose, of his patriotic fervor. In her marriage with Chiang Kai-shek she saw her great opportunity to help the people of China.

A private Christian ceremony was held at the Soong home, 139 Seymour Road, by the Reverend Dr. David Yui, on the morning of December 1. In the afternoon some two thousand guests, including foreign government officials and their wives, witnessed a second service held in the ballroom of the Majestic Hotel.

It was very impressive, very beautiful, a bit exotic—that ceremony with its touch of the East and the West.

Myriads of blossoms transformed the ballroom into a fragrant bower of loveliness, and the pathway leading to an improvised altar was marked with standards bearing great clusters of white chrysanthemums. On either side of the flower-banked altar stood tall white flower shields on which the characters translating "long life" and "happiness" were worked with red geraniums. Back of the altar a large photograph of Dr. Sun Yat-sen, draped with flags of the Kuomintang, was hung. With the first notes of the "Lohengrin" Wedding March, a hush fell upon the crowded ballroom. Flower girls came strewing rose petals; bridesmaids (beautiful girls in peach charmeuse costumes beaded with diamanté and pearls) followed, and then *the bride* on the arm of her brother T. V. Soong.

Mayling Soong was beautiful. Her embroidered satin gown fitted close her slim figure; her fragile veil of handmade lace was caught with orange blossoms; a long train of silver cloth embroidered with pearls fell from her shoulders. Little Miss Jeanette Kung and Master Louis Kung, children of Dr. and Mrs. H. H. Kung, were trainbearers. General Chiang Kai-shek, in foreign morning dress, awaited the bride at the altar under a large wedding bell.

The ritual was simple: There was the reading of the marriage ceremony by General Tan Yen-kai and the signing of official documents. Then the bride and groom made three formal bows. The first obeisance was to the photograph of Dr. Sun Yat-sen; the second, to the official witnesses of the wedding; the third was to the guests, in appreciation of their attendance. As I remember, someone sang "Oh, Promise Me."

During the reception Chiang Kai-shek smiled and bowed to everyone. He beamed as his lovely bride cut the glistening white wedding cake. His pride in her was delightful. He chatted and laughed. Apparently Chiang had not a worry on this, his most "joyful day." Yet the hotel and grounds, even the streets nearby, were under heavy guard. Secret service men mingled with the guests. The Chinese political situation was critical, tense. But Chiang, smart in his foreign costume — and Chiang wears even a wrinkled uniform with a certain flair — faced the day with the same dashing courage with which he meets each crisis.

After a time Chiang and his bride slipped away.

I talked with Madame Soong for a moment during the reception. She was to play an important part in Chiang's life.

Three women have done much in shaping the Chiang Kai-shek of today: his mother, his wife, and his mother-in-law.

Chiang Kai-shek issued a statement on the morning of his wedding day, which, in view of following events, has significance. He said in part:

"After our wedding, I know that my work for the Chinese Revolution will show great progress. With my heart filled with peace and great happiness, I can bear new responsibilities. From now on, my wife and I will do our best, give of our utmost, for the cause of the Chinese Revolution."

Only recently Mayling Soong Chiang, in talking with me, told of an incident of her honeymoon. She laughed a bit over it, then became deeply serious.

"When my husband announced that we two were determined to do our utmost for the cause of the Chinese Revolution, I warmly agreed; but I did not expect him to be called to attend a Party conference the first day of our honeymoon. That conference" — she laughed a bit ruefully — "lasted from eight o'clock in the morning until eight o'clock that night. I spent that day by myself. I thought most seriously of my new position as the wife of a Chinese leader. I saw quite clearly that my personal life must be lost in a larger life of service. I made a solemn vow on that first day of my married life that I would work side by side with my husband and strive to be worthy of the confidence people had placed in both of us. This I have tried to do — *to the utmost.*"

How little Mayling Soong Chiang, the bride, knew what that "to the utmost" was to mean in the years ahead!

A week after his marriage Chiang Kai-shek was invited by the Central Executive Committee of the Kuomintang, in session at Nanking, to become commander-in-chief of the Nationalist Armies. Telegrams poured in, urging that he accept; that he lead the People's Revolutionary Army northward on Peking.

Two attempts were made, by political enemies, to wreck the train which carried the Generalissimo and his wife to Nanking. But these experiences were forgotten in the cheers of the crowds which greeted them upon their safe arrival in the capital.

Chiang Kai-shek was back in the saddle; the Chinese Revolution, sans the support of the Communists, sans Comrade Borodin and General Bluecher, was marching on.

- 7 -

Shanghai was deliriously gay.

The disquieting, nerve-racking, sobering years of civil strife, of antiforeign uprisings and demonstrations in and about Shanghai were ended. The barbed-wire entanglements were down. Martial law and the curfew were off. Grim tanks of war no longer paraded the streets. The threat of a Sovietized China was dismissed. Everyone heaved a deep thankful sigh. Chinese and foreigners alike — together — celebrated. Shanghai had passed through another of her "ten thousand deaths"; had awakened to new life. New life: an expression which Chiang Kai-shek was to make famous as the name of his inspiring, regenerative "New Life Movement."

Business, which had been at a standstill during the uncertain years of Communist invasion, broke, like a long restrained tide, into an exciting boom.

The luxurious Cathay Hotel, built at the cost of five million (Shanghai) dollars by Sir Victor Sassoon of the wealthy Sassoon family of Bombay and London, opened in a blaze of sophisticated splendor, with a gala dinner.

In our party were a number of Chinese girls. We of the European world wore trailing French creations which bared our backs. But the women of the Orient wore clinging, seductive gowns which were made high in the neck and long in the sleeve, but whose scant skirts were cut with tantalizing slits up either side. Mildly shocking slits which extended from the ankle hem to the knee. And their gowns of shimmering flowered silks, of gold and silver brocades, were enhanced by diamonds, jade, and pearls.

When I first arrived in Shanghai, Chinese girls were not seen at the night clubs and hotels. The only Chinese woman I knew who danced was Princess Der Ling, who, as Mrs. Thaddeus White, moved much in foreign circles in Peking and in Shanghai; she had been reared in Paris, had grown up in Europe, had been lady-in-waiting to the Empress Dowager in Peking, and was in reality a Manchu. A new era in the social life in Shanghai began when the late Mrs. Edwin S. Cunningham, wife of the American Consul General, invited a few of the wives of distinguished Chinese to her famous curry tiffin parties, and asked them to stay on for mah-jongg. She added their names to her dinner-party list. In her boudoir over fragrant jasmine tea, candied ginger and almond cookies, I met many of the high-class younger women, informally; came to know and to like them. They were eager for life, and, with the poise and grace which characterizes everything they do, surprised Shanghai by their mastery of modern dancing; with the ease with which they fell into sophisticated foreign social life; with their ability to converse with foreign diplomats in French and English. They were utterly charming, those innately well bred Chinese girls. I liked them so much, delighted in their friendship.

About this time the first American sound film was shown in Shanghai—a "talkie" which thrilled the crowds of Chinese and foreigners who packed the theaters. As I remember, it was a Ruth Chatterton film, and I was enchanted by the timbre of her voice.

The dog races came into being. The Canidrome, the Stadium,

Luna Park, with pretentious grandstands and tracks, were built. Prize-winning whippets arrived from England. Throngs of Chinese and a sprinkling of foreigners rushed nightly to "the dogs," to gamble on the lithe runners after the elusive mechanical rabbits. A jai alai palace was built. Handsome Cubans in white flannels and brilliant red, yellow, blue, green shirts, each with a large number on his back, swung high on the hard, fast ball. Grandstands were filled with excited enthusiasts following each play with understanding eyes, backing their favorites with their money.

The city went mad over lights.

There were colored lights glowing red, green, gold, blue—dancing neon lights—lights sparkling like jewels; lights chasing up and down the sides of high buildings, to the tops of towers, far out over the sidewalks. Picturesque Chinese characters, sacred through the ages, enlarged to gigantic proportions, gleamed flamelike against a midnight sky; action lights, fascinated the Chinese even as the spectacular signs of Broadway thrill the man from out of town: Manhattan lights— Manhattan nights—set down in the mystery, the glamour of the Far East.

Overnight Shanghai became a city of Chinese cabarets, and of Chinese taxi dancers.

It was through a Chinese country girl with dreams of becoming a taxi dancer that I learned something of that tremendous industry; gathered material for a story.

We were having tea on the terrace one afternoon when the gardener and a young Chinese girl entered the gate.

"My plenty solly tlouble Master, Missie," said the man as he nervously twisted his battered straw hat. The three long black hairs which grew from the mole on his chin quivered. "This belong my girl. My number one angly he. Just now he talkee, wanchee do dance-girl pidgin. My talkee he—no can do dance-

272

girl pidgin! Please, Missie, my wanchee. go way two, three day. Must take clazy girl homeside."

She stood there, a sturdy country girl of about fifteen with an appeal about her which made me wish to help her. But a taxi dancer! Amah joined us.

"This girl talkee plenty nonsense," she announced. "Wanchee Missie lendee he fifty dollar. Fifty dollar! She wanchee buy new coat, cuttee he hair foreign-fashion—learn dancee pidgin. All finish can catchee job. Suppose wanchee do, must pay fifty dollar."

In other words, for fifty dollars a country girl would be streamlined into a taxi dancer. She could be launched on a career of a dancing partner, capable of earning a hundred to a thousand dollars a month, depending upon her personality and popularity. The gardener's daughter had learned of the taxi dance halls from a girl in the village whose sister danced at the Peach Blossom Palace in Shanghai. Tales of the incredible amount she was earning there had filtered back to the little farming community.

The next day I sought out the managers of the Peach Blossom Palace and the Moon Palace. From them I learned that the majority of the dancing girls were from the country. They were brought to Shanghai by respectable, responsible women who made a living by training likely girls. Frequently the success of a cabaret depended upon one or two dancers. They drew the crowds and were sought after by managers of rival establishments. A girl with personality and beauty could go far. She might marry a man of wealth, become a motion picture star, or eventually retire, a well-to-do woman.

The taxi-dance industry represented an investment of millions; employed some five thousand girls; supported a number of Chinese dancing schools, as well as beauty parlors. The Chinese cabaret boom had begun during the years of strife about the city.

Even at times when business had been at a standstill, the owners of cabarets had made money. There were thousands of foreign sailors, marines, soldiers stationed in Shanghai. They liked the Chinese girls with their strange beauty, and crowded the dance halls, bars, night clubs. Chinese men, tired of the novelty of Russian girls, sought their own kind, and, in consequence, the Chinese establishments began to crowd out the Russian. The taxi dancers organized, the "number one" Chinese dancing girl of the city being the beautiful "Rose-Marie" of the Lido.

The gardener's daughter?

Her father married her almost at once to a young second gardener. She would live close to the "good earth." When she married I sent her a silk coat and a bottle of perfume in the hope that it might help ease her disappointment.

With peace had come a real estate boom. An American company opened a new residential district in the outskirts of the city. For some three years the Chinese compradore of the company went about quietly buying up various tracts of farm land. There were difficulties about ancestral graves, about laying out roads, securing municipal water and lights, police protection; but eventually Columbia Circle materialized, became the smart suburban section of the city.

There we built our house.

Building is an exciting event in any land; but in China, where superstition, legend, old custom, "squeeze," and the geomancer have, through the ages, played an important part in the erection of any structure, it is an experience which leaves you limp, exhausted, thankful: thankful that your house, which has in the main been built by young apprentices (dozens of them), holds up; humble because certain ambitious ideas on your part—hand-carved, period stair railings and posts, for example—which in

America would be almost prohibitive, here are carried out by those same small apprentices on the lot at little, if any, additional cost.

Disturbing the earth to dig foundations is always a more or less dangerous undertaking in China. Evil spirits, which sleep peacefully in the earth, may be aroused. A friend was informed by her building foreman one day that the site for her home was unlucky — very bad, in fact. Years earlier many men had died there; their ghosts hovered round about. Fortunately her garden was large and she let her foreman lay the foundations in a location favored by the geomancer. Now her house is considered, by the Chinese, "very lucky."

We drove out almost every day to watch the work on our house. Even before we reached it, we could hear the Chinese workmen on the bamboo scaffolding singing as they pounded down the foundations. The leader would chant a line of the *ta chuang* ("hitting the foundations") song, then the workmen in chorus would intone, "Ah — ha-a-a! Ai-yah! Ai-yah!" as they dropped the heavy stone block patterned somewhat after a pile driver. It is most melodious and carries on the breeze like a song of spring.

One day I noticed that branches of trees had been fastened to the tops of high bamboo scaffolding poles. They now resembled trees and would fool the evil spirits.

Another day we arrived during a ceremonial feast. It is customary, when a new house is being built, to pay homage to Lu Pan, patron of the carpenters.[15] A square table was set in the midst of the lumber, shavings, cement, and bricks. On it, arranged

---

15   Lu Pan lived during the time of Confucius. He was so skilled as a workman that when he reached middle age he withdrew to the mountains, where for years he devoted himself to creating works of magic. He is credited with carving a bird which flew for four days, and a second bird on whose outspread wings he rode all the way from his home in Shantung to the Kingdom of Wu (Kiangsu). And this in 600 B.C.

in careful order, were symbolic dishes offered to Lu Pan. There were a brace of geese, indicative of conjugal fidelity; a pair of fish, symbolic of wealth; a bowl of bean curd, typifying joy; green candles (red would have suggested fire); silver paper money, to be burned for the use of Lu Pan in the Spirit World; incense sticks of sandalwood, whose sweet perfume augurs long life.

As the ridge beam of the house was fitted into place—a ceremony which in the building of Chinese houses is usually accompanied by the chanting of Taoist priests—hundreds of firecrackers were set off. Chinese from the Fah Wah village, just across the road, crowded about. A young workman, carrying a tray of round dumplings marked with green symbols, climbed up the scaffolding. As the crowd watched with excitement, he threw the dumplings to the four corners of the house, east, north, west, and south, and everyone scrambled to catch them. The characters on the ridgepole read, "May all good fortune come to this household." There was much bowing to the picture of Lu Pan; then his red and gold scroll was laid on a pile of silver paper money and lighted. The ceremony (one of good wishes for "thousand years of prosperity and position," for "ten thousand generations of glory") was ended.

The feasting and merriment for the workmen and apprentices began.

Ours was a three-story, white stucco, English-style house with gabled roof and dormer windows. Once again I had set aside my dream of a Chinese house with courtyards and moon gates and a spirit screen. Romantic—but not practical, I was told. We settled most comfortably into our new home, planted our garden. And life moved on its happy way.

From the interior came important news dispatches.

EDNA LEE BOOKER

The Nationalist army under Generalissimo Chiang reached Peking during the summer of 1928. Marshal Chang Tsolin, retreating from below the Great Wall to his Mukden stronghold, was killed when his train was bombed as it crossed a bridge. It is alleged that the bomb was set by Japanese militarists who were even then planning the seizure of Manchuria. Peking ("northern capital") became Peiping ("northern peace") and was recognized as such by the foreign powers. Nanking was proclaimed capital of a now united China — united in name at least — and the work was begun of transforming the ancient city into a great modern city, of organizing a strong central government of China. The Nationalists were faced with the task of bringing many troublesome factions to heel, a task which meant a ten-year war against the armies of the Reds, and union did not come in fact until the Japanese invasion of China in 1937.

- 8 -

Our family — John, the two youngsters, Amah, and I — sailed on holiday, John's home leave of six months, and returned in September of 1931 from a vacation spent in America and Europe.

In Europe, our happiness had been dimmed by talk of European war. It was more than the talk of war that frightened me: it was the expressions on the faces of the women and children; the trying on of gas masks, while stopping at a delightful château-pension in Meudon, outside Paris, horrible gas masks which covered the happy, shining faces of Johnny and Patty and transformed them into grotesque little animals. It was the continual crunch of drilling feet on ancient roads, the flash of bayonets across stretches of ripe wheat where poppies blossomed scarlet as blood. It was the hatred which had its roots in the past, its flowering in the present., and was so real that the children talked to us of wars which had taken place hundreds of

277

years ago as if they had just been fought. It was a smoldering, ever present hatred of which we in America have no conception.

John spent much of his time with the first officer of the German liner on which we traveled from Genoa to Shanghai. He was a big, aloof Prussian, with eyes as blue as a cold sea and as unfathomable. But he and John formed a boat friendship. Night after night as our liner rocked under the impact of the monsoon in the Indian Ocean, we would meet in a sheltered corner of the upper deck and talk of Germany's problems, of the Versailles Treaty, of the World War and its aftermath.

But when our liner finally skirted the China coast and we glimpsed distant pagodas against a sunset sky, coral and blue sampans, like fairy boats, off Amoy, amber sails of big-eyed junks swelling in the winds of the China Sea, all of us were glad to be "home" — glad to have left Europe before we were involved in a major cataclysm, before we had breathed too deeply of that atmosphere of hate.

However, that night at a dinner party I learned of the grave internal troubles which China was facing — troubles which read like a chapter out of the Book of Job.

Although northern and southern China had been united under Generalissimo Chiang Kai-shek in 1928, the unity, I was told, was as yet little more than name.

"It hasn't jelled," explained a man across the candles and flowers.

The Nanking government was fighting for its very life. In Canton the Leftists were endeavoring to set up a rival party; in the north recalcitrant war lords were plotting the recapture of Peiping; in the far interior Communist armies were on the march; and in Manchuria a number of alleged "incidents" involving Koreans and Japanese threatened war. The vast provinces of the northwest were suffering from famine, and during the summer 'certain other provinces had been struck by a prolonged plague of locusts. But the end was not yet. In August the turbulent Yangtze River had gone on a rampage, and a great flood—perhaps the most disastrous in her recorded history—had descended upon the very heart of China.

I rushed off to Hankow, flood-bound city six hundred miles up the river, to cover this unprecedented Yangtze flood.

"Mademoiselle," the middle-aged Frenchwomen who has been with us through the years, could be counted upon to meet any household emergency which might arise during the short time I should be away.

The tail end of a typhoon hit the steamer as I started up the Yangtze River: more rain!

There had been far too many days and nights of rain in the Yangtze valley during that spring and summer: rains which had swollen the rivers, lakes, and canals of the country into a devouring inland sea. There had been phenomenal snows high in the mountains of Tibet, mysterious land of the "Lost Horizon," in the glacial heights where the Great River is born; and a powerful torrent—uncontrolled, all-destroying—had swept through the narrow canyons of the Yangtze Gorges and rushed unchecked over flat, low-lying country, destroying dikes and dams, and enveloping towns, people, crops, animals, in its mad race toward the China Sea. Periodic are the epidemics, floods, droughts, famines, scourges, wars which take their mass toll.

The second day out, there was a sharp clanging of bells—a slowing of the engines.

Through the fog and mist I could see an upturned junk swaying with the swirl of the waters. A number of Chinese were clinging to it. Out of the wind came their pitiful cries as they struggled to maintain a precarious hold on the sinking boat.

Angry yellow waters pulled at them, and now and then a wave washed over the doomed vessel.

A lifeboat pushed off from our steamer and raced down with the current, toward the wreck. It required excellent seamanship to maneuver in the Yangtze waters at spate tide. The victims came to the upper deck of our steamer, a pitiful procession, to thank the captain: the elderly boat owner, who still wore his queue, his three grown sons, two women, and a little girl. They fell at his feet, eloquent in their appreciation. I knew that they would rise to face the future with an inherent courage. Another moon would find them again sailing the Yangtze with a favorable wind under a sunny sky.

The Yangtze was no longer a river, but a heavy, ponderous sea which stretched on and on and on, an endless sullen waste which covered villages and farm lands.

Somewhere upriver were the Lindberghs.

They had taken off in the *Sirius* from Flushing Bay in New York on July 27, had flown "north to the Orient," and had landed on Lotus Lake, outside the walls of Nanking, on September 19.

As we neared Nanking, everyone crowded the decks, hoping against hope that we should glimpse them. Cheers rang out when, as on the wings of the morning, their orange-winged *Sirius* rose over the ancient wall of Nanking, over Purple Mountain (where stands the tomb of the first Ming Emperor of China as well as the magnificent mausoleum of Dr. Sun Yat-sen), circled like a beautiful bird, paused a moment, then was off on an errand of mercy.

It was most dramatic: angry mud-yellow waters, forbidding, age-gray walls, and a bird of brilliant plumage against a sullen, low-ceilinged sky.

We stood watching as the plane soared off over that stretch of waters; then it was gone, and only the grayness and the drizzle remained.

Anne Lindbergh was at the controls. She sat there hour after hour, while Lindbergh made maps, took photographs, in an effort to chart the far reaches of the flood. The *Sirius* was the only plane in China at that time which had sufficient range to survey the farthermost limits of the flood waters. In Kiangsi Province alone, Anne Lindbergh flew the *Sirius* over more than sixteen thousand square miles, while her husband worked over charts, which were invaluable to the relief agencies — marooned villages here, hills there, crowded with Chinese refugees.

We passed boats where priests were chanting, beseeching the River Dragon to have mercy; saw Chinese on enormous rafts of logs throwing firecrackers into the air to drive away the flood demons; listened to the cries of mourners as a boat loaded with coffins passed us. I wondered where the living would bury their dead — there was no land for miles. I saw terrified Chinese huddled fearfully in narrow heavy coffins from which the dead had been thrown. They were using them as boats — using coffins, tubs, doors, upturned tables, anything that would float. And I saw sad-faced women placing little lighted cups on the water — lights which would guide their lost ones into the spirit world.

From Hankow, where vessels crowded the water front for miles, a relief launch pushed into an outlying district. We chugged over what had once been rice fields. We skirted a village where yellow water lapped the tiles of a temple roof. In the eddy about the temple enclosure, as many as thirty corpses rode on the water. Our boatmen were constantly on the watch to avoid dreadful bloated objects which gave off a nauseous stench — decaying bodies of men and women, carcasses of buffalo, pigs — shooting by in their rush to the sea.

About noon we came up on a high bit of land. Stupefied, half-dead Chinese crowded there. They showed little interest in our arrival. They had been starving in filth and mud for days, exposed to the burning sun, to torrential typhoon rains. They were as graven images sitting in the mud, too weak even to realize that help had arrived. A half-dozen gaunt women crouched in the shelter of a mat-shed of sorts. One of them was trying to nurse a skeletonlike baby that fretted pitifully as he sucked noisily, desperately, at flat, dry breasts.

"The hopelessness of it all!" exclaimed my escort as we turned back toward Hankow.

There were already some seven hundred thousand refugees in the emergency camps of the Wu-han cities of the Yangtze. More than one hundred thousand more were in Nanking, and about the same number in Shanghai. But in the marooned districts, isolated villages, tens of thousands perished.

En route back to Shanghai, our ship's radio picked up the news of the accident to the *Sirius* in taking off from the airplane carrier *Hermes* at Hankow. A wing of the plane had caught in the fast-moving current, and the Lindberghs were forced to jump into the turbulent stream just as it capsized. In her delightful book "*North to the Orient*" (Harvest Book Company, 1935) , Anne Lindbergh describes it all with charming nonchalance. But the story might have had a very different ending, for the undercurrents of the raging Yangtze seldom release a victim, and the *Sirius* narrowly escaped being bashed to bits.

The Lindberghs' visit to China was brought to a sharp, unhappy close by a cable telling of the sudden death of Mr. Dwight Morrow, father of Mrs. Lindbergh. They came downstream on the *Hermes* with their badly damaged plane. American Consul General Cunningham met them upon their arrival and whisked them away to the Consulate.

Shanghai is innately well mannered. She seldom gives way to enthusiasms, almost never intrudes upon the privacy of her visitors—although the famed of the world pass through her gates—and there was no curious crowd to greet them.

Several days earlier Mrs. Cunningham had arranged a small informal curry tiffin. With considerable graciousness Anne Lindbergh insisted that her hostess should not postpone it.

Just before we went in for luncheon, Anne Lindbergh came into the drawing room. She was homesick—homesick for America and for her baby who had been left in the care of her mother. She was small, slim, big-eyed, and possessed of a glowing loveliness which her photographs do not reveal.

After a bit Lindbergh came, stood somewhat abashed in the doorway, just as any man might before a room filled with women. Then he too entered. Just as surprising as the beauty of Mrs. Lindbergh, was the youthfulness of Lindbergh. His smile was a broad grin topped off by freckles. After a bit they retired to their sitting room, and we went in to our curry.

The Lindberghs were sailing with a broken-winged *Sirius*, yes, but they were leaving in China an inspiring example of the value of aviation—an inspiration which did much to open up air routes which six years later spanned the country.

- 9 -

Early in October, Shanghai took on a tenseness.

I had returned from Hankow to find the foreign and Chinese dailies full of the capture of Mukden by the Japanese. It seemed a blow below the belt in the light of the titanic flood which was demanding every Chinese resource.

Thousands of students from all over China, whole colleges of them, were pouring into the city. They were making their way up to Nanking. If the railroads refused them free transportation, they stretched out on the tracks and defied the engineers to run over them.

"War with Japan!" "Fight with Japan!" was their cry.

The seizing of Manchuria by the Japanese had been a clarion call, "To arms!" to the students of all China. In every part of the nation thousands of young men and women, boys and girls, ranging from twelve to twenty-odd years, had taken up the cry. And the Student Movement, which had been comparatively dormant since 1927, at once took the lead in a nation-wide anti-Japanese movement. By December, 1931, an army of some seventy thousand girl and boy students had invaded the Capital. They came from universities in Peiping, Hankow, Shanghai, Canton. They stood for hours in the cold before the government buildings, marched through the streets bearing slogans, "War with Japan"; held mass meetings.

Ten days after Japan's capture of Mukden, they stormed the offices of Dr. C. T. Wang, then Minister of Foreign Affairs (in 1936 made Chinese Ambassador to the United States), demanding that he support the "war with Japan" movement. In an effort to disperse the students Dr. Wang was badly beaten; and his offices were turned into a shambles before the police arrived. The students were put on trains, sent back to their universities under military escort.

The Sunday after the C. T. Wang incident I attended a gigantic student mass meeting with some Chinese students. It was held just outside the French Concession at a public athletic field on the Slanting Bridge Road (Jiao Jau Lu). Thousands of students were pouring into the grounds from every direction, and stirring music reached us, caught us up in the excitement of it all, even before we were inside.

From an improvised platform, draped with flags and hung with anti-Japanese posters, young men and women addressed the assembly. They were burning with patriotism — dramatic in their fierceness, their intensity. In impassioned voices the student speakers poured forth the wrongs of China at the hands of Japan; they deplored the chaotic conditions existing in their own country, exposed the fact that China was again on the eve of civil war, the Canton faction against the Nanking Government. They demanded that the Kuomintang heal internal differences and declare war upon Japan.

Out of their intensity was born a brand of patriotism, a sense of national unity, such as I had never seen before in China. As one great body they swore to carry out their "duties as members of the National Salvation Army, as workers in the Anti-Japanese Association." Thousands of hands reached high, pledging their loyalty to China, even unto the death.

In all leading educational centers of China similar student mass meetings were being held. During November more than 12,000 students marched on Nanking and stormed the Government buildings. Early in December large numbers of students were arrested in the Capital, and thousands of students protested. Just before Christmas an army of approximately seventy thousand young men and coeds from all over China quit their classes, and arrived in Nanking demanding action. They attacked both the Foreign Ministry and the central party headquarters, and destroyed the plant of the *Central Daily News*. So serious was the situation that local garrison troops were called out.

Their retaliation to Japan was a nation-wide boycott, a boycott such as China, the past master of the art of boycott, had never before known.

The headquarters of the Anti-Japanese Association were in the Temple of the Queen of Heaven (Tien Hon Kong) on North Honan Road. It was a popular temple, crowded during all festivals by the Chinese living in Hongkew. Massive stone lions, which were said to roam at night over the district, stood at each side of the great entrance gate. Off the main courtyard within one of the many high-ceilinged halls sat the big-eared god, Ching Tsiang Ching Chiang, who can hear anything said within a thousand Ii, and in the opposite chamber, Liu Tsiang Ching, whose great carved eye in the middle of his high forehead can see a thousand Ii. In the days ahead it was as if these two famed personages had imbued the students with their powers, so effective were they in their work of searching out buyers and sellers of Japanese goods.

I visited the temple, saw something of the work of the students; and I marveled at their efficiency.

The courtyards were teeming with students, young merchants from great Chinese hangs, apprentice clerks from wealthy Chinese banking houses, representatives of various labor and factory organizations. Many were enlisted as pickets. They literally policed Greater Shanghai, and the regular Chinese police did not interfere with their activities. To have done so would have brought fiery "unpatriotic," "proJapanese" accusations upon their heads.

A group of pickets were starting out to meet a train. They met every train and examined the baggage of all incoming Chinese for Japanese goods. Others departed to continue their daily search of Chinese shops for the sellers of Japanese merchandise. Many were off to incite factory and mill workers in Japanese plants to strike, to urge Chinese loaders of Japanese ships to go "Ningpo more far" (on a holiday).

Five or six pickets pushed into the courtyard, leading a loudly protesting man. He was a middle-aged, silk-coated merchant, opulent in appearance. An impromptu court was held — a court which administered "justice" then and there. He was declared a "national thief," and, before I could determine what was going on, he was led to a wooden, barred cage, thrown in, and the door bolted. His howls of rage were lost in the jeers of the Chinese milling about. He was left there to be gazed at by all—a strange "beast" who betrayed his country by selling enemy goods!

Another man, timid and badly shaken, was shoved forward. He was threatened with branding, threatened with having the characters "Yong Noo" (Foreign Slave) burned on his face unless he paid a fine of several thousand dollars for handling Japanese cotton cloth.

"Would they really brand him?" I asked.

"What do you think?" came the answer, eyes flashing. "It is an economic war! We must show a united front against Japan, or we cannot succeed. Branding is too easy for these bloody traitors—they should have their eyes burned out!"

We left the temple and joined a group of pickets who were headed for a crowded street off North Szechuen Road. The students entered every Chinese shop on that busy thoroughfare. They did not go into a Japanese shop, nor in any way molest the Japanese of the neighborhood.

In a systematic manner they went through the stock of each shop. In the sixth little store, a wool shop, they found goods marked "Made in Japan." The merchant protested that the wool had been purchased from Japan before the boycott had gone into effect. He was a young man, and he was trembling in his eagerness to convince the pickets. But one husky chap lashed him across the face. Others tied his hands; pushed him into a corner. They hurled insults, taunts at him. Then they left him and began to pull hanks of wool from the shelves which reached from floor to ceiling. Red, green, yellow, orange, purple wool—down it came cascading in a riot of color.

From another room hurried a pretty, bright-eyed young woman, the wife of the merchant. With her was a tottering Chinese woman who protested fiercely over the intrusion of the students. But by this time the pickets had dragged all of the wool from one side of the shop and were carrying it into the street. The elderly woman returned to the back of the store, where she hastily lighted incense and red candles which were arranged on an altar before the henna and gold gods of the household.

The young wife, however, did not depend upon the household gods. She brought forth a record book. She tried to interest the pickets, who were by then setting fire to the pile of wool. An enormous crowd of loud-talking Chinese had gathered before the stop. They entered into the general *walla walla* (loud talking).

In desperation the wife turned to a Chinese girl student with me for help. "*Ai-yah!*" she cried, as she finally hit upon an item in the account book which proved that the wool was old stock. The Chinese girl appreciated the situation, took charge and the two young women quickly settled the whole affair.

Ten years earlier this would have been impossible. China's women were now tackling her national problems. I felt that a powerful, stimulating, permanent force had entered into the building of the Republic.

A few nights later John and I dined at the home of a prominent Chinese banker. There were some thirty guests, the majority of them members of Shanghai's smart young Chinese set. The costumes of the women, made from shimmering brocaded metal cloth, lamé, cut velvets, rich silks whose colors changed with every movement under the lights, were very beautiful. The accessories were fascinating: flowers caught in curls, long bobs, chignons. I was amazed to hear a stunning girl across the table urge that the Shanghai Chinese Bankers' Association break off all relations with Japan. She was very Parisian in a form-fitting black metallic gown, on which gold flowers glowed. Long gold earrings dangled from her ears, while a spray of gold leaves sat as a coronet upon her sleek hair. Even her fingernails were tipped with gold polish. As the Chinese boys brought on the delicious feast dishes of a Chinese banquet, the hostess explained the absence of shark fins, a customary feast delicacy. The shark fins were imported from Japan, and smart Shanghai had boycotted them.

As the days passed, October fading into November, November into December, the seriousness of the situation grew.

Practically all of the smaller Japanese firms were facing bankruptcy. The doors of a large number of Japan's factories and mills were closed. One week after the invasion of Manchuria, Chinese workers had walked out of the Japanese textile factories in Shanghai, which represented an investment of some 200,000,000 yen; had deserted their posts generally in all Japanese mills. Japan's ships lay idle in the harbor; her shipping up the Yangtze had come to an absolute halt.

On January 18th, what is now known as the "Monk Incident" threw Shanghai into turmoil, and precipitated a crisis in the Sino-Japanese situation.

A group of Japanese monks left the Hongkew district and entered a thickly populated zone outside of the foreign concessions. They stopped in front of a Chinese towel factory and began to chant a Japanese national anthem. Almost at once a riot broke out. During the fray three of the monks were injured; one of them died.

The incident for which Japan may or may not have been waiting had occurred.

The next morning the Japanese Consul General presented General Wu Teh-chen, Mayor of Greater Shanghai, a note containing five demands: "a formal apology by the Mayor," "the immediate arrest of the Chinese responsible for the attack on the Japanese monks," "the payment of damages and hospital expenses of the victims," "the control of the antiJapanese movement," and "the immediate dissolution of the anti-Japanese agitation."

General Wu of Shanghai conferred with officials in Nanking.

Three or four days went by. The Japanese Admiral, with growing impatience, announced that, "should the Mayor of Greater Shanghai fail to give a satisfactory reply to the Japanese and fulfill their demands without delay, the Admiral was determined to take the necessary steps in order to protect Imperial rights and interests." The Japanese Navy moved on Shanghai. The affair reached a crisis on January 28th, when Admiral Shiozawa notified all foreign defense commanders in Shanghai that unless he received a satisfactory reply by the following morning he would take action. And it was on the morning of the 28th that Mayor Wu, in agreement with the Nanking Government, replied to the Japanese Consul. He replied accepting the Japanese demands in full. The Japanese Consul subsequently notified the Consular Body, of which American Consul General Cunningham was the senior member and Dean, that the reply from Mayor Wu had been entirely satisfactory.

Everyone was so keyed up over the situation that the apparent settlement of the issue between the two nations brought a tremendous relief. Even so, at four o'clock in the afternoon the Shanghai Municipal Council declared that "a state of emergency" existed; a plan for the defense of the settlements was announced; and the International defense forces including the Volunteers were ordered to "stand by."

It was cocktail time at the French Club.

Officers in uniform, men and women in evening dress, in sport clothes, were crowded about the little tables in the grill room. Seven o'clock, and the grill, always crowded with cosmopolites at this hour during the winter season, was filled to overflowing. The air was electric with excitement. The usual hum of cheery

EDNA LEE BOOKER

voices, the frequent tinkle of laughter, were missing. A staccato cacophony took their place. A purple smoke haze hung over the ornate room with its sophisticated decorations done by an artist from Paris, hovered over the framed silhouettes of French Club notables which lined the walls, over the bar whose shelves were laden with the bottled wines of France, and which featured a sign "Plat du Jour: Suprême de Volaille Casanova." There was the scattering of uniforms, of gold braid, brass buttons, decorations, service ribbons. Frenchmen, Italians, Scandinavians, Portuguese, Britishers, Americans milled restlessly about the room, expectant of they knew not what, on the *qui vive.*

Although word had been received from the Japanese Consul General that there would be no hostilities in Shanghai, still there was really no letdown in the tension which had enveloped the city during the past week.

The white-coated Chinese boy brought platters heaped with puffy French finger potatoes, pats of black caviar with chopped onion, slices of thick toast and curls of butter, specialties of the club at the cocktail hour. But no one paid any attention to these tempting bits. Everyone at our table and at the tables about us was talking excitedly, volubly. Everyone was trying desperately to believe that the crisis was over. But no one did.

With some friends we stayed on at the Club for dinner.

There was too much excitement in the city—everyone was too keyed up—to go calmly home. A cordon of barbed-wire and sandbag barricades again surrounded the settlements. American marines, British troops, Italians and French, and Colonials stood guard at strategic boundaries. There were so many rumors about that no one knew what to believe.

A little before eleven o'clock an American chap in the Shanghai Volunteer Corps strode into the room.

"The Japs are going to land troops and take over Chapei in

291

about an hour!" he informed the men at our table. "Admiral Shiozawa has announced that he feels nervous about the Japanese nationals living in Chapei; so he is sending in troops to protect them. Nervous—hell! This is even more brazen than the firing on Mukden!"

We sat stunned.

"But how dare they when the Japanese Consul General has declared the Chinese reply to his demands was satisfactory— when he has published to the world that there would be no invasion of Chinese territory?" I asked.

In the light of the Japanese activities in Manchuria it was a silly question.

An American business man at our table began to worry about his parents, elderly missionaries who lived in the Southern Baptist missionary compound on Paoshan Road out beyond Chapei. We decided to drive down and get them out of the possible danger zone. Our car, with Ah Ching asleep by the wheel, was waiting.

The city appeared calm. The gay laughing lights of Nanking Road, of North Szechuen Road, were shining in their usual riot of color. Music from the cabarets and night clubs, from Chinese theaters and restaurants rang out as we drove along. In the Hongkew district of the International Settlement the streets were quiet.

We began to hope that the report of a Japanese attack was just another rumor as we turned up Range Road to Paoshan Road.

The Nineteenth Route Army of Canton under the command of General Tsai Ting-kai was intrenched in Chapei, Chinese territory in Greater Shanghai, which bordered the Settlement on the north. But according to reports the army had only that day received orders from the Nanking Government to withdraw from the Settlement neighborhood in order that there might be no possible friction with the Japanese. Just why these Chinese troops were there at all was something of a mystery. They had arrived some two months earlier and had dug in as if they intended to stay. One rumor had it that Tsai intended to rush the International Settlement. But he had been in the vicinity for several weeks, and nothing untoward had happened. I was more inclined to believe that his move to Shanghai fitted into some intricate Chinese political pattern as he was at odds with Chiang Kai-shek. We wondered if Tsai had obeyed the orders from Nanking and had begun his evacuation of Chapei. We saw no preparations for war. We debated whether or not we should even carry on to the missionary compound.

Suddenly the stillness of the night was shattered.

At first I thought that the explosive sounds were caused by firecrackers at some Chinese celebration. Then came the *rat-atat-tat* of machine-gun fire.

"*Ai-yah!* Japanese soldier man come!" cried Ah Ching.

He quickly swung the car down a deserted side street and into the entrance of an alleyway.

We jumped out and crouched in the protection of a godown wall. Around this we could see a dimly lit cross street about half a block away. It was as if we watched a stage from the darkness of a theater pit.

On the run came Japanese marines. They lost themselves in the opposite "wings." More Japanese bluejackets. These set up machine guns and began firing into the rows of tenementlike houses which reared straight up from the sidewalk, houses which were packed with hundreds of Chinese workers. Unwarned, undefended houses!

Terrified screams of women and children rang out. These screams were lost in the shriek of shells, in the crashing of broken glass. We could see only a bit of that nightmare; but what we saw was shocking.

On and on the Japanese forces came, firing into houses as they ran: little men in dark uniforms, white leggings, with flashing guns and silver bayonets; marines; armored cars; motorcycles with machine guns mounted on side cars. All in a frenzy of haste—all on the run to take over Chapei.

Suddenly they were gone, like a cyclone or an earthquake which leaves destruction in its wake, gone on toward the North Station—toward Chapei.

After a time the men decided to turn back, to make a try for North Szechuen Road and the Garden Bridge. We stopped in a little restaurant and Tom telephoned his parents. They were safe. The compound, which so shortly was to be shellriddled, was as yet undisturbed. The elderly missionaries had lived through many exciting experiences during their long years of service in China, and were unperturbed.

"The fighting will in all probability be over before daylight," they predicted. "The Japanese will have taken Chapei by morning."

But Hongkew, the section of the International Settlement where some twenty thousand Japanese then lived, and which in time of trouble was allotted by the Shanghai Defense to the Japanese to protect, was now seething with excitement. The Japanese were violating their trust. Instead of protecting the district they were turning it into a shambles. The Japanese reservists and ronins[16] were literally taking Hongkew. Maddened armed gangs bent on revenge over the Chinese boycott, over the failure of their factories, mills, small business concerns, were abroad. There in the dead of night they were creating a reign of terror, secure in the protection of their bluejackets.

We were forced to stop at one corner because of the hand-to-

---

16   Wandering samurai who had no lord or master.

hand street fighting.

John ordered Ah Ching to crouch down on the floor in the back seat while he himself took the wheel. It was well that he did. Scarcely was Ah Ching hidden away when three or four ronins all set for trouble thrust a flaming torch toward our car. In the flickering orange light their faces looked like the masks of devils in a Japanese theater.

There was a tense moment. Seeing no Chinese in the car, but instead two husky foreigners in uniform, they gave way to wild, hysterical laughter, passed on.

As I looked out over that dark, seething mass, I could not believe that we were really in Hongkew. The Hongkew that I knew was a fascinating spot filled with bowing, smiling people.

We often went down there on sukiyaki parties. We would laugh as we took off our shoes and slipped into Japanese cloth sandals before walking over the thick mattings of some picturesque establishment, to a room reserved for us. A pretty little Japanese girl in a gay kimono would serve us rice from big wooden buckets, would cook the thin sliced beef and diced onions, cabbage, leeks, mushrooms, over a charcoal fire which glowed in the center of a little low table, about which we sat cross-legged on the matting or—any of us who might be very fussy or very fat— on a pillow. And when we left the whole family, from the refined-faced elderly grandfather, somewhat bent in his striped silk kimono, to the cunning bright-eyed youngsters, would bow us out.

"Sayonara, sayonara," they would say.

And there was the Japanese flower market, with the friendly, most polite little man from whom I always bought Japanese iris bulbs. I remember a dwarf quince tree he had given me. It was twisted—gnarled. War did that to people! And there was a young chap who for years had been waiting on me at a cloth shop on Boone Road. I took the children to him to be measured for kimonos. On the last trip I had ordered a kimono of dark blue cotton cloth on which gay dragonflies frisked for Johnny, one which was covered with little fans for Patty.

My thoughts of this delightful Hongkew were sharply shattered. John threw on the brakes. In front of us three or four rowdies were beating up an old Chinese woman. As we stopped to intercede, they threw her aside.

Chinese snipers had by that time found hiding places on roofs, in the second stories of buildings, and we speeded on. The lights of Shanghai's gay white way were still blazing – the music from her cabarets and night clubs was still echoing from the brightly lighted dance palaces, when we crossed the Garden Bridge and turned onto Nanking Road. It could not be real. Carefree, happy foreigners and smart Chinese dancing to the lilt of the latest Broadway dance hits, while less than an hour away men, women, and children were being terrorized – tortured – killed.

We stopped at the Little Club for a cup of coffee. A party of friends sat at a table near the door. We joined them. They did not even know that the Japanese had marched on Chapei.

On our way home we drove to the cable office, and I sent off a wire to Barry Faris asking the International News Service for instructions.

About five o'clock that morning the telephone rang. A friend living in the penthouse of one of the smart new apartment houses of the city was on the wire.

"The Japanese are bombing Chapei!" she cried excitedly. "The Chinese city is on fire. We can see it all from our terrace. It's pretty grim, but I thought you might wish to come over and watch it. You and John have breakfast with us." And we did.

Smoke and flames soared mountain-high over Chapei. Against that steel, murky sky, bombers from a Japanese airplane carrier in the river were flying—planes of death. In spellbound horror we watched the bombs being dropped on the positions held by the Chinese troops. We heard the booming explosions. In even greater horror—if there are degrees of horror—we watched other planes drop incendiary bombs upon the homes of the thousands of helpless, unwarned civilians who were trapped in that roaring inferno. At the drop of a bomb, a great sheet of fire would spread out like the flamecolored pleatings on a dancer's chiffon skirt, and then be lost in swirling smoke clouds.

"We were down there just a few hours ago," I whispered as the windows of the penthouse shook with the impact of every explosion.

"The cruelty of it!" someone muttered. "Bombing those unwarned thousands. They haven't a chance!"

I remembered this scene just recently when reading Henry L. Stimson's book *The Far Eastern Crisis*. Mr. Stimson, who was at that time Secretary of State, describes the bombing of Chapei as "an act of inexcusable cruelty which has stained the Japanese record at Shanghai for all time."

We paced the terrace in the cold January wind. Comments seemed futile, childish.

Slowly that scene before me became personally real, threatening to our little boy and girl. I was frightened and cried: "Those planes may fly over our home—those flames may spread into the Settlement! That fighting is taking place only a short distance away. What if we are all caught up in it?"

"By Jove, she's right!" broke in our host. "I'm for all women and children getting straight away. Why don't you girls go together?" he asked, turning to his wife. "Have a little holiday in Manila. Go to the Carnival."

The Carnival is to Manila what the Mardi Gras is to New Orleans. And so it was arranged.

After a time we went home. John wanted to catch a few winks before going downtown to his office—not that there was really much use in going. Business would once again be dead. The Sino-Japanese war definitely ended the boom begun in 1928. The local war and the world depression, which were only beginning to be felt in the Orient, had ushered in lean years, and only in 1931 was the city getting back to normal so far as foreign business in the Orient was concerned.

Mademoiselle took Pat and Johnny to school as usual that morning. I remember giving them an extra squeeze as I kissed them goodbye. Pat was so sweet with her curls blowing—her little chubby face glowing pink above the fur of her white rabbit coat. She was only five. Johnny was two years older. He was thrilled over the *boom – boom – boom* of the cannon. He was proud of his dad in uniform. In fact, Johnny was all for the war and could not see any possible reason for going to school.

At the corner sandbag barricades were being erected. Less than half a block from our house British soldiers were pitching tents and were unloading kitchen supplies. They were placing enormous searchlights to scan the distance and the heavens. They were setting up antiaircraft guns. On down the street at the Avenue Joffre corner, French soldiers were completing a fort on which guns were mounted. And beyond our house, out in the country just east of the railroad, the farthermost boundary guard was being strengthened. Additional barbed-wire entanglements were being laid—just in case retreating troops should menace the back door of the city. No wonder life had suddenly become exciting, thrilling to seven-year-old Johnny.

Even as they started off to school, a company of Fusiliers came marching by our house. A towering British chap with a leopard skin draped across his chest led the band. There were strains of martial music, the tramp of soldiers' feet, the boom of cannon in the distance, the whir of airplanes – and a sky to the north glowing crimson through black smoke.

Amah and I went at once to the box room to sort out the children's summer clothes. We should need white things for the tropics.

"How fashion Manila so hot wintertime, Missie?" Amah was asking as we packed the children's trunk.

The houseboy came to the door with a cablegram.

Only then I remembered the wire I had filed to Internews during the hectic hours of the previous night. Although but a few hours ago, it seemed ages in the light of all that had happened, was happening. The reply to my message read:

CONTACT JOHN GOETTE ARRIVING EXPEKING.
WORK WITH HIM. FILE ONE HUMAN INTEREST
STORY DAILY STRESSING WOMANS ANGLE UNTIL
FURTHER ADVICE LUCK
INTERNEWS

I stood in the center of all that packing and stared at the cable.
"What thing? What thing, Missie?" asked Amah anxiously.

Suddenly the mist seemed to lift. I was no longer caught up in the tentacles of terror. Instead excitement swept over me – the old familiar journalistic thrill. Cabled assignments arriving from New York! Rushing copy on the wire to make the deadline. There was now some point in staying on in war-torn Shanghai; I was going to be among those covering the war.

"We no go Manila, Amah," I answered. "We stay Shanghai. Plenty foreign soldiers have got this side. No trouble come Patty, Johnny."

"More better you talkee Master," scolded Amah. "How fashion Missie one time talkee go, next time talkee no go?"

"Because I was going soft, feminine, motherly — something, I don't know what, Amah," I answered as I rushed to the telephone to talk the matter over with John.

"Frankly," he answered over the phone, "I have never thought there was any immediate need for you to leave. The defense authorities have the situation well in hand."

I started in to town to contact John Goette at the Cathay Hotel.

We lived about five miles from the Bund, from the Cathay Hotel. Out in our neighborhood all was quiet as usual except for the incessant firing of distant guns, the explosions of bombs which were still being dropped upon Chapei. But after I passed the old Bubbling Well Temple the streets became more and more crowded. A whole city was on the move. Some two hundred and fifty thousand refugees were fleeing from burning Chapei, from terrorized Hongkew, into the International Settlement. On they came, their pitiful household possessions piled on rickshaws, on carts, on wheelbarrows, on bicycles, on their backs. But the possessions saved were few: in most cases just rolls of bedding, chests of clothes. Those Chinese had been lucky to escape that inferno with their lives. On they came, penniless, homeless, hungry, seeking refuge in the protected foreign settlements. And the men on guard at the iron gates let all unarmed Chinese into the fold.

The lobby of the Cathay Hotel teemed with excitement.

Everyone was loud in praise of the Chinese soldiers who were holding their lines, holding the North Station and Chapei, never yielding an inch despite the terrific drubbing the Japanese were giving them. No one knew how long the war would last. The Nineteenth Route Army, under command of General Tsai Ting-kai, held the limelight. Because of its proximity to Shanghai when the Japanese struck, the Nineteenth Route Army overshadowed the Fifth Route Army, which was made up of Chiang Kai-shek's crack Eighty-seventh and Eighty-eighth divisions.

Politically China was on the verge of civil war at the time. Chiang Kai-shek was out of office, his resignation having been accepted by the Nanking Government in December, 1931. Chiang's request that he be sent to the Shanghai front was refused by the Nanking Military Council, from fear that such a command would strengthen his position politically. Chiang was in a fume on the sidelines, his hands tied though he did what he could. (During the months ahead, however, when Japan's aggression in Manchuria and northern China became bolder and the Communist armies in central China pushed their activities, even Chiang's political enemies in the Nanking Government were forced to acknowledge that the Generalissimo was the only man who could cope with the desperate situation. On March 6, 1932, Chiang was reappointed chairman of the National Military Council and again became commander-in-chief of the National Armies.) The Shanghai war brought to China the realization that she must heal party differences at once, unite her forces, if she would face the aggressor, Japan.

Forty days of war — a mere fragment of time; but in that brief moment New China came to realize that, granted time, she had the possibilities of developing strength which would give her a real place among the nations.

The war at Shanghai was fought in a blaze of publicity. Correspondents and cameramen from Europe and America poured into the city. Floyd Gibbons and Karl H. von Wiegand arrived from New York, John Goette from Peking, to complete the I.N.S. staff in Shanghai. Every correspondent had a favorite lookout post. Almost every skyscraper had its correspondent. Peggy Hull (Mrs. Harvey Deuell), an old friend, who arrived as correspondent for the New York *Daily News*, and I "discovered" a marvelous lookout post in a flour mill. It was hazardous, but from its vantage point we could watch the progress of battle through field glasses.

Japan's military operations about the city were on the whole disastrous. The cost to Japan in marines and soldiers was high; the financial drain, heavy. She aroused Chinese resistance; strengthened the boycott against her; made plain her program of aggression against China. She stirred up world opinion. The League of Nations, together with the United States, talked of an economic boycott against Japan. The talk was faint, but Tokyo heard. Incidentally the fighting at Shanghai was a smoke screen to Japan's further penetration into Manchuria; and she was willing to talk peace. Japan was feeling her way — testing the Powers — seeing how far they would permit her to work her way into China.

A conference of Ministers sitting at Shanghai and a Committee of Nineteen acting for the League of Nations worked out a settlement of sorts. The armistice was signed on May 5, 1932.

In January of that year, in view of the Japanese military operations in Manchuria, Henry L. Stimson, American Secretary of State, drafted an important note which set forth plainly America's attitude in the complicated problems born of the crisis in the Far East. In the note, presented to China and to Japan, Great Britain, and France, Mr. Stimson stated in part:

The American Government continues confident that the work of the neutral commission [the Lytton Commission] recently authorized by the Council of the League of Nations will facilitate an ultimate solution of the difficulties now existing between China and Japan.

But in view of the present situation and of its own rights and obligations therein, the American Government deems it to be its duty to notify both the Government of the Chinese

EDNA LEE BOOKER

Republic and the Imperial Japanese Government that it can not admit the legality of any situation *de facto* nor does it intend to recognize any treaty or agreement entered into between those governments, or agents thereof, which may impair the treaty rights of the United States and its citizens in China, including those which relate to the sovereignty, the independence. or the territorial and administrative integrity of the Republic of China, or to the international policy relative to China, commonly known as the Open Door policy; and that it does not intend to recognize any situation or agreement which may be brought about by means contrary to the covenants and obligations of the Pact of Paris of August 27, 1928, to which treaty both China and Japan, as well as the United States, are parties.

American residents in China were gratified by Stimson's stand.

We looked to Great Britain for "possible cooperation," for "a sympathetic understanding." England had large interests in China. The Open Door policy had been determined by Lord Salisbury in cooperation with John Hay. Lord Balfour had worked for the Nine Power Treaty at the Washington Conference. Also, Anglo-American relations were cordial. Both governments had signed the Kellogg-Briand Pact. We in China were stunned by the British communiqué regarding the American note. It was as a snub.

The Japanese were jubilant. Honeyed words of praise for Great Britain's policy filled the editorial pages of Japan's newspapers. Japan laughed in the sleeve of her kimono, as she played England off against America. England was favored then, America reviled; even as today, seven years later, America is being courted because of desired trade treaties, and England stoned.

303

In part the British Government reply read:

Since the recent events in Manchuria, the Japanese representatives at the Council of the League of Nations at Geneva stated on the 18th October that Japan was the champion in Manchuria of the principle of equal opportunity and the Open Door for the economic activities of all nations. Further, on the 28th December, the Japanese Prime Minister stated chat Japan would adhere to the Open Door policy, and would welcome participation and cooperation in Manchurian enterprise.

In view of these statements, his Majesty's Government have not considered it necessary to address any formal note to the Japanese Government on the lines of the American Government's note, but the Japanese Ambassador in London has been requested to obtain confirmation of these assurances from his Government.

America was left standing alone—Sir John Simon turned a deaf ear to Stimson's suggestion, said Japan was moving Russiawards. America alone saw the handwriting on the wall and was prepared to do something about it.

That thought-provoking book *If, or History Rewritten* (book has title in quotes) was published about this time. If the Moors in Spain Had Won, If Napoleon Had Escaped to America, If Booth Had Missed Lincoln are the titles of a few of the chapters. I would add another "If": What would be the status of the Far East today if the Democracies had strongly backed up the American Government's note of January 7, 1932, to Japan?

Japan's successful grab of Manchuria paved the way for the seizure of Abyssinia by Italy, Czechoslovakia and Poland by Germany, the march on Finland by Russia and so on and on—to end who knows where?

EDNA LEE BOOKER

By the end of May the Japanese troops, with the exception of some two thousand left on regulation guard duty, had sailed for Japan; the barbed-wire barricades around the foreign settlements had been taken down, and Shanghai, resilient as a rubber ball, bounded back to life.

In Nanking, China's national leaders took stock.

Manchuria had been seized by Japan, and Nanking was faced with the grim realization that neither the League of Nations nor any individual nation was going to do anything about it. Bitter medicine, but China took it.

Old Cathay would have sat with her hands folded resignedly within her silken sleeve bands and waited on Heaven. Not so, New China.

In November, 1932, the National Government announced a policy of "self-help."

The Kuomintang was reorganized and a new Nanking began to rise on age-old foundations. A stupendous program of national reconstruction and rehabilitation under a National Economic Council was launched. The program stressed highway and railway construction, conservancy, public health, mass education, rural rehabilitation, currency stabilization, industrial development. The years immediately following saw China making great strides on many fronts into modernization, and the Republic entering upon the most progressive and prosperous years in its history.

As chairman of the Military Affairs Commission, General Chiang Kai-shek intensified his efforts to bring about a united national front against the day when China, as a nation, must meet an aggressive Japan.

He set about placating political enemies of the Kuomintang, bringing revolting factions into line, pressing his campaigns against the Chinese Communist armies in order to speed unification. Chiang worked against time to set China's great house in order, to build up her agriculture, industrial, and financial strength, to recruit armies and develop an air force.

"Give China ten years of peace," was the prayer of Chiang Kai-shek. She was to be granted but five.

It was during these years that New Life came to China.

PART III
NEW LIFE
(1933-1940)

NEW LIFE—Chiang Kai-shek's great vision of a rebirth for the Chinese masses, for the Chinese nation.

The New Life Movement began as a provincial experiment at Nanchang, Kiangsi Province, on February 19, 1934. On that day Generalissimo Chiang, outstanding military figure of China, stood before the world as the nation's reform leader as well.

I made a short trip to Nanchang to attend his New Life Conference and to talk with the Chiangs regarding the movement.

Conservative old Nanchang was astir. The city was experiencing its first American equivalent to "Clean-Up Week." Although many scoffed, the slogan "New Life for China" made an instant appeal to the progressive leaders, students; and from neighboring provinces government officials, civic leaders, student groups, Christian workers, trade-union representatives poured into Nanchang.

"We must set China's house in order if we would drive the invader from Manchuria," thundered Chiang at the fifty thousand persons attending the historic mass meeting at Nanchang.

"Why is a New Life for China needed?" demanded the Generalissimo even as a prophet of old. "I will tell you."

And tell he did.

"The general psychology of our people today can be described in one word—spiritlessness," Chiang hurled the words at his auditors.

"As a result, officials tend to be dishonest and avaricious; the masses are undisciplined and callous; the adults are ignorant and corrupt; the youth become degraded and intemperate; the rich become extravagant and luxurious, and the poor, mean and disorderly. Naturally, it results in the complete disorganization of social order and national life.

"Consequently, we are not in a position either to prevent or to remedy natural calamities or disasters caused from within or invasions from without. The individual, society, and the whole country are now suffering. It is, therefore, absolutely necessary to get rid of these backward conditions and to start to lead a new and rational life."

Chiang laid down precepts, working rules of moral conduct for the nation, which he summed up in four ancient virtues of Confucius: Li—regulated attitude of mind as well as of heart; I—right conduct in all things; Lien—honesty in personal, public, and official life; Ch'ih—real self-consciousness based on integrity and honor. He modernized, westernized their application.

Chiang laid emphasis on China's need for an intense patriotism; for good moral, hygienic, and economic habits; for a sense of responsibility toward the community; for pride in orderly, clean homes and civic places such as streets, parks, gardens; for social service as expressed in agitation against opium smoking, foot-binding; for free clinics and schools; for campaigns against corruption and squeeze, and so on. . . .

I was amazed at the simplicity of the initial step proposed by Chiang in his campaign of social regeneration. Good manners and cleanliness were to be first taught. To this end he harnessed the energies of hundreds of thousands of students.

A few evenings later, during a monster New Life parade, thousands of students marched in formation, bearing on standards illuminated, four-sided lanterns which were covered with inscriptions.

I had seen banners, carried in demonstrations in 1925 and in 1927, which denounced unequal treaties, the foreign concessions, the foreigner as the reason for China's ills. Never before had I read slogans which indicated a desire on the part of the Chinese to set China's house in order from within. China was growing in stature.

A pressman with me translated a number of the inscriptions: "Work harder and spend less," "Acquire habits of orderliness," "Teach others," "Be ready to die for China," "Strive for a spirit of self-sacrifice," "Corrupt officials and squeeze must go," "Be frugal;" "Develop a patriotic and a fighting spirit," "Learn to read," "Start a swat-the-fly-and mosquito campaign," "Be vaccinated against smallpox," "Politeness will carry you far," "Do not spit on the street." Slogans which in themselves spoke of a New China.

There in Nanchang I came to appreciate in part the mental and spiritual growth which were Chiang Kai-shek's, and I renewed my acquaintance with Mayling Soong Chiang.

She was gracious, lovely, full of enthusiasm, poised, sure of herself, very busy. She was unselfishly giving "of her utmost," in service to China. During the years since her marriage the attractive young bride had grown into the beautiful first lady of China. There was a radiance about her, a magnetism, a driving purpose, and she made an important place for herself in Nanking.

The Chiangs lived a full life, a disciplined life. They worked hard, they worked together. Their day began before six in the morning with Bible study and prayer. The Generalissimo did not smoke, or even drink tea or coffee. There were no mah-jongg parties in the Chiang home, nor elaborate social affairs with dancing or cards. They did not go out socially. There was no time.

Yet Madame Chiang could always find time to address a meeting conducted by the foreign missionaries of Nanking, to open a school or an orphanage, to "mother" the sons of men who had been killed fighting for China; to translate Chiang's messages, to consult with him, or act as his interpreter at important conferences; to write articles for the press of the world; to organize women's groups; to receive distinguished callers from many countries; to serve on committee after committee in affairs of government, to fly with her husband during his campaigns against the Red armies, to face death in order to be with him.

Chiang's explanation of the backwardness of the Chinese masses seemed to me most important. He said:

"For hundreds of years the people of China were discouraged from interesting themselves in the affairs of government and were taught, even with the executioner's sword, that the administration of the country was the exclusive concern of the official class.

"The people consequently, through the centuries, gradually ceased to have any interest in government and lapsed, as the rulers desired, into complete disregard of national affairs, confining themselves to seeking the welfare of the family and the clan, and knowing nothing, and caring nothing, about the responsibilities of citizenship, the requirements of patriotism, or the urge of loyalty to the country or its flag.

"In forced conditions such as these, the habits of the great population of China developed along lines quite contrary to those characterizing the peoples of other countries, with the result that when the political window opened (following the establishment of the Republic) they were, in a sense, blinded by the light that suddenly and unexpectedly poured in upon them.

They found themselves without understanding of political or official life, bewildered, owing to lack of universal education."

Psychologically Madame Chiang felt that the masses were ready for the New Life Movement, that under its national banner any number of lesser reform movements which had been groping about, struggling along for many years in scattered centers, would find direction, purpose.

But even as I rejoiced in Chiang's New Life message I remembered a day a few months earlier at Kweifu, far up the Yangtze Gorges, when the weight of ancient customs, of thousand-year-old traditions, of internal disorders was upon me. .. Could old China ever become a new China?

A friend from Los Angeles had arrived for a visit. One night at a dinner Mr. Lansing Hoyt, who had given up a diplomatic career to become president of the Yangtze Rapids Steamship Company, and his wife, Mrs. Josephine Cudahy Hoyt, invited Winifred and me to be guests of the company on a trip up the Yangtze Gorges to Chungking.

For years I had dreamed of making this most spectacular of all trips in China: of journeying fifteen hundred miles straight into the heart of old China, to Chungking[17] in faraway Szechwan.

At Ichang we changed ships, boarded the *Chi Chuen*. That stocky, shallow-draft ship, with its blunt nose and powerful engines, built to conquer the treacherous rapids of the Gorges, spelled adventure. Large American flags were painted on the bridge and on the starboard and port sides as well. Steel shutters, which could be lowered at a moment's notice, protected the bridge. Heavy steel plates lined the deck rails, while the

---

17   Now war capital of the Nationalist Government.

enormous fat funnel resembled a giant round cheese grater, so riddled was it with bullet holes.

"Fall flat in case the Reds start firing from the cliffs when we get into the Gorges," advised the captain. "Not much danger now, however; the government troops are cleaning the bandits and Reds out of the Yangtze valley."

Chiang Kai-shek's campaign against the Communist-bandits began to take on meaning.

This is no place to write of the grandeur of the Gorges; of the swirling, raging rapids, gleaming gold in the sunlight which on bright days penetrates the gloom of the lofty chasms; of the legends and poetry which envelop its overhanging peaks with their temples, caves, and pagodas; of the tales of tragedy, romance, mystery, which every old-timer of the upper river tells. The West falls away there in the heart of China, and only the East, strange, eerie, unfathomable, is real. Danger lurks there, from hidden rocks, from a sudden rise or fall of the river, from the treacherous rapids. The steamers do not travel by night, but seek safety in established anchorages.

Winifred and I were weak from excitement after that first day in the Gorges. The sturdy boat had rocked and panted in every fiber as we passed the first rapid; zigzagged across narrow stretches of tumbling water to avoid jagged boulders; dashed toward a wall of rocks, to be released just in time. Our boatmen had thrown strong wires to bare-backed trackers on the shore who had bent double as they heaved and strained — auxiliary engines. The grandeur of the dark, narrow gorge, with its black, mysterious shadows of late afternoon, cast a spell. The turmoil of surging waters ceased as we tied up at Wushan.

The River Dragon was in an ugly mood the following morning. Thunder rolled from his throat; smoky clouds, from his nostrils; lightning flashed from his eyes. The giant fish which hid in the great rapid was thrashing hungrily about, waiting for a ship to suck down his gullet: That night we reached Kweifu, ancient city that clings high on the cliffs, like a city painted on an ancient scroll. The moon came out, and against its brightness we could see sentries patrolling the top of the massive crenelated wall, a wall whose battlements and watchtowers spoke of a China centuries old. The city gates were closed, barricaded. We heard of General Ho Ong. He and his Red soldiers were somewhere on the river, and who could tell where the "old Ho with the white beard" might strike?

Late the following afternoon we were fired upon.

Winifred and I were on the upper deck, lost in the strange beauty of perpendicular cliffs rising high about us in solemn grandeur, when suddenly from one of the narrow trails cut in those miles of canyon walls came the *rat-a-tat-tat* of machine guns.

"Drop," shouted Winifred. And we made a dive for the deck protected by steel railings.

Our steamer made a perfect target there in the narrow chasm, but the Chinese pilot at the wheel remained as immobile as one of the Buddhas carved in the cliff shrines. His eyes followed the dangerous river currents as if magnetized. He did not move even when a bullet whistled past, and the steel shutters of the bridge were clamped shut by a deck boy. A sharp turn in the stream, and we were safe.

"Only some poor devil taking a few pots at us," the captain explained. "Probably a junk owner whose cargo business has been killed by foreign river steamers, or a boatman whose junk was damaged or perhaps sunk when caught in a steamer's wash. These boatmen of the upper river fight progress. Can't blame them: the steam vessels break their rice bowls."

Suddenly the canyon vibrated with sharp explosions. Again

we dived for the shelter of the steel railings. What now? Were the Reds about to get us? The captain's deep laugh rolled out, and cautiously we lifted our heads.

We were passing a village that nestled at the foot of the cliffs. It was Dragon Boat Festival day, and the entire countryside was stretched along the river bank watching the Dragon Boat races. What a din the firecrackers, drums, and gongs made, as the slim, long boats, with their elaborately carved and painted dragon heads lifted high at the bow, shot downstream!

Our fears were forgotten in this spectacle of old China, for the festival commemorates the death of the scholar Ch'u Yuan who drowned himself in the third century B.C., in despair over the corruption of the government. He was hailed as a great patriot, and. through the centuries the Chinese have made offerings to appease his wandering soul; the boat races are held in memory of that earlier day when every boat in his village raced frantically about trying to locate Ch'u Yuan's body. More than two thousand years ago, yet China remembers.

A day was "ten thousand years" there in the heart of old China. The world was far away, unreal. Inertia, which seemed to emanate from the very river mists, crept over me. I longed to charter a great junk with patched sails and travel slowly, day by day, on and on, into its mysterious reaches. The rhythm of the drums and tom-toms enmeshed my spirit, and I sank into insignificance—but a grain of sand lost in the immensity and solidity of old China.

For thousands of years, from generation to generation, life there in the heart of the Flowery Kingdom has carried on, secret and deep, according to an age-old pattern, a design handed down from the past. Even the people of that upper river seemed aloof, distant, wrapped in tradition. I had watched a master of junkmen dash the blood of freshly killed cocks over the bow of his boat, even as his ancestors, in sacrifice to the river gods before starting on the dangerous, torturous way upriver; had seen village women climb perpendicular cliffs better suited to the chamois, in order to light incense before some protector from mountain landslides; had seen a pagoda being built on a high point as appeasement to the *Feng-shui* of the neighborhood, and cargo junks loaded high with paper cash — the cash to be burned for use in a future world.

Inexplainable forces bordering on the supernatural seemed abroad there in Szechwan — jealous forces, jealous gods.

The captain told of strange illusions, ghostly mirages, which have driven the steam vessels of the foreigner upon the rocks. Late that afternoon, when we went ashore for a short walk, an aged Chinese priest who carried a willow branch was pointed out to me as a member of an order of monks who "walked the souls of the dead" back to their ancestral homes for stipulated fees. And there had been paper charms over doorways and amulets around the necks of naked children.

The weight of that vast China hinterland . . .

Kingdoms and dynasties had risen and fallen, yet the "ten-thousand-year-old" pattern of old China had not changed. A patriot had died in his despair during one troubled period, and his memory had been kept bright by the Dragon Boat Festival (rightly it is the summer solstice); and on the other hand Li Tai Po, poet of the upper Yangtze, had sunk down in the shade of a cypress grove with his jar of wine and sighed:

"Our time seems a disordered dream to me.
Why should my days be passed in struggle?"

What place had such philosophies — despair which seeks consolation in death, resignation which drowns responsibility in

Shanghai social leaders in amateur theatrical production for the benefit of the Chinese Woman's Club and The Child Welfare Association at the International Arts Theater. Left. Mrs. Ing Tang-lee. Right Mrs. Walter Kwok. (Photographs Sanzetti & Skvirsky and Dorothea Bertrand.)

Chinese girls in patriotic service for China in America under the auspices of American Bureau for Medical Aid to China. Top. Mrs. Hilda Yen, niece of Dr. W. W. Yen, and her Good Will ship. Lower left. Miss Virginia Chang (now Mrs. Yu Kien-wen), daughter of H. N. Chang, former Chinese Ambassador to Chile. Lower center. Mrs. Ernest (Averil) Tong, leader of the Chinese Cultural Mission. Lower right. Miss Ethel Chen, granddaughter of Sir Shou-Son Chow, who sang Chinese folk songs in the Mission's production "An Evening at Cathay." (Trans-Pacific News Service.)

the wine cup—in our modern world?

But a twentieth century soldier-statesman, Chiang Kai-shek, was offering China "New Life," was fighting ignorance, superstition.

Like all reform movements, Chiang's New Life program came in for ridicule during those first days. "How can preventing coolies from spitting on the sidewalks, or from turning street drains into open, odoriferous lavatories, affect the political situation?" was asked.

Undaunted by the tradition of the past or by the ridicule of many Chinese politicians, writers and cartoonists, the Chiangs set the machinery for the New Life Movement to work. Progressive leaders, soldiers, students, heads of government departments, Christian workers, and in time even the farmers (who were benefited by improved seeds and stock, as well as governmental loan banks and a certain land readjustment) were back of it.

Who could know that, some four years later, this group would provide the country with a nation-wide machinery which overnight could be used to educate the masses to play their part in the Sino-Japanese war? that New Life would usher in the greatest reconstruction movement modern China had known and an industrial progress which helped to stampede Japan into war?

Aviation came into China on the wings of New Life.

Madame Chiang was an enthusiastic supporter of commercial aviation, and quickly grasped its possibilities.

"One of my first trips by air was with my younger brother," Madame Chiang told me one day. "It was in a small open plane, and I sat on my brother's lap while he flew. We became lost and made a forced landing in a rice field in the heart of the bandit country when night came on."

Then she had journeyed by sampan in order to reach her

husband's camp. She had lived close to the farming people during this time, and had come to know something of their lives and problems.

During a campaign in Fukien against the Reds she flew from the headquarters of the Generalissimo at Chuchow, in southwestern Chekiang, straight into the Communist territory, where she made a secret landing at Kienyang. There, representing the Generalissimo, she received back into the Nationalist fold a number of officers of the Nineteenth Route Army who had rebelled a few months earlier. Her beauty, bravery, and sincerity won their surrender.

Madame Chiang has her own plane, delights in air travel, and has done hard, dangerous flying over uncharted spaces.

The flights of the Generalissimo and Madame Chiang into the distant provinces of the north and northwest in 1934 made history. It was a New Life tour, the first of its kind ever attempted in China, and it became a triumphal trip into ten far interior provinces.

Months later, Madame Chiang told me of the ovations received from the officials, of the gun salutes and the cheers of the multitudes. The interest of the masses was a revelation. At each stop, while the Generalissimo was occupied with the reviewing of troops and the discussion of government policies, Madame Chiang, smiling and friendly, explained the New Life Movement to group after group. The foreign missionaries working in each center were invited to attend and many of them in turn formed Sino-foreign New Life committees. The Chiangs flew to Lanchow in little known Kansu, and the famous General Ma Lin journeyed day and night to receive them. They flew over wastes of desert into Ningsia, land of the Chinese Mohammedans.

Chiang with his plane made strides in the unification of China. Back in Nanking he laid plans for a similar trip into the southwest. Thus the Generalissimo and Madame Chiang became known over the length and breadth of China, and they turn came to have a tremendous understanding of the country and its problems — an understanding which is of greatest importance during the Sino-Japanese war of today.

The building of powerful radio stations at Nanking and later at Chungking for the purpose of broadcasting directly to the people, after the manner of President Franklin D. Roosevelt, aided Chiang in his fight for the unification of China and in the spreading of his New Life doctrines among the masses.

- 2 -

Any newspaper story of China during the past eighteen years must be filled with high lights which spell news. But along with the exciting, stirring times of strife and danger, were days on end of charm and sheer delight.

We looked forward to the summer holidays, holidays given to the sample life in our cottage at Weihaiwei or passed with friends in their home at Shanhaikwan, a quaint city of north China where the Great Wall of China rises straight out of the sea. John, Jr., and Patty had a junk of their own and two boatmen to take them fishing. They had donkeys to ride with other youngsters — French, British, Swiss, Italian, as well as American — in mad gallops down the hard sandy beach to picnic teas on the Great Wall. Or we went up mountain trails, over which the Great Wall rambles like a great dragon, to picturesque temples from whose courtyards we could see far — over the green, unbroken stretches of Manchuria, It was vast and open and soul-satisfying.

We expected to go to Shanhaikwan the summer of 1935 and had even engaged a cottage close to the sea; but there were rumbles of Japanese activities in Manchuria, and we were advised against going. The previous summer we had watched the Japanese landing their goods in that far port, to be smuggled into China proper by rail. So the children and I sailed for America by way of Europe instead. John's home leave was due, and he expected to join us in California a few months later.

I had always wanted to travel by freighter. At the last minute we booked passage on a fast German cargo boat sailing for Bremerhaven, and the trip more than fulfilled my dreams of adventure. We stopped at fascinating out-of-the-way places.

While the ship loaded rice at Saigon we motored into the Cambodian jungles and explored the ruins of ancient Angkor.

At Djibouti, French Somaliland, where we loaded wild African animals for a Berlin zoo, the heat was so intense that one of the ship's cooks died from stroke; a sand storm brought devastating locusts, turning the sky a dull greenbrown; and Patty developed fever. We just made the little train leaving for Addis Ababa, mountain capital of Ethiopia, where we hoped to cool off. We had been in a monsoon in the Indian Ocean for days, knew little of world movements, and I was stunned, when we arrived at Addis Ababa, to see Ethiopian chieftains in gorgeous war trappings assembling for review before Emperor Haile Selassie.

We had reached the capital at the incipiency of the Italian-Ethiopian war!

My busman's holiday was over. News again became my job, and I set to work gathering colorful copy, seeking important interviews. Addis Ababa was exciting, fantastic — but this story is of China. Whenever I think of Emperor Haile Selassie, however, I remember with sadness his confidence and faith in the League of Nations. Until the end he believed that the League would save Ethiopia. I wanted to tell him about Manchuria . . .

We cut our days short in Germany, Italy, France. A tense Europe was no place for children.

The Italian-Ethiopian war was front-page news when we arrived in New York, and for several days I was busy in the East writing articles for the International News Service, for the Central Press Association, and for the Los Angeles *Herald*.

One afternoon when I dropped into the busy International News office, Barry Faris, as kindly, dynamic as ever, startled me by saying, "Why don't you write a book?"

"Write a book?" I echoed.

"Sure, write about your experiences out in China."

I laughed and shook my head. "No, indeed," I answered, "Anyone who lives in China during these hectic days has 'experiences.' Take some of the missionaries, for example."

"It's an assignment," insisted Barry Faris as I left.

But I was on a holiday and gave not a thought to writing a book of "personal experiences."

Summer days in California passed in a happy whirl, and late in July we planned to sail for Shanghai; there had been business complications in Shanghai, and John had been unable to get away. Always on the lookout for news from China, I read a casual mention of a Sino-Japanese "incident" at the Marco Polo Bridge near Peking. I feared those "incidents." There had been a Mukden incident before the seizure of that city, and there had been the "monk incident" in Shanghai before the Japanese attack in 1932. I hastened our packing, arranged an earlier sailing, for I wanted to get home. But within a week China was plunged into war, an undeclared war, according to the press. Japan had struck again!

I received a cable from John: "Delay sailing."

Days of anxious waiting followed, days in which the great port of Shanghai was laid low. I spent a Week with Mrs. John Beaumont, an old friend at the Marine Base in San Diego, where I watched General Beaumont and his marines sail off to reinforce American forces at Shanghai. Mothers and sweethearts and wives (many of whom had been married only after sailing orders had been received), cried as the transport pulled anchor. I too wept, but it was for joy and thankfulness. Thankfulness that additional marines were on their way to protect our homes, business enterprises, and missions in Shanghai.

Months later, the children and I sailed for Shanghai. In the meantime I began work on the "assignment" which Barry Faris had given me. I had to do something! Don Moore of *Cosmopolitan* liked the chapters on the war lords, and *Cosmopolitan* published them. There was an exciting day when I met Mr. Harold Latham, vice president of the Macmillan Company when he was on a western tour, and he too found the beginnings of my book of interest.

But at last the cable to sail for home came. I closed my typewriter, gathered up my partially completed manuscript and spun around in circles. We packed all one day and night and left for Vancouver, British Columbia, the second day. The American liners were not then calling at Shanghai.

- 3 -

A mesmeric wave of apprehension seemed to settle over our liner as she weighed anchor at Victoria, and set off on her run across the North Pacific for Yokohama, Kobe, Shanghai — set out for a Far East straining under the rack of war.

Somewhat mechanically the handful of passengers — officials, business men, foreign correspondents, missionaries, China-evacuated wives, aviators, adventurers — joined in tossing multi-colored serpentines from the decks to relatives and friends on the wharf below. But there was no laughter in that usually gay gesture of farewell. I wondered if they, too, felt that same uncertainty. The lilt was missing from this crossing. It was as if an arc of apprehension stretched right across our route. I did not even unpack my evening gowns.

A few hours out from Victoria we glimpsed a Japanese fishing fleet plying northward toward Alaskan salmon waters.

There was nothing picturesque about that fleet; nothing about those boats to suggest the quaint fishing smacks seen in colorful Hiroshige prints. Instead they loomed on the horizon as powerful, swift-moving craft capable of encroaching on any fishing waters, and built so as to be readily convertible into mine layers and torpedo boats... As I watched those mysterious gray-blue bodies disappearing like a school of giant porpoise into a thickening haze, I remembered a starless night in southern California a few weeks before. From the bluffs above San Pedro I had seen powerful searchlights from United States battleships in the harbor flash out across black waters: diamond baguettes set in ebony. They were seeking out just such alien fishing boats—boats allegedly manned, in part at least, by Japanese naval reserves and topographers.

Four or five days later the Aleutian Islands—glistening mountains of snow and ice—rose in majestic beauty out of the long rollers of a blue Pacific. They are the vanguard of Alaska; next-door neighbors to the Kurile Islands of Japan.

As we neared Yokohama the tension which had been with us throughout the voyage seemed to increase.

A gray transport crowded with Japanese soldiers cut past us. I was reminded of the Italian transports which I had seen in the Mediterranean headed for Eritrean ports during Italy's war on Ethiopia. A whir of bombers overhead caused a rush to the boat deck. In precise formation ships of death were heading Chinawards.

Everyone was nervous about landing.

Two customs men pounced upon the books and magazines in

my two bags as we went through the examination on shore. They discussed the titles. Their manner stiffened as one read aloud with the stilted precision of a child, "The — Red — Book."

The word "Red" hit them, and my magazine was confiscated. A fashion magazine caught their eyes. As I watched those men turning over the pages, I wondered what possible objection there could be to it. In the list of articles whose importation is regarded as most undesirable under the new war regimentation program of the Ministry's bureaucratic machinery, occidental publications now occupy an "honorable" place. Fashion magazines are frowned upon.

"Thoughts of Japanese women must not be disturbed by so-o frivolous books," explained the squat official who wore dark goggles with pale blue rims. "Japanese women live only for glory of Emperor. Japanese women so-o happy wear kimono."

The official's gaze lingered on a page devoted to glamorous negligees and undies.

"Women's underwear — ah-hi 'Women's naked buttocks' — ah-h! 'Naked female thighs,' also unpermitted showing in Hollywood moving picture in Japan."

Later I learned that in speaking of the "buttocks" and "thighs" he was actually quoting from the censorship laws of Japan.

We did not linger in Yokohama; I had a dinner engagement in Tokyo and set about hiring a motor car for the trip (this was still possible). A young chap, whose smart uniform was topped off by a black nose mask, offered his services. He drove a Datsun. A Datsun is Japan's idea of a motor car. It is her creation, her pride, her one ewe lamb. It is a top-heavy, poorly done imitation of a Citroen or an Austin. Hoping to cover son John's scornful "This is a heck of a Lizzie," I waxed chatty and inquired as to the horsepower. The driver regarded me with suspicion.

"So-o sorry," he rebuked me. "Datsun is big Japanese secret."

I engaged instead a middle-aged Japanese driver of the old school and his 1927 Buick.

There is only one motor road from Yokohama to Tokyo, and we made our way along mile after mile of depressing boxlike buildings, whose flat, corrugated-iron roofs are utterly devoid of charm. Great lorries loaded with soldiers and supplies tore past us. Time after time it seemed as if we must be run down. Flashing bayonets and black nose masks — germ-proof masks — rushed along. Every one wears these masks.

I remembered my first drive over that road a year or two before the earthquake. Gentle country laid out in neat rows of vegetables reached away on either side into paddy fields, iris and peony gardens, stretched on and on until lost in a silvery mist which blew in from the sea. Low thatch-roofed cottages with sweet flags waving from the ridgepoles nestled among clouds of delicate peach and plum blossoms. From ago-old temples seen through pines and vermilion torii came the throb of drums, deep and stirring as the Orient itself. Rows of quaint shops were there. It had been an exquisitely peaceful, most courteous, and utterly satisfying road; but it had become industrialized and had surrendered to the fierce military road of today.

I was glad when at last Tokyo loomed in the gathering dusk, for I was curious about this war capital of Japan.

I had seen modernism come to Tokyo. Wide streets and boulevards replaced the quaint byways of the pre-earthquake days. Seven and eight-story buildings of steel and concrete rose where once had been fascinating bazaars. Taxis with raucous horns, motor lorries, trucks, thousands of bicycles, relegated the leisurely moving rickshaws to the country districts. A few cocktail bars and tawdry dance halls crowded in upon the ago-old teahouses and geisha palaces. The mysterious glow of lanterns was forgotten in the novelty of neon lights. The Japanese radio silenced the samisen. Sprawling slums grew up where once were avenues of plum blossoms. Great factories took over industries heretofore carried on in the homes and in small shops. Tokyo had become one of the great cities of the world; and Japan was rated as a first-class power. Her control reached out to cover vast shipping yards whose ocean liners and weighted cargo vessels called at ports great and small. Under the direction of her industrialists, hamlets and towns in the back country of Japan had mush roomed into throbbing factory centers from which her varied merchandise flooded the markets of the world. Her financiers, headed by the five great families of Japan, matched their wits with the Rothschilds and the Morgans. Her militarists, having successfully defied the world in the seizure of Manchuria, at once set about intensifying their preparations for future land grabs; rounding out their program of cold blooded, deliberate aggression, which had been drafted years before. I refer to the Tanaka document.

The year 1937 saw Japan engaged in the China "incident." The military had the ear of the Emperor. Japan was riding the tiger, had been riding him hard for nearly a year when we arrived.

What about the people of Japan? Were they back of the military? Were they on the point of revolting, as certain wishful thinkers in America had prophesied?

Our friends in Tokyo had arranged an informal dinner party. I was full of questions, but when I asked my hostess about Japan at war I was silenced by a look. She suspected her servants were government employees, had reason to believe they reported every conversation, read all papers, examined any papers.

I was reminded of my visit three or four years before to an old Shanghai friend in Italy. After luncheon, when seated on the balustrade overlooking Milan, I had said, in anticipation of receiving some real information, "Now — tell me what you really think of Mussolini." My friend looked about to see if a maid had overheard, then exclaimed, "Dio mio!"

People in Italy did not discuss the government—no more do they in Japan.

After dinner we went down to the Ginza, the so-called Gay White Way of Tokyo. On my last visit, walking along the Ginza (modernized though it was) had been fun. Happy, carefree, well dressed Japanese had crowded the street, the bazaars, restaurants, motion picture theaters, and you met members of the international community and tourists from the ships, sauntering along. Now I saw only a few Japanese, and they moved by, silent and unsmiling. We did not meet any foreigners. What with earthquakes, war regulations, restrictions, "spy weeks," lack of business, many of the Americans and British had pulled up stakes and sailed for home.

Neon lights gleamed overhead, but they seemed as futile as illuminations on a deserted beach pike during the off season.

Doleful strains of Japanese martial music attracted us to a cinema entrance. The billboard showed Japanese airmen blasting Chinese soldiers to death on the Great Wall. Later we visited a theater. Here the play was of war—a revue of sorts, with Japanese girls marching on in Nazi, Fascist, Nipponese uniforms. They sang the national songs of Germany and Italy, gave the Nazi salute, and there were German, Italian, and Japanese flags everywhere.

In a shop selling materials, we came across a sign which (translated) read,

Buy no more American cotton,
Buy Japanese cotton from Shantung.
Buy no more Australian wool,
Buy Japanese wool from Manchukuo.

A radio announcer was broadcasting war news in a bookstall. According to him the honorable soldiers of Dai Nippon were advancing on every front. The handful of Japanese in the shop showed no particular interest.

Suddenly a boyish voice called out. Across the room I saw John, Jr., in the hands of two Japanese officials. My throat became so dry I could not speak; but one of the men in our party, an old Japanese hand, inquired as to his offense.

The officer flourished a cartoon before us. John, Jr., who has an unholy gift as well as a passion for caricature, had drawn a picture of a Japanese policeman standing in the doorway. A single line of whiskers stretched from ear to ear by way of the chin, while his nose mask was worn at a rakish angle.

· I could only express my feeling in a glance of agonized appeal. "Why," I asked John with my eyes, "why, with sketches of policemen from all over the world in your notebook, why did you have to draw one in Japan?"

He had sketched tall, bronzed Sikhs in red turbans in Shanghai, sturdy brown Igorot police in short coats and Gstrings, up in Baguio, Arabs in flowing white robes patrolling the Suez Canal on camels, fierce gendarmes in Paris, stalwart Beefeaters at the Tower in London, an Irish cop all smiles in New York — and now this Japanese!

"We'll have to get in touch with one of our American officials unless we can explain things satisfactorily, I'm afraid," someone offered. "I have known a number of foreigners who have been taken up to the Dangerous Thoughts station for less."

It seemed incredible that the drawing of a boy of thirteen should be taken seriously! Then I remembered the printed warnings against sketching as well as taking photographs, which were posted on the boat. Question after question. I answered them all, and the officials wrote my responses down in their books. Our passport was examined, and the fact that I was a journalist discussed at length.

But not for nothing has John, Jr., grown up in the Far East. In the midst of the questioning he bowed politely and presented one of the men a most flattering sketch of himself. Surprisingly he bowed in return. Then John, Jr., set to work on a second. Dangerous Thoughts official or not, the Japanese struck a pose. A final dash — another bow — and the second officer received his sketch. There were more bows, a pleasant "*Sayonara*" (Goodbye), and we went on our way! I was limp.

We had arrived during "National Spy Week." A Wartime Thoughts Control Exhibition, organized by the Cabinet's Information Bureau of Tokyo, was being shown at the Takasimaya department store. It was soon to begin traveling about Japan very much as the old Kickapoo Indian medicine show with its quack medicines moved about America in the nineties.

Its purpose was to expose to a credulous Japanese world the so-called tricks of foreign spies (from the United States, England, France, and Russia).

During our stay in Tokyo I saw long processions of school children filing into and out of the exhibition. They were required to write essays on foreign spies, to draw posters illustrating their activities, and to listen to lectures on the subject. This education of the children of Japan in antiforeignism was to me very depressing.

Enormous maps of the Far East, with the ever growing Empire of Japan marked by lights, were a feature of the exhibition. I had never really appreciated the size of that empire. The lights blazed from the frigid north of Manchukuo westwards to inner Mongolia, covered Korea and a large section of China, centered in Japan proper — then took in Formosa, and stretched, a formidable Asiatic barrier of two thousand islands, southwards to the equator.

Other exhibitions going out from Tokyo depicted the rich homelands offered in China for Japanese families. Brides were wanted for soldiers. Inducements were offered for colonizers of lands from which the Chinese have been driven by the tens of thousands. Provision had been made even to free convicts who would settle in the newly acquired lands, doing their bit for Dai Nippon.

On every hand I heard discussions of Japanese monopolies in China — monopolies which, if achieved, would effectively close the Open Door.

There were astonishingly few outward signs of conflict. I had come with an undefined conviction that there would be concrete evidence of war strain — perhaps Freda Utley's book was responsible — and went about expecting to see street riots being suppressed by the police, evidence of an undercurrent of unrest which would break forth in revolution. But no. The millions of Tokyo seemed to have settled down to the business of war with China in a matter-of-fact, unhysterical manner. They were cogs — pinched, heavily taxed cogs, to be sure, but cogs which worked in rhythm with the powerful, well organized, most efficient war machine. Eighteen months later however I was to sense unrest, hunger, revolt.

"What do the women of Japan think of the war with China?" I asked a Japanese woman acquaintance.

She explained: "From the time a mother nurses her first son, she is taught to regard him, not as a son, but as a loyal subject to Japan and a follower of the Emperor. She tells him stories of the heroes of old Japan; she teaches him the glory of dying for the Emperor. Naturally, when a mother raises her son for the Empire, she sees in a call to war but a fulfillment of destiny.

Intense patriotism is fed into the child with his mother's milk. This same patriotism is causing parents to sell their daughters as honorable comforters for the Japanese soldiers sent abroad."

"Honorable comforters?" I questioned.

"Hundreds of Japanese village girls are being sent to Manchukuo and north China for the pleasure of the soldiers," she explained. (I saw a boatload of these fresh country girls sail out from Kobe a few days later.)

That evening I accompanied her to a meeting of more than one hundred girls conducted by a Japanese Christian worker. To all appearance the girls were gathering for lessons in flower arrangement.

They were young, pink-cheeked girls, and in their colorful kimonos they were as lovely as the blossoms they handled. I slipped off my pumps in the hallway, then entered the reception room, where I was seated on the thick-matted floor before a low table. It was fascinating to learn something of this art of flower arrangement, an art which, even in wartime, Japan is teaching her daughters along with the tea ceremonial.

After a time the girls began to slip away to an upper room, an assembly room. Downstairs the rooms were closed. The lights were extinguished. By the glow of a lantern I followed the others. The girls had gathered to pray for peace. For more than an hour they remained there knelt in silent prayer. It was most impressive.

This was my first glimpse below the surface.

The Japanese woman told me of the government organization of ten million Japanese women for war duty. In every city, town, and countryside, the women are enrolled by the military. They are required to make a semimonthly contribution to an official who comes to the door and collects. The contribution is in proportion to their means.

Whenever troops are dispatched, women are summoned to the station or wharf to wave farewell to the men. They carry flags made of paper, with the emblem of the Rising Sun stamped on only one side (an economy measure), and wear patriotic aprons over their kimonos, which are "honorably shabby." On a number of occasions I saw these groups of several hundred women waiting at stations, wharfs, crossroads, to greet the troops.

And once at Kobe I saw them receiving the little white boxes containing the ashes of soldiers who had died in China for the glory of the Emperor.

There was little expression on their faces.

So far as I could learn, only a small number of middle and upper-class women who had received western education, a larger number of Christian women, and certain suppressed Communist groups take exception to Japan's war with China. For the most part the masses of women follow blindly the orders sent out by the military. All their lives they have obeyed, like their grandmothers for generations before them.

I visited a school attended by young boys. Their textbooks told of the sacred origin of "holy" Japan. The militarists are playing up these old beliefs as national propaganda.

Millions of Japanese children are today being taught that the Emperor (God) feels that it is his sacred duty to protect, not only the "divinely conceived" islands of Japan, but all of the misguided peoples of the outer world—the "Under Heaven." They are told that, if any unlawful peoples attempt to hinder the actions of their Emperor, he must apply force. I saw these boys marched to a Shinto shrine about eight o'clock one morning. They bowed before that unpainted, unadorned temple, mystically silent among the pines, erected to the souls of warriors who had died "tranquilizing" China.

While I watched, a steady stream of Japanese men on their

way to their offices appeared and paid homage. A busload of sight-seers under the guidance of a brisk Japanese girl stopped on their tour. More processions of school children filed past.

Out near the entrance of the temple I saw a Japanese woman collecting stitches for her *Sennin-musubi,* or "One Thousand Persons' Knot," band. She was a plain little woman in dark kimono, her hair drawn into a simple knot at the back of her neck.

Each woman entering the towering temple gate paused to take a stitch in the amulet against sudden death. They did not cut the threads, but broke them; for if the thread should be cut by metal, a metal ball would be attracted to the soldier wearing the band. (Weeks later in Wuchang, across the river from Hankow, China, I was to see a number of these amulets which had been taken from the bodies of Japanese shot down in battle. One worn by an air pilot was encased in a bag containing dried peppers.)

Several of these early morning worshipers paused at a bazaar in the temple grounds. Chatting merrily they purchased for a few sen a vivid pink silk handkerchief showing the figure of a Chinese soldier being blown into bits — bits which splashed blood-red against its surface.

I noticed a number of women carrying their bundles wrapped in *furoshiki* (squares of silk or cotton cloth), which were highly decorated with cannon, bombers, machine guns: and with horrible scenes of carnage and death. They sickened me.

We traveled from Yokohama to Kobe by fast deluxe train. We passed signboard after signboard, miles of them planted along the tracks, on which painted flags of Japan, Germany, and Italy stood out in sharp relief.

Wishing to see something of the country during wartime, we stopped at a village for a few days. Fuji rose in all its majesty against a blue sky, but there was no beauty in the scene for me.

Factories of war belched out smoke at the base of the sacred mountain.

The scene from our rooms in the quaint Inn of the Dragonfly, however, was one of exquisite beauty.

In the valley below, rice paddies stretched on and on like little brown and green patches of an old-fashioned crazy quilt — oblong, square, triangular, round — so closely cultivated that the stubble hedges outlining them appeared to be but the threads of the cross-stitch. Women — old women, for there are no longer any young faces in the village — like blue-coated figures in a *nishiki-ye* (brocaded picture), worked in the fields. An old farmer, whose three sons were fighting somewhere in China, bowed before the shrine of Daikoku, the happy god of wealth and the patron saint of the farmers. Despite Japan's veneer of bayonets and steel, her masses are stolidly superstitious — superstitious in a heavy, serious way — and would never dream of playing a joke on their gods, or making amusing puns at their expense as do the Chinese. Nearby, a waterfall blew its sparkling spray into the sunshine.

A young wife had committed suicide among the ferns and rocks at its base a few days before, I learned. The village police found her lying there, correct, even in death, to the ancient traditions. Her glossy black hair was arranged in high swirls; her flowered kimono was carefully bound below her knees so as to keep its folds in place. In her throat was a deep dagger wound. She had committed suicide in the name of patriotism. Word had been received in the village that her husband, a soldier, had been taken prisoner at Hsuchow. Honorable soldiers do not allow themselves to be captured. They perform hara-kiri rather than bring the disgrace of their imprisonment upon their Emperor. She had been scorned by the other women in the village, and she had wiped out her husband's dishonor, saved the family name

Upper left. United States Marines on the Bund, Shanghai during the Sino-Japanese war, 1937. Upper right. Admiral Harry E. Yarnell, Commander-in-Chief of the American Asiatic Fleet, discussing plans with General John Beaumont, Commander of the U.S. Marines. (Courtesy U.S. Marine Corps.) Lower left. War refugees fleeing from burning Chapei into the International Settlement. (Photograph Richard Hubert.) Lower right. Burning of Chapei (Courtesy U.S. Marine Corps)

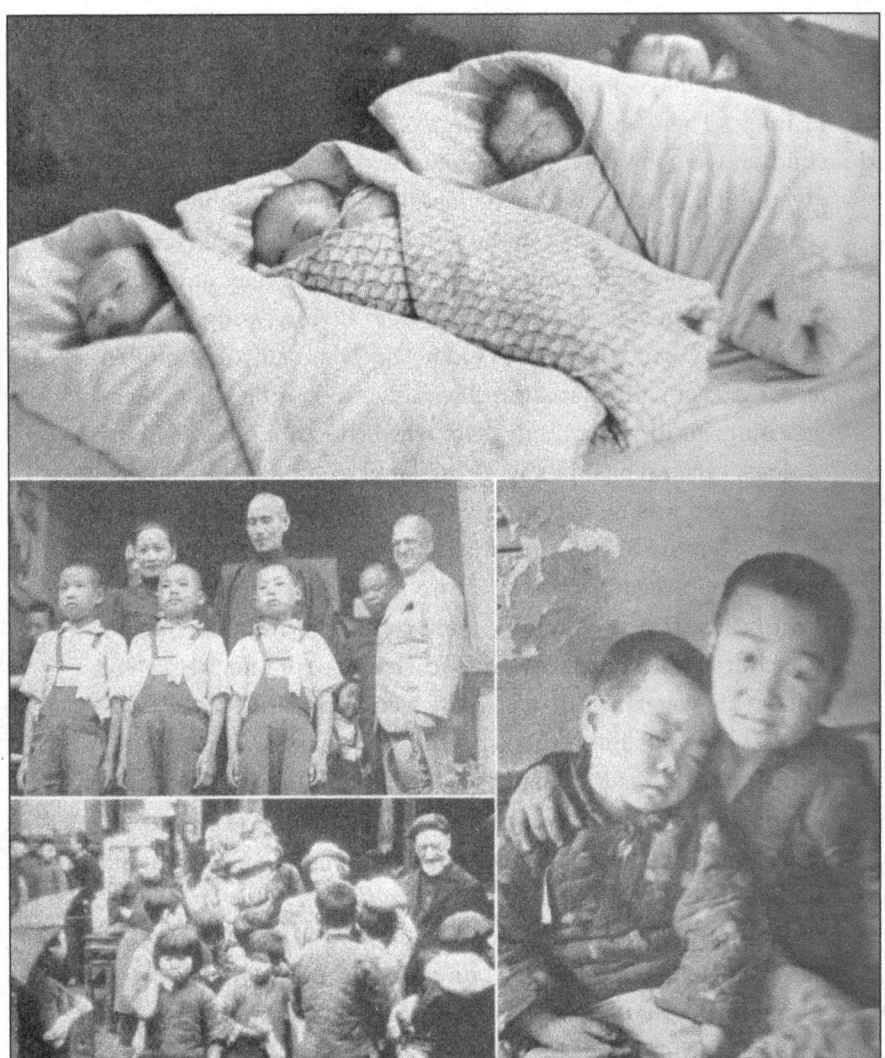

Top. War victims cared for under the direction of Madame Chiang Kai-shek with support from the Church Committee for China Relief, the Bowl of Rice Fund, and the United Council for Civilian Relief. (Trans-Pacific News Service.) Middle left. War orphans and their benefactors: Madame Chiang Kai-shek, Generalissimo Chiang, and Mr. W. H. Donald, close friend and unofficial adviser to Chiangs. Bottom left. Father Jacquinot de Besange and the author on a tour of the Nantao Refugee Zone, founded by Father Jacquinot. (Photograph Richard Hubert.) Bottom right. Orphans of the storm, after bombardment of their village. (Trans-Pacific News Service.)

for her sons. The Japanese press acclaimed her action.

In that village I saw more of the pinch of war than I had seen in Tokyo. There were few men left, or boys over fourteen. Little children were marched to the Shinto shrine; and at school were given military drills with wooden guns. At the bathhouse, the center of community life, radio announcers told of the victories of Japan's honorable armies. Any villagers who may have once owned foreign-style leather shoes, were then wearing wooden geta or straw sandals. But this did not spell hardship. It is only in recent years that the Japanese have worn shoes of leather. There was no meat to be had, but there was fish in abundance. Skins of dogs, cats; rabbits, rats were prepared as linings for soldiers' coats. There was no cotton or woolen cloth in any of the small bazaars, but there were substitutes. Some iron railings and posts had been replaced by cement, the iron being taken for scrap iron. Soya beans, rich in vitamins, were coming in from conquered Manchuria; and there was no food shortage: the markets were full of fish, vegetables, fruits. There were prohibitive restrictions on gasoline, but these did not affect the masses. The greatest hardship, so far as the small home workers was concerned, was the difficulty in getting certain raw materials, due to import restrictions. In consequence substitutes are used, and the goods are poor in quality.

We went on by train to Kobe. As we wound through the picturesque mountain country—how lovely it is in the springtime!—I jotted down a few notes for my journal. I was writing of drifted snow in the crevices of high peaks, of waterfalls, of thatched-roof houses perched high on hillsides terraced with tea bushes, squatty as mushrooms, of any bit that pleased my fancy.

A hiss from son John, Jr., warned me of trouble.

A "Dangerous Thoughts" official stood beside me. He bowed,

asked for my passport, also for "the writings." Without a word I gave him my notes.

After a time the official again appeared, bowing politely. "Ah," he said, "you are a poet! You write so lo-ve-ly poetry about our so beautiful country."

The stigma of being a journalist was gone!

In Kobe I saw Japanese families starting off for China, for conquered Shanghai, Nanking, Peking. They were jubilant, full of the get-rich-quick spirit. Dreams of conquest, of empire building are held before the people of Japan, preached daily to young Japan.

There was a boy of eleven at a cake shop there in Kobe. He had just returned from Shanghai, where he had served his country as a spy. Dressed as a Chinese urchin, he had secured information for the military map-makers. He was a hero! And there was an older boy who told me that his father and mother must commit hara-kiri of disgrace if he should object to his country's holy war.

We reached Nagasaki late in the afternoon. A shipbuilding plant loomed against a sunset sky. It was enclosed in miles of matting, and all shipbuilding operations within were shut off from public view. Here too I saw the flags of Japan, Germany, and Italy.

A Japanese on the boat explained that this was Japan's year of the Tiger. I remembered certain wild dogs in China, northern cousins of the family of red dogs of India, of which Kipling sang. Dogs of this breed fight tigers in great bands, using guerrilla tactics. They wear out the tigers, then kill them. . . And I wondered.

- 4 -

Rain swirled about our liner as it made its slow way up the Whangpoo toward Shanghai. We were on deck, eager for our first glimpse of Shanghai's sky line; but, long before we saw the tower of the Cathay looming against a leaden sky, the knowledge that we were returning to a Shanghai very different from the gay, prosperous city we had left many months previously was brought sharply home.

On either side of the river was desolation: aftermath of war. A large portion of Shanghai's great industrial district lay in ugly ruins. Gutted roofs, jagged walls loomed through the rain, mute evidence of the terror which had so recently broken over the city. There was no life about those ruins. It was as if time stood still there.

Patty began to cry.

One afternoon shortly before we sailed for China, we had gone to a children's cinema matinee. The newsreel had shown the bombing of Shanghai. In horror I watched great black clouds of smoke, shot with flame, engulf buildings crashing with the explosion of bombs. Patty became hysterical; John, Jr., joined in the hisses which filled the house. We left at once.

And now on the boat—face to face with the reality of it all— Patty had again broken into sobs. The sight of those crooked walls from which empty windows stared like crazed eyes was too much for her. Only the sight of her dad on the landing wharf, waving to us through the rain, finally quieted her.

When we landed, Patty clung to her father as if she would never let him go. It was only then I realized that she had been fearful for her dad during those weeks in California, where radio commentators and newspaper headlines had recounted frightful events in the Sino-Japanese war over Shanghai.

Rain, which fell from low-hanging, gloomy skies for days after our return, intensified the misery met on every hand in the settlements, and outside the foreign protected areas where all was chaos.

Greater Shanghai was a mass of ruins.

Practically all that was left standing of the teeming port city was the comparatively small foreign protected areas of the International Settlement and the French Concession, with certain outside roads, and a few blocks of the Chinese city bordering the French Concession which had come to be known as the Nantao Refugee Zone.

Later my husband drove me through the war areas of Chapei and the northern and eastern districts.

The sight of endless blocks of sprawling ruins was shattering. Previously two million hard-working Chinese had lived there. Now not a soul was to be seen; not a child or even a wonk dog. Those sodden piles of ruins which stretched so grotesquely in every direction had been mills, filatures, factories, tenements, schools, shops, temples, homes. There was an eerie silence over all.

A Chinese with us explained that the ghosts of all those thousands who had been killed round about hovered there.

He pointed out a partially wrecked terrace from which strange noises, like the clanging of gongs, were heard at night. Innumerable "devils" gathered at the ruins of the North Station after ten o'clock, he said; and Japanese sentries seldom ventured abroad after sundown in those stretches of waste. On certain nights, when the moon was bright, *kuei huo* (devils' fire balls, *ignes fatui*) could be seen bounding down the broken streets and passageways. Japanese guards that followed those will-o'-the-wisp lights were found dead in the morning.

The gutted walls of the splendid Civic Center buildings seemed mockeries of lofty aspirations to me. In their architectural beauty they had pictured the ancient glories of the emperors, but the dreams and hopes of a progressive New China were implanted in their foundations. Less than a month before the outbreak of hostilities, the Greater Shanghai City Government had celebrated its tenth anniversary with a gala twelve-day festival in the Civic Center, and the foreigners as well as the Chinese had shown pride in this splendid achievement of the Kuomintang. Rain swirled in devilish glee through the wrecked wing of the Museum building, which had—oh, so recently! — housed art objects, valuable scrolls and rare volumes of ancient Chinese literature. A sagging telephone wire whined crazily in the wind.

It was too depressing to look further. I wanted to get away from that maze of destruction, back to the comparative normality of the International Settlement.

We went on to a tiffin party given by the Cornell Franklins in honor of Mr. and Mrs. John Gunther.

As we drove up the wide driveway of their spacious grounds and saw the tall, white pillars of their southern colonial home through the trees, the peace and beauty made the morning experience seem but a nightmare.

Judge Franklin, American attorney from Mississippi, former Judge of the first Judicial Circuit Court of Hawaii, was the Chairman of the Shanghai Municipal Council. "Mayor" of International Shanghai, as it were. Yet friends in America had asked me what interest Americans had in *British* Shanghai. Forty years ago they might have asked that question; but as I write Americans hold several of the highest positions in the government of the Settlement, while American business and American money play an important part.

John Gunther, author of *Inside Europe*, was in the Far East gathering material for his *Inside Asia*. He, too, for all his experience in Europe during exciting years, had been shocked by the magnitude of the chaos of Chapei. John Gunther is big and likable, and full of questions. His first query of the guests seated about the long luncheon table was, "How do you tell a Chinese from a Japanese?"

We all answered at once! It was most amusing.

I, too, was full of questions. What of Shanghai during those three long months of war?

A few days before the ill fated August 13, 1937, masses of Chinese from the northern and eastern districts of Greater Shanghai began pouring across the bridges over Soochow Creek into the comparative safety of the foreign settlements.

By tens and hundreds of thousands they came.

They pressed toward the settlements even as birds fly before a threatened storm, or as creatures of the forest flee from some major catastrophe which they sense.

They came in seemingly endless streams—in motorcars, busses, trucks, handcarts, wheelbarrows, rickshaws, on foot. The weak and aged and very young were carried on the backs or in the arms of others. Babies were packed into baskets which swung from the carrying poles over the shoulders of coolies. Boys of eleven or twelve struggled with the burden of their aged grandmothers. Little girls fought their way through the crowds with babies tied on their backs and arms filled with rolls of bedding. Each little family brought what it could carry away of the household belongings; but in that struggling sea of humanity mothers lost their children, husbands their wives and old ones.

A million destitute refugees settled down over the foreign settlements in a vast swarm, and took possession.

Every nook and corner which could receive man, woman, or child was occupied. They sank down on the grassplots and landscaped flower gardens of the Bund. Every doorway, window ledge, vacant bit of ground, alleyway in the downtown districts was appropriated by them. They struggled to find even a bit of

343

sidewalk, backed by a building, where they might huddle; and, having found that sidewalk space, they unrolled their bedding, settled their young and ill thereon, hoisted a matting or cloth roof of sorts, fanned the charcoal in the clay "stove" and, if fortunate enough to have saved a few handfuls of rice, set it to cooking. If not, they just sat in patient apathy, to wait—wait on the will of Heaven. But for several days the settlement streets were a seething mass of hungry, homeless Chinese, desperate, terror-stricken. Among those hundreds of thousands of hard-working ones who had lost their all, were lepers, criminals, madmen—those unfortunates whose "hearts have been turned."

Some five hundred thousand were taken in by Chinese relatives. Literally dozens of them packed into each room; hundreds in one house or flat. Months after the outbreak of hostilities some forty thousand refugee families, according to official reports, were still occupying many of the buildings, despite the repeated protests of the owners. Hundreds built shacks along creek banks, of anything on which they could lay their hands: flattened five-gallon oil tins; packing boxes; rice straw, lifted, regardless, from loaded cargo barges; oil paper; bamboo strips torn from fences of private residences; strips of cotton cloth which Chinese dyers had spread to dry in fields adjoining their establishments; branches broken from the trees which lined wide avenues. They camped in buildings under construction. They even invaded the coffin shops which sprang up like mushrooms, and slept at nights in the wooden coffins.

The problem of feeding, providing clothing and shelter and sanitation, caring for the sick of such a multitude, was colossal. One hundred fifteen refugee camps—mat-shed cities—each housing from 500 to 7,000 Chinese were erected. The Salvation Army opened two large mat-sheds for lepers in its Ferry Road Camp. The sum required to meet the daily expenses of those refugee camps was staggering. Contributions poured into the relief organizations of Shanghai from all the world. "Bowl of Rice" parties in the United States had an immediate appeal.

Refugees died in large numbers. Burial in the country round about was impossible. Shanghai found itself a haven not only for the living—but also for the dead. Relatives could not move their dead to the country, to their ancestral burial grounds, as the land was in Japanese hands, but must store the bodies in hastily erected mat-shed "mortuaries." The smoke rose night and day from the municipal crematories, which gave the last poor service to Shanghai's abandoned dead, gathered up where they fell.

The refugee problem seriously increased with the fall of the districts to the south and west of Shanghai, including the old Chinese city.

The establishment of the Jacquinot Refugee Zone on the border of the French Concession probably saved the lives of a quarter of a million Chinese.

In the midst of this refugee situation, war broke over Shanghai in earnest.

Great shells rumbled high over the settlement housetops, now and then exploding in some unexpected spot because of faulty range. Bombers roared away to the north. Machine guns kept up their deadly *rat-a-tat-tat*. Lights from the battleships in the river played over the heavens. What with wild rumors, the heat and humidity of August, the closing of the Yangtze to foreign vessels, the worry over business, uncertainty as to what the next hour would bring, and the refugee multitudes, the situation was tense. Then came a fateful day in mid-August when bombs accidentally released over the International Settlement, killed hundreds of helpless civilians.

Panic gripped the city.

The evacuation of foreign women and children began at

once. An SOS was sent out for all boats in the China vicinity. Authorities of Great Britain, America, France, Germany, and Italy moved fast. Events were happening rapidly, unexpectedly.

Admiral H. E. Yarnell, Colonel Charles F. B. Price of the United States Marines, American Consul General Clarence E. Gauss and Mr. O. G. Steen, Far Eastern head of the American President Lines, together with members of the American Emergency Committee headed by Mr. R. T. McDonnell began the evacuation of American women and children.

"I will never forget those hectic hours," a friend told me. "One minute I was playing mah-jongg on the terrace of the Columbia Country Club, trying to be nonchalant over the noise of the guns and bombers; and the next, all my worldly goods were packed into *one* suitcase and I was kissing my husband goodbye on the jetty. The baby and I were both crying, as were all the other wives. We were leaving our husbands to face — what?

"As for the trip down the river, it was one ghastly experience.

"From the jetty to Woosung our tender ran a war gantlet. We were in danger every minute. What with flying shrapnel, anti-aircraft shells, the crossfire on the river, and bombs aimed at the *Idzumo*,[18] it was a miracle that we reached Woosung.

"But just when I was getting back to normal, an earthquake welcomed us in Manila."

The men remained in Shanghai. What else could they do?

One of the members of the Shanghai American Chamber of Commerce said to me:

"I am a representative of an American company which has millions of dollars invested in China. It was up to me, and to the other Americans in our Shanghai organization, to do what we could to save our companies' business and property. Believe it

18   The Japanese battleship moored in the river

or not, our trade with China gives employment to hundreds of men in America. American business men in the Far East don't quit under fire!

"During the past ten years the National Government of China has been bringing about the modernization of the country in an amazing way. There was a growing demand for American machinery, materials, products needed to build this new China. All American business houses did a record business here during the first months of 1937. Furthermore President Roosevelt and Secretary of State Hull had given a tremendous impetus to our foreign trade in to the Far East. There was a growth in appreciation of Americans at home as to the importance of foreign commerce to the economic life of the country. Then came the Sino-Japanese undeclared war: a war in which Japan was fighting China with her right hand, and all foreign interests in China with her left. Japan began to close the Open Door . . ."

In the ten square miles or so of territory to which the settlements were reduced by the Japanese seizure of the Hongkew area (once known as the American Settlement) as base for war operations, the population figure mounted to three million.

All around the perimeter, guarding every possible entry, were thrown up miles of tangled barbed-wire meshes, sandbag barricades, redoubts at strategic points giving sweep far into the outside areas. Members of the Shanghai Volunteer Corps, the United States Marines, the French, British, and Italian defense forces, were on guard. And in the river, in "Battleship Row," with the United States ship *Augusta* and Admiral H. E. Yarnell at the head, the foreign squadron stood in line. All ships were fully manned and armed; on the *qui vive*, with guns and anti-aircraft defense directed for *protection*, protection for this City of Refuge.

And outside those barricades was chaos, destruction, frightful loss of life. War!

American business men, as well as other nationals, settled grimly down to make the best of things until the fighting around Shanghai should end. They confidently expected that Japan would then open the China trade door, closed under excuse of war.

The days dragged along.

After three long months the war moved on!

But trade did not open up—the refugee problem did not lessen—the barbed-wire barricades still held.

The Shanghai picture, brought up to date for me (spring of 1938), was not a particularly happy one.

The glamor of Shanghai, for the time at least, was gone.

Only the depressing aftermath of war remained: a war which announcedly had moved on into the interior of China, yet which hung like an all-enveloping cloud over Shanghai. There was no peace in Shanghai. I found life to be very different; difficult.

I thought longingly of the charm of Shanghai in the early twenties; of the romance and color of Nanking Road; of the peace of tree-shaded boulevards and of gardens quiet and beautiful. There had been an intimateness to life then, and there had been leisure, time to enjoy one's friends. There had been houseboat trips up the river and Easter holidays at Mokan-san, and the whole vast expanse of China's hinterland waiting for exploration. Calling.

And now?

Houseboats, yachts, motor boats owned by the foreigners rot at anchor because the Japanese military chooses to say, "So sorry."

I found that we were shut up in an overcrowded oasis, which was surrounded by a series of high walls. Miles of barbed-wire barricades set up by the Municipal Council. Beyond the barbed wire was the Badlands, then a wall of Japanese bayonets. Beyond that, Chinese guerrilla patriots. Then scorched earth. Japanese-controlled territory and no man's land, and war! On the other side of the Japanese lines was Free China!

It was difficult even to obtain a pass to enter the Nantao Refugee Zone, founded by Father Jacquinot de Besange on the border of the French Concession. A visit to the Safety Zone, for an interview with Father Jacquinot, brought home to me even more sharply than my trip through the Chapei devastated areas the fact that Japan was in control of Greater Shanghai.

My husband accompanied me, and I was glad. A messenger with a symbol of the Red Cross on his sleeve met us at the boundary gates of the Boulevard des Deux Républiques. He had been sent by Father Jacquinot, who had lived for months in the heart of the Zone, to escort us through the maze of passageways of the old Chinese city. Mr. and Mrs. Richard Hubert, keen amateur motion picture photographers, who were to make a film of the refugee zone for Father Jacquinot to show in America on a cross-country lecture tour, joined us.

We crossed through the barbed-wire barricades of the crowded, noisy French Settlement into the empty silence of the Japanese-controlled area. It was a bit frightening. Japanese soldiers with fixed bayonets examined our passes. After a long delay we were permitted to proceed.

It might be well to explain in brief the establishment of this refugee zone which commanded the interest of the world. When war moved from the northern districts toward the Chinese city to the west and south, tens of thousands of terrified Chinese remaining in the old city clamored outside the gates of the French Concession for admittance. The foreign concessions with their million refugees simply could not accommodate this additional surging mass of humanity. Yet something must be done—and

349

done quickly — Father Jacquinot, kindly French priest, who has had many years of experience in ministering to Chinese victims of flood, famine, civil war, and plague in the interior, initiated a move whereby a section of the old Chinese city would be maintained as a neutral zone. Overwhelming difficulties rose on every hand. But the consent of the Chinese and finally of the Japanese military was secured; and on November 9 the Safety Area of Nantao was established. An estimated quarter of a million Chinese were sheltered there. Just beyond the Zone boundaries war had raged. The sky had flamed red for days. The Japanese forces took Nantao on November 15, but that part of the district which had been set aside for refugees remained more or less under the control of the foreign committee. The work was too great for any single organization — winter was approaching and there was need of clothing, bedding, food for those tens of thousands — and a gradual evolution of responsibility brought into operation various relief groups working in coordination with the supervisory committee. The Red Swastika Society took over the refugee work; the National Child Welfare Association, the care of destitute children; the International Red Cross Committee and the Franciscan Sisters, the medical work; and so on. It was to raise additional funds for carrying on the vast enterprise that Father Jacquinot went to America during the summer of 1938.

We left the French Concession and, under guidance of our escort, entered the old Chinese city.

I remembered my first visit, to cover a "Parade for Hungry Ghosts" in 1922. I had been enchanted, and there had been innumerable jaunts to the old city through the years. But the life and color of the district was gone. There were no crowds of Chinese jostling along; there were no food sellers, nor story-tellers, nor countrymen from Pootung selling ducks and greens. Shops where once I had poked for hours, delighting in the ivories, silks, jades, and furniture, were closed and barricaded. The "Willow Pattern" teahouse, where always before carefree Chinese had been whiling away the hours at tea, and loitering on the Bridge of Nine Turnings to watch the antics of the turtles and fish in the lake, was silent with the silence of death.

The streets were empty, void of life, and the only sound was that of our footsteps through the rain. *Crunch – crunch – crunch.* Even the smells of the Orient were missing.

"Foul weather, definitely foul," Mr. Hubert commented as he began shooting pictures of the "Willow Pattern" teahouse through a silver rain curtain.

It was not until we reached the Temple of Mercy that we came upon the Chinese refugees, and Father Jacquinot.

Thousands of Chinese were there, standing patiently in the drizzle. They formed a long line through the courtyards – a rice line. Father Jacquinot was in the midst of them – a veritable Good Shepherd – and he had a word of cheer for each destitute one filing past, each gratefully clutching the tin containing his daily ration of rice.

We talked long with Father Jacquinot. He told us of the sufferings of the 140,000 refugees still there under his protection; of the nine camps where those tens of thousands must be cared for until they could return to their normal pursuits.

"It costs so little for each individual, but so much for the whole mass," the kindly priest explained. "A sum of $1.00 (U.S.) a month will provide frugal food and medical care for one Chinese. A bit more will supply a farmer with sufficient seeds and native implements to put his small farm into fruition again." And he sighed.

Father Jacquinot, possessed of a courage that pressed him to carry on in the Safety Area of Nantao despite the rents in his dark robe caused by shrapnel bits, is still waiting for the situation to open up, so that the farmers may get back to their farms.

Japan is now in her third year of war on China, and Nantao is still closed – tight.

J. B. Powell prints in his *China Weekly Review* a conversation held between a foreigner and a Japanese official on this subject:

"Why do not the Japanese 'open up' the Nantao section and allow the tens of thousands of Chinese who are now spending a miserable existence as refugees in the foreign settlements to return to Nantao and reopen their shops and residences?" the foreigner asked. "Why not allow the Chinese refugees in the safety area to spread over the whole of Nantao and begin their normal life again?"

The Japanese official answered:

"But we haven't sufficient troops here to police Nantao."

"Japan has 'conquered' Nantao: why not permit the Japanese-sponsored Chinese Ta Tao administration to assume responsibility for policing the district?" he was asked.

The official replied, "But we dare not give them guns because they might turn against us!"

The July 22, 1939, issue of the *North China Daily News* gives an account of such an event at Pootung, across the river from Shanghai, stating:

Most of the 200 Japanese soldiers who escorted about 350 Chinese youths recruited for fighting the guerillas in Pootung were wiped out on Wednesday when the youths suddenly staged a mutiny not far away from their destination, Pootung, where they were supposed to fight their own countrymen. The Chinese youths were said to have had the upper hand throughout the battle after which they went over to the guerilla leader. The Japanese gave firearms to the youths only when they were about to go to the front.

In the foreign settlements our life moves on, after a fashion.

Scarcely a week passes that we are not awakened in the night by the *rat-a-tat*-tat of machine guns off in the distance. Chinese guerrillas fighting Japanese sentries out Hungjao way.

The only daughter of a wealthy Chinese friend ran away from home to join her brother, who was a guerrilla leader near Shanghai. Large numbers of students were slipping out of the city to join these bands or to make their way into the interior and join the army. Girls from good homes, in fact it is these girls of education and means, who work with the guerrilla units both inside and outside the city.

Just across the street from where we live is Fah Wah village, a typical little Chinese settlement which was the center of life for the Chinese farmers all about.

Our suburb, Columbia Circle, was set down in a farm district. The foreign children had cut through the narrow passageways of the village, across an arched bridge or two over sluggish canals, to the back entrance of the Columbia Country Club. They had friends among the Chinese shopkeepers who sold "useful" wares in their bazaars, especially for boys in their teens: strings of firecrackers; small tortoises; singing crickets in little bamboo cages—crickets reputed to be excellent fighters in a ring; devil masks; red candied apples on a stick; strange knives or maybe an old sword. And there was usually something going on, on those busy village streets: a Chinese Punch and Judy show; a tumbler or a magician in some courtyard; priests chanting before a coffin; a row between two countrywomen; any number of things which might interest a boy.

Now Fah Wah village had become part of the Badlands. It was cut off from the outside settlement roads by barbed wire. Gambling houses have opened there, and cook told me of opium dens—small, cheap affairs of only three or four beds, which cater to the poor of the village. The village school, where until the war some two thousand boys were being educated along modern lines, were inculcated with the New Life principles, was closed.

The village, because it was located in the midst of a suburban foreign area, bordering "outside settlement roads" which were foreign-policed, had grown unbelievably. New houses lined the canals, even resting on stilts reaching midstream. Chinese factories, moved in from the devastated areas, have opened all about us. A big tannery is just down the street, and along the road are lines of easel-like frames with stretched hides. There is a glue factory nearby, and just at the corner, across from a pretentious foreign residence, is a sewer-pipe pottery and kiln. Close upon a friend's home a cotton mill is crowded. Its shrill whistle blows into her bedroom window at five o'clock each morning. And there are silk filatures, and some kind of chemical plant. Heaven only knows what else. They all give off the most sickening odors. The factory workers clatter by at dawn, whereas formerly only the hoofbeats of the ponies of early-morning riders were heard, and the song of birds.

Even at that, we in Columbia Circle are better off than many of the foreigners. They may have a mat-shed refugee city with some seven thousand Chinese backing their garden wall; or even a mat-shed "mortuary." The ground floor of an apartment house in which friends live has been partitioned into cubicles and rented to hundreds of Chinese refugees. A scholarly Chinese family who for years has held a salon of sorts for foreign and Chinese friends now shares their apartment with thirty relatives and servants. Their rare porcelains and ivories are packed. Other friends live in the very heart of the Badlands—we are but on its edge. The famous old American Episcopal St. John's University is there, as is the beautiful Jessfield Park. While the streets through this section are owned and policed by the International Settlement, the district itself is now under control of the Japanese-sponsored puppets.

Wang Ching-wei, the one-time Kuomintang official who allegedly is being groomed by the Japanese militarists to head the puppet government which the Japanese are hoping to set up at Nanking, lives there. Forbidding walls enclose his fortresslike, heavily guarded palace. Machine guns are mounted on corners, 'and a charged electric wire tops the wall. Wang lives in constant fear of his life. His wine, tea, and food are tasted. His motor car is bullet-proof, and he wears a protecting vest.

It was here that Wang in the fall of 1939 held a "peace conference—a conference whose policy was dictated by the former Japanese Premier, Prince Konoye, in December, 1938— attended by 240 Chinese officials.

Each of those 240 men has received a threat warrant from the secret China Forever Brotherhood, a Chinese girl patriot confided to me. Wang heads the "threat" list of the patriots, who implacably, relentlessly, hunt down the men they believe to be "traitors" to China. Some of those officials entered the conference by stealth at night, others arrived in motor cars with drawn shades. But members of the Brotherhood watched the great gates as they swung open to admit each puppet official. In the guise of hawkers of sweet cakes or sellers of flowers they moved along the street, or squatted in near-by doorways as shoe cobblers.

I was reminded of Dickens' account of the old women who sat knitting in the sunshine along Paris streets, during the time of the French Revolution, and worked into their shawls the names of the aristocrats who rode past in their carriages. But the girl patriot who told me of the activities of the Brotherhood in Shanghai was young, ardent, the essence of refinement, an aristocrat. Throughout China similar secret organizations of patriots are at work. Their members are greatly feared as they bring swift judgment of death to "traitors," death which comes by poisoning, shooting, knifing, beheading, or ax blow.

Because of these secret patriot organizations, which work even under the very eyes of the Japanese military, Japan is finding it increasingly difficult to set up any permanent puppet governments in conquered territories. Surprisingly few of the patriots have been captured. Some of them have even accepted positions in the puppet government in order to betray its members.

They baffle the Japanese militarists and break down the morale of puppet henchmen, many of whom are disgruntled politicians who have been expelled by the Chinese Nationalist government, opportunists out for money, opium addicts, or recalcitrant, lesser war lords.

Near Wang Ching-wei's fortress is the most notorious gambling hell in the Far East.

Gambling houses have mushroomed in the Badlands since the capture of Shanghai by the Japanese. (Under the Chiang Kai-shek government such places were forbidden by law, and opium smoking was punishable by death.) Chinese gangsters, terrorists, opium barons, traffickers in women—the riffraff of the China coast—are said to operate from them. Members of the dare-to-die Brotherhood send blood-curdling warnings to the owners and promoters of these establishments. Regardless of armed guards and puppet police, they sometimes rush the entrances, or in disguise mingle with the crowds and single out their marked man. Pretty Chinese girls are there as patriotic spies. The grapevine functions, and sooner or later the whereabouts, habits, plans of "traitors" are revealed. Foreign residents seldom "go gambling" in the Badlands, for shooting frays, cold-blooded murders, abductions, bombings occur almost daily. The Shanghai newspapers are full of such accounts.

I made a quick visit to two of these gambling establishments for "copy" in company with my husband and a newspaper friend. Frankly I was nervous.

Down a long narrow passageway, far back from the foreign-policed road, we entered a low building whose maze of rooms, covering something like a city block, seemed to stretch on and on. A silvery haze hung over all, a haze which rose from incense curling before the gods of good luck who sat in the entrance and from the pipes of the smokers of opium. The air was cloying, heavy, drugged.

We made our way through the crowds of Chinese milling about, into rooms where roulette, fan-tan, and dice games were being played. Along the walls of many of those rooms, in small curtained cubicles, men stretched on divans smoking opium. Free smokes were provided for the "guests." Guards with drawn guns paced back and forth, ever on the alert. We stopped at one of the tables. A boy rushed tea, oranges, a dish of sweets for the foreigners, but we did not play. About that table were gaunt-faced Chinese, a few Russians, and European refugees, a number of Japanese (although according to Japan's plan it was only "weak Chinese" who were to be caught in these hells). The Chinese looked as if they might have stepped from the pages of a sordid thriller, or a Chinese melodrama such as Rohmer writes.[19]

It was horrible, depressing. In my many years in China I had never seen anything like it before, nor Chinese of this type.

I learned of drug-dispensing stations there in the Badlands where wretches who slept on doorsills and ate from refuse buckets left their coppers for a bit of white powder; of alley-ways along which heroin slaves stood in line to receive a shot

---

19   Sax Rohmer, author of Dr. Fu Man-chu detective stories.

of cocaine water from a rice bowl which relieved the wildness of their eyes, the twitching of their muscles; of the "red pill" resorts where men smoked a deadly mixture of opium, heroin, arsenic. Lower in the scale than even the poorest opium den was the "red pill" dive.

There was no romance in the place which we visited: only unmitigated horror.

We entered a shabby building on a squalid alleyway and made our way up stairs that sagged. A thin, hanging light cast weird shadows. Now and then a figure brushed past us, then faded into the semidarkness below. We climbed one stairway then followed a narrow passageway until we faced a stairway so rickety that our Chinese "guide" called it a "chicken ladder." We followed him to a low door opening on a small landing. From the shadows emerged a watchman, who admitted us.

It was ghastly, a room filled with living dead. Panic caught me as the door was closed, shutting us into that appalling place with its reek of filth, its nauseous, choking odors: the sickeningly sweet scent of opium—black rice, the common people call it—mingling with the somewhat less discernible odor of the "red pills." There were no windows, and I could have touched the fuliginous rafters overhead, so low hung the ceiling. The only lights were the flickering flames of two candles and the glow from the *ven teng*, smoke lamps. There were a few opium bunks; but for the most part just mats crowded on the floor and on a sort of raised platform. All was quiet with the exception of the slight movements of the few who were making their pipes. The soon-to-die seemed to me already dead—inert figures, human beings, material manifestations of the degradations and depravity to which men seem to fall.

As we grew more accustomed to the gloom we made out forms of men, women, and even babies, stretched out in the shadows. Skin and bones hung with padded rags. Out of that silvery fog, pallid faces peered at us, the faces of *va p'ien kuei*, opium devils. There were faces like awful temple images; impassive faces so sunken and wan that they seemed but palest amber wax; unwashed, leering faces whose eyes were obscene depths; death's-heads covered with unkempt hair. . .

"Red pill" victims. Debauchees whose systems could no longer be satisfied with opium but craved, demanded something stronger; who stole, begged, starved to satisfy that craving.

Crowded on a mat almost at my feet lay a dull-eyed, unkempt beggar woman, and huddled near her, in a bundle of rags, a baby. He fretted as will an infant hungry for his mother's milk. The woman lighted the rag wick in a low brass "red pill" lamp on the wooden tray which rested beside her on the mat. For three or four pennies she had bought enough bean-oil dregs to burn the night. From the wide-mouthed glass chimney top to its squat base the lamp was less than four inches high. Opening a small paper packet, she chose a small pink pellet, worked it onto the sharp point of a long needle as if it were something precious. Then with experienced gesture she held the ball over the chimney top, as swiftly removed it (the "red pill" cooks quickly) and pressed it into the hole in the bowl of a common, bamboo pipe — "smoke gun," it is sometimes called. She took several long inhalations, and a thin haze of silvery smoke curled about mother and child. The fretful whimper of the baby ceased as he inhaled the scented vapor, sank into a coma-like sleep.

Somewhere I heard the story of a mouse that lived under an opium couch. One morning the smoker was called away. When he returned after four days, he noticed a small mouse lying weak and thin on the floor. Instead of killing him, he blew a few puffs of opium into his face. At once the mouse — an addict — revived.

Opium was not a stranger to Shanghai, nor was it the first time that a foreign country had thrust opium upon China.

The first period of Sino-foreign opium relations lasted from the opening of the port to foreign trade in 1843 until 1858. Opium was then the most important import of the city, and the newspapers quoted the daily rates on opium, as they do today on cotton, rice, silver. It was classified as "Malwa," "Patna," and "Benares." Fortunes were built upon the trade. Woosung, the anchorage some twelve miles down the Whangpoo from Shanghai, was the most important opium station along the China coast. It was there that the fast opium clippers discharged their valuable cargoes into opium hulks before proceeding up the river with the superficial cargo which must go through the Chinese Customhouse on the Bund. Opium was exempt from duty, for Emperor Tao-kuang, who fought its importation, held that China would not derive revenue "from the vice and misery which opium brought to his people."

A second period ran from 1858 until the enforcement of China's anti-opium legislation in 1907. The outlawing of all licensed opium houses and dens within the Settlement marked a third period which extended from 1907 until 1918. Public sentiment against opium in the Settlement continued to grow until all trade in opium was abolished by the Municipal Council in 1918 and the Shanghai police authorities, together with the National Anti-Opium Society and the International Reform Bureau, sought to wipe out smuggling, to root out illicit dens and trade. This was also a time of propaganda by the youth of China, who made much of the public burning of opium and opium pipes. I remembered one such burning I had seen shortly after I arrived. A great crowd of Chinese had cheered as opium confiscated by the officials went up in a great bonfire.

Since 1918 the authorities of the Settlement have waged an

unceasing war against opium possession, sale, or individual smoking within its boundaries.

With the capture of Shanghai by the Japanese the opium suppression problem within the Settlement has become acute. The wide-open dens licensed by the Japanese-sponsored Ta Tao Government which now operate in the Badlands have their repercussions in the Settlement, and public opinion has little force in the Japanese conquered areas against either opium or gambling.

Thus had Japanese "culture" and the Japanese "New Order" come to Shanghai.

Spring advanced, and the leaves opened on the willows. But tension in and about the city grew. Fighting between the guerrillas and the Japanese troops on the outskirts was intensified. Almost every night we were awakened by machinegun fire. And the list of "incidents" between the Japanese military and Chinese civilians continued to grow.

One afternoon we were disturbed by wails from the servants' quarters. We found cook's wife in a critical condition. She had been caught by two drunken Japanese soldiers just beyond the railway. They had tied her to a tree, torn off her coat, and slashed her naked back with their bayonets. They had also cut the shoes from her poor bound feet, had pricked the ugly stumps, held her up to ridicule. We got her to a hospital, but I thought cook would lose his mind; for days he brooded.

After breakfast one morning, when he came to receive orders for the day, he said, "Little time my stoppie work this side, Missie."

I could not believe it. Cook had been with us the fifteen years of our married life. Leaving? Never! But there he stood in his white apron, his round face sober under a stiffly starched cap.

And then he told me.

He, together with seven other equally substantial cooks in Shanghai, was leaving for Kunming, capital of far-away Yunnan. They were going to open a "Free China Forever Restaurant."

I was desolate. No one can cook a chicken curry like Ah Kun; but what could I do? The spirit of New China burned fierce in his soul. So he determined to take his family and go west, for freedom. And in the end my husband said, "More power to you, Ah Kun," and helped him with his passport.

Strange how things work out.

In less than a week, I too was off for Free China.

I was to interview Generalissimo and Madame Chiang Kai-shek, then proceed to the Sino-Japanese war front and write personal experience stories of a China at war for Internews and for the *Cosmopolitan Magazine*.

Because the Japanese gunboats blockaded the Yangtze River, it was necessary for me to go south to Hongkong and from there travel north by train to Hankow. It was a long, roundabout way. Hongkong was crowded with refugees and was incensed over Japan's bombardment of Cantonese civilians.

Although warned of possible danger, I boarded the train for Canton and Hankow.

- 5 -

It was midnight.

We had been waiting hours, it seemed, at a small station on the Kowloon-Canton line while a Chinese train crew repaired tracks somewhere ahead which had been damaged by Japanese bombardment earlier in the evening. We were well within the range of Japanese bombers, and I was nervous — anxious to get on. The Japanese had a habit of returning again and yet again to the scenes of their destruction.

The setting did not quiet my apprehension.

Piles of debris, of ghostly arches, of broken walls — mute evidence of repeated bombardments — marked the station. Tunneled deep in the heart of the ruin was a small, compact room with matting sides and ceiling where, in the faint light of lanterns, telegraph operators and train officials were at work. At every station along the way I glimpsed these *heroic* men, men who had remained on duty despite almost daily bombardments.

I was having a late supper of sorts in the compartment of two American men, missionaries, who were returning to their stations upcountry.

With us was a happy-go-lucky young Swiss adventurer, an aviator, with the blue of Alpine skies in his eyes — eyes which had seen much. He was hoping to join the Chinese air force.

We were long delayed in arrival at Canton, and one of the missionaries had suggested coffee.

Upon their insistence, I was sitting back, a lily of the field (a somewhat grimy, wilted lily, because of the smoke and cinders of the railway tunnels, and the humid heat of the tropic night), fanning myself.

With adaptability which comes from long experience in hard travel in the interior of China, the men began making coffee over a little kerosene pressure stove which they carried in their bulky kit along with dishes, canned provisions, and insect powder. There was no diner; but somewhere in the rear there was a "chow kitchen" where, over a charcoal fire, a train boy had steamed rice for us.

Tan ch'ao fan — boiled rice scrambled with eggs, bits of ham, and soya sauce — I welcomed it. There is nothing exciting about rice, but there is something strengthening, courage-giving; a substantial "hominess" which checked my mounting imagination by its very prosaicness.

The Swiss, who traveled light as if *en marche*, contributed a tin of dried prunes, a bar of chocolate. He was fussing with a train boy because he could not get a cold dark beer.

I was trying to be chatty, but all the time we sat there I was growing more and more concerned—jittery. I seemed to have a prescience of danger, a sense of impending evil, yet when trouble struck I was unprepared . . .

Suddenly, without warning, the lights blinked out. We were in darkness.

A wartime black-out!

For a moment all was quiet. Then from out of the silence, the dimness, came the calm, utterly unconcerned voice of the train boy:

"*Tih nyoh le lah*—Iron bird come!"

My heart leaped.

"No, No! This can't happen to me," I wanted to protest. "No! Why must I know the ghastly horrors of a Japanese air raid?"

And then I remembered that only a few months earlier practically all foreign women and children had been evacuated on specially beflagged refugee trains from the Hankow area. I remembered also H. R. Knickerbocker's remark in a *Cosmopolitan* article:

"Wherever you find hundreds of thousands of sane people trying to get out of a place and a little bunch of madmen struggling to get in—you know the latter are newspapermen." Gunther, Fleming, Snow, Mowrer—so many of these experienced newspaper correspondents had headed toward Hankow during the weeks just previous.

I made a determined effort to stop the trembling of my chin.

From all about us came the whispered "*Fei gai! Fei gai*!—Air raid! Air raid!"

A trainman with a flashlight stopped for a moment. He talked rapidly. I was thankful for the missionaries — big, granite-faced, granite-haired men, who were calm in the face of crisis, who remembered even to extinguish the fire under the coffee. They translated:

"Japanese bombers are heading toward Canton. . . They may pass our way, bomb the station — fire the village. . . Everyone must scatter and hide in the rice paddies — might be machine-gunned if seen."

"How can anyone hide in a shallow rice paddy?" I whispered. Everyone was whispering.

"Must dig into the mire, wallow deep like a water buffalo or a hog — something less than a man," came back a low-pitched answer.

I filed out of the coach with the others. There was no panic. The Swiss made light of it all, and I laughed with the rest; but inwardly I was scared to death.

In quiet orderliness the Chinese with their babies, young children, bags, baskets, teapots, fans and bird cages began to scatter out in all directions. There were elderly ladies of wealth and position among them, who were calling down curses upon the Japanese even as they tottered along on their "golden lilies" (bound feet) assisted by sturdy amahs. There were pregnant women heavy with their precious burdens. There were students in uniform, girls as well as boys, members of a patriotic propaganda group. There were great numbers of bewildered Cantonese refugees from the Shanghai areas, who had lost their homes, their relatives, their livelihoods, their all, going back to their ancestral southland.

North of the Yangtze there were then some thirty millions of these homeless Chinese refugees on the move, roughly four times the population of Greater New York.

The train, with fire slacked down, now backed away from the station where we had stopped, until it was partially hidden in the shadow of the trees which lined the tracks for a short distance. A crew of Chinese workers began to erect a matting roof over the engine—a roof covered with branches of bamboo. Incredibly swift, they were, in their work of camouflage.

We hurried on. From the air, I thought, the paddies would look like the squares of a chessboard, and we, like so many helpless pawns.

Suddenly I realized the moonlight.

Overhead like a circle of luminous white jade hung a great glowing moon. It was a perfect night, a lush night, with all the warmth and color and mystery of the Orient. The air was sweet about me with the scent of the white orchid lilies which were caught in the chignon of the Chinese woman just ahead. It was all so utterly lovely, so peaceful in its age-old calm, that the thought of an air raid seemed absurd. But I shuddered as I realized what the daylight brightness of that moon might mean.

During May, when the moon had been at its best, the Japanese had bombed Canton unmercifully; night after night, for ten ghastly nights, they had brought terror to that ancient city. But though I had read the newspaper headlines, "Japanese Bomb Canton," my abhorrence had been vicarious. Now I was to experience an air raid first-hand. But the thrill which usually goes with writing a first-person, eyewitness story, was missing.

We moved faster. . .

All about was young rice, emerald-green, mirrored in water which was silvered by the moonlight—young rice growing in terraces like the tiers of an amphitheater done in green velvet, until lost in the misty light which hovered over the distant cliffs and mountain walls; rice for the bowls of China's hungry millions.

Late that afternoon from the train I had watched the farmers with their blue cotton trousers rolled up to their loins cultivating the rice with their feet; had seen them scattering the powdered lime which was to sweeten the soil. Now and then we had passed little clusters of picturesque farmhouses with courtyards and patios which resembled the thick-walled adobe houses of early California. It had been so utterly peaceful then.

It was hard going across the narrow ridges, but we hurried on and on and on. . . . I had an urgent sense of haste, and slipped as I ran; but the Swiss laughed at my excitement.

"Those bombers may not even come here," he commented. "It may be what you Americans call a false alarm."

But even as he spoke a droning of planes came from the direction of the Pearl River.

"Drop flat," he called to the missionaries and me.

He was suddenly on the *qui vive*. With that quick, cool resourcefulness which comes from much experience in danger, he aided a Chinese mother with her babies, planted them at the edge of the nearest rice paddy, and stretched flat on the ridge protectingly near them. Their little round heads dropped sleepily against the bank above the water which half covered their bodies.

I simply could not drop flat into that water. Frogs croaked there. Slimy things hid there. Ugh! In panic I looked about as the whir of the planes grew louder.

Some distance beyond I glimpsed a somewhat pretentious Chinese grave built above the ground on an elevated bit, and rushed toward it. One side was broken, caved in, and I thankfully concealed as much as possible of my five-foot length under its protecting gray tile roof. My navy blue linen slacks and shirt toned into its shadows.

The air was dank, but I gave no thought to grave or to grave ghosts. The Chinese preferred the rice paddies: Chinese people are much too considerate, too polite to disturb the peace of a ghost in his snug grave house (they have definite etiquette regarding ghosts).

Then I saw the white machines of death circling high in the moonlight.

They moved slowly, deliberately, steadily, as if toying with us — and all the time the roar of their engines . . . . I had never known such suspense.

A second later the world went mad.

Explosions tore up the earth and flung it high. Water from the paddies shot into the air, carrying showers of mud and rice plants. Loaded freight cars on a siding cracked up like kindling wood. Bits of steel whistled about.

I crouched deeper into the grave, thankful for even its doubtful protection. My ears seemed to burst; my throat was parched as if I had been wandering in a desert; I held my arms tight, to keep them from being torn from me.

Again and yet again came those roaring power dives — those deafening discharges which rocked the earth.

The station walls, such parts as remained, crashed in thick clouds of smoke and debris. The stands where hawkers had bargained out delicious, pink-shelled lichees, pork and noodle soup, flat meat cakes in which white orchid lilies were chopped (much more poetic than hamburgers with onions), were suddenly gone.

A lambent flame rose from the village. I wondered if its farmers had been warned.

A fleeting memory — more a sensation than an actual memory — flitted through my mind: the deafening turmoil of the air raid in that last scene of "Idiot's Delight." The drama had gripped me then; but the reality —

One of the planes circled low—so low that I could see the enormous red sun symbols of Japan painted on its silver wings and could glimpse the face of the pilot as he peered down upon us. I saw him dip his plane; heard the rataplan of machine-gun fire, the spit of bullets. He was gunning the rice fields.

Hot, fierce anger—primitive anger—surged through me, wiping out all thoughts of fear, of personal danger. Somehow I seemed to know that I should not be hit by those bullets; but what of the Chinese women and children trembling in the fields about me?

I wanted to scream out in protest against the cruelty, the barbarity, the inhuman savagery of it all—scream out as did the fierce *lau ta ta* on the path just below me. While evidently just an elderly coolie woman, she had the soul of a Barbara Frietchie, and I loved her.

She stood boldly upright, her stocky figure silhouetted against the moonlight, shaking her fist in angry defiance at the plane. She spat, again and again, then called down curses upon that flier.

"Dead man's head!" she shrieked, and when a Cantonese flings that curse upon you it is indeed a terrible malediction. A man, whom I judged to be her son, prevailed upon her to crouch low. She finally did so, but continued muttering. I have heard Shanghai coolie women "reviling the street" until they could no longer speak, over some quite trivial matter— and this old grandmother gave no evidence of being "beaten to her knees." Her *ch'i* (wrath) was up; as is the *ch'i* of all China.

I prayed for an Old Testament visitation of divine wrath, but only the *rat-tat-tat-tat* of the machine guns answered.

There was nothing to stop those gunners in their savage sport. There were no anti-aircraft guns, no Chinese pursuit planes. Nothing—only farmers in a near-by village, a few hundred

Chinese passengers and four foreigners hiding ignominiously in the rice fields.

After a time I became conscious of the volley of the frogs, of the shrill chorus of cicadas, of fireflies dancing about me.

The planes had gone.

Had they been *American* made . . .

Slowly we made our way back to the train.

There were great bomb craters in the earth, and in some places it was difficult finding a path around them. Once I nearly stumbled over a man whose face was blown quite away...

Even before we reached the chaos of the station, the train Salvation Crew was at work clearing the debris from the tracks; the Volunteer Red Cross Scouts (students in their teens) were carrying away the wounded on stretchers to an emergency hospital. They seemed so young, those boys and girls in khaki uniforms marked with the red cross of service; but the young of China have become old during the past year. They worked fast, expertly, for they have had much experience.

Fortunately our engine and the tracks ahead had escaped injury, and after a time the "All clear" was sounded.

It seemed strange to find the coffee pan still resting on the stove, the prunes and the chocolate bar undisturbed, everything quite as usual when the train boy unlocked the compartment door. It was unreal to me, as is the waking from a nightmare.

I was limp, shaken. The Swiss, with Noel Coward irony, made light of it all; the missionaries said nothing. Then one of them sent out for hot rice. I noticed that his face was slategray, and that his hand shook as he lighted the fire under the coffee pan. He served the *tan ch'ao fan* in an assortment of bowls, poured the coffee, then bowed his head. In a voice vibrant with emotion, he offered a prayer of grace, of thanksgiving . . .

We arrived at Canton with the dawn.

There was a tenseness about the station, a sense of pending disaster, such as I have felt before a typhoon breaks at sea or an earthquake strikes. The Chinese passengers from the train seemed caught up in that tenseness and rushed about after rickshaws, hand carts, taxis. The station, I learned, was subject to frequent bombardment. The neighborhood was not a safe one in which to loiter.

By the time the missionaries and I finally managed to get a car, the Swiss had disappeared, with most of the other passengers.

Where a moment before I had been in the midst of an exciting turmoil, now all was silence. The bizarre reds and blues and golds had been swept away, leaving only drab gray.

I was glad when we too were clear of that desolate, partially wrecked station and all that it signified, and were on our way through streets already teeming with a blue-coated throng, toward the Pearl River bridge which led to Shameen, the foreign concession of the city.

Like a street scene in an Oriental film, the early-morning life of an awakening Canton was projected before me: countryfolk with baskets of green vegetables swinging from poles over their shoulders; hawkers calling seven o'clock congee; fishermen displaying buckets of fish, eels, strings of crabs; blind beggars tapping their way; sellers of *vah tsu*, that strangely scented golden-fingered fruit known as Buddha'shand, which transforms white wine into a glowing amber of strength-giving virtue; small boys singing out the sweetness of their sugar cane; fat merchants smoking water pipes in shop doorways; a crowd of stripped-to-the-waist fellows talking of war over their melon seeds in a teahouse; soldiers smart in new uniforms, on the march; Red Cross nurses riding by in ambulances. Over all a sky hung with dark clouds.

I had an appointment to interview his Excellency General

Wu Teh-chen, governor of Kwangtung province, at ten o'clock that morning. I had known General Wu when he was mayor of Greater Shanghai, and was anxious to see him again.

But I was not to keep that appointment.

The wail of a siren spiraled up and down the closely built street, cutting through the tranquillity, and brought me up with a start to the horrible realities of 1938.

Ah-ou-ou-ou, it wailed, again and again, like the voice of Canton's Old Calamity Bell, reputed to sound only to foretell disaster.

"*Chin pao* — Air-raid warning," explained the driver.

Although his voice was matter-of-fact, his actions were fast, definite. He drove close to the side of a concrete building; jammed on the brakes; hurried us out of the car. The crowds on the street were equally precise in their movements, automatic from force of habit.

Traffic stopped. The street was emptied as if by magic.

In the confusion I was carried along into a shop where bundles of incense sticks, silver paper "ghost" money, red candles were sold. A squat, round-faced Chinese with loose white cotton shorts wrapped around the many rolls of his fat belly and rivulets of sweat running down his bare chest and back, offered me a stool and a fan. His bright-eyed young wife, slim and cool in a porous gown of lacquer black silk, brought me the customary bowl of tea.

More and more Chinese crowded into the shop. They overflowed into a back room and courtyard, which I glimpsed through an ornate arch of latticed wood enhanced by gilded water lilies carved in high relief.

There was no confusion, but there was a tension in the little shop which I did not like.

A second alarm sounded – staccato, sharp, urgent. Japanese planes had been sighted!

Even then I was not particularly alarmed, being certain that I was not near any military objective. That was before I learned to allow for Japan's campaign of terrorism – to destroy the morale of the Cantonese by systematic, indiscriminate bombings-in which she reckoned without the fiery spirit of Canton.

From the distance came ominous warnings: the drone of approaching planes, the muffled detonations of the anti-aircraft shells, dull explosions.

Then suddenly, close upon us, came a shattering crash. The walls of the shop rocked, and I seemed to feel the force of its thrust on the air. Out of the echoes of that explosion came confused sounds of crumbling walls, breaking glass. . .

The faces of the Chinese about me turned olive-green. Instinctively they shielded their heads with their arms and crouched low on the floor.

As for me – it was all I could do to control my panic, to keep my "face." One moment, I wanted to hide under the counter, for the roar of those planes had some resemblance to rolling thunder; the next, I thought I should die if I could not get out into the open where I could run blindly on and on. . .

Again and yet again came those death-dealing blasts. Where would the next bomb drop? And the next?

An elderly woman huddled near me began to whisper a Buddhist supplication. Over and over, like a monk with his carved peach-stone beads, she chanted in my ear, "*Ou mi tau fah. . . Ou mi tau fah.* – All-highest Buddha. . . . Allhighest Buddha." Then she added, "May the exploding eggs fall not on my unworthy head."

The shopkeeper lighted incense sticks before the scroll of T'ien Ti (God of Heaven and Earth), hanging on the wall behind the counter; he kotowed before it. His old father did likewise.

And all the time the world was crashing about us. I wondered if the end had come...

A long wait — strained, tedious — then at last, the "All clear!"

The Chinese hurried off to search for their families; to learn if their homes and shops were gone.

I found that I must rest yet awhile — another bowl of hot tea might help. News was my job, but I shrank from facing the aftermath of that raid. I must move on.

Down the street from the incense shop, what had once been a long arcade housing prosperous little shops was now a shambles. Hundreds of Chinese had crowded there for refuge with the sounding of that first *chin pao*. What of them?

Piles of debris, jagged walls, drunken doorways, broken windows loomed as I drew nearer, and all about on the street, in the ruins, everywhere lay mangled victims.

Across the way the skeleton wall of a building was literally stuccoed with flecks of gray — bits of human flesh — as by a plasterer's trowel. And piled in the doorway were what appeared to be life-sized figures — grotesque, misshapen — made of gray putty

A peculiar, awesome silence hung over the scene.

Where one might have expected screams, agonized cries, all was hushed. My first thought was that *all* of those hundreds of Chinese were dead. Then here and there I became conscious of movement; of life. But there were no outcries, no agonized moans — just dumb silence.

Some who were whole were beginning to move gropingly away; some with blackened garments were attempting to stanch the flow of blood from their wounds. But there were no calls for help.

I began to single out first one and then another: a man was

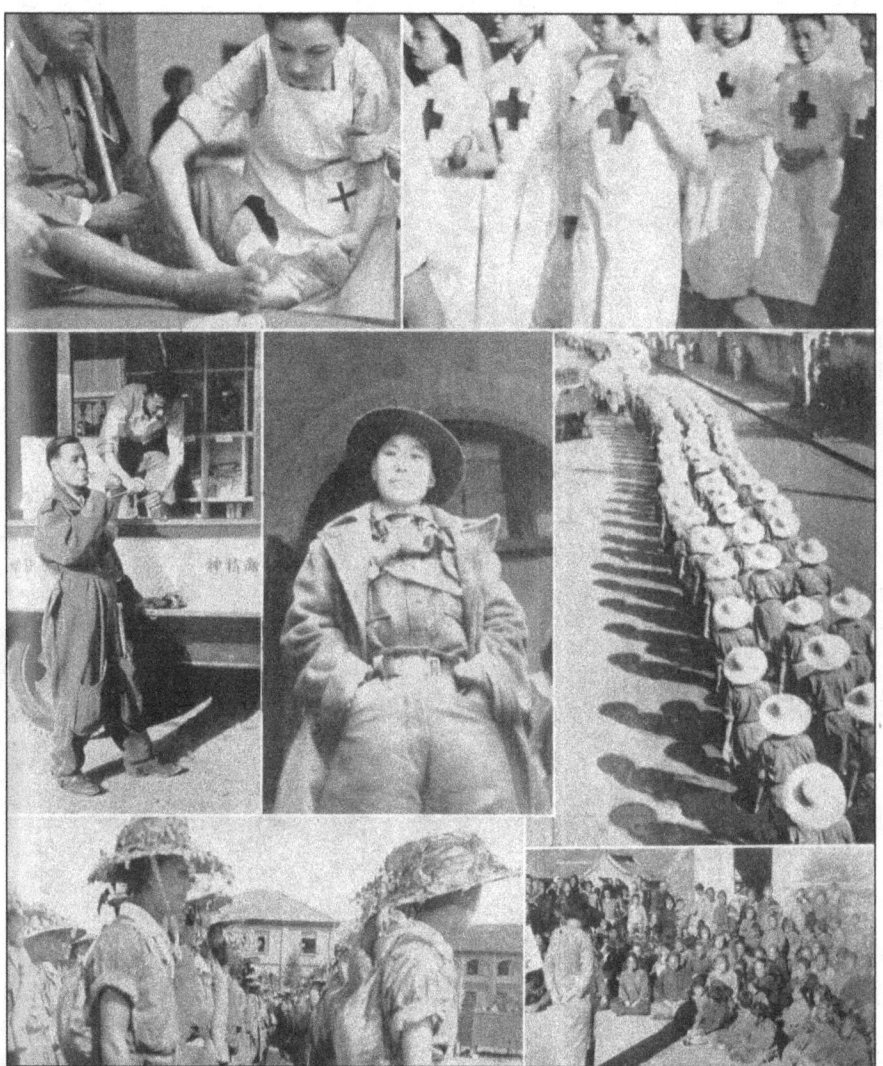

Top left. Madame Chiang Kai-shek in hospital work in Chengching. (China Information Committee.) Top right. Shanghai schoolgirls in a patriotic drive for the Chinese Red Cross. Middle left. Chinese aviator at the supply truck on the aviation field. Middle center. Miss Yang Hui-ming, heroic girl guide, in war uniform. Middle right. Chinese girls in war workers' uniform in patriotic parade. Lower left. Chinese girl war workers about to leave for the Eastern war front after three months' intensive military training, being reviewed by General Chen Cheng, Vice Minister of War. (China Information Committee.) Lower right. Girl propagandist explaining Japanese aggression to villagers in the interior.

375

Top. Filming of Chinese motion picture "Resist to Our Last Man," for propaganda purposes for the War Bureau. Lower left. Rose Marie, taxi dancer in Shanghai, head of the Taxi Dancers' Patriotic Union. Lower right. Golden Flower, famous patriotic singsong girl, singing at benefit given by the Singsong Girls' Gold Offering National Salvation Association in Hankow.

fitting a dangling arm back into place. Close to a wall a woman, in last feeble effort, was trying to draw back to herself her poured-out entrails. A rickshaw stood intact, the coolie sprawled between the shafts; but his head was gone, his torso putty-gray and naked. Nearby lay a dead mother mangled and torn, the body of her baby crushed into her own. A woman stumped along on bound feet, her face smokesmeared — but her head was entirely hairless, one of those weird tricks of explosions. Then almost at my feet was the body of a young girl who seemed to be sleeping, but was dead from concussion.

The thousands of Chinese women who have perished in the past few months at the hands of the Japanese invaders — died horrible deaths from bombing, rape, wanton murder, shock, burning — seemed to narrow down to that one young girl. I remembered a bewildered refugee in Shanghai saying to me, "But why do the Japanese kill our *women?*"

Chinese in ever growing numbers began crowding in. Many of the women were wailing loudly, as they clawed at the debris; a number were quite deranged. Men, more controlled, were viewing first one body and then another in the search for relatives.

The silence gave way to activity, movement. Ambulances, carts, trucks arrived; foreign and Chinese doctors, Red Cross nurses, officials began their work of rescue. But in most cases an attendant would raise a head, an arm, give the victim a quick look; then a quiet verdict — "Dead." Into that ghastly picture came a song, a stirring, stimulating song of patriotism, sung by fresh, young voices. It thrilled — like the tempo of the *Marseillaise*.

In quick step there appeared a band of Chinese Boy Scouts and Girl Guides, in uniform, equipped for relief service. They stood for a moment as they sang eagerly, fiercely:

"Arise! Let our millions unite as one,
Brave the enemy's cannon and planes.
Forward! Ye who refuse to be slaves,
Forward! Forward! Forward!"

The effect of their singing on the people was electric. The youth of China were showing the way. It was as if they had cried: "Come! There is work to do. 'Let the dead bury their dead.'" And all over that stricken city, where in many places the dead were laid out in long rows, the girls and boys in their teens were marching, singing, quieting the panic-stricken by their brave young courage.

Girl Guides tackled a pile of debris to release a woman pinioned beneath. In orderly teamwork, as if following a rule in their Guide Handbook, the girls formed in line; began lifting and passing the heavy chunks of masonry, brickwork, timber pieces, which cut into their hands and made them bleed. I spoke to one of the girls, a student, and expressed my surprise at the sight of Chinese girls in the midst of such chaos. She gave me quick reply:

"Wouldn't your American girls volunteer for duty if your country were invaded — if your people were being forced into slavery?"

As the morning matured, a sweltering hotness settled down on the city like a quilted bedcover stuffed with Chinese raw silk. No air penetrates such a cover. The stench of blood, together with the innumerable smells peculiar to the Orient, was heightened by that nauseous heat vapor, and even the Red Cross nurses held handkerchiefs to their nostrils.

I went with one of the groups to the Canton Hospital.

In every hospital in the city, American, European, Chinese surgeons operated throughout that day as fast as the cases were brought in — amputating limbs, extracting shrapnel — operating while the drone of airplanes still sounded overhead, while bombs were bursting in their very compounds.

Dr. J. O. Thomson, for twenty-eight years surgeon at the Canton Hospital, stopped his work a moment to speak with me.

"The hospitals of Canton during these terrible days," said Dr. Thomson, "resemble field hospitals after a large battle. But the wounded are not soldiers; they are ordinary people like you and your loved ones. As many as one hundred and sixty wounded civilians are admitted to each of our several mission hospitals within the period of an hour. Ninety-nine per cent of the deaths are due to high-explosive bombs — the same as are being used by Japan to blast the Chinese armies.

"We, the foreign physicians and nurses, who have witnessed these ruthless and barbarous bombings, and have cared for several hundred severely wounded noncombatants in our hospitals, have cabled to America and Great Britain, appealing to the humane people of the world to take decisive steps immediately to stop these persistent and terrible mass massacres."

Messages were cabled to all parts of the world by foreign and Chinese organizations during the next few days. One message sent to a member of the House of Representatives in Washington stated:

Terrible suffering and death toll have been caused here by wanton bombing. For God's sake will you help us?

In time I made my way to Shameen Island — to the comparative safety of the foreign concession — and sank down in a big wicker chair on a veranda of the Victoria Hotel, gay with flowers and shaded by banyan trees.

But before the boy had had time to bring me a long cold drink, those dreaded air-raid signals again sounded.

The Japanese planes came four times that day, flying at a great height among the clouds, over the densely populated open city of Canton. Only now and then could I glimpse a plane as it dived down through the haze.

I was with a Chinese official nearing the governor's headquarters when the third alarm sirened through the city. Soldiers on guard admitted us, and we hurried down the long flight of steps which led to the official dugout. It was a bit like going into a subway in New York, or like heading down into an excavation near the foot of the Sphinx in Egypt.

I had envisioned (along with Webster) a dugout as "a rude shelter, as one dug in a hillside": a hole in the ground.

The dugout in which I found myself was a most substantial affair, built forty feet underground at heavy cost, to accommodate some two hundred persons. The walls were tiled, the ceiling whitewashed, and there were electric lights, electric fans, a telephone, food, water, bedding. Along the walls hung pickaxes and shovels.

"In case of a direct hit, even the strongest dugout suffers," some one explained. "Perhaps half of us would be killed. With the axes and shovels, the survivors might dig their way out."

An official report which was issued in Canton on June 20, 1938, stated: "No less than 1,400 Japanese air raids were made on undefended villages and cities of Kwangtung Province, including 800 on Canton, from July 1, 1937, up to June 7, 1938."

I pushed on for Hankow that night.

The train was packed with refugees fleeing from the city. They crowded the aisles, rode on the roofs of the coaches. How "Erny" Tong, then Councilor to the Canton Provisional Government (his wife, Averil, was one of my most delightful Chinese friends), secured a compartment for me, I do not know; but I have an idea that some Chinese government official lost his berth.

Shortly after we were under way, a heavy rain blotted out the moonlight. Thankfully I welcomed its coolness, its protection.

The journey turned out to be of considerable interest, for it was through much of this land that Chiang Kai-shek and the Red Army had battled back and forth for a number of years. We jerked along at a snail's pace around mountains green with bamboo and pines; alongside swift-moving rivers, carrying junks with widespread sails; through valleys of rich rice lands. We passed blockhouse after blockhouse. These heavy stone forts had been built by Chiang Kai-shek in his campaign against the South China Communists.

Those Communist armies, against which Chiang had waged war for some ten years, had put aside the past and were battling with the Generalissimo against a common enemy — Japan.

At each station on the way, trim, smartly turned out young soldiers were on guard. They stood at attention when the train pulled out.

Four days after leaving Canton we arrived in Hankow. Dr. Hollington Tong, graduate of the University of Missouri School of Journalism and head of China War Publicity Bureau, had arranged for me to stop in the home of Bishop Logan H. Roots, of the American Church Missions (Episcopal) during my stay. Everyone in the Yangtze valley knows Bishop Roots' house. During his long years of residence in the city, he had opened his doors to foreign business men, refugees, traveling diplomats, missionaries from the interior, newspapermen, writers, tourists of note. The Bishop was then in America; but his home was open, and I was shown to a large cool room. It was a bit of heaven after the train.

Although exhausted from the hardships of the past few days, I could not sleep that night. Whenever I turned off the reading lamp, tucked in the mosquito net, and decided that at last I was off, I would find myself stark awake, waiting—waiting for the jerk of the refugee train on which I had ridden from Canton; for the roaring zoom of a bomber about to go into a power dive; for the weak moan from a peasant cut by shrapnel.

I was living in suspended time.

The war pictures which crowded upon me might have been grouped by Salvador Dali as a surrealist composition . . . And when I went down to breakfast in the morning, there in the wide hallway leading to the dining room, an abnormality in the sunshine, was a great pile of sandbags!

War—ugh!

- 6 -

My assignment was *war*. But suddenly I wanted none of it. I had gone to the Wu-han cities of the middle Yangtze to write exciting personal-experience accounts of narrow escapes behind the Chinese front lines, eyewitness stories of Japanese and Chinese troops locked in battle; but I had seen too much of war in Canton and could not face more of its horrors.

Down the Yangtze River the armies of China and Japan were at each other's throats. The heavily mechanized forces of Dai Nippon were pushing with concerted action upon Hankow, the objective of Japan's militarists in their war to "beat China to her knees." The capture of Hankow, they announced, would definitely cause China to *k'o t'ou*, to knock her aged forehead on the ground in homage to Japan.

But even before arrangements had been made for me to go to one of the fronts—out from Changsha in company with one of Dr. Robert Lim's Red Cross units—I knew that Japan's premise regarding the collapse of the China front with the capture of Hankow was wrong. With this certainty came the knowledge that I had a story which outclassed *war*; that story was "The Miracle of New China."

There in Hankow I came to realize that Japan was fighting a force more powerful than China's armies. It was a baffling, cogent force which Japan did not and does not understand. Her bombs cannot destroy it. It is a force motivated by a fire of Patriotism, Nationalism, New Life.

Generalissimo Chiang Kai-shek was at one of the fronts when I arrived in the city. Madame Chiang was conducting an important women's conference at a resort high in the mountains above the heat and strife which hung over the valley. Some fifty influential, well educated women leaders from various provinces were in session with Madame Chiang. They were planning work for China's women in the nation's fight against aggression. China's new woman has gone far under her leadership; is a force in China's war of defense.

I was glad to have a few days before my interviews with Generalissimo and Madame Chiang in which to familiarize myself with this embattled war capital of China during the summer and fall of 1938.

The streets of the French Concession and of the former British Settlement of Hankow seemed silent, empty as I made my way in a rickshaw to a press conference called by the Chinese military.

Some twenty correspondents sat about the long table in the press headquarters. There was only one woman among them, Agnes Smedley. Campaign maps lined the walls, and almost at once a Chinese officer began pointing out Chinese and Japanese troop movements and answering the questions of the correspondents.

The military was confident, cheerful. Hankow was conceded

to the Japanese, yes—but the evacuation of the populace, the destruction of much of the city, the withdrawal of Chinese troops would follow a carefully laid out plan which bespoke a long period of national resistance. There was no defeatism: on the contrary I was caught up in a confidence of ultimate victory for China—a spirit which I met everywhere in the Wu-han.

Generalissimo Chiang's war program was twofold. He headed two armies: his army of combat in the front lines; and the army of reconstruction, China's second line of defense, behind his far-reaching battle line. It was this second army which interested me.

Although at war China was engaged in an extensive program of reconstruction—a program which set up industrial cooperatives in the provinces of the southwest, which stimulated the farmers to intensified farming in order that the troops might be fed, which promoted education of her students although their universities in the coastal cities were destroyed, which took care of her war orphans, which undertook the building of new roads and the development of her mineral resources: a program which would have been important during peace, but which was thrust forward with amazing speed under the pulse of war.

Dr. Tong turned the facilities of his press bureau over to me. Through him I came to know a China behind the lines, a China which showed a spirit of determined resistance, a willingness to die if need be for the country, a unity which China had not known during my years in the Far East. Japan had fostered that unity; nursed it.

I talked with students who had trekked hundreds of miles to Hankow, and who were setting off for interior points where they would carry on their studies in temples, caves, hastily constructed buildings. Whole universities were on the move.

Guerrilla organizers told me of their plans for slipping

through the Japanese lines to carry on their fight as guerrillas and as propagandists in Japanese occupied territory. Some of these were known as pen guerrillas.

I interviewed artists, cartoonists, writers, actors, motion picture promoters and singsong girls; wounded soldiers and young aviators who had brought down enemy planes; girls who were off to the front-line trenches as soldiers or as entertainers. I went about with New Life workers, Chinese Y.M.C.A. and Y.W.C.A. leaders and talked with factory girls (thirty thousand of them were evacuated by Madame Chiang), with refugees.

The courage and fire of those young Chinese was exemplified for me in the story of a Boy Scout hero, Ng Chee Keng, whom I met in the Military Hospital of Hankow. He had been wounded on duty in the front lines.

Along with eight other Scouts and seven Girl Guides, he had arrived from Singapore with the volunteer, War Front Service Corps, in October, 1937. Most of these teen-age boys and girls came from good Chinese families in Malaya, their leader being Miss Mack Swee Cheng, only daughter of a wealthy Singapore sugar merchant.

The corps was detailed for duty in the Shanghai sector to serve as stretcher-bearers and as dispatch runners.

The story of those ardent young patriots was tragic; one of the Scouts was killed while carrying a message to battalion headquarters; another died when the Japanese bombed a Red Cross truck carrying wounded to a field station. A Girl Guide, while aiding in the evacuation of women and children war refugees at Lotien, was machine-gunned by a Japanese airman. Two more Scouts died during the withdrawal of Chinese troops from Soochow; one was killed while driving an ambulance, another while rescuing wounded soldiers under fire. Captain Mack, the girl leader of the Corps (with a relative, Miss Mack

Kock Nan), was trapped in Nanking when the city was captured. Miss Mack was killed, but her companion was seized by Japanese soldiers entering the city, and later died. One of the Scouts was killed during the fighting.

Only seven of the corps were left. They were dispatched to the Shansi front. There, five were killed in action. Out of the sixteen only two, Ng Chee Keng and a Girl Guide, Miss Chong Yen Tack, remained. Both were in the hospital. Miss Chong was recovering from the amputation of her right leg.

I left the hospital sick at heart—bitter against war—but thrilled over the heroism of Young China.

I was taken to the Wartime Educational Propaganda Building, where artists, writers, musicians, dramatists, actors who had been commandeered by the National Government for propaganda purposes were hard at work. Even the temperamental Chinese artists of the type I had met from time to time in Shanghai had settled down to purposeful, creative work.

Gone were their long hair, their Left Bank mannerisms, their futile dreams spun over teacups in the Russian tea shops of Avenue Joffre. They had become cogs in the impressive patriotic machine operating back of the front lines.

The posters on which artists were working were strong, virile, ultramodern in treatment, harsh in line and color. But each carried a rousing propaganda message. One which especially interested me depicted an incident in the life of General Yoh Fei, hero out of history. The mother of General Yoh Fei was shown tattooing four Chinese characters upon the back of her son with her silver hairpin as he knelt before her. The message read: "*Tsing tsung pao kuo*. The essence of loyalty is the service of one's country."

Even before the Japanese invasion Chinese art students had become experimentalists; had revolted against classical academicism and developed a living contemporary art. Thus it was easy for them to abandon the more aesthetic mediums of expression and serve their country as cartoonists, illustrators, as Chinese Walt Disneys. Their posters plastered city walls, buildings, temples, trees, railway stations. Their banners and placards were carried by the war service groups who comb the villages of Free China.

The first Cartoonist Propaganda Corps was organized in Shanghai in August, 1937, with eleven members. After the capture of Shanghai the corps moved its offices to Nanking, then on to Hankow. They were prepared to open a studio in Kunming, capital of Yunnan Province.

War movie cartoons were being made by the motion picture studio of the Political Training Board of the National Military Council. In the cartoon rooms of the studio (Shanghai's Hollywood had moved to Hankow) expert movie cartoonists were turning out war propaganda films. China's war slogans and her patriotic songs were given a vivid interpretation upon the screen.

They ran off part of a film, *Resist to Our Last Man*, for me. As if in answer to that charge, Chinese farmers, students, merchants, laborers, boatmen were seen dropping their chattels, grabbing up arms, and as they ran taking up the cry of the untold marching thousands, "Fight on and on and on." There was no end to those marching men. . .

I set off on a tour of rural districts with a movie van manned by girl propagandists. The girls were trim, efficient in their khaki uniforms. We rolled along over a pleasant countryside and stopped at a village temple.

As the girls began unpacking their motion picture equipment, a crowd gathered. In that ancient temple, amidst old gods at whose feet incense and red candles burned, the girls hung their screen and began the explanation of the war cartoons which they projected. The words and music of the Chinese National Anthem were thrown on the screen. The Chinese girl patriots began to sing; and, as they sang, the characters from each stanza appeared. Never within the memory of the most aged village elder had such a thing as a patriotic mass meeting been held. Responsibility of the common people toward the country, toward its government and defense, was a strange doctrine. Soldiers, it seemed, were no longer as weeds in the rice fields, but as the very rice itself. And the village elders smoked their long water pipes and listened to the children joining in the singing. . .

"*San Min Chu I,*" they sang, the song written by Dr. Sun Yat-sen:

"Be diligent, be brave,
Be true, be loyal,
With one heart, one mind,
Carry through to the end."

Bands of students, literally *hundreds* of them, under National Government sponsorship, are working among the villages back of the firing lines, arousing the masses. They are giving the farmers lessons in citizenship. They are slipping through the Japanese lines into the provinces whose main arteries and chief cities are in Japanese hands, carrying their patriotic songs, posters, and movies with them. Every day they face capture, and death.

One evening I went with friends to an entertainment at the New World in Hankow, given under the auspices of the Singsong Girls' Gold Offering National Salvation Association of Hankow. The singsong girls had launched the movement, "Give your gold and silver to China," and had set the example by stripping themselves of gold and silver ornaments. And through the main streets of Hankow and Wu-chang, the most beautiful of the entertainers canvassed in groups of ten. They extended their graceful little hands, sans jewels, and cried, "Please do as we have done." The war-aid movement caught the imagination, and heirlooms, jewels, treasured possessions were received.

The stage of the theater was hung with patriotic banners, while the auditorium was crowded with soldiers in uniform. As each graceful, slim young singer appeared in turn, the Chinese pressman with me explained that their songs were no longer the love lyrics of yesterday, but war ballads written around the heroism of China's ancient warriors, as well as dramatic episodes of the Sino-Japanese war. "Hao! Hao!" the soldiers would cry, as a singer, with face as expressionless as a beautifully painted mask, would reach her flutelike heights and recount a moving tale. One, "The New Moon over Marco Polo Bridge" described the heroism of the Chinese soldiers during the Lukouchiao fighting in July, 1937: the now historic Incident which precipitated the present war.

One girl sang a Mongolian folk song of such pathos that I asked to have it translated:

A Refugee's Lament

The Great Wall is ten thousand li long, and beyond it lie our beloved villages and farms.

The kaoliang is ripening, and the soya beans grow sweet; prosperity is everywhere, and of famine there is none.

Then like a thunderbolt from the blue comes the Great Disaster,[20] and the invaders kill and rape and plunder.

Unable to endure such suffering, we flee; today our kinsmen are separated and our parents are dead.

To the end of our lives, we shall never forget our hatred for the enemy as, day and night, we long for our homes.

---

20   The Japanese invasion of Manchuria in 1951.

However fierce and strong are the dwarf tribesmen,[21] they shall never hold us.

> The Great Wall is ten thousand li long, and beyond it lie
> our beloved villages and farms.
> Let four hundred million souls have one heart, and the
> protecting new Great Wall be just as long.

I talked with one of the singsong girls after the performance. She was from Soochow, and was slight as a willow wand and lovely as a spring blossom. She was so quiet in her remarks that I almost missed her meaning:

"If the Japanese succeed in taking Hankow, I will not evacuate. Six of my friends and I have taken a blood oath to mutilate or kill as many Japanese as we can. We have embroidery scissors and hair ornaments sharp as death itself and rings in which are poison. If we die?" She shrugged a silken shoulder. "We will not have lived in vain."

I wonder what has happened to those girls — for Hankow was even then on the verge of falling.

I recently heard of a Japanese officer and four of his men, a sentry group who were killed in a "singsong" house somewhere up the Yangtze. The men had been wined, fatally drugged. The bodies of the four soldiers were discovered in' the house. It was several days before the officer's body was found, half buried in a field. The pretty little singsong girls had disappeared from the Sweetly Peaceful Mutual Happiness House established for the soldiers. It was all a great mystery to the Japanese.

Small things, yes — but, multiplied again and again, important in this Far Eastern drama.

---

21   The term applied to the Japanese because of their short stature.

Dr. Tong conducted a press trip to the Japanese War Relic Museum, where armaments, munitions, airplane wreckage, parachutes, uniforms, war diaries, etc., captured from the Japanese were on display. I shuddered as I examined the silver wing of a bomber with a blood-red sun on its tip. The "Thousand Stitch" belts, such as I had seen the women making in Japan for their sons and husbands called to arms, and the translations of the rows of Japanese war diaries interested me especially.

Most of these records of the Japanese soldiers had a pessimistic note. It is with the permission of the Chinese military that I quote from the translated diary of one Captain Ishiguro Yeichi:

October 23. — Just back from the front lines after having been at it for twenty-four hours. Tired, hungry, thirsty. Consider myself extremely lucky for having been able to survive the intense fire and brave defense put up by the enemy. But how long I can last is a question. It is rumored that the war will be over soon. I shall be thankful if I can ever get home safely.

As result of the fierce barrage laid by the enemy this morning, only forty members of this company are left, while over half of our 68th Company are either killed or wounded. Every time I see a funeral pyre, my heart feels acute pain. After each battle, a fire is made with wood or charcoal, and the bodies of our dead comrades burned. Their ashes will be sent back to Japan. Why is it all necessary?

October 25. — It is strange that I am not at all hurt, though bullets have been flying all around me. I attribute my luck to the speed I run. During the training period at home, I learned that the best way to dodge firing is to keep away from the range of the bullets. As a captain, I am usually with the first few in advancing. But I run directly forward regardless of the support of the people following me. In this way, I have succeeded in avoiding disaster so far.

October 26. — We received an urgent order to move forward to commence attack at one A.M. of the 26th. All of a sudden, I heard the shouting of Mishima. When I looked back, he lay dead on the ground with a bullet wound through his chest from the right to the left. It is lucky that I could return unhurt and write this.

October 27. — This morning we collected the dead bodies. It was a horrible job. The unpleasant duty fell on me of gathering the wrist watches, pocketbooks, and the belts of "One Thousand Stitches," to forward to the relatives of the deceased.

October 28. — This morning we cremated the body of Mishima among others. When I thought of his parents, who were still ignorant of his death, I could not help crying. What will tomorrow bring to me? Will I follow Mishima? . . .

I watched Chinese girl soldiers drill. They were dressed in Chinese army uniforms of dark green cloth with military caps leather belts, and canvas shoes. Their hair was bobbed short, their faces so tanned from exposure that it was difficult to tell them from the boys. Their training had gone through three stages: military, espionage, and propaganda. Only those physically fit were allowed to undergo the hard military training which prepared them for fighting. The others took either of the other courses. During training all rose at five A.M., lived on two meals a day, which consisted of millet and vegetables shared from a common pot by each eight girls; and they were given training under military instructors.

It was a gripping experience to be in Hankow during those tense days before the evacuation.

I watched refugees without end pour into the Wu-ban. They came by sampan, steamer, boat train, and junk. They traveled over a vast network of roads. They came by the modern highways laid down by the National Government during the past ten years; along roads worn into ruts by heavy cart wheels, by the feet of their ancestors; by country paths, through the paddy fields. They packed busses, lorries, wheelbarrows, rickshaws, carts. And they trudged the weary miles on foot.

As one of the river steamers disgorged its bewildered refugees, I remembered that throughout Chinese history there have been mass migrations of momentous importance. These have also been the result of invasion. Each of these migrations had a profound effect upon China, and resulted in the absorption of the invader.

In A.D. 307-312, during the Ch'in Dynasty, invaders laid waste the capital, massacred its people. All who could, fled from the Yellow River, migrated south of the Yangtze. Another noted migration took place in 1126, during the Sung Dynasty, when great hordes of Chinese were forced southward. This powerful stream from the north injected new life into southern China. Those who remained in the Yellow River valley, who clung, even as clods of yellow earth, to their lands, in time assimilated their very conquerors.

What effect will this migration into the southwest today have upon Chinese history?

This, the greatest of all mass migrations in China's history is advancing those · backward, far inland provinces centuries overnight. Factories, colleges, new roads supporting motor travel, air services are being built. The cities have become boom towns. The ancient tribute routes, the old Silk Road, the highways traveled by Marco Polo and by the Turks and by the Jewish traders are once again opening up; pretentious new highways are begun.

The best of China's middle schools and colleges are coming in from as far north as Mukden, Peking, Tientsin; banks, factories, mills; industries, from Shanghai; culture and government, from Nanking; orphaned children are called from the whole war area.

I talked with a number of the refugees. Many of them represented. families of some substance, who were waiting for passage on boats to upriver ports, or on trains, busses, carts, headed into the southwest. Others on foot joined the long line, which undulated like a dragon, on and on . . . These were definitely settlers, who would carry New Life into the little known back lands.

One day I witnessed the aftermath of a Japanese air raid on Hankow in a patriotic demonstration which would have startled even Broadway. Tens of thousands of Chinese — young Chinese — packed the grounds of a large park where Japanese planes, brought down during that raid, were placed on display. Throughout the afternoon and on into the evening the celebration continued.

There was no sang-froid there. Instead there was a stirring patriotism which, I believe, has gone too deep into the fiber of Young China ever to be wiped out by the Japanese bombs.

Madame Chiang Kai-shek arrived from Kuling the day of that Japanese bombardment of Hankow. Obviously the demonstration by the Japanese was given in her honor!

The day following, I set off for Wuchang, where I was to have tea with Madame Chiang.

- 7 -

Swiftly, under the instinct-guided touch of the vigilanteyed Chinese pilot at the wheel, our launch swung downstream. Although I could see the historic old city of Wuchang crowding the distant shore, the pilot did not head the vessel directly toward our landing. Instead, he worked his way carefully down the dilated, tossing current to a point far below Wuchang, cut across the river at an angle, then turned sharply upstream, hugging the shore.

"The Yangtze takes a bit of doing at Hankow, especially when the water is rising," explained Dr. Tong, my escort.

We elbowed for a place in the river traffic, and zigzagged with the current as did the boats ahead. It was like a game of Follow the Leader. The river told its own story of war as did the land. Some four thousand junks had been commandeered for war service. We passed a string of tugs crowded with war orphans; lighters carrying Chinese troops, and others bearing wounded men. One houseboat bore a coffin draped in the red, blue, and white of the Kuomintang flag. Two great figures, guardians of the dead, rose in grotesque fierceness at the bow, while priests clanged their cymbals to keep away evil spirits. And there was a river steamer bringing its hundreds of additional refugees.

Tall and black, the smokestacks of the Hanyang Arsenal—a dismantled shell—rose in hazy clouds. We turned toward the Wuchang shore and, as we neared the picturesque Temple of the Yellow Stork, were caught in the wash of the lighters on which hundreds of Chinese soldiers were embarking. They were smartly uniformed men, many of them with broadswords strapped to their backs along with their knapsacks, blanket rolls.

These were men of the *Ta Tao Tui* (Big Sword Troop), who wield the heavy, broad-rimmed, ancestral swords, with razor-sharp edges. In 1932, during the fighting about Shanghai, the big-sword men played the Japanese. They would approach the enemy line, throw a few hand grenades at a Japanese post and when the marines rushed out, would cut at their white puttees, then swiftly at their necks. In the north, during fighting at the Great Wall, wide dog-collars of steel were worn by the Japanese engaged in hand-to-hand combat.

Members of the Big Sword Troop obligingly permitted me to take photographs. They were proud of their swords.

According to ancient lore, the swords made by King Wu of *Mo-kan-shan* many centuries ago were the most famous in all China. Placed under the pillow of a good general, such a sword would make a noise in the night if a robber, a ghost, or a wandering devil approached. If the light of the moon, or of a candle, were reflected on the blade, evil spirits and enemies would flee. King Wu's swords were reputed to have power of speech. If the day were not propitious for a battle, the sword would warn the general. Such swords were priceless. "A sword is equal to one city." Big-sword men "worshiped their swords." I heard of one officer who had placed his sword in the sunshine for forty-nine days, and in the moonlight for forty-nine nights. His sword was placed on a high table as if a Buddha. Only men were permitted in the room. Candles and incense were burned before it, and priests offered prayers. It was only then that the officer placed his sword in its case, swung it over his back, and deemed it worthy of battle. Some swords are thus worshiped for one year, others for as long as three. If a BigSword man kills an enemy with his sword, he does not dry off the blood; on the contrary, he smears the blood from his sword on the entrance gate of his home when possible, thus frightening off devils. Old customs, fast disappearing.

Madame Chiang's car was waiting. It was a car of good, substantial make, just as any one might own, except that it was bullet-proof.

The Generalissimo and Madame Chiang rode about the Wuhan much as did other Chinese. There were no machine guns mounted on their car, no guards riding on the running boards; there was no clearing of the streets.

Wuchang is one of the most historic old cities of China, and it was Wuchang's uprising in 1910 which touched off the revolution against the Manchus. But as we passed along the wide, carefully laid out streets of the modern Wuchang there was little to remind one of old China. At each corner, a policeman in trim uniform stood upon a massive pillbox marked with machine-gun openings. Banners with pictures of Dr. Sun Vat-sen and the Generalissimo, and the flags of the Kuomintang, flew from the shops which lined the main business street.

We turned into an unpretentious driveway, wound through a large garden whose paths were bordered with flowers and trees, and stopped before a large two-story house, somewhat on the early California type of architecture. Only one soldier stood at the entrance. He appeared to be an orderly rather than a sentry.

I was amazed at the simplicity, the lack of pretense, the absence even of usual protection measures about the Generalissimo's ménage.

Madame Chiang received me upstairs in her private apartments, where she and the Generalissimo lived *en famille*. She greeted me cordially, with the smile which is so much a part of her. She was more beautiful than I had ever seen her — slender, graceful, lovely in the Chinese-style gown of soft blue brocaded satin, her only ornament the large diamond-studded "wings" which the Generalissimo had given her in appreciation of her work as Minister of Aviation. Her large, dark eyes glowed like carnelian, and her pale oval face, smooth as a petal of the magnolia, was framed with black hair which waved softly back from a high forehead to a smooth knot at the nape of her neck.

We sat at one end of a long table in a simply furnished room, and as the boys served tea in fragile cups of the Thousand Flower pattern I felt the magnetic charm which Madame Chiang radiated. There was force, power, strength back of that rare beauty. Every minute of her day was booked: official interviews; committee meetings; visits to hospitals caring for wounded soldiers; New Life rehabilitation meetings; dictation of newspaper and magazine articles; directing activities of the Chinese Women's Association of War Relief; advising with heads of refugee groups; personal attention to war orphans; sitting in on important government conferences; advising with promoters of cooperatives. Each day brought new responsibilities, duties. Madame Chiang is without doubt one of the busiest women in the world today. She grudged a scant five or six hours out of the twenty-four for sleep. She was at her desk early each morning, following a "quiet time" of prayer and Bible study with the Generalissimo, and she was hard at it until well into the night. There was no time for relaxation. One (sometimes two) of her corps of secretaries was on duty for night dictation. She was giving of her utmost to a China fighting for life. She worked under high pressure, and as she talked I sensed the strain she was under. I admired her tremendously.

She was so intense as she talked, so ardent and indomitable, that I had a vision of her crushing the whole of Japan's army in the tight grip of her slim white hand.

"The soul of China will emerge triumphant from this ghastly war," she declared, with unshakable conviction.

As she talked, sometimes quietly, sometimes fiercely (for Madame Chiang is no meek soul afraid to express her opinions), my fears for China vanished. The spiritual stamina, the power of recuperation which had enabled Chinese civilization, Chinese millions, to survive for some five thousand years, would not be snuffed out.

Madame Chiang spoke of an old stone above a portal of St. Paul's Cathedral in London, upon which the one word, *Resurgam* (I shall rise again), is carved. The broken stone, which was found in a graveyard, so impressed Sir Christopher Wren that he had it placed where all could see it and be heartened by its message.

"I could not know, when I was studying Latin at Wellesley," she commented, "that one day I would emblazon this Latin word, *Resurgam*, on my heart. It embodies the spirit that is China today.

"China will continue to fight. We shall live and thrive and multiply even through adversity, even in the regions where the enemy imagines he is supreme, but where, in reality, he has but a precarious hold."

Madame Chiang's eyes glowed as she spoke of her war orphans. She was eager, determined to save China's children. I had seen hundreds of those children who had been picked up in the wake of retreating armies in the great migration from the coast cities and from the Yellow River valley, arrive in Hankow. They were little wild things — terrified, starving, tattered — as a result of the horrors they had been through. In the clearing houses which Madame Chiang had established, the children were fed, bathed, given new clothes, and sent out of the city in groups to centers of safety far inland. Incidentally the Bowl of Rice parties given under the United Council for Civilian Relief in China, and the substantial donations received from the Church Committee for

China Relief,[22] were helping to feed those thousands of orphans.

"We must save our young," she said, "teach them to grow into future leaders. We are creating a new China for our children, a China tempered in the fires of war, which will emerge wise (I hope), progressive, indomitable, and unafraid."

There was a step in the hall. A pleasant voice called, "Mayling?"

A delicate coloring pinked Madame Chiang's cheeks. Her dark eyes, so fiercely serious, became tender, radiant.

"It is my husband," she explained somewhat shyly. "He always calls to tell me when he is going out."

I felt as I do in the theater, in the hush before the hero comes on stage.

The Generalissimo entered, greeted his wife affectionately; warmly. There is a deep love between the Chiangs; they are everything to each other. They work together, advise one with the other; face life and death as one. Yet make no mistake—the Generalissimo is the great *man* of China, the leader.

Chiang looked surprisingly fit; smart in his uniform; cheerful. Yet I knew that only a few days earlier he had come through an adventure with death. He had remained until the last moment at his headquarters in a village near the front. Even as he took off in his fast private plane, Japanese bombers appeared, began firing. But to the Generalissimo narrow escapes are just so many notes jotted down in his diary. His career as a revolutionary leader has been marked with hairbreadth escapes. Of them all his miraculous release from Sian following his kidnaping (December, 1936) was the most spectacular.

I asked Chiang his opinion of the effect of the Japanese

---

22   Headquarters in New York.

bombing upon the morale of the Chinese people:

"The cruel and inhuman, indiscriminate bombing of nonmilitary objectives and of civilians by Japan has dealt a hard blow to China's progress, and actually to her civilization. An enormous number of innocent Chinese people, including old women and young children, and charity and relief workers, have been mercilessly murdered.

"If such barbarous acts were expected by Japan to break the morale and destroy the fighting spirit of China, the results have been just the reverse. The bombings by Japanese airplanes have taught the people in every part of the country that those crimes have been deliberate, and have made them realize that, if the Chinese do not now defend their country successfully, their lives and property will have to pay Japan's price.

"The bombings by Japan have educated the Chinese in courage and death-defiant patriotism. Those ill advised acts only serve to mark Japan's efforts as crimes against humanity and against international law; but they shall never weaken China's spirit of resistance."

The Generalissimo and Madame Chiang were warm in their praises of the missionaries who have stood their ground in the interior of China despite the bombings; who had been "articulate eyewitnesses to the barbarous behavior of the Japanese troops on Chinese soil."

So outspoken was Madame Chiang during an address delivered before a Wu-han Prayer Meeting, in which she thanked the missionary body for "succoring wounded civilians, feeding and housing countless destitute refugees, and saving numberless Chinese women and girls from the lust of the Japanese soldiers, from a fate worse than death," that members of the Japanese Women's National Defense Association, through the Tokyo press, declared the accusations of Madame Chiang "shocking."

There are two "ways of life" taught in Japan. Those following the Way of Peace, *Ando*, with its doctrines of kindliness, politeness, and courtesy (characteristics which the tourist so often meets), have little knowledge or understanding of the Way of the Warrior, *Bushido*, nor of the callous brutalities to which the soldier of Japan is trained. Consequently the Japanese women were sincerely "shocked."

As I rose to leave, Madame Chiang expressed the hope that America would never know the horrors of enemy invasion; that the women of America would never suffer as the women of China have suffered.

But she sounded a warning.

Before leaving Hankow Mr. Tong arranged for me to interview Mr. Ong Wen-hao, Minister of Economics and educator. A slight man, with keen, alert eyes, greeted me at the Bureau's headquarters. Without waste of time or words, smacking of modernism, Mr. Ong explained the herculean feat of moving inland China's universities and her coastal industries.

Under his direction more than 100,000 tons of modern machinery was being moved fifteen hundred miles inland by junk, handcart, train, coolie caravan, muleback, from industrial centers endangered by Japan; was being set up in and about Chungking; and thousands of workers were being trained for work in the steel mills, munition plants, textile mills.

Under his direction, returned students (the majority, graduates of American universities) were working coal, tin, mercury, and gold mines: students who only fifteen years earlier had returned from technical colleges and fretted on the side lines because the old-type Chinese scholars and officials refused them positions in the government or in industry.

Today graduates of Cornell University, the Massachusetts Institute of Technology, the Colorado School of Mines, are among the men who are building roads, railways; who are operating and building steel mills, working out new methods in industries to meet urgent requirements such as the extraction of gasoline out of vegetable oils, and inventing a new-type machine gun.

As Mr. Ong talked, I could see the old inventive, creative spirit of China—the spirit which invented gunpowder, paper, etc.—springing to new life under the pressure of modern civilization. Primitive tools were being used there in Chungking, but in a few months these tools were being improved and China launched on a productive industrial program far behind the fighting lines such as she has never experienced in her long history.

China's second line of defense was operating from Chungking—a Pittsburgh which has risen overnight in the heart of old China.

- 8 -

Returning to the strife, the tenseness of Shanghai, from Hankow was like awakening from a mountaintop experience to harsh reality.

The Whangpoo had broken out in a red rash with the flags of Nippon. Practically all boats moving on the river flew the Japanese flag; especially was this true of the cargo vessels headed for the Yangtze River ports. The Open Door was shut and bolted, in most cases without so much as a "So sorry," to the boats of other nationals.

John arid I dined with Admiral H. E. Yarnell, then commander of the United States fleet in Asiatic waters (retired with highest honors, July, 1939), and his wife, on the U.S.S. *Augusta* shortly after my return to the city. There were other Americans present, and we were all proud to be there. The U.S.S. *Augusta* had stood as a bulwark to Americans in Shanghai during those months of Japanese attack, and Admiral Yarnell was making a determined fight to protect American interests in the Far East. Incident after incident was piling up—some six hundred having been reported to the State Department.

Day by day, Japan's dual war—the war against the Chinese Nationalists and the war to oust all foreign interests except her own—carries on, anti-British today, anti-American tomorrow. Our future in China is tied up with Britain's and France's.

Admiral Ando with unequaled candor is urging that Japan peel off the thick skin of the British in the Far East. The British ambassador, Sir Archibald Clark Kerr, who has received Japanese-inspired letters threatening his life, wore a bullet-proof jacket to a dinner party recently. I learned then that he had been wearing such a protector for several weeks. Friends arriving from Tientsin bring shocking stories of the treatment of foreigners in the electrically charged barbedwire entanglements about the foreign concession. One British woman was stripped, slapped, and exposed to the public gaze under pretense of "searching."

The Munich pact, which brought to light Britain's lack of readiness to make a stand in the critical European situation, brought immediate repercussions in the Orient. In Tokyo the somewhat restrained, "moderate" Prince Konoye and his cabinet fell. Canton was taken, and we learned that Hongkong was threatened. Hankow fell, an empty shell after the systematic evacuation of its schools, industries, masses, by the Nationalist government. But the former British Concession, where American and British interests are tied alike, was at once seized by the Japanese. The enforcement of drastic exchange restrictions set by the Japanese "Federal Reserve Bank" greatly increase the difficulties of American and British firms in carrying on trade. And Japan timed her occupation of the Spratly Islands and of Hainan according to European movements.

Because of Japan's increasingly belligerent attitude, rumors abound in Shanghai—the most persistent of which is that she plans to seize the International Settlement. Several of my friends have packed their silver, curios, linens in order to be able to evacuate upon short notice.

Day by day, our settlement is becoming more and more an armed camp, although there is no war. Armored cars and tanks are on patrol day and night. Barbed-wire barricades close certain streets, line others. "Newspaper Row," "Fleet Street," with its foreign-edited newspaper and magazine plants, is under heavy guard as a result of bombing incidents and published threats against the lives of certain foreign editors and writers. The terrorists from the Badlands grow bolder in their defiance of municipal authority. And rice riots are breaking out.

Rice, the food of the Chinese masses, which until recently sold for $12 Chinese currency a pecul, now sells (first quality) for $50. We have had to increase the wages of our servants substantially by a "rice allowance." Practically all foreign firms and households are also giving the "rice allowance." All imported goods have skyrocketed. We have to pay $6.40 a pound for butter, $104 a ton for kitchen coal, and in proportion for everything else imported. Exchange, which normally is $3 Mex for $1 U.S. has within a few days dropped to $15 for $1 gold. The American sailors in Shanghai are having a wonderful time—their small U.S. pay multiplied by 15 buys the town. It is amusing to see them piled into taxis instead of rickshaws.

But the big United States Marines—the American Devil Dogs, the local press calls them—are respected by all nations in Shanghai—especially by the Japanese. Colonel Joseph C. Fegan, in command of the Marines stationed at Shanghai to protect American interests, is on the job day and night for the Japanese-provoked incidents occur daily.

In the midst of all Shanghai's troubles, thousands of Jewish refugees from Europe are arriving. I talked with Sir Victor Sassoon about the refugee situation. The committee in charge is providing schools for children, arranging shelter camps which will house thousands, is providing money to equip as many of the professional men as possible with offices, manufacturers with plants; to get positions for the musicians, journalists, singers.

I went with Sir Victor's secretary to meet the *Conte Rosso* with its refugee passengers. While there were many penniless, others arrived with household goods and money. Still others were to receive money from relatives in America. One Shanghai daily estimated that the collective moneys of the refugees equaled approximately $2,500,000 Chinese currency. But the cost of living in Shanghai today is fantastic to those with Chinese currency, and the committee staggers under the weight of housing and feeding their needy. Mr. M. Speelman has gone to America and Europe in the hope of raising large sums. The most grateful of those thousands arriving – who come by every ship from Europe, are those who have escaped from German concentration camps and prisons. Their stories are tragic. One elderly woman, dazed from shock, asked me if I could help her find her great-grandfather's clock. She had been long in prison, her mind deranged, and she worried about the little things which had been her life in happier days.

As I talked with a number of those refugees from Europe I was reminded of a day some fifteen years earlier when I had interviewed White Russians arriving from Vladivostok. They too were fleeing for their very lives from an ism. They had managed to dig a place for themselves in Shanghai, to open their shops along Avenue Joffre, to establish their homes. Even as they, the Jewish refugees are striving to open tailor shops, restaurants with the charm of Vienna where Viennese dancers and musicians entertain, small manufacturing plants, I know of one man who formerly supplied smart handbags to a New York house. He is now carrying on from the International Settlement. Instead of breaking the rice bowl of the Chinese, these new industries which spring up against overwhelming odds in Shanghai, are giving employment to Chinese workers.

Shanghai to me is not a city of high adventure but a city of refuge: a gallant city which opens its gates to the refugees of the world. There is no sanctuary for suffering refugees — Chinese, Russian, or European — in any of the Japanese-controlled areas, however. Quite the contrary!

Against us in Shanghai is hurled the expression, "Japan's New Order in East Asia."

The American Information Committee, consisting of some fifteen men and women — missionaries, business men, journalists — all long in China, made a study of life in nine Japanese-controlled cities.

A letter delivered by hand from an interested friend in Peking told of the Japanization of that ancient city. The fascinating streets — Jade, Embroidery, Lantern, Silk, Curio, Furniture, Flower streets — had taken on the modernity and tawdriness of a Kobe bazaar. The *clack, clack* of the wooden geta worn by the Japanese in kimonos is heard on every hand. She wrote:

The Japanese came into Peking the last of July, and now for a year and a half we have been living under conditions most trying and insidious in the undermining of morale and the breaking of the spirit of the people. There is something much more terrible than physical suffering and death, and that's the warping and strangling of life and spirit through the deadly grip of fear! Waves of terrorism sweeping the city have made the masses the prey of unscrupulous Japanese. All Chinese of means and of political affiliations fled; their homes and property were confiscated. Japanese. adventurers and Japan's edition of carpetbaggers flooded the city. Within a year, thirty thousand Japanese had settled in Peking and more continue to come. There is no recourse to justice for the Chinese, whatever happens. There is a semblance of law and order in the Legation Quarter, for the Embassies are still in Peking and communication with the outside world is quick and sure. That is the only thing that has saved Peking from the more blatant and hideous crimes of Mukden oppression and Nanking occupation.

Large districts of the city have been taken over by the Japanese. Their flags fly over many, many shops and houses. On the main streets, every second or third shop is Japanese. Hundreds of small drugstores and so-called clinics have been opened, which deal in drugs and narcotics—opium, heroin, morphine, red pills, etc.; and there are hundreds of brothels, cabarets, and geisha houses (one report says two thousand). The streets are lined with Japanese signs; the shops with "modern" fronts. Instead of the stately measured tread of the past, there is the quick, broken cheap *clack, clack* of the worst of dissipated modern life. I've never seen so much drunkenness in all my life—the once quiet peaceful streets of Peking are now devastated by wild midnight orgies of drinking and quarreling. I have to remind myself continually that only the worst elements of Japan have come in, and that the people at home in Japan would be heartsick if they knew and understood what was actually happening under their flag in Peking.

She described the enforced participation of Chinese in the Japanese victory celebrations:

The people are required to march in parades, carrying

banners decrying the tyranny of the Nationalist Government of China, praising the Japanese for their sacrifice in *saving* China, etc. One enterprising newspaperman somehow succeeded in getting pictures showing such a parade being photographed by a Japanese movie man, with the machine guns mounted along the street, in the background.

In spite of everything Japan can do, however, a new spirit is being born in Peking. Under the surface. The masses are waking up.

Following the capture of Nanking by the Japanese, accounts of atrocities so shocking as to be almost unbelievable had come. I was inclined to think them overstatements until a letter-diary from a serious-minded old China hand, who had lived and worked through the days of the capture, was presented to the committee and forced the truth upon me. The letter-diary from which I quote is not pleasant reading, and at that I have used the blue pencil freely, having no desire to dwell on war horrors unnecessarily. But what happened to civilians in Nanking, has happened in countless villages in the conquered areas:

Nanking, December 2, 1937
I am working day and night with a small but splendid international group trying to secure a safety zone for refugees and other civilians in the expectation of military operations here. After difficult negotiations we have a reasonable and most specific proposal with all but formal agreement with Chinese military, civilian authorities and the detailed approval of several embassies, who have transmitted the plan to the Japanese command. We can only hope for merciful consent on behalf of the wretched remainder of this city that yesterday had a million people.

NEWS IS MY JOB

We know it is a great gamble, but the stakes are big stakes: the lives, welfare, and safety of over two hundred thousand Chinese who are unable to get out of this city. If we can in any way make a safe spot for them, it is worth all the effort and risk. We are supported by loyal groups of Chinese pastors, Y.M.C.A. men, and business men, who are carrying out much of the administrative work. The heartening thing is that local foreign business men, as well as missionaries, of Germany, Denmark, England, and U.S.A. immediately responded to the idea because of its pure humanitarian appeal. Now with the British and American business men ordered onto the boats, the burden of the work is being carried by a group of German Nazi business men and a group of American missionaries.

Wednesday, the 15th.

The battle of Nanking is finished and gone. The Japanese big guns shelled the city throughout the night. On Monday, the 13th, exactly four months after the trouble started in Shanghai, the Japanese entered the city by several gates at once.

We had all thought that the actual change over from the Chinese to the Japanese would bring order out of the confusion and peace would soon come. But how different the actual outcome! From the beginning of the entry of the Japanese army into Nanking, confusion of the greatest kind ensued.

It is a terrible story to try to relate. I know not where to begin nor end. Never have I heard or read of such brutality. Rape! Rape! Rape! We estimate at least 1,000 cases each night and many by day. You can scarcely imagine the terror and anguish. The whole Japanese army seems free to go anywhere it pleases and do anything it pleases. There is no discipline whatever, and many of them are drunk. A Japanese official told us that the generals were angry at having to complete their occupation under the eyes of neutral observers.

December 18, 1937

Today marks the sixth day of the modern Dante's Inferno. Murder by the wholesale and rape by the thousands of cases. In the — — — school, where there are eight thousand people, the Japs came in ten times last night, came over the wall, looted and raped until they were satisfied. One girl, whom I am treating, clawed at a Japanese soldier. Her reward was a bayonet thrust which cut away half the muscles on one side of her neck.

December 21, 1937

This is the shortest day in the year, but it still contains twenty-four hours of this hell on earth.

December 23, 1937

One of my patients, admitted this afternoon, represents about the last word in fiendish brutality. He is the sole survivor of 140 who were led from one of the refugee camps to the hills. They were first sprayed with gasoline, then set afire. His eyes are burned out.

February 18, 1938

The Japanese are wrestling with the problem of sanitation. Still no night-soil collection since the occupation on December 13th. Dugouts are about full of night soil and dead bodies. They are vaccinating and dosing people, but how they can avoid an epidemic is more than I can see.

A committee of foreigners is now trying to make plans to help the people to return to their homes and get started in some economic activity. The problem is increased because three-fourths of the shops in the city have been burned by the Japanese. No production in any form is going on. The glory and joy of China's capital is now in ashes and the only economy is grubbing economy, grubbing in the ruins for something to be salvaged, to be sold to buy some food.

Our whole time in the hospital is spent in trying to patch up and save the lives of victims of Japanese guns and bayonets. They are all Chinese civilians, whom the Japanese have come to help. When they made their fine speeches on New Year's Day, telling us that the Kuo Min Tang had no regard for the needs of the common people, I could not think of anything but of our whole hospital full of their victims. I have buried thirty-eight bodies, myself, in the hospital dugouts.

Every day we call at the Japanese Embassy and present our protests, our appeals, our lists of authenticated reports of violence and crime. We are met with suave Japanese courtesy, but actually the officials are powerless. The victorious army must have its reward — rewards of plunder, murder, rape, and acts of unbelievable brutality and savagery, upon the very people they had "come to protect and befriend," as they have so loudly proclaimed to the world. In all modern history, surely there is not a page that will stand so black as the rape of Nanking.

When the Red Sun of Nippon flew over Nanking, Japan's "New Order" replaced the teachings of New Life laid down by Generalissimo Chiang Kai-shek. Japan's "culture" filled the once prosperous main streets of the city with brothels, opium dens, gambling houses.

A *China Weekly Review* man photographed a poster advertising a brothel established by the Japanese army. The sign is typical of the many which today are seen along the streets of Nanking. It is written in a vulgar mixture of Chinese and Japanese.

The translation reads:

"Designated by the Base Camp Authorities, House of Restful Consolation Chinese Beauties. No. 4 Hall for Friendly Relations Between Japan and China, 600 meters along the bank of the stream from here."

In the brothels, gambling houses, and dens, opium, morphine,

兵　站　指　定　支那美人

慰　安　所

第　四　日　支　親　善　館

是ヨリ河ニ沿ヒ先方六〇〇米

and heroin are openly sold. The drastic and extremely effective measures taken by the Chinese National Government's Opium Suppression Commission during recent years, are not continued in effect by the new Japanese-sponsored government.

Before the war, the Opium Suppression Commission, a bureau of the Chinese National Government, was realistic in effecting its six-year program for the complete elimination of drugs. Heroin, morphine, and cocaine were to be completely suppressed in the first two years, while the following four years, ending with 1940, were to see the extinction of opium. Clinics were set up throughout China, and addicts were forced to register and take the cure within a set time. The death penalty ordered for users and venders of heroin and morphine went into effect in 1936, and action was swift and merciless. Just before hostilities began, a review of the Commission's program showed suppression far ahead of schedule, opium-selling firms being gradually reduced in number, the cultivation of opium poppies drastically discouraged, and the educational program accomplishing results far beyond expectation.

A published report by Dr. M. S. Bates, American missionary educator of the University of Nanking, gave a factual account. He addressed his report to "The Japanese and Chinese Who Care for the Welfare of the People of the Nanking Area."

I heard Dr. Bates speak before the American Information Committee in Shanghai.

"The present generation had not known large supply and consumption of opium in Nanking, nor open sale in a way to attract the poor and ignorant," said Dr. Bates. "Particularly during the last five years has the use of opium been slight, because of the fairly consistent and cumulative government pressure against the trade, plus the result of educational effort during the past thirty years.

"Under Japan's new order it is possible for everyone to secure narcotics conveniently and cheaply."

A missionary from Soochow told us an amusing story of how Chinese, forced into posts of puppet guards, are outwitting the Japanese. These puppet police stand at the city gates and search all who come and go. They have orders from the Japanese to arrest all attempting to smuggle in arms. Suspecting that the Chinese on duty at the gates were permitting a free flow of contraband goods, two Japanese disguised themselves as Chinese and entered carrying hidden munitions. But the Chinese puppet police set upon the two disguised smugglers, gave them the beating of their lives, then turned them over to the Japanese gendarmes for the death sentence. They had been tipped off!

The "new" newspapers of the city, addressed to the "Beloved People of the Occupied Areas," bombard the populace with propaganda designed to destroy their faith in the national cause, to ferment antiforeign trouble for the democracies, to urge them

EDNA LEE BOOKER

to turn to Japan as their "friendly neighbor." But practically every teahouse in the city is a grapevine center, and newspapers from Shanghai are smuggled in daily and rented at ten cents an hour. Three victory arches built by the Japanese to celebrate the first anniversary of the Reformed Government were mysteriously burned, and three of the Chinese puppet officials were killed. A secret patriotic society sent threatening letters to seventy men slated to head the city's puppet administration, and the majority of them fled in terror.

But the economic life of Soochow is coming more and more under Japanese control. The main streets are lined with Japanese stores. The Native Products Emporium, once a "Buy Chinese-Made Goods" enterprise launched under the New Life movement, has become the Dai Maru. All foreign business is finished. The door is closed. The district's rich silk industry has been taken over by a monopoly with Japanese "advisers," who control the stock.

Soochow was an educational center; but the majority of its schools have been bombed, looted, or are now occupied by the Japanese.

City after city, each with its shocking story.

And the Yellow River valley, China's "Good Earth"?

As a member of the American Advisory Committee in Shanghai (an allocating organization which works with the Church Committee for China Relief, the China Famine Relief, Red Cross, and Bowl of Rice and other committees), the picture of a suffering, broken hinterland opened before me.

Report after report was received from the stricken interior. Since midsummer of 1937 *war* like a scorching shuttle of death, had moved back and forth, back and forth over many of the provinces north of Yangtze River and south of the Great Wall. The Yellow River valley with its millions of peasant farmers was

415

hit hardest of all north China areas. Requests for relief presented to the American Advisory Committee tell of mass suffering, mass death, throughout the length and breadth of the Yellow River and Hui River valleys. For miles on end stretches a no man's land: blood-sodden, charred, bomb-torn, flood-swept. The floods resulted from the cutting of the dikes as a war measure; and even worse floods have since swept the Tientsin area.

Japan's New Order has descended like a blight on China. Instead of accomplishing her boasted reconstruction of the conquered areas, she has brought about conditions far worse than even a year ago; and the end is not yet.

Many of our Chinese friends were out of the city.

The group of young Chinese intellectuals who had met so informally in the colorful rooms of the International Arts Theater for four years was widely scattered. Shanghai was "not healthy" for them, I was told. There were artists, dramatists, musicians, writers, poets among them—young experimentalists in the arts. They had done some interesting work in adapting historic Chinese plays to a modern theater; in composing music for instruments such as the ancients played; in translating poetry into French and English. The workshop where we had worked together so pleasantly was closed. Even many of the foreign members, Italian, American, French, British, German, had been evacuated and as yet had not returned. Lovely Hilda Yen, niece of Dr. W. W. Yen, Chinese diplomat, one of the most modern of the Chinese group, was in the United States as an airplane pilot, a flyer of a "good-will ship" for China. Mrs. Bernardine Fritz, organizer of the theater, was in Hollywood while Dr. Lin Yutang was in New York. It was through the International Arts Theater that a number of young Chinese girls and matrons of the smart set had first appeared in public on the stage.

I had been back in Shanghai from Hankow but a few days when the wife of Judge Milton J. Helmick of the United States Court for China invited me to tea. Three Chinese friends from the International Arts Theater days were there. Mrs. Ernest (Averil) Tong, whose husband had befriended me in Canton; Miss Virginia Chang, attractive daughter of H. N. Chang, former Chinese minister to Chile, and Miss Ethel Chun, granddaughter of Sir Shou-Son Chow, who had been knighted by King George V.

The girls were eager, full of ambitious dreams—dreams of going to America with a Chinese Cultural Mission.

"We will raise funds for Madame Chiang's war orphans," explained gentle-voiced Ethel. "We'll try to win friends for China," cut in the beautiful Virginia, while Averil, who has a real love for the theater as well as the emotional depths of a great actress, told us of her desire to give the little theater audiences of America a glimpse of the culture of old China. As the girls talked, we also caught their enthusiasm, and Mrs. Helmick, who gives lavishly of her time to Chinese charities, agreed to act as chairman of a committee of American sponsors. Through long months the girls worked. They collected donations for their costumes, scenery, transportation; they overcame objection after objection, and they assembled a group of remarkable amateur Chinese musicians to accompany them. When they finally sailed, a party of eleven with limited funds, without a foreign manager, and with no definite bookings, I waved a nervous goodbye. They were so brave, so courageous, so ardent in their desire to serve China, that I prayed America would appreciate their fine spirit and receive them warmly.

And America did!

Averil returned to Shanghai full of praise and appreciation for the reception given the Chinese Cultural Mission group.

Again we met at Mrs. Helmick's, and we listened eagerly as she told of their experiences. She was full of gratitude to her own people in America, to the dramatic critics, who had been most generous, and to members of the American Bureau for Medical Aid to China who had sponsored their American tour.

Ethel Chun was not with Averil, nor was Virginia. Ethel had remained for the time in Paris as the guest of Madame Wellington Koo, wife of the Chinese Ambassador to France, and Virginia had married Mr. Kien-wen Yu, second secretary of the Chinese Embassy at Washington and was acting as hostess at the Embassy for Dr. Hu Shih.

Averil, however, was a shadow of her glowing self. She was pale and worried. She returned from her undertaking to raise funds for China's orphans to find her own small daughter seriously ill. Canton had fallen and certain ancestral lands of the Tong family had been seized. Her home in Canton was gone. There is much sorrow in China.

Life in Shanghai was so charged with suspense, hatred, danger that it seemed as if a climax must be reached. Much is going on that the public at large only senses. Rumors that Japan will attempt to seize the settlements — today? tomorrow? next week? — persist. Yet on the surface life is gay.

John, Jr., had not been well, and we decided to send him "home" to school. Boys living in the Orient are often sent to America a year or so before college in order that they may make certain readjustments. Educationally it is not necessary, for Shanghai boasts an excellent American preparatory school. But John and I wanted to get our son out of the turmoil of the Far East, into the peace and beauty of a New England countryside. We wanted normality for him even if it meant an ocean between us. We who live in the Far East have roots down in two lands, roots that pull in opposite directions, and the heart is never quite at rest.

I packed lightly, for after getting John, Jr., settled and turning my book manuscript over to my publisher in New York I planned to return at once to my husband and little daughter in Shanghai.

- 9 -

John, Jr., and I were at dinner in mid-Pacific when a brief message received by the ship's radio brought a chill to every passenger aboard. War had been declared in Europe. . . War!

Just opposite, a titled Polish woman on her way to Warsaw to visit her parents grew pale, while a young Canadian next to John, Jr., on his way home to college in Ontario said slowly, "I'll be just old enough to enlist when we dock."

Day by day, night by night, we hung onto each garbled, censored war bulletin and speculated in little groups on the deck, in the smoking room. A pall hung over the ship. It was the longest Pacific crossing I have ever experienced. A strange, unpredictable war, which threatened civilization, democracy, even Christianity, had begun. . .

We stopped for only a few hours in California with relatives, then rushed on East, for John's school had already opened.

I was invited down to Washington to speak before the Women's National Press Club on the Far Eastern situation. It was intensely interesting to me, who lived so out of American life, to meet the brilliant women of the press assembled. After the luncheon meeting I rushed with Doris Fleeson, a Washington correspondent for a New York daily, to the press conference being held by President Roosevelt.

We worked our way through the crowd of newspapermen waiting for the doors to open, and when they were opened by the guards, joined in the scramble for front-row standing room. We made it! It was the first time I had ever seen the President, and I was struck by the lines of care which cut into his face when his smile relaxed.

At once, even as a corn in a popper, the questions of the newspapermen began: question after question on domestic and foreign affairs. Mr. Roosevelt answered them as fast as they came. Once he sidestepped with a remark that was a subtle one.

Doris introduced me to Mr. "Steve" Early, the President's secretary, and he asked us to wait a moment after the conference. It was then that he presented me to the President as "Little China." The President was in excellent form, and I ventured a question. I was glad to learn that America was not withdrawing her marines nor her ships from Far Eastern waters.

Mr. Early asked me how I enjoyed the conference, and without thinking I answered, "Very much indeed, except that in China tea and watermelon seeds are served." The President laughed, instructed Mr. Early to look into the matter of watermelon seeds for the newspapermen, then began a story about a press conference in Paris when there had been caviar and champagne and the newspapermen had worn tails and white ties. It was all delightfully informal, unexpected.

I was shocked a few days later when scanning the New York dailies for news of the Far East to read of the sudden death of General Wu Pei-fu: Wu Pei-fu, "my war lord," from whose ancestral halls I had gone to cover my first Chinese civil war. I was shocked, very; yet for days I had had Wu in my thoughts—I had been a bit afraid for him.

For more than two years the Japanese military had announced at intervals that General Wu was to head the new central puppet government which Japan hoped to set up in China. For more than two years Wu had smoothly outwitted the militarists. During this time he had lived practically a prisoner in Peking, buried in his Buddhist books and his poetry. The European war and an economic crisis in Japan had sharpened the purpose of the Japanese militarists, and additional pressure was brought to bear. The story going about was that a certain Japanese, appointed to bring Wu to heel, had threatened to commit hara-kiri in Wu's courtyard if he longer refused to head the puppet government. Wu had taken to his bed. It was reported that even "stacked" joss sticks in the diviner's bamboo could not shake him when he sought an answer from temple gods. Wu died, even as he had lived, a patriot.

Had Wu in desperate resignation mounted the dragon when pressure had become too strong? Did he die from a carefully plotted "political illness," as some reports seem to indicate? Or was the strain under which he had lived for the past two years, too great even for his brave heart?

Whichever the answer, Wu's death and the mystery surrounding it have stirred Chinese millions to new patriotic heights (for Wu was recognized as an "honest war lord" and was greatly liked by the people) and has brought loss of face, as has nothing else, to the handful of Chinese anti-Chiang officials who have sold out as puppets. Wu has set the example. Wu was wily, experienced in things political. I remember a time when he declined the gift of a beautiful concubine with the excuse that he was not worthy. He suspected her of being a spy.

Magazines and newspapers which my husband was sending to me from Shanghai began arriving. One publication spoke bitterly of "Stalin's Rape of Poland," and saw in Russia's march on Finland a "warning to China." The *China Weekly Review* carried in full an address delivered by Generalissimo Chiang before the People's Political Council at Chungking in which Chiang reaffirmed China's policy of resistance to Japan, regardless of European war developments or reports that a "central regime" under Wang Ching-wei would enable Japan to settle her "China incident" at an early date.

"The Chinese-Japanese problem is a world problem," said Chiang. "The Chinese people constitutes one-fourth of the world's population. We realize our responsibility in the noble task of promoting permanent world peace. But world peace is far distant as long as our conflict with Japan is not terminated. Even if the Japanese succeed in organizing a puppet regime, a regime such as a handful of traitors may establish in Japanese-occupied territory, treaties such as they may sign with the enemy will not have the slightest effect upon China's war of resistance."

Even as the European war moves on, certain leading American magazines and newspapers sound a warning to America of "danger in the Far East."

Captain Joseph M. Patterson, publisher of the New York *Daily News* and co-publisher of the Chicago *Tribune*, wrote an editorial under the heading "Europe Grabs the Headlines," in which he stated:

For all this European headline copping, the European war story is not, for Americans, the most important news story now running in the papers. The Japanese war story is. If we have any native sense at all, and if we learned anything from the one time we mixed into a European war, we'll resist to the end the temptation to send over another A.E.F. And we won't lose sight for a moment of what Japan is doing in China.

Japan is doing the same thing Russia is doing. Japan is utilizing the war in Europe to get things it wants in Asia.

These things include the freezing out of British, French

422

and American business in China. If China is subjugated, the sky will be the limit to Japan's ambitions. The Japanese have always been a warlike race. One tenet of their national philosophy is that Japanese culture must eventually become the culture of all mankind.

So it is up to us to keep our eyes on Japan: and to do what we can to stymie Japan at every opportunity — as, for a current example, by taking appropriate and self-interested action when the Treaty of Commerce and Navigation with Japan expires January 26, 1940.

Japan is our real foreign problem and our ever-present threat. The sun of empire moves westward. If we don't stand ever on guard, it may jump the Pacific before we know what is happening.

Two ships for one.

Japan "freeze out American business in China"?

The "freeze" has already set in. Japan has a carefully worked out program for which she is spending life and money; and that program, if accomplished, will "freeze out" all other interests in China. It will also freeze out American missions and schools, tend to undermine Sino-American friendship.

Japan needs capital in order successfully to set up her "new order in East Asia." She is looking to America to supply that capital and credit. A pamphlet published recently by the American Junior Chamber of Commerce in Shanghai states:

With American capital Japan hopes to set herself up as a military and economic overlord of the Far East in preparation for her ambition to dominate the entire Pacific regions. Thus the fate of our future on the Pacific will depend upon the wisdom displayed by us in the handling

423

of our capital resources. The principle of two-way traffic in Japanese-American relations is the only one which can make for permanent peace on the Pacific.

At the moment Japan hopes that America will continue to play the role of the crow and drop the cheese into her mouth whenever she flatters or dangles a promise.

The spring of 1937 saw China launched on a five-year industrial program of tremendous proportions. Mr. Julean Arnold, who for twenty-five years has served the United States Department of Commerce in China and Japan, says in *Amerasia*:

A China free to work out its own destiny would undoubtedly offer opportunities which, within a decade or two, would surpass those of Japan and most other countries, giving us an export trade with China probably tenfold that of the year 1936. Thus at the beginning of 1937, America was at the threshold of realizing in a big way on the potentialities in China's vast modernization program.

In the face of this ambitious, eager New China, Prince Konoye announced to the world on August 28, 1937, that Japan must "beat China to its knees." Gone was Chiang Kai-shek's hope for a ten-year peace. Communism was practically a dead issue in China. Konoye could no longer herald its threat. It was then that he proclaimed Japan's "new order" program.

The program announced by China and the one outlined by Japan in that fateful spring were directly adverse to each other. China's program was built on peace; Japan's, on war.

China had begun a railway network of many thousand miles in the interior. Great Britain, France, Germany, and Belgium

424

EDNA LEE BOOKER

had signed loan agreements with the clause that the materials used be ordered from their respective representatives in China. The Export-Import Bank of Washington was arranging credits for many hundred million dollars which would have benefited American manufacture and labor. For example: for each 1,000 miles of railroad $50,000,000 (U.S.) worth of material was needed. The laying down of 50,000 miles meant the purchase of 100,000,000 wooden ties from America's Northwest.

Again. During recent years China has constructed more than 50,000 miles of highway and was engaged in a far-flung road program. Approximately 80 per cent of the 75,000 automobiles used in China were American. Plans for the coordination of roads with railways and waterways meant the ordering of large numbers of motor cars, trucks, and busses.

China's air program was important. By 1937 China had installed a network of airways which reached all important cities and had made air connections with America, England, France. A Chinese-American company led the field in commercial aviation, with some 3,000 miles of lines, and was making plans for substantial extension of operations.

Radio broadcasting stations had been installed in all important cities, and a network of long-distance telephones established. The largest telephone company in China was American while the greater part of the radio equipment was purchased from the United States.

Smokestacks of modern industrial plants were rising on the China sky line in ever increasing numbers, not only in the coastal cities but in the interior as well. Mr. Arnold gives such figures as cotton spindles, 5,000,000; looms, 50,000; flour mills, yearly capacity 25,000,000 barrels; cigarette factories, yearly capacity 80 billion. Again America owns the largest electric power plant in China. The importation of American-made industrial machinery was increasing.

China embarked on a modern building program in 1937 which offered America big trade possibilities. Also improvements among the farming millions had been a successful weapon in combating communistic activities. Credit cooperatives has greatly increased the purchasing power of the rural districts.

Currency was being definitely stabilized in 1937. Long-term loans to the Nationalist government for industrial development by foreign powers indicated improved national credits.

America for the five years preceding led the world in both China's exports and imports. Our imports from China amounted to more than $100,000,000 a year, representing raw materials necessary to our manufacturing industries. Mr. Arnold gives the aggregate figure of American investments in China in 1937 as about $250,000,000 (U.S.). One of these which has done much toward popularizing things American in the interior is the American motion picture film industry: 80 per cent of the films shown are imported from America.

Japan's 1937 program definitely hopes to change this picture — to freeze out these opportunities for other foreign powers in China.

Mr. Arnold points out that this program includes the subjugation of China's masses by terrorism; the impressment into Japan's armies of China's man power; the building up on the Asiatic mainland of a Japanese military machine in preparation for further conquests; the securing of monopolistic control of China's economic resources, thus freeing Japan from dependence upon foreign powers for cotton, wool, tobacco, steel, etc.; to build up Japanese-controlled regional puppet governments; to wipe out westernizing influences and to substitute for English the Japanese language and Japanese textbooks: to make China one great Japanese concession.

Japan is a realistic nation, and her program must be met with realism, not "wistful thinking." In a Japanized China there will be no place for America. As it is, American exports to Japan and to Japanized Manchuria during the past few years have been chiefly in materials which figure in Japan's war industries. More than one Chinese friend has asked me: "Why is America rendering far more material aid to Japan than to China?"

In a paper "The Effect of the Sino-Japanese Crisis upon the Future of America" in *Amerasia*, Mr. Arnold states, "The longer we delay taking positive action to protect our interests in Asia and the Far East, the more difficult will become the task because, the more deeply the Japanese penetrate China, the longer the sources of supply upon which Japan will be able to draw for assistance in carrying on the war."

I was glad to see leading magazines and newspapers in America pointing out these facts.

There had been much anti-American feeling in Japan when we passed through, due to plain talking of American Ambassador Drew regarding treaties and trade. I remembered a recent letter from Madame Chiang Kai-shek, in which she had warned America. I share it with you:

GENERALISSIMO'S HEADQUARTERS
Chungking, Szechwan, China

Dear Edna Lee Booker:
Your letter reached me yesterday. Thank you for your expression of sympathy for the bomb victims.

We are hoping the United States and Great Britain are at last awakening to a realization that their interests and their prestige are definitely menaced by the policies which the Japanese have revealed as responsible for their invasion of China. It has taken months for the Democracies to realize that Japanese aggression was intentional in fulfillment of their ambition to establish a continental empire. Japan says that she is devoting her altruistic energies, and, incidentally, bankrupting herself, for the benefit of the Chinese people, and what she calls "East Asia" in general. It was only the announcement of Prince Konoye of this aim chat awoke the United States and Great Britain to an understanding of the dangers that were ahead of them and the interests of their citizens in the whole of the Pacific. That is very strange to me. We, in China, understood from the outset what Japan was up to because we had been witnesses, and sufferers, under the development of the old Tanaka Memorial.

When I broadcasted to America on September 12, 1937, I said: "They [the Japanese] are convinced that the Powers dare not oppose them. So they are proceeding with plans of conquest confident that they will be able to devastate China, and, in time, drive out western cultural and commercial influences, so that, if we Chinese cannot prevent them, they may erect upon the ashes of China a world-shaking Japanese continental empire. It will not be founded upon international ethics (for Japan has already crippled those), but upon militarized force. At least they expect to control all lands where the Oriental races live, and eventually determine international conduct and policies."

This is not quoted now with the idea of saying "I told you so." It is only mentioned to emphasize the astonishment we feel that the Governments of the great Democracies did not long ago understand the motives of Japan when she overrode them and their treaties in Manchuria, and subsequently scorned them all in China.

Japan has done more than scorn the Democracies. She has openly insulted them, deliberately worked to oust their trade and interests, and always has endeavored to stir up Asiatic hatred against them.

Before this "incident" occurred Japan was busy trying to persuade China to abandon her friendly relations with both the United States and Great Britain. When persuasion had no results Japan tried threats, and these threats must have been plain to the great countries concerned, since Japan openly demanded that China should give up expectations of economic assistance from the western countries and cling to Japan.

Naturally China refused to accept any suggestion of this kind, since we knew that to fall in with such an outrageous proposition would be to sacrifice our independence. Japan was certainly endeavoring to get us to sell our birthright for a mess of pottage. Because we would not do that, and because the militarists of Japan were intent upon making a drive to seize the complete hegemony of Asia and the Pacific, they took advantage of what they believed to be the weakness of China and the occupation of the Democratic Powers in Europe to get by force what they had failed to obtain by cajolery or threats.

We are hoping that both the United States and Great Britain will understand that the deliberate impoverishment of China which the Japanese have been endeavoring to effect by the employment of the most ferocious means they could contrive signifies the ultimate destruction of the purchasing power of the Chinese people, and consequently the ruination of this market for American and British products.

If the Democracies realize that the loss of the China market — which has tremendous possibilities — will do more to affect their workmen and their output of manufactured products than anything else that could happen in the world, they might take steps to curtail the sinister activities of the Japanese.

The Democracies, even if they do not wish to uphold treaties, or adhere to their espoused principles, or their humanitarian ideals, can protect their own interests by preventing Japan from continuing the desolation of China. They can do this by refusing to allow Japan to buy the wherewithal to manufacture munitions to use on our country.

With best wishes,

Yours sincerely,

Mayling Soong Chiang

(Madame Chiang Kai-shek)

GLOSSARY OF PLACE NAMES

Canton	Guangzhou	廣州
Chapei	Zhabei	閘北
Hangchow	Hangzhou	杭州
Hankou	Hankou	漢口
Hongkew	Hongkou	虹口
Ichang	Yichang	宜昌
Nanking	Nanjing	南京
Ningpo	Ningbo	寧波
Lo Yang	Luoyang	洛陽
Mukden	Shenyang	瀋陽
Paotingfu	Baoding	保定
Soochow	Suzhou	蘇州
Tientsin	Tianjin	天津

Afterword from the Publisher

I HAD THE PLEASURE to meet Patricia Luce Chapman when she contacted me with regard to her memoir of her early years growing up in Shanghai, which we published as Tea on the Great Wall.

But Patty also wanted very much to revive the memory of her formidable mother, Edna Lee Booker, and so we have here re-published, with Patty's approval, Edna Lee's ground-breaking account of her reporting years in China, News Is My Job.

As a journalist myself, I admire Patty's mother for her intrepid style and her wonderful scoops. I envy her the opportunity to have been in Shanghai, Peking, Canton, Baoding and Luoyang in those years, and I know I would not have handled it as well as she did.

But as a human being, I more admire Patty for the way she has led her life, faced down the challenges that have arisen, continuing to be positive, creative and productive in the face of an often unconcerned world.

The way to lead life is with the passion that leads to pushing for such projects as the re-publication of this book, in honor of her mother, and Patty gets it.

Graham Earnshaw
Publisher

INDEX

www.ingramcontent.com/pod-product-compliance
Lightning Source LLC
Chambersburg PA
CBHW011233120626
46549CB00009B/3251